1 8 JAN 2013

EXPLORATIONS IN SOCIOLOGY
British Sociological Association conference volume series

Sami Zubaida (*editor*)
Richard Brown (*editor*)

1 *Race and Racism*
2 *Knowledge, Education and Cultural Exchange*

Paul Rock and Mary McIntosh (*editors*)
3 *Deviance and Social Control*

Emanuel de Kadt and Gavin Williams (*editors*)
4 *Sociology and Development*

Frank Parkin (*editor*)
5 *The Social Analysis of Class Structure*

Diana Leonard Barker and Sheila Allen (*editors*)
6 *Sexual Divisions and Society: Process and Change*

Diana Leonard Barker and Sheila Allen (*editors*)
7 *Dependence and Exploitation in Work and Marriage*

Richard Scase (*editor*)
8 *Industrial Society: Class, Cleavage and Control*

Robert Dingwall, Christian Heath, Margaret Reid and Margaret Stacey (*editors*)
9 *Health Care and Health Knowledge*

Robert Dingwall, Christian Heath, Margaret Reid and Margaret Stacey (*editors*)
10 *Health and the Division of Labour*

Gary Littlejohn, Barry Smart, John Wakeford and Nira Yuval-Davis (*editors*)
11 *Power and the State*

Michèle Barrett, Philip Corrigan, Annette Kuhn and Janet Wolff (*editors*)
12 *Ideology and Cultural Production*

Bob Fryer, Allan Hunt, Doreen MacBarnet and Bert Moorhouse (*editors*)
13 *Law, State and Society*

Philip Abrams, Rosemary Deem, Janet Finch and Paul Rock (*editors*)
14 *Practice and Progress: British Sociology, 1950–1980*

Graham Day, Lesley Caldwell, Karen Jones, David Robbins and Hilary Rose (*editors*)
15 *Diversity and Decomposition in the Labour Market*

David Robbins, Lesley Caldwell, Graham Day, Karen Jones and Hilary Rose (*editors*)
16 *Rethinking Social Inequality*

Eva Gamarnikow, David Morgan, June Purvis and Daphne Taylorson (*editors*)
17 *The Public and the Private*

Eva Gamarnikow, David Morgan, June Purvis and Daphne Taylorson (*editors*)
18 *Gender, Class and Work*

*Gareth Rees, Janet Bujra, Paul Littlewood, Howard Newby and Teresa L. Rees (*editors*)
19 *Political Action and Social Identity: Class, Locality and Ideology*

Howard Newby, Janet Bujra, Paul Littlewood, Gareth Rees and Teresa L. Rees (*editors*)
20 *Restructuring Capital: Recession and Reorganization in Industrial Society*

*Sheila Allen, Kate Purcell, Alan Waton and Stephen Wood (*editors*)
21 *The Experience of Unemployment*

*Kate Purcell, Stephen Wood, Alan Waton and Sheila Allen (*editors*)

*Jalna Hanmer and Mary Maynard (*editor*

D1333673

*Colin Creighton and Martin Shaw (*editors*)

*Alan Bryman, Bill Bytheway, Patricia Allatt and Teresa Keil (*editors*)

*Patricia Allatt, Teresa Keil, Alan Bryman and Bill Bytheway (*editors*)

*Jan Varcoe, Maureen McNeil and Steven Yearley (*editors*)

*Maureen McNeil, Ian Varcoe and Steven Yearley (*editors*)

David McCrone, Stephen Kendrick and Pat Straw (*editors*)

Stephen Kendrick, Pat Straw and David McCrone (*editors*)

*Lynn Jamieson and Helen Corr (*editors*)

*Helen Corr and Lynn Jamieson (*editors*)

Geoff Payne and Malcolm Cross (*editors*)

Pamela Abbott and Claire Wallace (*editors*)

Robert Reiner and Malcolm Cross (*editors*)

Pamela Abbott and Geoff Payne (*editors*)

Claire Wallace and Malcolm Cross (*editors*)

Malcolm Cross and Geoff Payne (*editors*)

*Sara Arber and Nigel Gilbert (*editors*)

*Roger Burrows and Catherine Marsh (*editors*)

*Nigel Gilbert, Roger Burrows and Anna Pollert (*editors*)

*Catherine Marsh and Sara Arber (*editors*)

*Lydia Morris and E. Stina Lyon (*editors*)

*Colin Samson and Nigel South (*editors*)

Joan Busfield and E. Stina Lyon (*editors*)

*Janet Holland and Lisa Adkins (*editors*)

*Lisa Adkins and Vicki Merchant (*editors*)

*Jeffrey Weeks and Janet Holland (*editors*)

24 *The Sociology of War and Peace*
25 *Rethinking the Life Cycle*

26 *Women and the Life Cycle*

27 *Deciphering Science and Technology*
28 *The New Reproductive Technologies*
29 *The Making of Scotland*

30 *Interpreting the Past, Understanding the Present*
31 *State, Private Life and Political Change*
32 *Politics of Everyday Life: Continuity and Change in Work and the Family*
33 *Sociology in Action: Applications and Opportunities for the 1990s*
34 *Gender, Power and Sexuality*

35 *Beyond Law and Order: Criminal Justice Policy and Politics into the 1990s*
36 *New Directions in the Sociology of Health and Illness*
37 *Youth in Transition: The Sociology of Youth and Youth Policy*
38 *Work and the Enterprise Culture*
39 *Women and Working Lives: Divisions and Change*
40 *Consumption and Class: Divisions and Change*
41 *Fordism and Flexibility: Divisions and Change*
42 *Families and Households: Divisions and Change*
43 *Gender Relations in Public and Private*
44 *The Social Construction of Social Policy*
45 *Methodological Imaginations*
46 *Sex, Sensibility and the Gendered Body*
47 *Sexualizing the Social*
48 *Sexual Cultures*

From the same publishers

Sexual Cultures

Communities, Values and Intimacy

Edited by

Jeffrey Weeks
Professor of Sociology
South Bank University
London

and

Janet Holland
Senior Research Lecturer
Institute of Education
University of London
and
Lecturer in Education
The Open University

© British Sociological Association 1996

All rights reserved. No reproduction, copy or transmission of this publication may be made without written permission.

No paragraph of this publication may be reproduced, copied or transmitted save with written permission or in accordance with the provisions of the Copyright, Designs and Patents Act 1988, or under the terms of any licence permitting limited copying issued by the Copyright Licensing Agency, 90 Tottenham Court Road, London W1P 9HE.

Any person who does any unauthorised act in relation to this publication may be liable to criminal prosecution and civil claims for damages.

First published 1996 by
MACMILLAN PRESS LTD
Houndmills, Basingstoke, Hampshire RG21 6XS
and London
Companies and representatives
throughout the world

This book is printed on paper suitable for recycling and made from fully managed and sustained forest sources. Logging, pulping and manufacturing processes are expected to conform to the environmental regulations of the country of origin.

A catalogue record for this book is available from the British Library.

Printed and bound in Great Britain by
CPI Antony Rowe, Chippenham and Eastbourne

ISBN-13: 978-0-333-65003-5 hardback
ISBN-10: 0-333-65003-4   hardback
ISBN-13: 978-0-333-65004-2 paperback
ISBN-10: 0-333-65004-2   paperback

Contents

Acknowledgements   vii

Notes on the Contributors   viii

Introduction   1
    Jeffrey Weeks and Janet Holland

PART I   APPROACHES TO SEXUALITY

1 From Sexual Divisions to Sexualities: Changing
    Sociological Agendas   17
    Sheila Allen and Diana Leonard

2 Intimate Citizenship and the Culture of Sexual
    Story Telling   34
    Ken Plummer

3 Gay Brains, Gay Genes and Feminist Science Theory   53
    Hilary Rose

PART II   HISTORICAL EXCURSIONS

4 The Shock of the *Freewoman* Journal: Feminists
    Speaking on Heterosexuality in Early Twentieth-century
    England   75
    Lucy Bland

5 Mass Observation's 'Little Kinsey' and the British
    Sex Survey Tradition   97
    Liz Stanley

6 From 'Immorality' to 'Underclass': The Current and
    Historical Context of Illegitimacy   115
    Andrew Blaikie

PART III   IDENTITIES, COMMUNITIES AND CONTROL

7   Medicalisation and Identity Formation: Identity and
    Strategy in the Context of AIDS and HIV   139
    Brian Heaphy

8   Community Responses to HIV and AIDS:
    The 'De-Gaying' and 'Re-Gaying' of AIDS   161
    **Jeffrey Weeks, Peter Aggleton, Chris McKevitt,
    Kay Parkinson and Austin Taylor-Laybourn**

9   Prostitution and the Contours of Control   180
    Julia O'Connell Davidson

PART IV   INTIMACY

10   Intimacy, Altruism and the Loneliness of Moral Choice:
     The Case of HIV Positive Health Workers   201
     Neil Small

11   Whose Orgasm is this Anyway? 'Sex Work' in
     Long-term Heterosexual Couple Relationships   220
     Jean Duncombe and Dennis Marsden

12   Reputations: Journeying into Gendered Power Relations   239
     **Janet Holland, Caroline Ramazanoglu,
     Sue Sharpe and Rachel Thomson**

13   The Conundrum of Sex and Death: Some Issues in
     Health Care Practice   261
     David Clark and Julia Hirst

Index   284

Acknowledgements

This book consists of essays originally delivered as papers at the 1994 British Sociological Association (BSA) Annual Conference, on the theme of 'Sexualities in Social Context', held at the University of Central Lancashire, 28–31 March 1994. It is one of three volumes produced from the papers given at that conference. The companion volumes are: *Sex, Sensibility and the Gendered Body*, edited by Janet Holland and Lisa Adkins, and *Sexualizing the Social: Power and the Organisation of Sexuality*, edited by Lisa Adkins and Vicki Merchant.

The conference itself was one of the largest ever held by the BSA, and these three volumes offer a distillation of the 258 papers given at the conference. The editors of all three volumes had great difficulty in making a representative selection of the papers, and we would like to thank the forbearance and patience of all the contributors while we reviewed each paper and came to our often painful decisions concerning them. The editors of this volume would particularly like to thank the contributors for the speed and efficiency with which they responded to editorial comments and revisions. More broadly, we would also wish to thank all the participants at the conference, both those who gave papers, and those who participated in the various streams. We feel that all who participated in the conference gained enormously from the intellectual vitality and excitement that was apparent there. We hope that this volume and its companions reflect some of that excitement, and contribute to the growing recognition of the significance of sexuality in understanding the social dynamics of contemporary societies.

That the conference was such a success is due to the efforts of countless people. We would like to thank members of the British Sociological Association staff for their support throughout this venture. We are grateful for the support given by staff at the University of Central Lancashire both before and during the conference itself. The editors of this volume owe a great debt of gratitude to their colleagues at the University of the West of England, South Bank University, the Institute of Education, University of London and the Open University. We owe personal debts to our immediate partners and friends; they know who they are.

We dedicate this volume to the many young sociologists who attended the BSA Conference, many for the first time. Their enthusiasm for the subject, and for the theme of the conference, gave us great hope for the future of our discipline.

Notes on the Contributors

Peter Aggleton is a Professor at the Institute of Education, University of London, and is co-director there of the Health and Education Research Unit. He is the author of numerous articles and several books, and is editor of the Social Aspects of AIDS series of books. He was co-director (with Jeffrey Weeks) of the ESRC-funded Voluntary Sector Responses to HIV and AIDS project.

Sheila Allen is Research Professor of Sociology at the University of Bradford and University Adviser on Equal Opportunities. She researches and publishes in the areas of sociology of work, gender relations and ethnic and race relations. She is currently engaged in writing a book on feminist contributions to sociology.

Andrew Blaikie is a Senior Lecturer in Sociology at the University of Aberdeen where he teaches courses on Sex and Gender, and The Body, Self and Society. Recent publications include *Illegitimacy, Sex and Society* (1993), and he is currently researching the connections between infant life chances and unmarried motherhood in Scotland between 1845 and 1945.

Lucy Bland is a Senior Lecturer in Women's Studies at the University of North London. She has written extensively on feminism and sexuality in the late nineteenth and early twentieth centuries, including *Banishing the Beast: English Feminism and Sexual Morality, 1885–1914* (1995).

David Clark currently holds the Chair of Medical Sociology at the University of Sheffield, where he is actively involved in a wide-ranging programme of research relating to sociological and policy aspects of palliative care.

Julia O'Connell Davidson is Lecturer in Sociology at the University of Leicester. She is currently involved in research on prostitution in Britain and sex tourism to economically underdeveloped countries.

Jean Duncombe works as Senior Research Officer at Essex University on an ESRC-funded project (with Dennis Marsden) on 'The Role of Ideologies of Love in the Social Construction of Coupledom'. She has previously been involved in research on extra-marital sexual relationships, Alexandra Kollontai, YTS, women's work and Household Allocative Systems.

Brian Heaphy is currently a Research Fellow on the 'Families of Choice' project at South Bank University, London. His first degree was in cultural studies, and he is currently completing a PhD in sociology on the theme of medicalisation and identity in the context of the HIV/AIDS epidemic.

Julia Hirst is a Senior Lecturer in Health Promotion (HIV/AIDS) at Sheffield Hallam University. She has extensive teaching and research experience in sexuality and sexual health. She is author of *Not in Front of the Grown Ups* (1994) and co-author of *The Place and Meaning of Drugs in the Lives of Young People* (1994).

Janet Holland is Senior Research Officer in the Social Science Research Unit, Institute of Education, University of London, and Lecturer in Education at the Open University. Recent publications include: (with C. Ramazanoglu) 'Coming to Conclusions: Power and Interpretation in Researching Young Women's Sexuality', in J. Purvis and M. Maynard (eds), *Researching Women's Lives from a Feminist Perspective* (1994) and (with C. Ramazanoglu, S. Sharpe, R. Thomson) 'Power and Desire: The Embodiment of Female Sexuality', *Feminist Review*, no. 46, 1994. She was co-organiser of the 1994 BSA Annual Conference.

Diana Leonard is a Senior Lecturer in Sociology and head of the Centre for Research and Education on Gender at the Institute of Education, University of London. Her publications include *Sex and Generation* (1980), and the A-level textbook *Families* (1988, with John Hood Williams). She is co-editor with Sheila Allen of the BSA publications *Sexual Divisions and Society* (1976) and *Sexual Division Revisited* (1991). Her most recent book, written with Christine Delphy, is a theoretical work, *Familiar Exploitation: A New Analysis of Marriage in Contemporary Western Society* (1992). She has just completed translating and editing with Lisa Adkins a collection of papers by French radical feminists, to be published by Taylor and Francis as *Sex in Question*.

Dennis Marsden is a Professor in the Sociology Department at Essex University. He has published *Education and the Working Class* (with Brian Jackson, 1961), *Politicians, Equality and Comprehensives* (1967),

Mothers Alone (1969), *Workless* (1979), and *Scheming for Youth* (with David Lee, 1990). Other research areas include family violence, the social costs of community care and stepfamilies.

Chris McKevitt is a social anthropologist currently employed as a Research Fellow in the Department of Public Health Medicine at the United Medical and Dental Schools of Guys and St Thomas's. He was a member of the ESRC-funded Voluntary Sector Responses to HIV and AIDS research team.

Kay Parkinson was formerly a Research Officer at the Health and Education Research Unit, Institute of Education, University of London. She was a member of the ESRC-funded Voluntary Sector Responses to HIV and AIDS research team and is presently researching youth workers' training needs in the areas of sexual health, drugs, HIV and AIDS. She is co-editor of *Pleasure Principles* (1992) and her current research interest is women and infidelity.

Ken Plummer is a Professor in the Sociology Department at the University of Essex, and was recently Head of the Department there. He is the author of *Sexual Stigma* (1975), *Documents of Life* (1983) and *Telling Sexual Stories* (1995), as well as the author of many articles and editor of a number of anthologies.

Caroline Ramazanoglu is a Reader in Sociology at Goldsmiths' College, University of London. Recent publications include *Feminism and the Contradictions of Oppression* (1989); (as editor) *Up Against Foucault: Explorations of Some Tensions between Foucault and Feminism* (1993); (with J. Holland) 'Coming to Conclusions: Power and Interpretation in Researching Young Women's Sexuality', in J. Purvis and M. Maynard (eds), *Researching Women's Lives from a Feminist Perspective* (1994); and (with J. Holland, S. Sharpe and R. Thomson) 'Power and Desire: the Embodiment of Female Sexuality', *Feminist Review*, no. 46, 1994.

Hilary Rose has published extensively in the sociology of social policy and also science. She was appointed to the Chair of Social Policy at Bradford in 1975 and was Director of the West Yorkshire Centre for Research on Women between 1985 and 1993. She has a current honorary attachment to the Social Science Research Unit at the Institute of Education. Her most recent book is *Love, Power and Knowledge: Towards a Feminist Transformation of the Sciences* (1993).

Sue Sharpe is a freelance writer, researcher and consultant, whose main interests are the lives and experiences of young women, but include work on young men and heterosexuality. Her books include *Just Like a Girl* (1976, 2nd edn 1994), *Falling for Love* (1987), *Voices from Home* (1990) and *Fathers and Daughters* (1993).

Neil Small is a Senior Research Fellow in the Trent Palliative Care Centre and the University of Sheffield. He is the author of *Politics and Planning in the National Health Service* (1989) and *AIDS: The Challenge. Understanding, Education and Care* (1993).

Liz Stanley is Reader in Sociology at the University of Manchester, currently seconded to act as the University's Director of Women's Studies. She is working class and Romany by birth, a Northerner in England by choice, and lesbian by luck. Her main preoccupations concern books, music, food, cats and wine, in changing permutations of that order. She is interested in the epistemological dimensions of all forms of social investigation. Her recent publications include *The Auto/Biographical I: Theory and Practice of Feminist Auto/Biography* (1992), *Debates in Sociology* (editor, 1993, with David Morgan), *Breaking Out Again* (1993, with Sue Wise), and *Sex Surveyed* (1995).

Austin Taylor-Laybourn was formerly a Research Officer at the Health and Education Research Unit, Institute of Education, University of London. He was a member of the ESRC-funded Voluntary Sector Responses to HIV and AIDS research team. He has been involved in a variety of aspects of HIV and AIDS research, with a particular emphasis on the health needs of gay, bisexual and other men who have sex with men.

Rachel Thomson is Senior Development Officer for the Sex Education Forum at the National Children's Bureau. Recent publications include 'Moral Rhetoric and Public Health Pragmatism: The Recent Politics of Sex Education', *Feminist Review*, 48: 40–60 (1995); 'Desire, Risk and Control: The Body as a Site of Contestation' (with J. Holland, C. Ramazanoglu and S. Scott) and 'Achieving Masculine Sexuality: Young Men's Strategies for Managing Vulnerability' (with J. Holland, C. Ramazanoglu and S. Sharpe), both in L. Doyal, J. Naidoo and T. Wilton (eds), *AIDS: Setting a Feminist Agenda* (1994).

Jeffrey Weeks is Professor of Sociology at South Bank University, London. He is the author of numerous articles and books on the social organisation of sexuality. Recent publications include *Against Nature: Essays on History, Sexuality and Identity* (1991) and *Invented Moralities: Sexual Values in an Age of Uncertainty* (1995). He was co-director (with Peter Aggleton) of the ESRC-funded Voluntary Sector Responses to HIV and AIDS project and is currently directing an ESRC-funded project on 'Families of Choice'. He was co-organiser of the 1994 BSA Annual Conference.

Introduction

JEFFREY WEEKS and JANET HOLLAND

The theme of this book is 'sexual cultures'. The plural form is central to the argument of each of the essays in this volume. The underlying assumption of all the contributors is that sexuality takes many forms, is patterned in a variety of different ways and, moreover, cannot be understood outside the context in which it is enacted, conceptualised and reacted to. The subtitle of the volume, 'Communities, Values and Intimacy', underlines a more specific focus. Sexualities today are lived in a variety of communities of identity, of interest and of politics. They express and delineate a plurality of values. But in all sorts of ways they relate to the question of intimacy. In the English language, at least, the term 'intimacy' tends to indicate a link with the sexual. But the question of intimacy has also become the focus of much recent speculation and theorisation within broader fields of sociology (Giddens, 1992). Sexuality is not necessarily co-existent with the intimate; nor does intimacy always connote the sexual. Yet modern forms of intimacy tend inevitably to throw up significant questions about sexual belonging, ethics and choice. So although for the sake of convenience this book is divided into sections, with their own titles, these themes, summed up in terms of community, values and intimacy, are reflected in all the contributions.

In this, the contributions to this volume reflect the wider concerns of the 1994 British Sociological Association Annual (BSA) Conference on the theme of 'Sexualities in Social Context'. For the organisers of that conference, the theme was an important one for two key reasons. In the first place, it represented an acknowledgement that sociological explorations of sexuality had now achieved a critical mass that deserved wider recognition within the sociological community. It has become a major concern of now well-established sociologists but, perhaps more importantly for the future of British sociology, a major preoccupation also of a younger generation of researchers and practitioners in the broad sociological domain. Some of the reasons for this are explored below, but it is important for us to signal here that the entry of a serious concern with sexuality into the mainstream of the sociological endeavour is a major achievement for a broad range of scholars.

But the second element behind the theme is equally important: a dawning recognition that an understanding of sexualities in their broadest sense must now be central to the understanding of wider social developments. Just as, twenty years ago, a recognition of the significance of gender helped to re-energise and transform sociological investigation, to the extent that no serious sociologist today can ignore the relationships between men and women, so in the 1990s it has become impossible to think of such issues as power, the family, the organisation of work, identity and politics without an understanding of sexuality.

This emphasis has, however, not been without its hazards. In a contribution to an earlier volume of essays from a BSA Conference, one of the editors of this volume commented that 'Writing about sex can be dangerous' (Weeks, 1990, p. 31). Researchers on sexuality are less likely today than in the past to be faced by explicit forms of censorship, but an air of anxiety, combined with prurience and nervous humour, all too frequently still surrounds the subject. This was made glaringly obvious to the organisers of the 1994 conference by the press reaction to it that suddenly burst upon us on the eve of the conference opening. *The Sunday Times* broke the story to its avid readership in the edition of 27 March 1994, with the headline 'Sex from Every Angle from the Sociologists'. The article's author, Stuart Wavell, began his piece as follows:

> The anticipation has been tantalising, the foreplay unbearable. Tomorrow the earth will move for 600 sociologists at the biggest gathering on sexuality since the orgies of ancient Rome. The venue is Preston in Lancashire, where Arkwright invented the water-powered spinning frame.

The reduction of the conference to this degree of frivolity was echoed in other broadsheet, and therefore to British assumptions, 'serious', newspapers. David Ward in the *Guardian*, the embodiment of British liberal journalistic values, noted 'sociological enquiries into chewing gum, stockings, Finnish nocturnal activities – and Blackpool'. The *Independent*, on its front page, headlined 'Sexual Congress for Sweet-talking Sociologists'. The more conservative press took a slightly more political line. The *Daily Telegraph* headlined its story 'Everything you need to know about Sociology and Sex', and began:

> The politically correct prevails at the four-day British Sociological Association Conference at Central Lancashire University, Preston,

this week . . . some of the papers would indeed be regarded as mumbo-jumbo in Coronation Street. Sociologists' dress is alternative and informal: many women were yesterday wearing workman's boots and many of their male colleagues favour earrings.

The enthusiasm of the serious press for the theme of the conference was soon echoed by the investigative prowess of the tabloid press. The *Sun* and the *Daily Star*, in competition for the bottom end of the market, sought scandal at the conference. The *Daily Mirror* sent its top investigative journalist to stay in the best hotel in Preston, but then failed to print a story in the national editions.

These excursions by the press into the BSA Conference were unprecedented. On one level it perhaps indicates a typically British prurience when attempting to discuss sexuality seriously. A wider unconscious assumption may also be detected, and one which still informs the work of many sociologists themselves, an assumption that as sexuality is a 'natural' phenomenon it is scarcely worthy of serious sociological investigation. This notion was belied, however, by the very attendance at the conference. But there is a serious lesson that can be drawn from this almost unanimous press reaction. People are still vulnerable, especially the less well-established and younger researchers and teachers, when attempting to study sexuality seriously. Several people felt compelled by the publicity given to their papers to withdraw them at the last minute, either because they were attempting to submit proposals for grants, and were nervous of sensationalist coverage, or because the research findings summarised in the papers were of a controversial and sensitive nature, which might then reflect back on the subjects of the research. Ironically, nothing more indicates the necessity of serious sociological investigation of sexuality, and of proper dissemination of research-based findings, than the suspicion and merriment reflected in the press coverage.

The initial proposal for a conference on the theme of 'Sexualities in Social Context' came from the BSA's Standing Committee on the Equality of the Sexes (and it is worth noting that the plural form 'sexualities' was in the initial proposal submitted to the BSA Annual Conference in 1992). To quote from the initial proposal:

Sexuality is an intrinsic aspect of social relations, which can be studied in relation to all areas of life and the organisation of society . . . until recently, sexual relations were relatively neglected in the development of theory and empirical work. There is now, however, a growing interest in the area, reflected in increasing research in a wide range of contexts. A conference on sexuality offers the possibility of linking the existing theorising and practice of sociology ... and provides a catalyst for reconceptualisation of traditional themes within the discipline. The study of sexuality can challenge pre-existing knowledges. As sexuality is linked to all aspects of social life and implicated in the construction of individual identity, it invites an integrated approach to other key social issues – age, gender, 'race', class, and culture.

These themes were reflected in the structure of the conference itself in 1994. Just as the 1974 conference on sexual divisions in society (see Allen and Leonard's chapter below) put gender at the centre of the sociological endeavour, so we hope that the 1994 conference has helped to widen the understanding of the significance of the sexual in structuring the social.

There has in fact been a transformation of the sociological approach towards sexuality. Just twenty years ago, Plummer (1975) commented on the absence in Britain of a sociological understanding of sexuality. Today, as John Gagnon observed in his plenary paper at the 1994 conference, sexuality has moved from the periphery to the centre of sociological concerns. Gagnon's own work has made a significant contribution to this development. His book, with William Simon, *Sexual Conduct* (1973) was for many of us a revelation. It made the now widely accepted, but then revelatory, observation that sex, far from being the most natural thing about us, was to an extraordinary degree subject to socio-cultural moulding. This rejection of what has come to be known as the 'essentialist' approach in favour of what is now called 'social constructionism' forced many of us, who were then putting a tentative foot into these dangerous waters, to ask what were the social forces that had given such a centrality to the sexual in our culture.

As Gagnon and Simon (1973) noted, there may have been a need at some stage in the distant past to 'invent' an importance for sexuality. It forced us to ask the simple question: why? It helped to propel us along the road of asking what the sources of the invention could be. It forced us to ask historical as well as sociological questions about the sexual. Above all, it led to the simple, but transforming, conclusion that if the forms of sexuality as we knew them were social inventions, then sexuality could be re-invented, re-made according to changing social, cultural and political needs.

It is important to make this chronological point about the work of

Gagnon and Simon, because it is all too easy to see the contribution of Michel Foucault (1979) as the key moment in transforming serious understanding of the sexual. The first volume of Foucault's *The History of Sexuality* was a major event, because he was able to link up developing sociological concern with wider philosophical preoccupations that were already making an impact on the sociological community in Britain and elsewhere: a preoccupation, in other words, with what came to be know as post-structuralism. In terms of the emphasis on the invention of sexuality, Foucault was not strikingly original. Nevertheless, by linking that historical emphasis with wider analysis of the dispersed and pluralistic form of power in modern cultures, Foucault did open up a broader recognition of the links between the sexual and the wider social and cultural milieu. The preoccupation with power as at the heart of the working of sexuality is widely reflected in a number of essays in this volume (for example, Heaphy, O'Connell Davidson, Plummer, Holland *et al.*). No doubt, the general remarks by Foucault on power have needed much development since. Their opacity on issues of gender, for example, have occasioned much comment, particularly from feminist critics (see essays in Ramazanoglu, 1994). Yet Foucault did help to create the space within which these questions could be asked.

That space was necessary because of a third element which has contributed massively towards the development of a sociology of sexuality: the rise of a radical sexual politics from the late 1960s, particularly that associated with contemporary feminism and the lesbian and gay movements. That political context is vital in understanding recent sociological explorations. The challenge to embedded hierarchies of authority posed by the new sexual politics could draw on Foucault, but had its own sources in the deep questioning of the power relationships embodied in institutionalised heterosexuality and in what came to be called homophobia or heterosexism. These sources of revealed authority included sociology itself (as Allen and Leonard illustrate in their account of the battles within the BSA to put gender and sexuality on the agenda) and the wider field of scientific knowledge (Rose's discussion of feminist critiques of the epistemology of science, below, illustrates this graphically). The various vicissitudes of feminist and gay and lesbian politics can be traced in the changing preoccupations of sexual study: from the preoccupation with female and gay sexuality and identity in the 1970s, through an exploration of issues such as rape, sexual violence and child sex abuse in the 1980s, to the great concern with sexual health and the body in the AIDS dominated 1990s. The questions posed within sexual politics have forced questions to be asked of the forms of regulation and control of the sexual, and in turn have opened up new vistas for research (and indeed political activism). The reference to AIDS reminds us that although the deep structures of sexual regulation have a long history, and cast their shadow over current concerns, we must also expect the unexpected. The emergence of HIV and AIDS as both a serious health issue and a major challenge to our cultural assumptions from the early 1980s onwards has posed sharp new questions about identity (see Heaphy), female sexual autonomy (see Holland *et al.*), values (for example, see Small) and attitudes towards death (see Clark and Hirst), amongst many other issues.

A history of the sociological approaches towards sexuality still awaits its chronicler. Our perception of that history is necessarily partial, perhaps polemical, and committed. It is clear that there are many approaches to the sociology of sexuality, as this collection, and its two accompanying volumes, underlines, and it has not been our intention to offer a single approach to the understanding of human sexualities. Diversity is a theme of this book. But it is worth adding here a further comment on the use of the term 'sexualities'. Implicit in Allen and Leonard's comment on the use of our term for the conference title is an assumption that there are common structures of sexuality which need to be understood. We agree with that in the sense that there are certain hierarchies of power and domination in our culture which both shape its form and limit its various expressions. But it is also true that today sexuality is lived in many diverse ways. The changes of the past generation, which have made possible a sociology of sexuality, have also transformed the ways in which sexualities are lived. It is no longer possible, if it ever was, to see our society in terms of a hegemonic form from which everything else is a bizarre deviation. Increasingly today we have to recognise that sexuality is as much about self-making and self-invention as it is about dominant forms of regulation. Foucault (1979) talked about power and resistance. For many of us today it is the resistance, or to put it another way, the forms of agency that shape personal life and collective identities, that needs expression as much as the structures of power and domination. In fact it is impossible to understand one without the other. The chapters in this book, in their various ways, deal with both structure and agency, and the recognition of the dialogical forms of the sexual is one of the major breakthroughs of the past twenty years of sexual sociology.

Part One of this volume provides different perspectives on the theorisation of sexuality. One of the unifying preoccupations, however, is precisely the difficulty of combining a recognition of diversity with the need for a broader understanding of the forces that shape the erotic. As John Gagnon described in his contribution to the conference of 1994, the progress of sex in sociology is precisely a development towards the recognition of plural forms, from gender differentiation and diversity of sexual preference to a recognition of the elements of difference provided by ethnicity and race. But there is a danger in this emphasis on pluralism, as Allen and Leonard note in their contribution: a perception that some of the papers delivered at the 1994 conference appeared either to confuse sexuality and gender, or to imagine that sexuality had nothing to do with gender. The theoretical trajectory of the sociology of sexuality has been to recognise the way in which sexuality impinges on the social, but also the way in which the social shapes the sexual. There is a danger that in simply celebrating the glorious efflorescence of sexual form, the continuing existence of structural limitations will get lost. In other words, an emphasis on the 'experience' of the erotic at the expense of understanding the embedded resistances to individual choice poses the danger of pushing the study of sexuality 'a large step backwards'.

Ken Plummer's paper on the culture of sexual storytelling offers a way out of this impasse. The emphasis on narrativity pays homage to recent post-modernist emphases, but also builds on Plummer's continuing preoccupation with the strengths and weaknesses of symbolic interactionist approaches to sociology. The contemporary growth of sexual stories, Plummer argues, can best be seen through a recognition of the shifting of social spaces in which listeners and audiences break down traditional boundaries around narratives. Today we are experiencing, in Foucauldian terms, an explosion of the possibilities of talking about sex. Some of these possibilities are the result of long-term social transformations, from the globalisation of experience to the revolution in communications and the creation of cyberspace. But other spaces are the result of long-lasting social struggles, which now make it possible to talk about the sexual and to explore sexual possibilities. As Plummer puts it 'Stories come into their time when a community has been fattened up, rendered ripe and willing to hear such stories.' Sexual storytelling is therefore a political process. The stories we tell of our lives, as Plummer argues, are 'deeply implicated in moral and political change and the shifting tales of self and identity [which] carry potential for a radical transformation of the social order'. The new politics of sexual storytelling, aware of diversity and contingency, democratic in their participatory forms, opening up the possibility of different life choices, open also the possibility of what Plummer calls 'intimate citizenship'.

But what we put into our new stories is not necessarily what 'good scientists' think ought to be there. This is the theme of Hilary Rose's critique of the epistemological assumptions of recent discussions of the 'gay gene' and 'gay brain'. The scientific discussions of sexuality, as Rose notes, have their own stories: of origin, of aetiology, and most recently, in the wake of HIV and AIDS, of epidemiology. One of the temptations of insurgent sexual communities, as the experience of the lesbian and gay communities over the last twenty years illustrates, is to seek validation in science, even as the politics of those movements and communities critiques established science. The politics of minority status, especially of the American lesbian and gay movement, seeks its theoretical justification in precisely those notions of a homosexual essence which it has been the task of the sociology of sex to critique over the past twenty years. As Rose comments, 'the problem for sociology in responding to such technically elaborate essentialist accounts of sexuality', as put forward by the advocates of a 'gay brain' and a 'gay gene', is that social theory has tended to exclude the body. This points to the dangers, Rose argues, of a social constructionist account which ignores the embodiment of sexuality. The inability of sociology until recently to confront the body, as well as the social forces that invest it, has created a space, Rose argues, which has allowed the new genetics to be linked with a generally reactionary social policy.

Part Two, 'Historical Excursions', takes up some of these challenges by exploring in a historical perspective the construction of sexual knowledges. In her analysis of the 'shock' of the impact of the *Freewoman* journal in 1912–13, Lucy Bland documents the hazards of attempting to create a space for the discussion of what was hitherto taboo, in this case the possibilities of female sexual autonomy. Outrage was a major initial response to the appearance of the *Freewoman*, even from amongst other feminists. For what was scandalous to many about the articles published in the journal was not so much the fact that they were about sex – feminists had been talking about sex at least from the 1860s onwards – but what was talked about. Whereas previous discussion had primarily been about the ways and means of protecting women from undesired sex, the *Freewoman*, Bland argues, was now beginning to claim the right for women to be sexual. The publication of the *Freewoman* was a brief moment in which a space was opened up for feminists to discuss sexuality in this way, a moment that was soon to disappear with the increasing eugenicist emphasis on 'fit' motherhood, the tightening up of the definition of appropriate sex and increasing emphasis on heterosexual reproductive sex. This paper should remind us that what matters is not so much whether sex is discussed, although clearly that is important, but how it is discussed, and the possibilities opened up by that discussion for increasing autonomy.

This theme is taken up again in Liz Stanley's study of Mass-Observation's 'Little Kinsey' survey in the late 1940s. This was another moment when new sexual possibilities were under discussion, in the wake of the publication of the first Kinsey surveys in the USA (Kinsey *et al.*, 1948). As Stanley points out, the more modest Little Kinsey is a valuable source of information about sexual behaviour, sexual attitudes and sexual change in Britain in this post-war period. The survey contains a coherent, if largely implicit, attempt to theorise as well as to research people's own constructions of sexuality. But as Stanley goes on to demonstrate, despite its generally 'liberal' approach, the Little Kinsey has an implicitly essentialist approach which in the end vitiates its own would-be progressivism. The dominant assumption in Little Kinsey is of the naturalness of heterosexuality, along with an associated assumption that sex is synonymous with penetration. Although the focus of the survey was women, the framing of the questions and the analysis was with reference to a widespread assumption about the impact of the declining birthrate. So although the Little Kinsey, in contrast to other contemporary surveys of sexual behaviour and attitudes, does focus upon changes regarding women's sexual expectations and marital behaviours, the possibilities opened up by these changes are underplayed because of the survey's normative assumptions.

The gap between official ideology and lived realities is one of the themes of Andrew Blaikie's chapter. Current preoccupations with the 'underclass', and particularly its propensity to produce unmarried mothers and supposedly uncontrollable illegitimate children, is not new. Blaikie illustrates the way in which 'epidemics' of teenage pregnancy and rises in illegitimacy reflect a recurrent social preoccupation with the implications of sexual nonconformity. As Blaikie notes, 'Moral panics have often used the language of epidemics to equate social ills with a medical vocabulary of causation and a moral vocabulary of motive.' In nineteenth century Scotland the advent of civil registration of births, marriages and deaths (in 1855) meant the need to accept new and apparently startling facts, facts so stark, Blaikie notes, that whole new ideologies had to be invented to explain them. The high incidence of bastardy in rural Scotland disrupted the assumption that it was only the urban slums that were hotbeds of vice. But in the new ideological response 'immorality' became a culturally convenient myth by which to maintain a

safe distance between classes: 'it created the fiction of a racially distinctive sub-group, habitually "incontinent" and politically threatening
to the nuclear family as the mainstay of national stability'. But as in
today's anxiety about the underclass, these responses signally fail to
explain the motivation of unmarried mothers. Blaikie's chapter provides a signal service by reminding us that current preoccupations have
a long genealogy, and that we sometimes need to beware of social
scientists bearing apparently neutral statistics. It also reminds us, however, as do the other pieces in this section, that historical sociology
has a dual purpose: to understand the past, of course; but also to provide a 'history of the present'. Our contemporary anxieties and fears
have a history, and the ideological formulations in that history still
bear on our ability to understand changing patterns of sexual behaviour.

The historical nature of sexual identities has been a major theme in
recent sociological studies, and this provides the unifying preoccupation of Part Three of the book, with HIV and AIDS as a thread running through most of the chapters. In his contribution, Brian Heaphy
explores the role of medicalisation, particularly around HIV and AIDS,
in shaping sexualised identities. Drawing on the experience of some
people living with HIV and AIDS, and providing an account of how
the meanings of HIV and AIDS could be seen to be negotiated by
some of those most closely affected, Heaphy illustrates the tension
between history, scientific discourse and agency in shaping contemporary senses of self and social belonging. The theoretical framework
draws both on Foucault's analysis of power and discipline, and on
Giddens' (1992) emphasis on the reflexive project of the self. Giddens'
concept of 'fateful moments' provides a fruitful way, Heaphy argues,
for understanding the construction of the self in the wake of epidemic.
But in the context of AIDS and HIV, he goes on, there are limits of
reflexivity to be considered: 'These can be seen in terms of both the
limit of choice and limit of reskilling.' He concludes that while the
early work of Foucault, and the recent work of Giddens, can be useful
in providing a theoretical approach to the problem of identity, both
have their limitations: Foucault's overemphasis on domination and
Giddens' overemphasis on reflexivity must be tested and refined in
relationship to the lived experience of those infected and affected.

A sense of 'community' has been central to the experience and politics of self-defined 'sexual minorities' over the past twenty years or
so. In their exploration of community responses to HIV and AIDS,
Weeks *et al.* focus on a particular aspect of the contemporary meaning
of community. One of the noticeable features of the early response to

AIDS in Britain was an identification of the epidemic as a 'gay disease'. It was one of the tasks of the first generation of AIDS activists to attempt to break this link. So successful was this, however, that in terms of social policy the gay community was not targeted either in terms of funds or of public advertising around safer sex. This has led, some activists suggest, to a complete 'de-gaying' of the epidemic, with the result that the impact of the epidemic on the gay community has been downplayed. In response, activists argue for the importance of 're-gaying' the epidemic, so that proper priorities are reassessed. This controversy within the AIDS activist movement is important not only for measuring appropriate responses to people at risk, and the lineaments of government policy, it also poses important questions about the meaning of community in the contemporary world, and the shifts in identity that this involves.

In her essay on 'Prostitution and the Contours of Control' (Chapter 9), Julia O'Connell Davidson explores another form of sexualised identity, that of the female sex worker. Drawing on an ethnographic study of a successful and independent white British prostitute, O'Connell Davidson offers a sharp insight into the transactions 'Desiree' enters into with her clients, and therefore highlights a number of theoretical problems: 'In particular, her experience suggests that issues of power, control and consent in prostitution are rather more complex than either the radical feminists or the liberal sex work model imply.' On the surface, 'Desiree' seems to be in a position to decide for herself on her life situation. But, O'Connell Davidson argues, in pursuit of this end she must repeatedly transform herself into 'an object who is not an object, a person who is not a person, a slave who is not a slave and a wage labourer who is not a wage labourer'. It seems, she concludes, a high price to pay for a kind of liberty that is supposed to be everyone's birthright in contemporary capitalist democracies.

This brings us to the question of autonomy, sexual values and the concept of intimacy in the final section of this book. The fraught implications of these issues are reflected in Neil Small's contribution on the loneliness of moral choice, especially as confronted by HIV-positive health workers. The variability of 'risk' in confronting the likelihood of HIV transmission challenges notions of identity and community. As Small puts it: 'The aim of health educators appears to be to break through the barriers of personally constructed risk identities and so insert the scientific into the reflexive. But the reflexive is well protected.' The ethics of the group and the morality of the individual can often meet in head on collision. In this situation, Small asks, to what extent is it appropriate for the interests of society as a whole to impinge upon individual control of the body. HIV-positive health workers have been instructed to sacrifice confidentiality on the grounds of furthering the social good. The claims of the social, Small argues, are strengthened by evoking risk and HIV-positive health workers are therefore forced to act altruistically by revealing their status. Small argues for the importance, however, of recognising the need to protect the intimate: 'From the intimate can grow acting for, acting altruistically, consistent with a morality that belongs with the self and not with the ethics of the powerful.'

In their chapter, Jean Duncombe and Dennis Marsden explore the tensions between the increasing cultural emphasis on the 'pure relationship' as the ultimate source of emotional and sexual fulfilment, and the actual sex lives of heterosexual couples in long-term relationships. They ask whether individuals may be seen as performing a kind of 'sex work' analogous to 'emotion work', to bring their sexual feelings more into line with how they believe sex ought to be experienced. In exploring this question, Duncombe and Marsden also raise major questions about the continuing power disparities between men and women. The necessity to 'perform' sex work reveals the heightened expectations about sexual fulfilment; but they also reveal that in the pursuit of 'authenticity', sex work has to be done differently by men and women.

This fraught encounter between expectation and the reality of gendered relationships is continued in the chapter by Janet Holland *et al.* on sexual reputations. Sexual reputations, they argue, can regulate behaviour, knowledge and expectations, since they are formed through very powerful normative assumptions about what it is to be masculine and feminine. As young people become heterosexually active, they argue, they have to engage with gendered relations of power, even though they may actively resist specific aspects of this power. In their accounts of sexual reputations, they find clear expressions of a double standard of sexual behaviour for men and women, and also a more hidden area of power relations in which the masculine dominates the feminine. The tension between this apparent dualism of masculine/feminine sexual reputation, and feminist conceptions of male power, provides the focus of the chapter.

Finally, Clark and Hirst explore the interrelationship of sex and death which brings together many of the other themes explored in this volume: normative assumptions about sexuality, the impact of health crises, including AIDS, on a sense of sexual wellbeing; and the growing sociological preoccupation with cultural attitudes to death, made vivid both by the AIDS crisis and by the growing numbers of ageing people in the population. The aim of the chapter is to understand many of the connections between these themes, and in particular to illustrate the ways in which they are represented in the particular context of health care and the work of professional carers. Within the contemporary social world, sexuality has become an integral part of an individual's identity. The acknowledgement and expression of sexuality from birth to death has been seen as a basic human right, and a right which has no age limit. Yet, Clark and Hirst argue, although health care has recognised the importance of treating the whole person, sexuality is rarely seen as integral to the treatment process. For those who are dying, of AIDS or of old age, the 'importance of tenderness, touch and affection is paramount. For many, expressions of love and affection through sexual behaviours will not be possible. Is this not more reason to support a move towards a vigorous reappraisal of the focus of health care for this expanding group of service users?'

As the various chapters in this book illustrate, the study of the sexual touches on many, if not all, aspects of social life. Far from being an esoteric preoccupation of a minority, the theoretical and empirical work summarised in these chapters underlines the reorientation of thinking of the social that an awareness and sensitivity to the sexual brings. Sexuality is shaped within society, and in turn helps to make and re-make the variety of social relations. It is the underlying theme of this book, as well as of its companion volumes, that a sociology which ignores the sexual will fail to grasp the complexity of identities, belongings, personal relationships and social meanings in late modern societies.

REFERENCES

Foucault, M. (1979) *The History of Sexuality*, volume 1: *An Introduction* (London: Allen Lane).

Gagnon, J. and Simon, W. (1973) *Sexual Conduct: The Social Sources of Human Sexuality* (London: Huchinson).

Giddens, A. (1992) *The Transformation of Intimacy: Sexuality, Love and Eroticism in Modern Societies* (Cambridge: Polity Press).

Kinsey, A. C., Pomeroy, W. B. and Martin, C. E. (1948) *Sexual Behavior in the Human Male* (Philadelphia and London: W.B. Saunders).

Plummer, K. (1975) *Sexual Stigma: An Interactionist Account* (London: Routledge & Kegan Paul).

Ramazanoglu, C. (ed.) (1994) *Up Against Foucault: Explorations of Some Tensions between Foucault and Feminism* (London: Routledge).

Weeks, J. (1990) 'Sexuality and History Revisited', in L. Jamieson and H. Corr (eds), *State, Private Life and Political Change* (Basingstoke and London: Macmillan).

Part I

Approaches to Sexuality

1 From Sexual Divisions to Sexualities: Changing Sociological Agendas

SHEILA ALLEN and
DIANA LEONARD

Twenty-four years after the founding of the British Sociological Association, its first annual conference to give major attention to 'Sexual Divisions in Society' was held in Aberdeen in 1974. Eight years later, in 1982, the focus was 'Gender and Society', and in 1994 the theme was 'Sexualities in Social Context'.[1] We thought it useful to look at how sociology has changed over this period, reflecting particularly on whether these titles reflect more general conceptual/political shifts, and what this means politically and conceptually in relation to feminism.

The substantial historical research required to write about sociology as a discipline (and the BSA as a professional organisation), its engagement with the women's and other movements, and its relation to feminism, has still to be done. This chapter is therefore simply a contribution from two[2] of those involved in a variety of ways and with differing perspectives throughout the period. We owe an immense debt to many other women in terms of sharing ideas, research, supportive networks and struggles which we wish to acknowledge fully.

Arguably, space in sociology for work on sexuality/sexualities became available in large part because of previous work on sexual divisions and gender. It is important to maintain a sense of this history, and never to lose sight of the importance of the hierarchy of relations between men and women when studying sexuality. Both seemed to be lost in some of the 1994 conference papers (though cf. Gagnon and Plummer in this volume). But without a recognition of feminist work on sexuality (and also of the debates *within* feminism), the significance of the shift from sexual divisions to sexualities, and the processes which have brought this about, cannot be evaluated.

THE CONTEXT OF THE 1974 CONFERENCE

Preparations for the 1974 conference had an inauspicious beginning.
That year's theme was to have been 'Europe', to mark Britain's entry
into the EEC; but when it became apparent that this would not be
possible, 'the family' was suggested as an alternative at a BSA executive committee meeting.[3] As organisers, we moved the format and title
provisionally from 'the family' to 'the political economy of the family' and then to 'sexual divisions in society', because of our involvement with the women's movement and in line with then current thinking
in critical sociology and in the class based analyses of society which
had re-emerged in the late 1960s. There was a great deal of scepticism
in the BSA executive about whether there was sufficient work being
done to warrant such a change of theme.

The 1974 conference took place in a period when there had been a
marked trend in British sociology to see itself as a critical discipline.
There was in many quarters a questioning of abstracted theoretical
approaches, and a (renewed) concern with major social changes and
the problems to which they gave rise. Sociology in Britain was, despite its lack of any attention to sexual divisions, an exciting discipline to work in, and it covered the gamut from pure empiricism to
theoretical Marxism (i.e. it was broader than in many European countries,
and certainly more radical than the dominant paradigms in the USA).
Many, including ourselves, believed it had much to offer, through its
analyses, to the social, political and economic struggles taking place.
As women sociologists, we saw ourselves not as being in opposition
to sociology-as-we-would-like-it-to-be, but to the intellectual straightjacket
of existing dominant paradigms; and to women as a whole being
marginalised in the sociological labour market and within the professional
association. We had, through discussions and experiences in the women's
and other movements, become acutely aware of all the processes and
the structures that systematically cut out all consideration of women,
and all but a very few actual women[4] from the discipline. Aberdeen
was about changing this intellectual and societal state of affairs: about
transforming knowledge and professional power relations.

In tune with the times (and specifically Women's Liberation Movement (WLM) practice), we wanted the conference to be more open,
for more women to participate – to attend, to give papers and to chair
sessions in greater numbers than was usual.[5] This could not have been
done had we not changed the format and moved beyond the confines
of academe, as there were relatively few women sociologists holding

full-time jobs in departments or as office holders in the BSA committees. The worries expressed by the BSA executive that there would not be enough material was not shared by the organisers, who adopted a different method of recruitment,[6] advertising widely in the women's movement's publications as well as along networks in sociology, history and anthropology and outside academe (including race-relations groups, women trade unionists and various community groups). We were clear, however, that it was a sociological, and not a WLM conference, though, as we have said, sociology in the UK was a broad church and it enabled many strands of feminism to come together. We did, however, specifically want to open up debate *within* sociology, rather than holding a conference 'about women'.[7] We therefore also wrote to several leading sociologists encouraging them to present papers reassessing their work from a sexual divisions perspective. Most declined our invitation.[8]

REORGANISING THE BSA

At the Aberdeen conference, women working in sociology and other social sciences therefore came together to discuss what changes we wanted to see and how these could be brought about. The theme and the format helped women from all parts of Britain and beyond to get to know each other and realise we *could* work together, and that there was something we could do worth doing *inside* the BSA. We were not unaware of some of the difficulties likely to be encountered, but we were surprised by some of the attitudes and behaviour, ranging from incomprehension, through ridicule, to outright hostility, which we met with from some of the men in sociology.[9] However, values learned from the women's movement and skills learned in women's meetings *were* introduced into the BSA.[10]

Many of those at the conference remarked on the difference in the ambience from past meetings, and some wrote to us later about this, and about the quality of the presentations and discussion. The latter was facilitated by having only one paper in each $1\frac{1}{2}$ hour session and time for discussion being given at least equal weight – a practice rarely followed in the subsequent 20 years.[11]

Much of the change emanated from the women's caucus, which first met at the 1974 conference as an informal group. In the following few years the caucus acted to keep issues alive, introduced new ones and

regularly reviewed progress (and backsliding) in the BSA. The existence of the women's movement, the experience of those who had attended the Women's Liberation meetings begining in 1970, and the
black and women's caucuses in the American Sociological Association, were direct influences in the decision to set up this group. In
Aberdeen, notices were pinned up announcing a meeting for women
participants, almost all of whom came – leaving the men to go to the
bar and wonder what was happening. We had debates on what to call
the group, because while caucus was being used in North America, it
was not familiar in Britain. Finally we agreed it was the only choice.
The caucus was outside the formal organisation of the Association.
For several years it received no funding for its meetings and had no
access to the facilities of the BSA. But, none the less, it held meetings
in different parts of the country, set up regional groupings, produced a
newsletter and provided a network to discuss sociological issues and
matters of concern among women sociologists.[12] For some years we
produced a sheet on 'What is the women's caucus?' for each annual
conference, which was given out to those attending its meetings for
the first time.

Several resolutions were put to the Annual General Meeting in 1974.
Some of these had been anticipated, but much last minute organising
went into mobilising support (*Times Higher Education Supplement*, 15
March 1974). A working party on the Position of Women in the Profession was set up, together with one on course content, both of which
were to report to the AGM the following year.[13] As a result of these,
the Equality of the Sexes Committee was established in 1976. It has met
regularly since and, being a sub-committee of the BSA Executive, members' fares are paid. Discussions on the gender balance of BSA committees and editorial boards followed, and the organisation of the annual
conference and domestic arrangements in the universities where they
were held were revised (including allowing children to sleep on campus).

Out of the caucus, too, came the proposal that discussions of research and teaching on sexual divisions become a formal part of the
Association. The mechanisms for establishing a study group already
existed, and this was the route we followed. One obvious advantage
was that study groups, unlike the caucus, had budgets and access to
the Association's facilities.[14] The Sexual Divisions Study Group was
established in 1974 and has had a more or less continuous existence
ever since. It has provided a venue for discussion and greater visibility
for some women in subsequent generations, but we feel it has never
fulfilled its intellectual potential.

Two other groups emerged from the caucus. First, as more post-graduate women students became involved in the caucus and in the BSA,[15] they set up a group which met to discuss their research interests, their conditions and problems (on at least one occasion obtaining financial help from the then Social Science Research Council). Two members of the group edited the Women's Caucus *Newsletter* in the early 1980s. Towards the end of its life, it became the Patriarchy Study Group, narrowing the research field it covered. Second, a study group on Violence against Women was started after the 1975 BSA conference on 'Violence, War and Social Change' at the University of Hull. This second group continues to provide a space for some who work in the research area, including postgraduates, to meet. Although it receives a small amount of funding from the BSA, it remains part of the caucus and is open only to women.

Despite the success of the 1974 format, the next year's conference at the University of Kent in 1975 – when 'Into Europe' finally happened, at a place where the boys were sure people would turn up[16] – to our anger had almost nothing on women and few women speaking or chairing.[17] But from then onwards, there have been more women elected to the executive of the BSA, a sliding scale of subscriptions according to income has been accepted (though this initially caused financial problems for the Association when many senior men resigned), and the caucus has often influenced the choice of conference theme. In addition, the Equality of the Sexes Committee has helped individual women. But the solid research of the working group on women in the professions and curriculum content has never been repeated.

THEORETICAL ISSUES IN 1974

How important was the 1974 conference as a turning point in sociological theory and empirical research? The two volumes that came out of it (Barker and Allen, 1976 a, b) were considered path-breaking across many substantive areas in sociology. But, perhaps more importantly, they demonstrated the ways in which theory and methodology required overhauling if they were to encompass the gender dimension of social relations. They made the discussion of approaches, ideas, issues and explanations which were formerly excluded, possible. Areas which sociological theory did not address or dismissed as peripheral were opened up, and questions about taken-for-granted assumptions and research methods were asked. This explains why new generations of sociologists still see the volumes as having really changed ways of thinking, and why a volume containing a selection of the papers has been republished (Leonard and Allen, 1991) – the only BSA conference volumes to have been reissued.

A more interesting question, perhaps, is why we used the concept of sexual divisions rather than, for example, gender inequalities. An immediate response must be that 'gender' was not, in fact, a term in common use in the early 1970s and, where it was used, for instance in anthropology, it was usually associated with cultural relativism and neglected power relations.[18] We did, however, specifically reject 'sex roles' as an alternative on theoretical grounds, as deriving from a static, non-conflictual model aligned closely with the functionalist analysis of social relations (Coulson, 1972).[19] The title 'Sexual Divisions in Society' came from a political economy trajectory which stressed the oppositional nature of the relationship and linked it with both the division of labour problematic and the mutual definition of two groups (classes). It was intended to move beyond the then dominant conceptions of, for example, the family and the labour market, towards a paradigm in which questions of power and control, oppression and exploitation between men and women (and within these categories) would be addressed.[20] The ideological boundaries constructed in sociology, as well as the wider society, between what later became known as the 'public' and the 'private' spheres were challenged as inadequate and distorting.

It has to be said that the 'sexual' in 'sexual divisions' certainly did not mean sexual in the sense current at the 1994 conference. In 1974 we talked about sex not sexuality (meaning by the latter sexual practice). Sexual practice was one area of sexual division/within gender relations – but one which was even less easy to research than, say, the family. It was also not a good career choice: it had you labelled as a pervert. Nor was there any money available.[21] The four papers on sexuality given in 1974 were notably all by men, including one we published (Brake, 1976).

What is interesting in retrospect is that the problems with the term 'gender' are now becoming clear in English-speaking debates (see Gatens, 1983; Edwards, 1989; Evans, 1991; Butler, 1993; Delphy, 1993). In 1974, because 'gender' was not dominant, 'sex', 'sexual' and 'gender' were not analytically separated, and all were seen to be social constructs by most feminists, and certainly by feminist sociologists. So can we claim to be forerunners of Judith Butler? Or is it, rather, that Butler has laboured mightily to counter a problem which itself is the product of anglophone (and particularly United States) feminists' over-use of the politically less contentious term 'gender'? Certainly theoretical problems connected to the concept of 'gender' have long been recognised by some French speakers (see Mathieu, 1980, 1991; Guillaumin, 1982, 1995; Wittig, 1992; Adkins and Leonard, 1995).

THE CONTEXT OF THE 1994 CONFERENCE

In the 1990s, some posts within sociology departments are advertised with gender as one of the desirable specialisms; and gender is seen as an important *option*, though not as part of the core of the discipline. Unfortunately, many of the women who now get such jobs see the jobs' existence, and their being available to women, as givens, or as a natural progression within sociology, rather than making a link with feminist struggles. And also unfortunately, it is notable how feminism has always been kept out of the BSA Theory Group. It is apparently OK for feminists to keep running round the periphery so long as we are kept out of the true heart of the discipline.

This also seems to apply to the funding councils, which favour those who stress 'what feminism leaves out' (often the old familiar tunes of the 1960s like 'emotions in marriage'), rather than feminist cutting-edge work. Certainly a major aspect of the Economic and Social Research Council's policy from the mid-1980s, identifying and funding research initiatives (now called programmes), has never included one focusing primarily on sexual divisions. The opportunity to build on theoretical and methodological breakthroughs and to have a co-ordinated series of empirical projects has thus not been taken. Further, whole areas of debate – around work, for example – opened up by feminist scholarship in the 1970s, are still being researched in funded programmes with little or no consideration of sexual divisions. For instance, the research programmes on globalisation, economic and social change in Central and Eastern Europe, the single European market, environmental change, and governance, to give just some major examples.[22]

Alongside the continued marginalisation of sexual divisions in the core of sociology and by funding agencies, there have, however, been fundamental changes within higher education, and so in the conditions of academic labour. Those entering the profession now commonly face casualisation in the form of short-term contracts, extensive use of lowly paid teaching, and teaching/term-time-only contracts. At the same time, they are under pressure to present and publish academic papers. The tight job market forces contract researchers into short-cut production of hurriedly executed funded research, resulting in papers based on raw or at best semi-digested data, as they move on to the next project – a situation described by Holland *et al.* (1993) as 'Kentucky fast research'. In 1994, those in part-time and/or temporary academic posts are more firmly trapped there than their counterparts in 1974.

Other changes, especially the increase in student numbers without new resources, and finance-led pressures to reach higher and higher research ratings, are leading to a widening gap between staff and students, and between those who teach undergraduates and those who research. Except for a diminishing minority, those working in universities have little time to reflect and to read, and discussion with peers is replaced by writing the next research proposal or completing a research degree in record time. The demonstration of quality is formally through conformity to measures any sociology graduate would reject as methodologically inadequate; and, informally, in terms of powerful networks well understood by political sociologists.

This situation contrasts markedly with the 1970s. Those were not golden years, but the resource base at least gave time and space for doctoral students, for staff and for contract researchers to think through, to question and to build on the work of their predecessors. These conditions are now largely absent.

Attendance at the BSA conference in Aberdeen was not tied to looking for research funding: there *was* no money for work on sexual divisions. In 1994 it was, however, noticeable how people were using the conference as an opportunity to talk to those they thought had access to funds. In addition, there was little intellectual challenge offered to paper-givers. This was partly because there were five times as many papers (258 as against 58) in a conference of roughly the same length, with several grouped in each session, leaving the audience little chance to discuss any particular one. But partly also because the emphasis seemed to be on respect for diversities, rather than engagement. Hence, the 1974 conference was heady and political; and the 1994 one friendly and professional.

While the women's caucus met as usual in 1994, given the decline of the women's movement, such a group is more difficult to organise and programme. There is no outside agenda, no source of political training, and no-one who holds us, as academics/sociologists, accountable. The caucus's grounding in the political experience gained in the years from 1968 to the early 1970s (from the Vietnam Solidarity Campaign and radical politics more generally) is rarely known. Consequently, elements from the current political and intellectual climate, including distrust of structure and promotion of diversity, are influential. In the workshop we held in 1994 (from which this paper derives), women talked a lot about the problems they were having with 'post feminist' students – those who think the battles have been won; those who think 'battles' were never necessary; and those who say that because some men now teach or attend courses on gender, things are well on the way to being all right – and how different these students are from those with a feminist consciousness. However, given the present political and intellectual climate and the conditions in which sociologists research and teach, a clearly political, feminist caucus would seem even more necessary than it was twenty years ago – but by the same token, that much more difficult to organise effectively.

One factor contributing to this is certainly the way women's studies has drawn energy from sociology. The first feminist courses in higher education in Britain began as 'women and society' and 'sexual divisions', usually as final-year sociology options. In the caucus itself we debated, on the one hand, whether to develop informal courses outside academia (because the inevitable corrupting influence of universities would dilute feminism),[23] and on the other, whether to establish formal adult education, masters or full-time undergraduate degree courses in women's studies, or to aim for mainstreaming into the existing discipline(s). In the event, women sociologists virtually created women's studies in Britain (unlike the USA) – as is evident when one looks at who were the main movers to establish it in the late 1970s at the universities of Kent, York, Lancaster and Bradford (as well as, unsuccessfully, at the LSE, Essex and Sussex). (Again the history remains to be written.) In consequence, many of the women sociologists most active in 1974, who had or who subsequently got teaching jobs, are no longer in sociology. They want to work on women/gender, and women's studies offers a more (theoretically, collegially and now institutionally) congenial environment. Some are even pushing to separate women's studies from sociology to become a discipline in its own right – all of which has taken much of the focused look at sexual divisions away from sociology.

But there is more to women's studies than sociology – and from the first MA established at Kent in 1980, women's studies has been multidisciplinary in the social sciences and humanities – albeit heavily reliant on sociology. And other disciplines now challenge sociological analyses within women's studies (or rather, they challenge their own constructions of sociology) – as we shall see.

THEORETICAL ISSUES IN 1994

Members of The Equality of the Sexes Committee proposed the theme of 'sexuality' for 1994 to the 1992 AGM. How and when this was transformed into 'sexualities' and the arguments put forward for the change will, we hope, be part of the editorial contribution to the conference volumes. It is possible that the change signalled nothing more than a wish to convey an anti-essentialist standpoint. Or it may indicate an approach to sociology more broadly in which the very fact of difference justifies the impossibility of any generalisable theoretical statements or political practice.

In some of the papers presented in 1994, sexuality was used interchangeably with gender. While feminists have always been very clear that sexuality is part, but not the whole, of sexual divisions, it is possible some were chosing to conflate sexuality and gender for political reasons. But other papers appeared either *to confuse* sexuality and gender or to think that *sexuality had nothing to do with gender*. For instance, some had sexuality in their title, but then talked only of gender; while much of the work on AIDS did not look at gender at all. Where the power divisions between men and women *were* recognised, heterosexuality was usually taken for granted and critiqued, but not problematised. That is to say, the issue was presented as being the problems women face in their sexual relationships with men (infection, contraception, emotional witholding) and the problems men have with women – not why women have relationships (sexual and other) with men; nor indeed why 'men' and 'women' exist as social groups defined by having sexual relationships. Thus it appears that in much of the recent research on sexuality, sexual practice has somehow become detached from gender – or to have superseded it. If this is the case, the disconnection needs to be examined and explained.[24]

The WLM challenged sociology in 1974, and got some response in terms of both changing the organisation of the profession and the BSA itself, and encouraging the development of empirical and theoretical research. But most of the latter has not entered the sociological mainstream, so students can still reach the third year of a sociology degree and find Mary Maynard's article on reshaping sociology (1990) a revelation.

As we have said, partly as a result of this, many of the individuals who did the challenging on sexual divisions within sociology, have left it for women's studies. Here, however, they are now confronted by those from literary backgrounds who have discovered postmodernism – *and* some from sociology itself who have moved into cultural studies and now eschew 'the social' (see Barrett, 1992, and the critique in Adkins and Lury, 1996). Both the latter groups attack sociology, and suggest that in terms of 'smart' work on gender, sociology is not the discipline to be in any longer. They question its ability to get to grips with issues around gender and sexuality (and environmentalism and science and . . .).

Postmodern feminism is actively rewriting the history of feminist theory, (re)discovering the importance of context, (re)discovering that actors make their own history and (re)discovering that the meaning of things is not inherent in them but socially given. It dismisses as naive taking a 'pro-woman stance' or 'networking', and asserts that deconstructing texts is as important and as political as research on rape.

This causes many of us to despair – not as a function of our age, because young feminist sociologists feel it too – that women do not read, and specifically do not read and think, sociologically. Instead, many dismiss sociology on the basis of their uninformed presumptions about it. Hence arguments are now recurring – around action versus structure and the supposed 'victimisation' of women, around 'respecting' women's experience and appropriate methodologies for feminist research, around diversity and fragmentation,[25] around the use of the term 'materialist feminism', and around identity, etc. – which have already been fought through several times before during the last twenty years. Arguments are not being moved on because new gurus have not read the literature and because some do not understand issues which could be sorted out in the first term of the first year of a course in sociology.

In the late 1960s and the 1970s, it became fashionable in some quarters to counter abstracted theory by concentrating on the situation, without placing the directly observed or experienced relations of individuals into a framework capable of explaining or understanding them. Peter Worsley, referring to ethnomethodology and symbolic interactionism, argued that they

> have no explicit conceptualisation of the supra-situational, of social structure or culture, as societal phenomena, even less of inter-societal cross-cultural or world-systemic relations . . . To work with a social theory that . . . has no concept of society . . . makes it impossible to

produce a sociology which can answer to most of the major problems of understanding social life. (1974, p. 9)

Different names are now used, but we would maintain that these criticisms are equally applicable to much of the work adopting a
poststructuralist or postmodernist approach. Moreover, some cultural
studies re-invents modes of thinking which incorporate all the shortcomings of symbolic interactionism, without its descriptive strengths.

The conference in Aberdeen was avowedly a sociology, not a women's
movement conference, though it took up a women's movement agenda:
'sexual divisions in society' was arguably a translation of WLM
understandings into sociologese. But much research on gender/sexual-
ity in 1994 is done by those with AIDS research or women's studies
or cultural studies rather than sociological backgrounds – and sometimes with a hearty disrespect for sociology and for feminism (hence
the dominant debate in 1994 between queer theory and feminism).

CONCLUSION

One of the aims of feminist research since the emergence of the new
feminist movements has been a concern with developing an active relation between research and feminist political practice, so that the knowledge produced contributes to changing gendered inequality and
domination of existing social relations. Substantive concerns influenced
the subjects investigated and the kinds of questions asked and the types
and range of research methods adopted. This approach has produced a
very considerable empirical and theoretical literature on women's location and experience and on structural inequalities between men and
women. It has also developed over the past decade a body of work on
feminist epistemology, methodology and methods (Harding, 1987;
Maynard, 1990, 1994). The expansion of women's studies and the
development of optional courses on gender in academic institutions
have been a feature of the period which is believed in some quarters
to reflect an acceptance of feminism.

The women's movement that we knew and the wider radical political
groupings we mentioned as part of the context of the early 1970s are
virtually gone.[26] It is therefore not surprising that the development of
theory in relation to the politics of feminist practice has declined sharply,
though it has not disappeared entirely. The interrelation of theory and

practice is never unproblematic, but in 1994, in contrast to 1974 or even 1984, it is not perceived as relevant, let alone central, to developing feminist thought. There is an absence in some research and in writing about theory of the sharp critical edge which marked much of the earlier work. Within the discipline this is seen in 'the turn to culture' and 'the turn to masculinist theory'. Feminist academics who take cultural accounts as 'factual', for example, or personal experience as a prime ground for validating knowledge, are in danger of ignoring the social processes by which interpretations are reached and knowledge produced. Interpretation and knowledge are never neutral. They are linked to political (value) positions and nothing is to be gained by denying that this is so, certainly not by feminists who are interested in transforming the hierarchies of gender. Respecting and being informed by experience is a beginning not the end of feminist scholarship. Analysis of cultural phenomena is one part of sociology. It is not the whole, and to try to make it so is a large step backwards.

NOTES

1. The volumes produced from the 1974 conference were Barker and Allen (eds) (1976a, b) and from the 1982 conference, Gamarnikow *et al.* (1983a, b).
2. With thanks to Jalna Hanmer, who organised the workshop with us at the 1994 BSA conference and contributed to our subsequent discussions.
3. In 1971 a conference on women had been proposed at the BSA executive committee, but rejected (*Times Higher Education Supplement*, 15 March 1974, p. 8). It was not the case, as some believed, that what they saw as an 'inaccessible' conference venue was chosen for 1974 because of the theme. Aberdeen was booked *before* the theme was changed to 'sexual divisions and society'.
4. Most at the end of their undergraduate years and some when they were no longer needed as research assistants.
5. Of the 58 papers, 32 were by women and a further seven had women co-presenters. Neither the title nor the format nor the selection of papers met with approval in many quarters.
6. Previously BSA conference organisers had invited individuals to offer papers and some screened out oppositional views. Keynote speakers were invited and, as with the majority of paper givers, these were usually elite males. Our attempts to involve keynote speakers, at the express request of the BSA executive, failed because it was too late in the day.
7. Robin Oakley wrote to the *Times Higher Education Suplement* (29 March 1974) complaining it was not on women (and he and Ann Oakley also spoke to us at the conference).

8. Two responded positively (Brown, 1976; Frankenberg, 1976) and other
   more junior men also took up the challenge (e.g. Bell and Newby (1976)
   with the concept of deference; and Barron and Norris (1976) with dual
   labour market theory).
9. A *locus classicus* being men at Birkbeck College who had written a letter saying 'whatever next? Green Studies?' [*sic*] – but a 'sister' saw it
   and persuaded them they would look stupid if they sent it.
10. Unlike the Political Science Association, the British Psychological So-
    ciety and the Institute of Historical Research, which remained resolutely
    elitist.
11. Which would currently be impossible, given the number of papers. There
    were 31 papers in Surrey in 1973; 58 in Aberdeen in 1974; 50 in Kent
    in 1975; 187 in Kent in 1992; 265 in Essex in 1993 and 258 in Central
    Lancashire in 1994.
12. This was managed by members pooling travelling expenses and then paying
    according to income, the provision of free food and accommodation by
    those living locally, and the use of the facilities of organisations and
    institutions to which women had access. No one counted her time.
13. See BSA (1975, 1976).
14. This was not without considerable discussion, since there were fears that
    it would lead to the area being claimed and controlled by those in the
    Association who were opposed to it or did not share the aims of the
    caucus.
15. The lifting of the age bar (of 27) by the SSRC in 1970s, with pressure
    exerted by, among others, the BSA, enabled mature students to apply for
    studentships. This was especially important for women.
16. Organised by Richard Scase on 'Advanced Industrial Society' (see Scase,
    1977).
17. By the 1975 conference, there had already been some regrouping. One
    male professor from an eminent university argued in the AGM that it
    was perfectly appropriate to ask women questions at interviews about
    their domestic situations, because as good sociologists we should be con-
    cerned about the well-being of children. At this conference also some
    men came to the women's caucus and refused to leave when asked. So
    we went to another room and refused to let them through the door.
       The history of the BSA, which has recently been commissioned, will,
    we hope, provide a comprehensive account and fuller analysis of these
    events than we have space for here.
18. Ann Oakley's *Sex Gender and Society* was published in 1972, but as
    Delphy (1993) points out, it has little on oppression. It is in a 'Margaret
    Meadian' tradition of cross-cultural comparison, stressing the variety of
    the division of tasks between men and women, but with no Marxian sense
    of exploitation associated with a division of labour. It stresses how the
    variety of human potential is divided up very differently in each society
    and the variations in hierarchy between men and women; but sex div-
    ision is taken as given, and gender is argued to be culturally elaborated
    on biological sex.
19. The current Research Committee on Women of the International Socio-
    logical Association, when established as a Working Group in 1974, was

called 'Sex Roles and Society' to make it acceptable to the hierarchy, despite strong opposition to the title. Shirley Nuss has recorded how it took almost a decade of pressure on the ISA before the title was changed (Nuss 1994). It appears that currently the replacement of the word 'women' by 'gender' is being canvassed in this as in many other international organisations.

20. Anthropologists took a more holistic view of societies than sociologists in the early 1970s, and had long talked of the sexual division of labour and of the position of men and women in relation to each other, but with little or no sense of women's being oppressed, and giving most attention to men. See, for example, *Cambridge Anthropology*, vol. 1, no. 3 (1974); Ardener (1975); *Critique of Anthropology*, vol. 3, nos 9 & 10 (1977); and Mathieu (1991).

21. In 1985, when Diana Leonard was funded by the ESRC to look at ongoing research on women/gender, she and Margaret Littlewood found that, even at that late date, almost all the (relatively sparse) work on sexuality was being done unfunded or by PhD students.

22. A few seminar series, workshops and conferences have, however, been funded.

23. We even had discussions around establishing a women's university.

24. This would include exploring the relationship (if any) to the availability of financial support for AIDS research, the influences of gay and men's studies, and the growth of queer theory.

25. We should, rather, stress concentration of capital and power and wealth, which does women down rather well.

26. Cf., however, the Editorial in *Trouble and Strife*, no. 27, by Adkins and Leonard (1994).

REFERENCES

Adkins, L. and Leonard, D. (1994) 'Editorial: Then and Now', *Trouble and Strife: The Radical Feminist Magazine*, **27** (tenth anniversary issue), pp. 3–6.

Adkins, L. and Leonard, D. (1995) *Sex in Question: French Materialist Feminism* (London: Taylor & Francis).

Adkins, L. and Lury, C. (1996) 'The Cultural, the Sexual and the Gendering of the Labour Market', in L. Adkins and V. Merchant (eds), *Sexualizing the Social: Power and the Organization of Sexuality* (Basingstoke: Macmillan).

Ardener, S. (ed.) (1975) *Perceiving Women* (London: Dent/Malaby).

Barker, D. L. and Allen, S. (eds) (1976a) *Sexual Divisions and Society: Process and Change* (London: Tavistock).

Barker, D. L. and Allen, S. (eds) (1976b) *Dependence and Exploitation in Work and Marriage* (London: Longman).

Barrett, M. (1992) 'Words and Things: Materialism and Method in Contemporary Feminist Analysis', in M. Barrett and A. Phillips (eds), *Destabilizing Theory: Contemporary Feminist Debates* (Cambridge: Polity).

Barron, R. and Norris, G. (1976) 'Sexual Divisions and the Dual Labour

Market', in D. L. Barker and S. Allen (eds), *Dependence and Exploitation in Work and Marriage* (London: Longman).

Bell, C. and Newby, H. (1976) 'Husbands and Wives: The Dynamics of the Deferential Dialectic', in D. L. Barker and S. Allen (eds), *Dependence and Exploitation in Work and Marriage* (London: Longman).

Brake, M. (1976) 'I May Be a Queer, But at Least I am a Man: Male Hegemony and Ascribed versus Achieved Gender', in D. L. Barker and S. Allen (eds), *Sexual Divisions and Society: Process and Change* (London: Tavistock).

British Sociological Association (1975) *Working Party on the Status of Women in the Profession: Report to AGM*, April.

British Sociological Association (1976) *Sociology without Sexism: A Source Book* (London: BSA).

Brown, R. K. (1976) 'Women as Employees: Some Comments on Research in Industrial Sociology', in D. L. Barker and S. Allen (eds), *Dependence and Exploitation in Work and Marriage* (London: Longman).

Butler, J. (1993) *Bodies That Matter: On the Discursive Limits of 'Sex'* (London: Routledge).

Coulson, M. (1972) 'Role: A Redundant Concept in Sociology? Some Educational Considerations', in J. A. Jackson (ed), *Role* (Cambridge: Cambridge University Press).

Delphy, C. (1993) 'Rethinking Sex and Gender', *Women's Studies International Forum*, 16(1): pp. 1–9.

Edwards, A. (1989) 'The Sex/Gender Distinction: Has it Outlived its Usefulness?', *Australian Feminist Studies*, 10 (Summer): pp. 1–12.

Evans, M. (1991) 'The Problem of Gender for Women's Studies', in J. Aaron and S. Walby (eds), *Out of the Margins: Women's Studies in the Nineties* (London: Falmer Press).

Frankenberg, R. (1976) 'In the Production of their Lives, Men(?) . . . Sex and Gender in British Community Studies', in D. L. Barker and S. Allen (eds), *Sexual Divisions and Society: Process and Change* (London: Tavistock).

Gamarnikow, E., Morgan, D. H. J., Purvis, J. and Taylorson, D. (eds) (1983a) *Gender, Class and Work* (London: Heinemann).

Gamarnikow, E., Morgan, D. H. J., Purvis, J. and Taylorson, D. (ed) (1983b) *The Public and the Private* (London: Heinemann).

Gatens, M. (1983) 'A Critique of the Sex/Gender Distinction', in J. Allen and P. Patton (eds), *Beyond Marxism? Interventions after Marx* (New South Wales: Intervention Publications); republished in S. Gunew (ed.) (1991) *A Reader in Feminist Knowledge* (London: Routledge).

Guillaumin, C. (1982) 'The Question of Difference', *Feminist Issues*, 2(1): pp. 33–52.

Guillaumin, C. (1995) *Racism, Sexism, Power and Ideology* (London: Routledge).

Harding, S. (ed.) (1987) *Feminism and Methodology* (Milton Keynes: Open University Press).

Holland, J., Hey, V., Mauthner, M. and Sharp, S. (1993) 'Behind Closed Doors: Researching the Family', BSA conference paper, University of Essex, April.

Leonard, D. and Allen, S. (eds) (1991) *Sexual Divisions Revisited* (London: Macmillan).

Mathieu, N.-C. (1980) 'Masculinity/Femininity', *Feminist Issues*, 1(1): pp. 14–19.

Mathieu, N. C. (1991) *L'Anatomie Politique: Catégorisation et Idéologies du Sexe* (Paris: Côté-femmes).

Maynard, M. (1990) 'The Re-Shaping of Sociology? Trends in the Study of Gender', *Sociology*, 24(2): pp. 269–90.

Maynard, M. (1994) 'Methods, Practice and Epistemology: The Debate about Feminism and Research', in M. Maynard and J. Purvis (eds), *Researching Women's Lives from a Feminist Perspective* (London: Taylor & Francis).

Nuss, S. (1994) 'A History of the ISA Research Committee on Women', unpublished paper.

Oakley, A. (1972) *Sex, Gender and Society* (London: Temple Smith).

Scase, R. (ed.) (1977) *Industrial Society: Class, Cleavage and Control* (London: Allen & Unwin).

Times Higher Educational Supplement (1974) 'Focus on Women', 15 March, p. 8.

Wittig, M. (1992) *The Straight Mind and Other Essays* (Boston: Beacon Press/ Hemel Hempstead: Harvester Wheatsheaf).

Worsley, P. M. (1974) 'The State of Theory and The Status of Theory', *Sociology*, 8: pp. 1–17.

2 Intimate Citizenship and the Culture of Sexual Story Telling
KEN PLUMMER

Oppressed people resist by identifying themselves as subjects, by defining their reality, shaping their new identity, naming their history, telling their story

bell hooks

'Stories' have recently moved centre stage in social thought: as the pathways to understanding culture; as the bases of identity; as the tropes for making sense of the past; as 'narrative truths' (e.g. Spence, 1982; Bruner, 1987; Maines, 1993). A 'narrative moment' has now been sensed. Elsewhere, in some considerable detail, I have presented the elements and questions that need to be adressed in a symbolic interactionist account of story telling (Plummer, 1995). My focus is on one kind of story, 'sexual stories': the personal experience narratives of the intimate. Examples include the stories told by men and women of coming out as gay and lesbian; of women who discover they 'love too much'; of tales told by the survivors of abortion, rape and incest; or of 'New Men' rediscovering their newly masculine roots through mythical stories (e.g. Norwood, 1985; Penelope and Wolfe, 1988; Bly and Wolfe, 1990). For in the late twentieth century, it could seem as if every sexual story that could be told is being told. Many desires have found a voice. From the well-rehearsed tales of 'coming out', 'surviving abuse' and 'recovery' found in every book store, to the continuing babble on TV programmes such as 'Donahue' or 'Oprah', the swirling simulacrum of sexual story telling seems everywhere. We have arrived in the Sexual Tower of Babel where a world of past silences has been breached. How have we come to this curious situation? What has led to this new culture where sexual stories are everywhere? When does a story come into its time? And what are the political implications of all this? These are the concerns of this essay.

CREATING A CULTURE OF SEXUAL STORY-TELLING

Sexual stories cannot always be heard. Lesbian and gay coming-out stories, could hardly be heard publicly before the 1970s, although they may have been secretly said. Survivor stories of sexual abuse were largely silenced until the 1980s. These were dormant stories. But since then there has been a flood of tellings for those who would hear – in books, in therapy groups, in TV shows. Would the damagingly different stories of sex and harrassment told by Clarence Thomas and Anita Hill in the autumn of 1991 have been heard at all in, say, 1960, or 1860? (cf. Morrison, 1992). And who could have said – and who could have heard – the stories of 'Women who love Porn' on Donahue in 1975?

Stories are best told when they can be heard. There is usually no point in telling a tale without a receptive and appreciative listener, and one who is usually part of a wider community of support. To publicly tell a story to someone who will then mock you, disbelieve you, excommunicate you, sack you, hospitalise you, imprison you or bash you bleedingly senseless to the ground may be brave but it is foolhardy: it is not a fertile ground for the amplification of that story. It may well be better to be silent, at least for the moment. But what has happened over the past few decades is the proliferation of an array of different audiences willing to hear some different voices and some different stories – and some of these audiences have then become tellers themselves, adding to collective communities of story telling. The contemporary growth of sexual stories – through books, media, new social movements – can perhaps best be seen through the shifting of social spaces in which listeners and audiences break down traditional boundaries around stories. Whereas once stories were largely part of a localised oral culture, told in small bounded worlds, the nineteenth century witnessed stories moving into mass print – into the tabloids, penny press and scandal sheets (cf. Bird, 1992); and the twentieth century has seen them become television docudramas, talk-show fodder and self-help manuals available for mass consumption. Modern mass media organisation has shifted access to worlds that may not have been visible, accessible or even thinkable before. Whilst in one sense it has rendered the world mass, in another it has rendered it segmented, fragmented, dispersed. Thus the new electonic media have blurred previously distinct spheres, such as those between men and women, young and old, gay and straight, black and white – making once segregated worlds more pervasively accessible (Meyrowitz, 1985). When our central

medium was face-to-face talk, separate worlds could be created in which
some stories were kept away from others or, indeed, not permitted at
all. Modern media breaks down such boundaries: telephones make sexual
communication across place more easy, travel and tourism opens wider
vistas of sexual possibility, television chat shows enable one to hear
about the sexual problems of all manner of groups over breakfast, whilst
MTV can tell its postmodern sexual stories twenty-four hours a day.
In England a child being sexually abused can come to hear of Esther
Ranzen, Child HelpLine, where to ring, what to say. For many, these
stories fall into an impersonalised mass: to hear a story of sexual impotence does not lead you to a community of impotence sufferers – or
even to a community of men keen to swap stories of their impotence.
But for others, communities of support do exist. So, simultaneously,
mass undifferentiated audiences are created side by side with new segregated worlds of 'specialist' consumers. The neophyte young lesbian
may first find herself through a lesbian popstar like k. d. lang on TV,
and may then find 'her story' in the more segregated world of the
lesbian community – with its own fictions, memories and magazines
stuffed full of the stories of gay life (Zimmerman, 1991). Modern audiences for stories are both more *and* less segregated.

Stories come into their time when a community has been fattened
up, rendered ripe and willing to hear such stories. Whilst they can be
heard amongst isolated individuals, they can gain no momentum if they
stay in this 'privatised' mode. And personal narratives do remain in
the private sphere of dim inarticulateness, having no group to sustain
them. For stories to flourish there must be social worlds waiting to
hear. Social worlds are not like communities of old: no locale is required, only a sense of belonging, sharing traditions, having common
memories. A key point about the 'coming out stories' is that they pro-
gressively acquired an *interpretive community of support* which enabled them to flourish. There is historical amplification and feedback
at work here. For sure, people could 'come out' as gay in the 1960s
and before: but then it really meant in isolation, to oneself, a solitary
lover or in the disguised, furtive 'twilight' worlds of the secretive
homosexual underworld. To turn this tale from a private, personal tale
to one that can be told publicly and loudly is a task of immense political proportions. It requires a collective effort, creating spaces in the
wider social order and the wider story telling spaces. Bit by bit –
through the leaflet, the pamphlet, the booklet, the book, the meeting,
the recording, the newspaper, the television programme, the film, the
chat show, the video – the voice gains a little more space, and the

claims become a little bigger. There will always be counter stories too, but these may also have their part to play.

Back to the Future: History, Contingency and Story Telling

A full social history of the rise of these new stories and audiences awaits writing. But the fragments for assembling it already exist. Foucault, for instance, has charted the long revolution. Starting somewhere back in the eighteenth century in the Western world, he locates the paths through which the modern period brought a 'discursive explosion', an 'incitement to discourse', a desire to 'tell everything':

> Western man has been drawn for three centuries to the task of telling everything concerning his sex; that since the classical age there has been a constant optimization and an increasing valorization on the discourse on sex; and that this carefully analytical discourse was meant to yield multiple effects of displacement, intensification, reorientation and modification of desire itself. Not only were the boundaries of what one could say about sex enlarged, and men compelled to hear it said; but more important, discourse was connected to sex by a complex organisation with varying effects, by a deployment that cannot be adequately explained merely by referring it to a law of prohibition. A censorship of sex? There was installed rather an aparatus for producing an ever greater quantity of discourse about sex, capable of functioning and taking effect in its very economy. (Foucault, 1979, p. 23)

Foucault's compelling account of the workings of power through this apparatus is too well known to repeat. And it is possible to take Foucault further, and like Baudrillard argue that all the stories that are now told bear no relation to reality at all, that anything and everything can be said about sex, that it is all simulation, play, hyperreality. Discourses have imploded into themselves, sex is dead, simulations are all we have. But I think both Foucault and later Baudrillard go too far. Baudrillard is the philosopher of excess, and provides little real aid in understanding the direct empirical world. It is not the case that everything can now be said about sex – much has been said, but not everything. And indeed many stories are a long way from the hyperreal – tell an abuse victim or a young woman coming out as a lesbian that their stories are mere simulations, mere excrements of a hyperreal reality, with no links to real pains, sufferings, life! But even the (slightly) more measured and much-cited account of Foucault is couched at a level of generality – of the deployment of discursive strategies and power/knowledge spirals – which is too opaque. Yes, 'sexuality' has been thoroughly reconstituted for the modern period and, indeed, 'sexual stories' could slot neatly into his schema. Yet his account neglects the rise of mass media in all its diverse forms, and it provides little space for the generation of particular kinds of stories at particular moments: it is all strangely undifferentiated. Stories about sex have not all been fashioned from the same cloth in the modern world. Indeed, to hark back to the gay and lesbian story, there is a world of difference between the morbid pathological stories so prevalent in the nineteenth century, and the 'liberating' coming out tales of the late twentieth. Power may be ubiquitous – for Foucault, as for me. But some forms of power expand choices (coming out stories) and are empowering; whilst other forms reduce choices (pathology/victim tales), and lead to control and domination. What hence needs to be explained is why specific stories have their specific times, whilst others do not. Why do some stories lie dormant, some become dominant (at particular moments), some take on a dissident position, whilst yet still others become dead, moving out of their time? And many stories, possibly most, undergo recycling – for example, the narratives of sexual danger so popular in late Victorian England returned to popularity in the late twentieth century, as did narratives of decadence and disease (Showalter, 1990; Walkowitz, 1992).

A first step in this task is to avoid talking in such grand historical sweeps as Foucault, and to turn to a more specific time. Whilst the seeds of modern sexual stories are there in the nineteenth century, it is to the last four decades of the twentieth that real attention must be paid. Whatever changes occurred in the nineteenth century to establish preconditions of sexual story-telling, a qualitative shift occurs in the mid-twentieth. Most analysts of sexuality agree that something dramatic happened to sexuality during the 1960s and 1970s. This was a time which saw 'the sea-change in the sexualisation of modern capitalist societies' (Evans, 1993, p. 65), a feminization of sex (Ehrenreich and Jacobs, 1986), and ultimately a democratisation of intimacy. (Giddens, 1993, p. 65).

There are many reasons for these changes. One factor is surely the growth and proliferation of communications. Not only have the major means of mass communication become widely available to most (from mass paperbacking to records, TV, telephones, videos, etc.), but enough stories have been told publicly and circulated freely to reach a critical take off point. A string of important narrative tales around the intimate pile up in the latter part of the twentieth century, each one making it more and more plausible for others to emerge. In the late 1930s, the cheap popular paperback was invented and 'the world of books – like the world itself – would never be the same' (Davis, 1984, p. 13). The late 1940s saw the bestselling Kinsey Reports on *Human Sexual Behaviour* – turgidly taxonomic and ponderously long as they were. And then a steady flow of major books raised their own story: Betty Friedan's *Feminine Mystique* (tales of invisible and oppressed womanhood), Masters and Johnson's *Human Sexual Inadequacy* (scientific tales of sexual dysfunction), Alex Comfort's *Joy of Sex* (tales of lovemaking practices), Nancy Friday's *My Secret Garden* (tales of woman's fantasies, updated seventeen years later as *Women on Top*), Susan Brownmiller's epic *Against Our Will* (tales of rape) along with *The Sensuous Woman, The Happy Hooker, The Total Woman* and hundreds of other delights. Throughout the 1980s, one sexual paperback after another became a bestseller in the USA: *The Intimate Male, The Hite Report on Male Sexuality, Pleasures, Swept Away, Sweet Suffering, Women who Love too Much, Rediscovering Love, Remaking Love, Men Who hate Women and the Women Who Love Them, The Cassanova Complex, Looking for Love in all the Wrong Places, Escape from Intimacy, Smart Love, Sex for One, Nice Guys Sleep Alone* – to name but a few!

Yet whilst the spread of the media and the cumulative proliferation of stories provide a context ripe for more and more sexual stories, other factors have played a part in creating a culture of sexual story telling. First is the major spread of consumerisms. The post war period is marked increasingly by the rise of a logic of consumerism, which leads to increasing advertising and marketing. 'Consumption objects' become a means to demarcate life styles and hierarchies. 'Sex' in all it forms is manifestly part of this Big Sell. Newspapers seek out sex stories, willing to pay a high price, because of the likelihood of increased circulation; publishers pursue more and more outrageous stories – Madonna's *Sex*, for instance – because they often sell well and, especially in the USA, frequently head the best seller charts; advertisers head for the chat shows and the soaps that peddle sex; therapists and sexologists may be less commercial, but still know where the money is (Featherstone, 1991). Everywhere, the expansion of capitalism brings with it the expansion of sex consumerism. And an important part of the consumerist culture has been the rise of 'youth culture' in the post-Second-World-War period. Of course, 'youth' existed before; but not within the space of such a well organised market – of magazines, films, television programmes (the whole of MTV seems marketed for youth). An array of super pop stars sing of sex and write their sexual stories. From the early furore that surrounded Elvis Presley's appearance on the Johnny Carson Show; through the 1960s with Jimi Hendrix copulating with his guitar and simulating masturbatory ejaculation on stage; through to the banning of the Sex Pistols, Frankie Goes to Hollywood and on to the ubiqitous Madonna scandals, sex stories have never been far away from the youthful consumer.

Alongside the rise of both media and consumerism, a new infrastructure of 'cultural intermediaries' has developed. This large occupational culture connects to media, advertising, and 'para' intellectual information, and generates a proliferating industry concerned with the production and selling of 'symbolic goods'. There were, for instance, no 'talk show' hosts who could invite you on to television to tell your sexual story before the 1950s; there were few 'celebrity intellectuals', there were no Dr Ruths. But in the late modern period, people with a word processor or a video or simply an enthusiasm can decide to tell their sexual stories and indeed to sell sell their sexual stories – making themselves into part of the sexual 'chattering classes' Everyone seeks their Wharholian fifteen minutes!

Closely allied to this rise of new cultural intermediaries is the acceleration of the indvidualistic 'therapeutic/expressive culture' which fosters the telling of self narratives. There is a long history in the USA of self-help development. Reaching back to Benjamin Franklin, amplified by Freudian thought, developing through the therapies of the 1960s, symbolised momentarily by the counterculture, and drifting into the New Age, this whole modern period has been characterised negatively as the *Culture of Narcissism*, and, more positively, as the *Psychological Society*.

All this telling of sex has consistently been surrounded in controversy, moral panics and a stream of moral crusades which have tended to polarise positions keeping 'sex stories' as contested stories well in focus in public debate (Starker, 1990). Indeed, without polarities the stories may have lost much of their potency: ironically, the protests may well have amplified the context for more and more stories, by bringing them constantly into sharp public attention (even if just to denounce them). The right contest the left; the orthodox contests the progressive; the romantic contests the libertarian; the right-to-lifers contest the right to choose; the moralists contest the causalists; and the traditionalists, modernists and postmodernists are all at odds with each other (cf. Davies, 1981; Hunter, 1991; Seidman, 1992). Conflict and contest each serve to extend and highlight the power of sexual talk, pushing the stories further and further. This, then, is the backdrop to the creation of the modern culture of sexual story telling. The growth of mass media, the expansion of consumption, the rise of new cultural intermediaries and the expansion of a therapeutic culture – all locked into conflicts which highlight stories in their warfare. It is against this backdrop that more and more stories can be told.

Making Stories Happen: A Formalist Account

Sexual stories told in the past may have little relevance for today, just as stories told today may have little relevance for the future. Stories have their times. Just as some voices from the past were not heard, some voices of today remain mute. Many of the silenced voices of the past – of women, of gays, of 'the other' – have created some spaces, told some stories, brought about some change; but there are also stories that still we have not imagined.

A number of themes suggest when stories can be told, what I will call *a generic process of telling sexual stories* (cf. Prus, 1987). I put them in a rough sequence which indicates necessary conditions for the full-blown 'successful' telling of a sexual story (or indeed any story): for a story 'finding its time'. These generic processes are:

1. imagining – visualising – empathising;
2. articulating – vocalising – announcing;
3. inventing identities – becoming story-tellers;
4. creating social worlds/communities of support;
5. creating a culture of public problems.

The process can be pictured as a move from an 'inner world' of telling stories to the self privately to an increasingly public one where the circle of discourse becomes wider and wider. In the earliest moments, the story can hardly be imagined: it may be told privately as a tale to oneself. Later it gets told to a few people – a lover, a friend, a psychiatrist. Slowly it can move out into a public domain where it comes to take on a life of its own. It becomes part of a public discourse.

Firstly, then, there are processes of imagining – visualising – empathising. Something – a feeling, a thinking, a doing – is to be envisioned. This can be a very simple task – an issue is felt, experienced, found and is brought into focus as a story. *But I am thinking also of a whole world of feelings and experiences about which we may not even initially know.* They inhabit worlds where it seems that 'nothing unusual is happening' at one moment, and then some kind of 'trouble' appears at another. This 'trouble' has to be recognised – by self or other. Just as in the past 'rape' happened in marriage but was hardly recognised, just as child abuse happened in families and was taken for granted, so what is taken for granted now will not necessarily be in the future. 'Nothing unusual' will become 'trouble'. Betty Friedan, over a quarter of a century ago, could sense 'the problem that has no name'. Oscar Wilde, over a century ago, could speak of the 'love that dared not speak its name'. And Rousseau, over two centuries ago, could save the unnameable for after his death! Good stories of course are intimately connected to the imagination; but much of modern life is also trapped in the conventions and rituals of pre-existing stories which prevent, conceal, and block other ways of seeing. There is a need to recognise *the blocks to imagining* stories that could be told but are currently not.

I am speaking here about experiences hidden from awareness and part of this means entering the world of the unconscious: of repressions, masks, denials. Much of the inner life is kept at bay, sealed off from any potential for story telling. But it also means understanding better the processes of feeling helpless, incapacitation and loss of control. Traditionally, for example, women have sensed less control over their lives than men, and may have been less able to voice their stories because of this. In any event a crucial emergent from this process must be a growing awareness of languages that mask, hide, deny, or erase experiences. To take a major example: menstruation. All girls experience this, and yet it exists largely in a world of silence. Girls may experience a shock, a pain, a concern and yet the public narratives of menstruation are few. Much of the existing story telling around menstruation often cloaks it in myth and danger – the film *Carrie* opens with a menstrual scene, but this in turn places it firmly in a world of danger. Some girls may find communities of support but there is little public discourse that facilitates this often isolated experience.

A myriad of little sexual stories may be imagined – stories of intrigue and romance, stories of extreme eroticism thwarted in everyday life, stories of unhappiness built up through frustrations, stories of wives leaving their partners, tales of divorce through 'bad sex'. But such stories, whilst commonplace, remain culturally insignifcant as long as they fail to enter the more public domain: as long as they are silent.

Hence, crucially, a second generic process – of articulating – vocalising – announcing becomes crucial in the making of stories. To breathe life into the imagination, a language must be found for it. For what has to be seen, there may often not be words. Or if words exist, they may be the wrong words – words which place a wedge between the being and the telling. A space needs to be found where languages can be invented, words can be applied, a voice can be found, a story can be told. This will be a language explosion; from small words whispered alone to the self to whole rhetorics shouted in public spaces – from the trauma of naming your abuse to yourself to the public story at a 'Take Back The Night' rally. Language may not just be a matter of words said, but how the words are said. Thus some words may become little crimped tales told in small corners whilst others become shouted expansive stories told by people aware of power dressing. Here are matters of control over space, body, face, dress, eyes and touch.

Thirdly, there are processes of inventing identities and becoming storytellers. The image I have is that bit by bit stories move out from a small space of imaginings into a language, through a few tellers and into a community ripe and ready to hear. Crucial in this process therefore must be a time when story tellers come into public view: writing books, magazines, appearing on other media, etc. To work at their best they will be 'the stories of our lives' not stories of others co-opted, although in early stages these may be of value. Hence the stronger stories will be those of community – providing programmes and maps where others may be able to sense themselves. Highly individualistic stories without a sense of community will just 'float', with less chance of reaching a critical take off point. Grounded in this will usually be a story of indentity – of who one is, of a sense of unity yet difference. At this moment, the experience and a faltering language gains a voice and a personhood. The 'Gay', the 'Survivor', the 'Recoverer' becomes recognisable, an identity emerges with a sense of past, present, future: history, difference, anticipation. And the narratives of this new personhood start to enter public worlds of talk. The basis of a politics of identity is formed (cf. Calhoun, 1994).

Fourthly, then, this implies creating social worlds (Strauss, 1978). The story has moved out beyond the individual story teller to a community of reception. It is being heard by others. Social worlds must be invented which will hear the story. These 'others' must in some way identify with it, feel it to be part of their 'story'. The correct audiences become crucial. Some of these social worlds may already pre-exist, whilst others may actually be formed by the stories. Thus, many pre-existing social worlds of age (youth worlds, childhood worlds), of race (black worlds/hispanic worlds/asian worlds), of gender, of class provide forums for talk and telling stories. Often such worlds are seg-regated – the stories young men tell each other in the factory are not to be shared with parents or female friends. Other 'worlds' seem to come into being around the stories. The critical take-off point comes when social worlds come together around the story. These interpretive communities exist in and through social worlds of power: they are hierarchically arranged, and some are marginalised whilst others are prioritised. Thus, just having a com-munity will not be sufficient: the more power the community has, the greater the chance of the story of taking hold. Hence the story needs a visible public community of alliance and allegiances which facilitate the telling of the tale.

Fifth, and finally, then, are the generic processes involved in creat-ing a culture of public problems. Here the story moves out of a lim-ited social world and enters an array of arenas of public discourse. Sociologists have long studied the mechanisms through which social problems are socially constructed: 'How the dimensions are carved out, how the number of people drawn into concern about these discussions is increased, how a common pool of knowledge begins to develop for the arena participants, and how all these subprocesses increase the visi-bility of the problem' (Wiener, 1981, p. 14). Telling personal stories is a crucial part of this public process: the human-interest story is one of the key foci in getting issues on agendas. A 'good personal story' will advance a social problems agenda signficantly. For the culture of public problems is a competitive one: many stories are available, but few are chosen. How stories get selected for public attention will de-pend upon such matters as novelty, drama, saturation, the 'carrying capacity' of media, and the competion from other stories. At this stage, the kinds of stories being told will matter enormously, for the story has to attract allies and fend off opponents. It is at this 'stage' that rhetorical work matters most (although clearly it comes into play with most of the other processes, cutting across them). It has now entered a wider discourse, which will involve claims, grounds and warrants pitched against counter-claims, grounds and warrants (cf. Best, 1992). Stories whose time have come will be those that have entered this culture of public problems, the political spectacle. With this, there will be: (a) a large number of people willing to claim it as their own; (b) a willing-ness to tell the story very visibly so that others can identify with it; and (c) the presence of alliances who do not claim the story as their own, but who are keen to give it credibility and support. Indeed, it is in part a measure of political success when allies claim its legitimacy and give it support in large numbers.

INTIMATE CITIZENSHIP: THE POLITICS OF SEXUAL STORIES

Sexual story telling is a political process. Such stories play a prominent role in understanding the workings of the political and moral life of late modern societies. The stories we tell of our lives are deeply implicated in moral and political change and the shifting tales of self and identity carry potential for a radical transformation of the social order (Connolly, 1991; Fraser, 1991; Giddens, 1991; Benhabib, 1992; Fitzgerald, 1994). Stories work their way into changing lives, communities and cultures. Such changes are signs of a new pattern of politics emerging: a weakening of a single-minded and often absolutist concern with the now traditional politics of emancipation (whilst still assuming it as a vast backdrop) and a suggestion of a multiplicity of new projects, new constituencies, new strategies for the future: something new is afoot. This new politics comes in a plethora of forms and labels, moving under various, often contradictory, names: a politics of difference, radical pluralism, communitarianism, a new liberalism, cultural politics, life politics. In short, *a radical, pluralistic, democratic, contingent, participatory politics of human life choices and difference is in the making* (cf. Okin, 1989; Young, 1990; Connolly, 1991; Giddens, 1991; Barber, 1992; Benhabib, 1992).

This new politics has one major axis in 'gender/sexual/erotic' politics, and is heavily dependent upon the stories invented about 'intimacy'. Thus, 'coming out' narratives of gay and lesbian personal experience, no more than the 'breaking the silence' stories of rape survivors, played crucial and critical roles in the development of gay and feminist politics. Moving out of a silence, the stories helped shape a new public language, generating communities to receive and disseminate them on a global scale, ultimately creating more and more spaces for them to be heard. New social movements appear and, in their wake, a whole string of smaller, less organised, and less powerful communities and claims have developed which speak to a wider range of differences. These movements have shaped new stories of identity, and new cultures of political action. 'Rape Stories' and 'Gay Stories' may be seen as emblems of many other potential stories that could be told in the future. And new forms of being have emerged alongside these new stories. Indeed, the (late) modern period has invented stories of being, identity, and community for both rape survivors and gays that has made it increasingly possible to claim 'rights' in ways that could not be done until these stories were invented. The old (and still important) communities of rights spoke of political rights, legal rights or welfare rights of citizenship: the language of women's and gay communities certainly draws upon this – such gains should not be lightly lost – but takes it further. A new set of claims around the body, the relationship and sexuality are in the making. This new field of life politics I will call 'Intimate Citizenship'.

Stories of Intimate Citizenship

Citizenship has been a major concern of Western-style democracies throughout the twentieth century. In the classic formulation of T. H. Marshall, three clusters of citizen rights have emerged chronologically during the past two centuries to deal with concerns over civil, political and social rights – to justice under the law, to political representation and to basic welfare (Marshall, 1963; Turner, 1990). Despite many criticisms, it remains a useful model to sense a general and slow expansion of the idea of the citizen in modernity. In my view, it should not be seen as a necessary, evolutionary or essential concept, but a loose conglomerate of spheres of action whereby communities are developed which attribute certain rights and responsibilities to human beings around the zones of law, politics and welfare. Telling the personal stories of 'their rights' is a crucial part of this. There is hence nothing 'inalienable' or 'given' about such citizen's rights: they are, rather, heavily contingent and dependent upon the communities through which they grow. And, in turn, the stories such communities create help to shape the rights which develop.

To the existing three realms of citizenship, a fourth could now be added at century's end: that of *Intimate Citizenship*. This speaks to an array of concerns too often neglected in past debates over citizenship, and which extend notions of rights and responsibilities. I call this 'Intimate Citizenship' because it is concerned with all those matters linked to our most intimate desires, pleasures and ways of being in the world. Some of this must feed back into the traditional citizenship; but equally, much of it is concerned with new spheres, new debates and new stories. For many people in the late modern world there are many decisions that can, and increasingly have to, be made about a life: making decisions around the *control (or not) over* one's body, feelings, relationships; *access (or not) to* representations, relationships, public spaces etc; and *socially grounded choices (or not) about* identities, gender experiences, erotic experiences. New kinds of new stories are in the making around our bodies, our reproductive capacities, our relationships, our ways of raising children, our feelings, our representations, our identities, our genders, our sexualities, even our spiritualities? An array of new personal narratives that may be told around the intimate are emerging: stories which suggest new living arrangements, new families, new ways of thinking about feelings, bodies, representations and identities, and new modes of the erotic. We can see a proliferation of stories in the recent past, and there is no reason to think they will suddenly cease. Old stories will, however, remain side by side with the new. And in this lies a major source of conflict.

THE WAR OF THE INTIMATE TALES: FROM TRIBALISM TO DIFFERENCE

For with every new story, there is a rival old one. Tales of new families are countered by tales of 'family values': tales of new bodies are countered by traditional values of the 'natural'; tales of new ways of being men and women – even to the point of their dissolution – are countered by 'backlash stories' with the reassertion of traditional masculinity and femininity; and tales of the new sexualities generate intense anxiety over traditional standards of sexuality. Traditional values and absolutist moralities are evoked in the presumption of decline and relativity. Indeed, traditional and largely authoritarian stories of the past are placed severely under threat from a multiplicity of conflicting voices. Will one drown the other out? Can they co-exist, and if so how? What are the possible relationships of different stories to each other? A difficult period awaits.

One recent account by Hunter (1991) has presented the clash in stories as a 'culture war': as the latest manifestation of a religious and moral combat. In the past, the battle grounds were drawn up *between* religions – Protestant versus Catholic, Catholic versus Jew. But now the battle grounds are being drawn up between those of different moral and political visions which cut *across* past schisms, suggesting new alignments. On one side are those of religious orthodoxy – Protestant, Jew, Catholic, Buddhist, Islamic alike – who continue to seek the truth in a fixed authority, usually through a canonical scripture. On the other side are those who look more pragmatically to the shifts in the modern world for clues as to how to live the new moral life. It is a divide between *cultural conservatives/moral traditionalists* and *liberals or cultural progressives*. The former cling to the old stories, the latter are writing new ones even with a sense of their past. But they are telling very different kinds of stories. Whereas the traditionalists tells stories which attempt to encompass all within an obdurate framework of authority and received truth, to lay out the one story which all should adhere to, the progressivists attempt to open up the range of stories, of possibilities. Hunter's account fails to acknowledge clearly, however, that some groups want to tell others what to do: their moral code is a code for themselves it is true, but they wish it to be extended to others. It is a politics of prohibition: they wish to stop abortion, single parent families, pornography, sex education, diverse sexualities, gay rights, etc. The other position is more pragmatic – looking for spaces to open up. It is a politics of possibilities – no one has to have an abortion, but it is possible to. As such the latter is more open and more pluralistic. It is, of course, a story of the right to choose.

The problem of conflicting and competing stories is a central political issue for the future. Can the divergent stories manage to co-exist or will certain tales triumph? There are a range of responses to the problem of competing stories – from fundamentalism and tribalism to a more pluralistic and participatory culture.

The first, and in my view the most dangerous and pessimistic response to the problem of conflicting stories, is the reassertion of *tribalism, fundamentalism* and *separatism*. Here is the affirmation of stories which are exclusive, closed, authoritarian. They prioritise one group, culture and identity over others, and provide one essential or foundational truth over and above others. In many ways it is the politics of the past, still alive in the present: it is the politics against which emancipatory models came to fruition. Some of its arguments may be vital in shaping debates, but their triumph would see the closure of proliferating stories and the triumph of *the* story. It has and will lead to tribal warfare. Today it can be seen in the dissolution of old nation-states, and it is present in religious fundamentalisms of all sorts. Likewise, both sexual and gender fundamentalism (so common in the past) is still on the agenda: with the potential for sexual and gender tribes to assert their own fundamentalist stories. Some of the new social movements around these matters generate 'true believers' in single stories which themselves create a new essentialism: women as superior, gayness as radical transgression, man as the warrior. The late modern world here will become an increasingly risky place.

A more benign response may be that of *communitarianism*. This is most clearly exemplified in the philosophy of MacIntyre, and in the sociology of Bellah and Etzioni. Here is asserted the need for 'tribes' with their own 'traditions', but it is a model of the tribes at least managing to live together. The source of moral value is to be found in the community. Here, as in the earlier tribal response, communities will build their own collective stories in which people can locate the shared traditions of their lives; but unlike the tribalism, their stories will not assert a moral and exclusive superiority.

But with such a model, how are people to live together without the conflicts becoming unbearable? The traditional liberal response to this has been to establish some sense of a *common framework*, a *minimum of ground rules* through which stories can be told. An intriguing variant on this is the necessary *constraining and limiting* of truly discordant voices. Becoming aware that some stories are so different, so at odds with each other, one suggestion is to create a silent pact: some things are best left unsaid, best left unspoken. It is easy to see how this works on the personal level: millions of people who see themselves as gay may simply avoid 'coming out' to non-gays; and non-gays just elect to ignore it. This way, (gay) life goes on and nobody is (too) threatened. People can live together through simply ignoring fundamental differences! It is simply better not to know, even when we might 'really' know all along. Here, 'keeping certain secrets secret is important to – the general balance of life, the common utility' (Leavitt, 1986, 173). At a wider level, this is the liberal political strategy advocated by Bruce Ackerman (1989) with his idea of of 'conversational restraint'. This is not always a very hopeful strategy – it means many voices will continue to be unheard.

Tribalism, communitarianism, constraint are all possible futures, but they all work to remove threatening or new stories: tribalism through its appeal to authority, communitarianism through its appeal to tradition, constraint throught its tacit agreement that some things are best left unsaid. A range of other responses, however, place the greatest emphasis upon different aspects of communication, dialogue and discourse. One strand draws from Habermas, and stresses a communicative theory of ethics. In a universal and seemingly ahistorical 'ideal speech situation', all must have equal chances to make their voices heard; it takes a 'pragmatic turn'. Deception, including self-deception, is eliminated, domination is removed, and intersubjective communication becomes purer! But communicative competence free from deception and domination is an ideal, and although Habermas's view has its followers it 'ignores the contingent, historical and affective circumstances which made individuals adopt a universal-ethical standpoint in the first place' (cf. Benhabib, 1992). The whole theory is too homogenising, too objectivist, too close to making external (and eternal) elite claims.

So what could possibly be the way ahead? The fundamentalisms on either side are now a dead end. Though they may have once been important in clarifying issues, they are now too well known to need such polarities. Conversational restraint is probably, in practice, what is taking place in many places: a tacit agreement to live together and ignore differences. Traditional communitarians – perilously close to fundamentalisms – seek out the history of their ethics through the religious or feminist community. An ideal speech situation where a communicative ethics may be established remains just that: an ideal. There is not a lot of guidance here.

Following this line, there can be no Grand Conclusion – no final story to be told. Indeed, if one analysis has come through it is surely that in the late modern period such Grand Stories are no longer possible. Indeed, such claims must be looked upon with suspicion. What we are left with are fragments of stories. What seems to be required is a sensitivity to listen to an ever-growing array of stories and to shun the all too tempting desire to place them into a coherent and totalising narrative structure. Indeed, as Jane Flax has so clearly suggested, it may be that 'structures' only appear clear from the false perpsective of the single unitary story of dominant groups. (Flax, 1990, 28). It is not an easy option to keep the pluralistic, polyvocal potential of proliferating stories open; but it is probably a very necessary one.

Following the pragmatist tradition, we need to hear new stories and anticipate how they might change our lives if we do. Richard Rorty is the contemporary heir-apparent to the pragmatist heritage. He has argued that human sufferings can only be reduced through an improved sensitivity to the voices of the suffering, and that this is 'a matter of detailed description'. The search for such narratives of self is the work of much popular culture, which cannot therefore be lightly dismissed. For him, 'the novel, the movie and the TV programme have, gradually but steadily, replaced the sermon and the treatise as the principle vehicles of moral change and progress' (1989, p. xvi).

Other writers on sexuality and intimacy have recently converged on a position not wholly disimilar to mine. Steven Seidman's (1992) study of *Embattled Eros* leads him to a 'postmodern position' which advocates a 'pragmatic ethical strategy'. This shuns strict moral hierarchies and grants respect to differences: 'Unless we are prepared to exclude all those sexual constructions that differ from "our own"', or to deny difference by interpreting them as minor variations of an identical phenomenon, we must concede that groups evolve their own sexual culture around which they elaborate coherent lives' (1992, p. 191). Likewise, Jeffrey Weeks has, for over a decade, espoused a position of 'radical pluralism' which pays partial attention to contrasting meanings and situations over sexuality (Weeks, 1991). A dialogue around a multiplicity of stories needs to be established.

A final word can be left, for the time being, with the prescient William James:

> No one of us ought to issue vetoes to the other, nor should we bandy words of abuse. We ought, on the contrary, delicately and profoundly to respect one another's mental freedom: then only shall we have the spirit of inner tolerance without which all our outer tolerance is soulless, and which is empiricism's glory; then only shall we live and let live, in speculative as well as practical things. (James, 1956, p. 30)

REFERENCES

Ackerman, B. (1989) 'Why Dialogue?', *Journal of Philosphy*, **86**: pp. 5–22.

Barber, B. (1992) *The Aristocracy of Everyone* (New York: Oxford Press).

Benhabib, S. (1992) *Situating the Self* (Oxford: Polity Press).

Best, J. (1990) *Threatened Children* (Chicago, IL: University of Chicago Press).

Bird, S. E. (1992) *For Inquiring Minds* (Knoxville, TN: University of Tennessee Press).

Bly, R. (1990) *Iron John* (New York: Addison Wesley).

Bruner, J. (1987) 'Life as Narrative', *Social Research*, **54**: pp. 11–32.

Connolly, W. E. (1991) *Identity/Difference* (Ithaca, NY: Cornell).

Davis, K. (1984) *Two Bit Culture: The Paperbacking of America* (Boston, MA: Houghton Mifflin).

Evans, D. T. (1993) *Sexual Citizenship* (London: Routledge).

Featherstone, M. (1991) *Consumer Culture and Postmodernism* (London: Sage).

Fitzgerald, T. J. K. (1993) *Metaphors of Identity* (New York: SUNY Press).

Flax, J. (1990) *Thinking Fragments* (Berkeley, CA: University of California).

Foucault, M. (1979) *The History of Sexuality*, vol. 1 (Harmondsworth, Middlesex: Penguin).

Giddens, A. (1991) *Modernity & Self-Identity* (Cambridge: Polity Press).
Giddens, A. (1992) *The Transformation of Intimacy* (Cambridge: Polity Press).
Herman, J. L. (1992) *Trauma and Recovery* (New York: Basic Books).
hooks, b. (1989) *Talking Back: Thinking Feminist, Thinking Black* (Boston, MA: South End).
Hunter, J. D. (1991) *Culture Wars* (New York: Basic Books).
James, W. (1956) *The Will to Believe and Other Essays* (New York: Dover).
Leavitt, D. (1986) *The Lost Language of Cranes* (Middlesex: Penguin).
Maines, D. (1993) 'Narrative's Moment & Sociology's Phenomena', *Sociological Quarterly*, **34**: pp. 17–38.
Marshall, T. H. (1963) *Sociology at the Crossroads* (London: Heinemann).
Meyrowitz, J. (1985) *No Sense of Place* (Oxford: Oxford University Press).
Morrison, T. (ed.) (1992) *Race-ing Justice, En-gendering Power* (New York: Pantheon).
Norwood, R. (1985) *Women Who Love too Much* (New York: Simon & Schuster).
Penelope, J. and Wolfe, S. (eds) (1988) *The Coming Out stories* (Freedom, California: Crossing Press).
Plummer, K. (1995) *Telling Sexual Stories* (London: Routledge).
Prus, R. (1987) 'Generic Social Process', *Journal of Contemporary Ethnography*, **16**: pp. 250–93.
Rorty, R. (1989) *Contingency, Irony and Solidarity* (Cambridge: Cambridge University Press).
Seidman, S. (1992) *Embattled Eros* (London: Routledge).
Spence, D. (1982) *Narrative Truth and Historical Truth* (New York: Norton).
Strauss, A. (1978) 'A Social World Perspective', in Norman K. Denzin (ed.), *Studies in Symbolic Interaction* (London: JAI Press), vol. 1, pp. 119–28.
Weeks, J. (1991) *Against Nature* (London: Rivers Oram).
Wiener, C. (1981) *The Politics of Alcoholism* (New Brunswick, NJ: Transaction).
Young, I. (1990) *Justice and the Politics of Difference* (Princeton, NJ: Princeton University Press).
Zimmerman, B. (1990) *The Safe Sea of Women* (Boston, MA: Boston Beacon Press).

3 Gay Brains, Gay Genes and Feminist Science Theory
HILARY ROSE

THE HOMOSEXUAL AS A SPECIES?

Foucault's argument in *The History of Sexuality* (1978) that until Westphal's (1870) article on 'contrary sexual sensations', 'The sodomite had been a temporary aberration: the homosexual was now a species' has been hailed by many as the defining social constructionist account of sexuality in general and homosexuality in particular. While most contemporary sociologists would flinch at the fixity of the metaphor of 'species', for many discussing sexualities in a social context Michel Foucault hovers above as a gay intellectual father; others will be also conscious of Mary McIntosh (1968) as an intellectual mother who made rather earlier social constructionist claims. It was eight years before the French version of *The History* that McIntosh wrote her groundbreaking analysis of 'The Homosexual Role', in which she directed attention to the historical emergence of the (usually male) homosexual whose social role defines acceptable and unacceptable sexual behaviours.

Recalling McIntosh's intervention is not unimportant, for the gay brains/gay genes interventions of LeVay (1991) and Hamer (1993), in their uncritical reproduction of mainstream biological research, which focuses on the lives and bodies of men, inevitably reproduce in a discomforting way the recentering of men in the discussion. The failure to consider lesbianism with equal seriousness is nowhere expressed more graphically than in the methodological treatment of the seven female brains in LeVay's post-mortem sample. He observes that because there was no indication in the medical record of these women's sexuality, they were therefore 'presumably heterosexual'. Yet the presumption of heterosexuality is itself part of the problem, nowhere confronted with more wit and style than by the seventies badge: 'How dare you presume I'm heterosexual?' From here on in, despite such underlying problems as the assumption of fixity and singularity in the categories of homosexual and lesbian, this paper focuses on the natural-science discourse concerning the nature of homosexuality – or at least of the brains and genes of gay men. It is also written by a heterosexual woman who suspects that being post-menopausal, and therefore with a flawed sexuality, somehow makes it easier – not easy – to discuss the scientific construction of the sexuality of 'Other Others'.

The biological claims of gay brains and genes, while power-charged interventions in the current cultural and poltical debates of difference, are by no means historically innovatory, as social historians of sexuality have long recognised (Weeks 1981). The claims instead resurrect the essentialist thesis advanced by politically engaged gay men and argued intermittently since the mid-nineteenth century to secure political and cultural space for homosexuality. In a context of widespread political moves within the US to deny homosexuals their constitutional rights, this oppositional discourse, with its twin location in the neurosciences and in molecular genetics, seeks to ground the claim for civil rights within the body.

What is new is that the claims are made from within major US institutions of contemporary science (the Salk Institute for LeVay and the National Institutes of Health for Hamer), and by scientists with solid professional reputations. They are also, (as discussed below) extensions from two powerful pre-existing scientific discourses: first, neurobiology's account of sexual dimorphism in the human brain and, second, molecular biology's claim of the determining role of genes for behaviour. Neither of these have been without challenge (Rose *et al.*, 1984; Fausto Sterling, 1992; Hubbard and Wald, 1993), but it has taken the specific claims of a biological 'third sex' to stir controversy, not least because significant numbers of the gay community in the USA have been attracted to the thesis. The line-up for and against 'biology as destiny' is, to say the least, untidy!

THE POWER TO NAME NATURE

It is readily apparent that these interventions are powerful precisely because they are made by natural scientists. They remind us of how, since the birth of modern western science in the mid-seventeenth century, one group – the scientists – have gradually achieved the power to name nature, not least human nature. It is they who construct for modern late industrial society the dominant representations of bodily functioning, of health and illness, birth and death. They have, with rather less authority, claimed to construct our representations of intelligence, race, homelessness, alcoholism, etc. and – crucially for this paper – homosexuality. This is not to say that exclusively biological accounts of, for example, birth have been allowed to remain unchallenged, but that over the course of the twentieth century the discourse of the human body has become the pre-eminent property of the life sciences.

Currently, postmodernism seeks to reduce the accounts of science to just one story amongst many, and the feminist critique of science which is sometimes recruited to the postmodern but which, as I have argued elsewhere (Rose 1994), is not reducible to it – to say nothing of anti-science and new age mysticism – lay different sieges to science. Despite these multiple critiques, science itself, not least the new genetics, is claiming unparalleled powers, both as culture and as technoscience, to name and fashion human nature. (A parallel account could be made for biotechnology and green nature, but that related issue is outside my immediate concern.)

ORIGINS STORIES – THE THREE SEXES

Foucault's origins story sees the construction of the homosexual as produced by the knowledge claims of biomedical experts who look at and within the body to name, explain and police particular behaviours. Medicalisation becomes another means of biomedical experts claiming to speak for biology as destiny. As such it is only sustainable as a strong thesis by erasing the cultural and political interventions of those homosexual theorists who also drew on biological explanations of difference – but to create political space. Although in later writing Foucault acknowledges resistance, at the time of *The History* he simply erases significant figures, not least Ulrichs and Hirschfeld (Weeks, 1977, 1981), from the nineteenth and early twentieth century century debates.

Ulrichs was a declared homosexual who pioneered essentialist explanation of homosexuality. (A move paralleled within both nineteenth and twentieth century feminisms, in which a powerful strand has claimed women's natural moral superiority, but feminist arguments in both centuries have been largely content to leave nature vaguely defined, not looking to science to generate an account of women's different and superior nature.) Although Ulrichs was a lawyer, in mid-nineteenth century Europe, where scientific expertise and institutions were still very much in the process of development, it was entirely possible for an amateur scientist to make a significant contribution to a scientific field. In that century, where the ideology of science as unambiguously progressive held much larger sway than today, knowledge producers frequently claimed to be doing science. Indeed, it was only during the nineteenth century that the term scientist, to indicate someone culturally authorised to discover and name nature, came into common usage.

Ulrich's conception of homosexuals as an intermediate sex – Urnings – effectively proposed that there were three, not two, sexes: Urnings, women and men. He characterised this newly discovered 'intersex' as individuals having the 'bodies of men with the minds of women'. This anomalous being was the result of faulty foetal development. By turning to an explanation of faulty development, Ulrichs moves the moral blame away from the individual onto the developmental process, for which the poor foetus (though maybe the mother as usual) could scarcely be held responsible. Although not a scientist, and so not feeling the need to generate much in the way of empirical biological evidence to shore up his claim, Ulrichs was well placed to understand the significance of legal accountability as a central issue for homosexuals. He proposed that far from the Urning being criminally motivated towards homosexuality, a sinner within Judeo-Christian discourse, he is simply living in accordance with his developmentally flawed nature (Kennedy, 1980).

Ulrichs was by no means alone. By the end of the nineteenth century the developing field of sexology had become a site of intellectual and emotional tension (Flugel, 1953). Krafft-Ebbing's monumental work classifying sexual variations was translated into English – with the more graphic passages in Latin so as to guarantee its medical status. The work of Havelock Ellis and Freud put sexuality and sexual reform onto the agenda of a small but influential group of intellectuals. It was in this context that the German sexologist Magnus Hirschfeld extended the third-sex thesis through reference to the new field of hormones (Weindling, 1989, pp. 373–8). This field initially emphasised sexual dimorphism, with hormones themselves classified – and the classification lingers on in present day popular culture – as 'male' and 'female' hormones (Oudshorn, 1990). Hirschfeld took a further step to 'scientise' the discussion, namely to calculate the incidence of homosexuals in the population.[1] Then, as now, such a statistic immediately became a matter of passionate controversy – heterosexists insisting the number was exaggerated and homosexual activists insisting that there was more of it about. While sexologists like Edward Carpenter pressed the claim of the third sex, the project was unable to overcome a massively homophobic culture and polis. Homosexuality was to remain simultaneously both a disease entity and a crime until well into the second half of the twentieth century.

Using nature as a resource to defend difference and create political space is rarer within biological politics than the long-standing enthusiasm visible within the the life sciences to produce accounts of nature which mirror – and amplify – existing unjust social relations. In the nineteenth and twentieth centuries, those biologists who are socially progressive have consistently attacked such repressive constructions.[2] There is a discernible actor network extending over time and across countries among those biologists who are intellectually and socially committed to contesting biological reductionism. But as well as discharging the negative responsibility of clearing away repressive biological constructions – which are frequently criticised as failing to meet the canons of their disciplines and are energetically denounced as 'bad science' – many socially critical biologists, whether radical or feminist, carry also a notion of the need to construct accounts of nature which are both faithful and foster gentler relations between people and between people and nature.

By contrast, Foucault sees biomedicine as inexorably coercive. Like Francis Bacon he acknowledges the intimate relationship between knowledge and power, but he reverses Bacon's political conclusions. Foucault sees no circumstances under which a republic of knowledge, let alone a democracy, might come into existence, only the extension of the power of the expert. The medicalisation of sexuality is the extension of power by the experts over the lives of those who are medicalised. One had, he writes, 'to go to try to detect it – as a lesion, a dysfunction, or a symptom – in the depths of the organism or on the surface of the skin, or among the signs of behaviour' (Foucault, 1978, p. 44). This theoretical dismissal of science to provide reliable accounts of nature, indeed to be anything other than an extension of the power/knowledge couple, was not without harsh implications for Foucalt himself. His death from AIDS can be read as the hard revenge of the real against the relativist.

'IN THE DEPTHS OF THE ORGANISM'

None the less, Foucault was right in that it is precisely within the depths of the organism that today's gay biological reductionists seek to locate homosexuality. The history of the turn to biology in seeking to 'explain' – that is, describe the origins of – male homosexuality is more or less contemporaneous with that of the other manifestations of biologically determinist thinking, which recrudesced from the early 1970s onwards and which have been massively amplified by the Human Genome Project which, with an initial budget of $3 billion, seeks to map and sequence the human genome.

The story of gay brains begins with a consensus within the neurosciences that there is a degree of sexual dimorphism in both brain structures and brain chemistry, scattered through many regions of the human brain. As with other animals, there are human nerve cells which contain receptor molecules which can interact with the sex hormones, oestrogen and testosterone. Both male and female brains contain receptors for both hormones, but the pattern and strength of the interactions differ between the sexes. These differences emerge during development, both in the foetus and during the years before puberty. The conventional story, as told by the endocrinologists, is that all brains are female to begin with, but that male brains become masculinised in terms of their hormone interactions at certain key periods during development. One brain region in particular, the hypothalamus, is associated with the regulation of production of the sex hormones and has become the site of intensive research, and evidence has accumulated that there is sexual dimorphism in both numbers of nerve cells and biochemistry in several areas of this complex brain region.

Within the neurosciences, the question of whether there are reliable and consistent differences in brain structures between male and female brains is the subject of continuing debate. During the 1970s and 1980s, the neuroanatomist Geschwind (Fausto Sterling, 1992) claimed that there were sex differences in the symmetry of the two halves of the brain; the greater male asymmetry, he and his school suggested, was associated with the greater incidence both of mental dysfunctions, such as autism, and of superior mental ability (for instance in mathematics) in men than women. Such ideas helped foster the left hemisphere/cognitive/masculine, right hemisphere/affective/feminine notions which became popular at the time. The arrival of new brain-imaging techniques, such as functional magnetic resonance, enabling living rather than dead brains to be examined, refined some of these notions and also led to new claims that the great band of connecting pathways between the two brain hemispheres, the corpus callosum, was differently shaped in men and women.

It is within these areas of claimed sexual dimorphism that the search for 'gay brains' has been located. Could it be that in gay men something has gone amiss with biological masculinisation? Intensive research had failed to come up with any convincing evidence for any gay/straight hormonal differences and the focus of attention turned instead to the possibility that there might instead be structural brain differences. In a late-twentieth-century reprise of the claims that homosexuals formed a third sex, intermediate between males and females, the search began for brain regions which might show this intermediate character. Swaab and Hofman (1990), in Amsterdam, first claimed to find it in some hypothalamic structures, a claim that failed to be replicated. Allen (1994), in California, claimed that a sexually dimorphic substructure of the hypothalamus was intermediate in size and that the shape of the corpus callosum was more 'female-like' in the brains of homosexual men.

These claims achieved little resonance either within or without the neuroscientific community. But when the neuroanatomist Simon LeVay, studying the brains of a small number of homosexual men who had died from AIDS, published a paper in *Science* in 1991 claiming that there were large differences in size in a region of the hypothalamus, INAH 3, in 'gay brains' the response was different. LeVay had a distinguished track record as a neuroanatomist, having worked with the Nobel Laureates Hubel and Wiesel, was now located at the prestigious Salk Institute, and was himself an out gay. The publication in *Science* ensured that his report was given the imprimatur of one of the world's two most influential scientific journals, and it was also accompanied by a press release which ensured it media attention. LeVay followed the paper with a book, *The Sexual Brain* (1993), and left the Salk Institute and scientific research to work full time among the gay community. Much about the process through which the gay brains thesis was launched matches Nelkin's *Selling Science* (1987) analysis.

The claims were immediately contentious both within and without science. Despite LeVay's evident cultural capital which would make him more publishable than an outsider, it is questionable whether *Science* would have published an article of similar methological vulnerablity had it focused on anything less charged than homosexuality. The sample was small, and AIDS commonly produces severe neurological consequences. There were no 'normal' controls, and he sought to measure a brain region whose boundaries are notoriously difficult to define. His findings have not been replicated. Thus it is not entirely surprising that at the symposium organised at the American Association for the Advancement of Science in San Francisco by the National Organisation of Gay and Lesbian Scientists and Technical Professionals (NOGLTSP) in 1994, the focus of attention returned to the claims made by Allen. While INAH 3 has been sidelined, the significant point is

NOGLTSP's (1994) continuing interest in biological difference and its link with issues of 'national health reform, civil rights legislation and the rights to privacy'.

Within the discourse of natural science the problem in relating brain structures to sexual orientation is that the post-mortem approach leaves open the chicken and egg question of cause or consequence. Does living as a gay man shape the brain, or does the brain shape the gay man? By contrast, claims for a genetic basis for homosexuality, above all when made by the new molecular genetics, are unequivocal about the arrow of causation. This new genetics lays more powerful claims than the older approaches to the nature/nurture question of the twin-studies pioneered by behavioural geneticists and psychometricians from the early twentieth century on. These sought to disentangle effects of heredity and environment by studies of identical and non-identical twins and, of course, in identical twins reared together or apart, as in the notorious IQ claims made by Burt (Kamin, 1974; Hearnshaw, 1979). In the context of sexuality, the main research claims have come from Bouchard, in Minneapolis, who maintains a major twin register and has used it to advance claims for the heritability of everything from job satisfaction to religiosity and the tendency to become divorced, and from Bailey and Pillard (1991), who were among the earliest to claim a heritable tendency to gayness. Bouchard's reticence about publishing in refereed journals has led to considerable doubts about the validity of his genetic claims. However, a paper from his group was included in an issue of *Science* which focused on genes and behaviour. LeVay's reproduction of Bouchard's evidence as if there was no widespread criticism of twin studies, where at best correlation rather than cause reigns and where there is very particular criticism of Bouchard, has added to the difficulties of his INAH 3 thesis.

However, these older genetic methods have very much been sidelined by the rise of the new molecular genetics, and it was the use of these techniques by Dean Hamer, in 1993, to claim that he had found a genetic marker for homosexuality, which catapulted the gay gene story into front page news. (A marker is only a proximate indicator for a gene not a gene.) Like LeVay's, his paper was published in *Science*, and was accompanied by a dramatic press release in which the finding was announced in apocalyptic tones, accompanied by an ethical statement that the author hoped that the finding would not be misused by opening the door to either amniocentesis and selective abortion or genetic engineering to eliminate gay foetuses – again matching the process documented by Nelkin. The subsequent book-length version of the paper *The Science of Desire* (1994), co-published with journalist Peter Copeland, suggests by its title, if not its text, that the claims of molecular biology are truly imperialistic.

Like LeVay's publication, Hamer's *Science* paper was taken immensely seriously by the gay community in the US, whose spokespeople rushed to comment on the potential ethical implications. Few paused to point out that even if Hamer's observations were validated (and they still have not been replicated) the maximal possible theoretical predictive value of any test based upon them would be 50 per cent – scarcely a sound base for action. Hamer's paper also produced an extensive statistical discussion. What the biological argument did do was to support a widely discussed feeling of inborn difference. Thus actor and gay activist Ian McKellan observed on a radio programme that he knew by the time he was thirteen that he had 'a different nature'. Others saw the benefit of being 'born homosexual', no longer could the gay school teacher or social worker be cast as the figure of the moral corrupter of innocent youth, for only those with gay brains or genes could become gay men. Arguably, the power of the US Judeo-Christian fundamentalist Right to use social constructionist arguments to show that some women and men were sufficiently morally perverse so as to choose same-sex relations made essentialism look like an ally.

What Hamer had done was to study a number of families in which there was a significant incidence of male homosexuality. He had shown that in these families, the homosexual men shared a genetic marker – that is, a gene whose product could be identified – located on the tip of the X-chromosome; that is, it was inherited through their mothers (women's fault again?). Like LeVay's work, Hamer's was immediately subject to technical criticism (Fausto Sterling and Balaban, 1993; Risch *et al.*, 1993; Baron, 1993). Most seriously, he had only studied the gay brothers, not the straight ones in the family, justifying himself on the grounds that you could not be sure of the sexual orientation of someone claiming to be straight, whilst the stigma against gays was such that only a gay would claim to be one. Such an argument underlines the peculiar conflation between natural and social categories in his reasoning.

He made no study of the alleged marker in women, heterosexual or lesbian, on the grounds that such studies are technically harder to make, echoing the old cry from an androcentric biology that women's bodies are somehow not normal, so are necessarily excluded from biomedical research. His estimate of heritability depended rather critically, for technical reasons, on assumptions concerning the 'background' level of gayness in the population, which he took to be much lower than the figures given by, for instance, Kinsey. And his findings clearly relate to particular pedigrees, families in which there is a high incidence of gay behaviour amongst the men. There are no data on how typical this is of the general population.

Such criticism of studies, of either the LeVay or the Hamer type, is of course to accept the definition of 'homosexuality' as a phenotype to which it is appropriate to apply the techniques of neuroanatomy or quantitative genetics. Thus the criticisms as to whether the work is 'good science' or 'bad science' referred to above, are made within a particular construction of the scientific canon itself. Typically, the conclusion of such criticism is that the hypothesis is 'not proven', rhetorically a fairly weak opposition to a politically potent thesis. To mount a more powerful attack on a well-developed field such as genetics requires the redefinition of the canon. What legitimately is within and without the field of behavioural genetics? Can the concept of homosexuality be theorised and operationalised in this way? Can the social sciences challenge such a unitary concept of homosexuality used in a different discipline? Questions of this kind challenge the boundaries of the disciplines; who is qualified to speak?[3]

MIS/REPRESENTING SCIENCE?

To no small extent, the amplification of the twin 'gay brains' and 'gay genes' theses has been produced not simply by the media misrepresenting science – as scientists commonly claim – but directly through the language and activities of the scientists themselves. This process has worked through a mixture of press releases, titles and public comment. The title of Le Vay's book reduces sexuality to anatomical form. In parallel vein Hamer, as a molecular biologist, knows the technical difficulty of moving beyond finding a marker to determining a gene for even a well-understood physical trait such as cystic fibrosis (to say nothing of the gene for 'homosexuality' as if that had the same kind of fixity). The gap between locating a possible marker and identifying a gene is the familiar stuff of molecular biology; claims for markers remind molecular biologists that other groups compete for each laboratory and its backers, the one which identifies the gene first gets both scientific prestige and, through diagnostic patents, material rewards. But what Hamer did in his press release was to set aside the problem of closing the gap, for he insisted in his press release that he would patent the gene in order to stop misuse. (He also displays a certain US centrism, for other biological patents such as the Harvard Oncomouse have been rejected in Europe, so his defence of homosexual foetuses would break down at the US borders.) But most of all, neither Le Vay nor Hamer reflect on the category 'homosexual': for both it is as fixed as, say, brown eyes. Le Vay in particular has a very simple-minded view of sexuality. Thus he reflects in passing that heterosexual copulation is 'so simple, one hardly needs a brain to do it '(Le Vay, 1993, p. 47). Thus it is not the media which biologises the category but the gay scientists themselves.

The preoccupation with gay men's sexuality witnessed some bizarre expressions of ethics and solidarity between gay scientists and feminism. These have further eroded the boundaries between representing and misrepresenting science (even a science with all the reservations about its categories I have tried to indicate). Thus LeVay, at the ICA in London, commenting on the ethical implications of Hamer's findings, claimed that he would support any woman who chose to have an abortion on the grounds that she was carrying a foetus with a gene for homosexuality. So while Hamer seeks to stop such a mythical test from coming into existence LeVay considers himself bound by it. When a biologist endorses such an argument it is unsurprising (if disagreeable) that his support for abortion by choice should be echoed with homophobic intensity, but probably a lesser knowledge of genetics, by the former Chief Rabbi Lord Jakobovits who euphemistically welcomed this opportunity to use science for sexual if not ethnic cleansing: 'We may practice medical ingenuity to relieve suffering or a human disability.'[4]

Perhaps even more disturbing is the more temperate review by Martin Johnson – both a Professor of Reproductive Sciences at Cambridge and a member of the Human Fertilisation and Embryological Authority. Johnson welcomes the Hamer and Copeland book as 'the best attempt at a genetic analysis of human sexuality that we have so far' and goes on to welcome the way that it will 'fuel the moral debate about what any genetic component to sexuality might mean for ethics and the law' (Johnson, 1994, p. 46).

DISEMBODIED SOCIAL THEORY?

The problem for sociology in responding to such technically elaborate
essentialist accounts of sexuality is that general social theory has excluded the body. As Turner (1984) rightly points out, this absence is
particularly notable in sociology; by contrast, other social sciences,
such as anthropology and psychology, have long taken the body into
their accounts. It is not my purpose here to explore the development
of that silence within general sociology (perhaps pursuing fascinating
clues such as what happened after the founding of Lancelot Hogben's
Chair in Social Biology at the London School of Economics), or to
elaborate why I think that even where such mainstream sociology does
discuss the body, it is one peculiarly composed of words. It seems
remarkably unlike the body I inhabit, which bleeds, smells, hurts in an
untidy intrusive way. Instead I want to draw attention to the theoretical and political costs of such a denial of nature and the body, for it
leads inexorably to a crude opposition between essentialism and social
constructionism. In this either/or debate, essentialism is claimed to indicate
fixity (and conservativism) while social constructionism offers plasticity (and change). The political price of social theory's purely
social-constructionist account simultaneously offended commonsense experience of living in a body and also offered a golden opportunity to a
biological New Right to fill the gap with accounts of nature which
both reflected and constituted the political economy of the market and
a racialised and gendered society. That the Right now appeals to social
constructionism, and is always capable of invoking divine law or biology to justify unjust social relations is integral to the workings of
what has been characterised as a scavenger ideology. Such repressive
ideologies are rarely troubled by a need for consistency.

Social theorising, even where it sought to address social movements,
made little or no space for the theorising which was developing from
either the radical science movement or the feminist critique of science
which had fostered critical analysis of science and technology's representations and transformations of nature. Thus despite the intense
struggles over the body in grass-roots feminism, not least for reproductive rights, feminist social theorists, influenced by Marxism during
the 1970s, theoretically silenced the body. Nowhere was this shewn
more graphically than in the debate between the influential Marxist
feminists Barrett and McIntosh(1980) versus Delphy (1977). The protagonists were at the polar opposites of Marxist and radical materialist
feminisms, yet in complete theoretical accord that the body had no

part in the real. For all three, to admit the body was to lapse into the theoretical sin of essentialism, the determining and deplored feature of a non-materialist radical feminism. The later attempts by Walby to integrate materialist and Marxist feminisms, again had no space for the body (Walby, 1986, 1990). It has taken a much stronger move towards poststructuralism, when the once fierce debates of radical and Marxist feminisms have faded, for Barrett at least to show signs of repentance and to permit the body to sneak back in (Barrett, 1990). The alternative essentialist current of radical feminism basically claimed that women are naturally nicer. While the notion that men's cruelty and violence is pretty much endemic to maleness and masculinity, radical feminism's essentialism has not been located in an appeal to those contemporary life sciences which have competed to offer explanations of sexual difference. Despite the presence of individual feminist sociobiologists such as Hrdy (1981), there has been no sign of an attempt to mobilise a discourse from the natural sciences behind the essentialist feminist project. Instead, appeals to nature work as an empowering political resource, the non-scientificity being a new ageish spiritual asset.

CONSTRAINED EMBODIMENT

By contrast, those feminists and others engaged in what Sayers (1977) fruitfully called *Biological Politics* could not, whether they were theorists or activists, dismiss the claims of claims of the body or collapse into essentialism.[5] From the late 1960s onwards, first scientific racism (Jensen, Shockley, Herrnstein, Eysenck) and then sociobiology, with its claims to pronounce as the eye of god on nothing less than Human Nature itself, (Wilson, Barash, Dawkins,) insistently proposed that socially unjust relations were simply a reflection of what was to be found in Nature. Within the self-accounting of this scientific quest into the biological bases of human nature, the scientist who 'discovers' the truth of nature is represented as a cultural hero (or even heroine), who bravely uncovers natural facts, however unpalatable they are to his or her humane and egalitarian feelings. The scientific culture thus represents itself as having no culture, and that is precisely its claim to a universal gaze.

During these years, 'biology as destiny' was systematically put back onto the conservative political and cultural agenda in a way that sociology and social theory were largely unprepared for. Long after a renewed scientific racism was reclaiming the concept of 'race' as rooted in biological difference, sociologists of race relations continued to insist that the biological concept of race had been laid to rest (as it were once and for all) in the post war UNESCO settlement written by cultural anthropologists and progressive biologists. Already able to think about claims that the body was real, it was not by chance that the key disciplines which moved to contest the recrudescence of biological determinism were biology, (Bleier, Gould, Hubbard, Lewontin, Rose, Tobach) anthropology (Liebowitz, Sahlins) and psychology (Chorover, Kamin, Sayers).

Sayers, academically a psychologist and politically a feminist Marxist, was located at a place where contrary intellectual currents met. Like the biologists, but unlike sociologists, she was both unable and unwilling to ignore the rising tide of claims of biological sexual difference.[6] A rather facile plasticity based on pure social constructionism dominated feminist debate; in those heady early years it seemed that with one bound the movement would overcome patriarchal structures surrounding our everyday lives and in our heads. The emphasis was on the similarity of women and men. Femininity was dismissed as simply an outcome of conditioning; if we gave our daughters trainsets they would be free.

Sayers understood that the problem was rather more difficult. Without entering into a discussion of the sterility and theoretical folly of dichotomous reasoning, she presciently argued for a limited essentialism and a constrained social constructionism. In similar vein, the Bressanone group, an international grouping of biological and social scientists engaged in biological politics, attacked biological reductionism as a main enemy, but went on to criticise all forms of reductionism, whether biological or sociological (Rose and Rose, 1980). They defined the task as to admit both nature and the social as real while insisting that knowledge, not least natural science, was socially shaped. More recently, Fuss (1989) has elegantly argued the impossiblity of separating the essential from the socially constructed.

Equally for those feminists engaged in the women's health movement, (and in one sense we all were in those early groups where everything about women's lives including our bodies was admitted) the reality of the female body was not an optional matter. To reflect on the routine experience of pain and bleeding, to live within a body whose boundary is ill defined, which can harbour the lives of others, give suck, and whose menopausal changes are flagged by sudden heat and dryness, and which gets sick or old and certainly dies, thought was necessarily embodied. While Benton (1991) cautiously welcomed a return of the repressed body to sociology, those engaged in biological politics had been there a long time; for them the pleasure has lain in the beginning recognition within sociology of the body as real. More recently, Murphy (1994) critically surveyed mainstream sociology of science and incisively demonstrated its inability to cope with nature; less encouragingly he manages to ignore the entire feminist critique of science – no small achievement after two decades of scholarship – which has had a distinctive agenda which meets a number of the problems Murphy raises.

To compress a lengthy feminist epistemological debate in science theory which extended throughout the 1980s and into the 1990s, the theoretical choice became not one between realist (or as feminism termed it standpoint epistemology) and relativist or pure social constructionist accounts, but how could feminist theorists plunder all the tool kits to serve a feminist political agenda. Among the feminisms the agenda was commonly spoken of as replacing 'either or' with 'both and'. (That the agenda of the feminisms had itself become both broadened and deepened beyond the classed and 'racialised' definition of feminism of the early years, is integral to this changing historical project.) As part of this process feminist science theorists reconceptualised both rationality as responsible, and objectivity as an embodied and situated knowledge, the old poles of relativism and realism as dichotomous choices losing their potency. While a less sketchy account of the debates within feminist science theory would bring out the nuanced differences between the leading protagonists (Rose, 1994, pp. 71–96), between, for example, Keller (1985), Harding (1986) and Haraway (1991), it is a sense of the possibility of more reliable accounts of nature, that is a cautious and limited defence of realism, which separates the feminist analyses of science as culture from feminist analyses of, say, film, psychoanalysis, literature or popular culture which display a strong constructionism. In the sense of wishing to hold onto a more reliable knowledge – however situated and embodied – they resist being swept away by the postmodern deluge; with the effect that the feminist critique of science has, for all its normativity, a distinctly conservationist (some would say conservative) aspect.

GAY BRAINS, GAY GENES AND BEYOND

While it is unquestionably important to resist the twin theses of gay
brains and gay genes as determinant, both for reasons within the canon
of their own particular discourses, and also because the history of grounding claims for rights in biological difference has been negative, it is
as, or more important, to see that this specific deterministic claim around
homosexuality is located within a massive genetic turn within the life
sciences. The new genetics is in the process of extending its claims to
explain – and solve – not just biomedical but also social problems.
The political economy of genetics as a technoscience, with the
possibility of making immense financial profits from diagnostic testing,
stands just behind the glitzy cultural debates. These new genetics offer, and the confusions of the LeVay/Hamer ethical contributions do
not escape this, nothing less than a consumer eugenicism. Radically
different from the state eugenicisms of the past, today the individual
consumer freely chooses – to use the favoured concept of the time –
to have diagnostic tests to determine their, or if they are pregnant women,
their foetus's, genetic future. Among the tasks of the social sciences is
to deconstruct that concept of 'choice' and to make careful ethnographies
of how people understand, experience, use and even resist the new technoscience of genetics in everyday life. But even more importantly, sociology
needs to reflect theoretically on the growing geneticisation of culture.
   Currently the extension of the new genetics beyond diagnostics (though
those have their own significance – Nelkin and Tancredi, 1989) and
into medical therapies is constrained by sheer technical difficulty, but
money and time will resolve much of that. My argument here is that
the extension into social policy is constrained by the weakness of the
ontological status of the category of 'behaviour'. Sexuality is not reducible to such a unitary category as if it was either singular or could
be suspended outside biography and social context. However, passively
relying on such weaknesses within the categories of the natural sciences is no substitute for improving our own or actively criticising
theirs. The ideologues of the new genetics, unlike the social sciences,
are in a position to command many millions of research dollars and
look to the new genetics to solve nothing less than alcoholism, violence, drug taking, criminality and homelessness (Koshland, 1989).
   The take-home message from the gay genes issue (much more than
the older gay brains issue) is that this is a foretaste of a cultural debate
where the ultimate consumerist stakes are nothing less than the physical re-construction of the flawed body and its flawed behaviours. As

Keller (1992) notes, the danger is the silence as to who is to define the 'normal'. This is far too important to be left solely to the producers of biomedical discourse, regardless of the sexuality and claimed good intentions of the producers. Gay politics turning to bodily difference for the site of its claim to civil rights is, even in the context of renewed sensitivity to arguments of equality and difference, unlikely to find this a rewarding political strategy. In this situation it becomes politically as well as theoretically important that sociological theory draws on feminist science theory to break out of the dichotomous choice between essentialism and constructionism, not least to mount an effective challenge to a growing and massively resourced biologism. To ignore the body as integral to nature as well as to culture is to ignore that a power-charged account of biological difference is currently being written by immense institutional forces.

ACKNOWLEDGEMENTS

My thanks to Wendy Faulkner, Catherina Landström and Steven Rose, colleagues at the 1994 BSA conference where an earlier version of this paper was given, and the editors for their helpful comments

NOTES

1. Hirschfeld and his colleagues at the Berlin Institute of Sexual Science were energetic sexual reformers, turning to the new medium of the cinema to extend their campaign. Thus Hirschfeld took the part of a doctor reformer in a story of unhappy denied, and happy recognised, homosexual love: 'Other than the Others' (1919). In the same year he produced his own film, an exegesis of his belief in the biological basis of homosexuality: 'The Laws of Love'.
2. Abolitionist biologists attacked the concept of Drapetomania (the inborn tendency of slaves to run away). Feminist biologists in the late nineteenth century attacked the assertion that a woman's brain was directly linked to her uterus and that excessive intellectual work would unquestionably threaten her reproductive functions. (It did not escape them that the thesis arose precisely at the time that bourgeois women were seeking access into higher education.) Despite a widespread prior enthusiasm for hereditarian thought and eugenicism, with the advent of Nazism Left and liberal scientists contested Aryan science's construction of the less than human. Anti-racist biologists attacked the energetic promulgation of scientific racism in the form of IQ theory in the 1970s – directed towards blocking educational

support to black children in the US and discouraging immigration in Britain. Nor did it escape notice of critical biologists at Harvard that the Harvard University Press launched E. O. Wilson's *Sociobiology* (1975) with an unprecedented publicity expenditure in the same year of the Equal Rights Amendment and a developing enthusiasm for cutting welfare. Raging hormones have been used both to block women's careers and to justify murder: both reductionist moves precipitating criticism from feminist biologists.
3. In Britain the discourse is institutionally policed, the MRC – and not the ESRC – control the programme designed to research the 'ethical legal and social implications' of the new genetics.
4. Reported *Sunday Telegraph*, 25 July 1993.
5. Actually this is not quite accurate, the radical science movement was divided between the pure social constructionism of 'science is (nothing more than) social relations' and the orthogonal position of 'science is both socially constructed and real' (Rose, 1994).
6. The sociologists of science retreated to spectator status, neutrally commenting as disengaged professionals on the IQ debate.

REFERENCES

Allen, L. (1994) 'Anatomical and Physiological Correlates of Sexual Orientation', *NOGLSTP Symposium*, AAAS Annual Meeting, San Francisco, CA.
Bailey, J. M. and Pillard, R. C. (1991) 'A Genetic Study of Male Sexual Orientation', *Archives of General Psychiatry*, 48: pp. 1089–96.
Baron, M. (1993) 'Genetic Linkage and Male Homosexual Orientation: Reasons to be Cautious', *British Medical Journal*, 307(7): pp. 337–8.
Barrettand, M. and McIntosh, M. (1980) 'The Family Wage: Some Problems for Socialists and Feminists', *Capital and Class*, 11: pp. 51–73.
Barrett, M. (1990) *Women's Oppression Today: The Marxist Feminist Encounter* (London: Verso).
Benton, T. (1991) 'Biology and Social Science: Why the Return of the Repressed should be given a Cautious Welcome', *Sociology*, 25(1): pp. 1–29.
Delphy, C. (1977) *The Main Enemy* (London: Women's Research and Resources Centre Publications: Explorations in Feminism, no. 3).
Fausto Sterling, A. (1992) *Myths of Gender* (New York: Basic Books).
Fausto Sterling, A. and Balaban, E. (1993) 'Genetics and Male Sexual Orientation', *Science*, 261: 1257.
Flugel, J. C. (1953) *A Hundred Years of Psychology* (London: Duckworth).
Foucault, M. (1978) *The History of Sexuality*, vol. 1 (New York: Pantheon).
Fuss, D. (1989) *Essentially Speaking* (Cambridge: Polity Press).
Hamer, D., Hu, S., Magnuson, V. L., Hu, N. and Pattatucci, A. (1993) 'A Linkage Between DNA Markers on the X Chromosone and Male Sexual Orientation', *Science*, 261: pp. 421–7.
Hamer, D. and Copeland, P. (1994) *The Science of Desire: The Search for the Gay Gene and the Biology of Behaviour* (New York: Simon & Schuster).
Haraway, D. (1991) *Simians, Cyborgs and Women* (London: Free Association Press).

Harding, S. (1986) *The Science Question in Feminism* (Milton/Keynes: Open University Press).

Hearnshaw, L. (1979) *Cyril Burt: Psychologist* (London: Hodder & Stoughton).

Hubbard, R. and Wald, E. (1993) *Exploding the Gene Myth* (Boston, MA: Beacon).

Hrdy, S. (1981) *The Woman that Never Evolved* (Cambridge, MA: Harvard University Press).

Johnson, M. (1994) 'Sexual Innocents and Serendipity', *New Scientist*, **12** (November): pp. 45–6.

Kamin, L. (1974) *The Science and Politics of IQ* (Hillsdale, NJ: Lawrence Erlbaum Associates).

Keller, E. F. (1985) *Reflections on Gender and Science* (New Haven, CT: Yale University Press).

Keller, E. F. (1992) 'Nature, Nurture and the Human Genome Project', in D. Kevles, and L. Hood (eds), *The Code of Codes, Scientific and Social Issues in the Human Genome Project* (Cambridge, MA: Harvard University Press).

Kennedy, H. (1980) 'The "Third Sex" Theory of Karl Heinrich Ulrichs', *Journal of Homosexuality*, **6**: pp. 103–11.

Koshland, D. (1989) 'Editorial', *Science*, **246**: p. 189.

LeVay, S. (1991) 'A Difference in Hypothalmic Structure between Heterosexual and Homosexual Men', *Science*, **253**: pp. 1034–7.

LeVay, S. (1993) *The Gay Brain* (Cambridge, MA: MIT Press).

McIntosh, M. (1968) 'The Homosexual Role', *Social Problems*, **16**(2): pp. 182–92.

Murphy, R. (1994) 'The Sociological Construction of Science without Nature', *Sociology*, **28**(4): pp. 957–74.

Nelkin, D. (1987) *Selling Science* (New York: Freeman).

Nelkin, D. and Tancredi, L. (1989) *Dangerous Diagnostics: The Social Power of Biological Information* (New York: Basic Books).

NOGLSTP (1994) Press release, AAAS, 12 February.

Oudshorn, N. (1990) 'On the Making of Sex Hormones', *Social Studies of Science*, **20**: pp. 5–33.

Sayers, J. (1982) *Biological Politics* (London: Tavistock).

Swaab, D. and Hofman, M. A. (1990) 'An Enlarged Suprachiasmatic Nucleus in Homosexual Men', *Brain Research*, **537**: p. 141.

Risch, N., Squires, C., Wheeler, E. and Keats, B. (1993) 'Male Sexual Orientation and Genetic Evidence, *Science*, **262**: pp. 2063–4.

Rose, H. and Rose, S. (1980) 'Against Reductionism', in S. Rose (ed.), *Against Biological Determinism* (London: Allison & Busby).

Rose, H. (1994) *Love Power and Knowledge: Towards a Feminist Transformation of the Sciences* (Cambridge: Polity Press).

Rose, S., Lewontin, R. and Kamin, L. (1984) *Not in Our Genes* (Harmondsworth: Penguin).

Turner, B. S. (1984) *The Body and Society: Explorations in Social Theory* (Oxford: Blackwell).

Walby, S. (1986) *Patriarchy at Work* (Cambridge: Polity Press).

Walby, S. (1990) *Theorizing Patriarchy* (Oxford: Blackwell).

Weeks, J. (1977) *Coming Out: Homosexual Politics in Britain from the Nineteenth Century to the Present* (London: Quartet).

Weeks, J. (1981) *Sex Politics and Society: The Regulation of Sexuality since 1800* (London: Longman).

Weindling, P. (1989) *Health, Race and German Politics between National Unification and Nazism 1870–1845* (Cambridge: Cambridge University Press).

Wilson, E. O. (1975) *Sociobiology: The New Synthesis* (Cambridge, MA: Harvard University Press).

Part II

Historical Excursions

4 The Shock of the *Freewoman* Journal: Feminists Speaking on Heterosexuality in Early Twentieth-century England[1]

LUCY BLAND

In August 1912, well-known South African feminist Olive Schreiner wrote disgustedly to her close friend, sex psychologist Havelock Ellis, about a new weekly feminist journal called the *Freewoman*:

> I think it ought to be called the *Licentious Male*. Almost all the articles are by men and *not* by women, and the whole tone is unlike even the most licentious females or prostitutes. It is the tone of the brutal self-indulgent selfish male. There is something that makes one sick, as if one were on board ship. It is unclean. And sex is so beautiful! (Schreiner to Ellis, 7 August 1912, in Cronwright-Schreiner, 1924, p. 312)

She was not alone in her outrage. Suffragist Maude Royden called it a 'nauseous publication' (*The Times*, 22 June 1912), while Millicent Fawcett, President of the National Union of Women's Suffrage Societies, was so appalled by the copy she read that 'she tore it up into small pieces' (Strachey, 1931, p. 235).

Why did these feminists react so strongly? Opposition to the paper was partly due to the editorial assault on the politics of women's suffrage. The editors, Dora Marsden and Mary Gawthorpe, had both been active members of the Women's Social and Political Union (the WSPU), but had recently left, Dora, far more than Mary, having become virulently opposed to a feminism which concentrated solely on the vote. She reserved her greatest hostility, however, for the Pankhursts and

75

the WSPU. Indeed, Mary's early resignation from joint editorship, although partly due to poor health, was also due to her anger at Dora's continual attacks on the politics of former colleagues.[2] But opposition to the paper, from Olive Schreiner's point of view at least, was also, if not centrally, to do with its explicit discussions of sex.

Olive Schreiner was wrong on one point at least: not more than about half the articles and letters in the journal were by men, with Dora Marsden writing one or two long articles each week. And the paper was explicitly open to a range of positions, from those which Olive might well have seen as licentious, through to those with which she is unlikely to have disagreed. It was true, however, that from the *Freewoman*'s beginning, sex, amongst other things, was a subject which it was keen to discuss. Indeed, within its first few months, several correspondents wrote to congratulate the paper for providing a public forum in which to discuss this controversial subject.[3] In reply, and displaying no false modesty, Dora Marsden maintained:

> We make bold to say that never before the advent of the *Freewoman* has the opportunity [to study sex], either for men or women, in England or elsewhere, been at hand. That is the reason why the *Freewoman*'s advent is phenomenal. (*Freewoman*, 14 March 1912, p. 332)

For the *Freewoman* to have been *able* to talk about sex, the groundwork had to have been laid. Nineteenth-century British feminists had, of course, been talking about sex for years before the appearance of this new journal, from the campaign against the Contagious Diseases Acts in the 1870s and 1880s onwards. But whereas previous discussion had primarily been about the ways and means of protecting women from undesired sex (a woman's right to sexual protection), and of preventing men acting out their undesirable sexual 'proclivities', feminists in the *Freewoman* were now beginning to claim the right to *be* sexual. This was, indeed, a radical development, given that for most of the Victorian period a *sexual* identity for a woman meant an identity as a prostitute. How was such a shift conceivable? The new openings for women on the job market, and thus the increased possibility of economic and social independence, contributed to the development in young women of a self-identity separate from marital status or familial obligation (see Vicinus, 1985). But for this younger generation to think about claiming a *sexual* identity required the appearance of new ideas about sexuality. The crucial contributor was the body of work being generated by sex theorists and reformers – the ideas of the new 'science' of sex, namely 'sexology'.[4] If we are to examine the ideas expressed in the *Freewoman*, it is important to begin by looking at this wider context: the current feminist ideas on sexuality, and the new and developing ideas of sexology. Both discourses – the feminist and the sexological – informed the *Freewoman* writers and readers.

FEMINIST VIEWS ON SEXUALITY

Since at least the 1880s, feminists had been discussing how to change sexual relationships between men and women. Many feminists believed that such a change was possible, but could only be realised through a multi-pronged offensive: firstly, by means of the law, attempting both to mobilise the current legal system, and also to transform it by the gaining of female suffrage, marital law reform and greater legal protection for women from sexual abuse; secondly, by means of economic changes which would facilitate women's economic independence and contribute to the elimination of prostitution and mercenary marriages; thirdly, by means of cultural transformation – changes in ideas and behaviour concerning sex and morality – realisable largely through education, and men's adoption of 'self-control'.

To many late nineteenth and early twentieth century middle-class women, prostitution haunted relations between the sexes. Combined with the sexual ignorance of so many women and men, the dominant idea that women did not experience sexual pleasure anyway, and the widespread notion that men needed an outlet for their sexual urges, many women, including many feminists, whether married or unmarried, were, at the very least, ambivalent about sexual relationships. They assumed that women's sexual relations with men were not always wished for, let alone enjoyed.[5] Feminists across the political spectrum shared the central belief that women must win the right to absolute control over their bodies, that all sexual encounters with men must be consensual and all motherhood voluntary. Feminist free lovers and anarchists[6] were as keen as other feminists for sexual relationships to be monogomous, for sexual encounters to be subjected to a degree of self-control and for them to be defined and experienced as other than simply physical.[7] They wanted sex to be more than a set of physical sensations, to be more, even, than an emotional, loving experience – to be what many of them termed an experience at the 'spiritual' plane. These hopes and desires had as a prerequisite the assumption that sexual

relations could, and would, radically change, and that *men* would have
to learn to be different.

THE RISE OF SEXOLOGY

In the mid to late nineteenth century, Britain, Europe and America
witnessed a new classification of multiple aspects of sexuality, including the specification of fantasies, fetishes and numerous pleasures of
the body, and new pathologised individual identities, such as the homosexual, the lesbian, the pervert, the sado-masochist, the nymphomaniac
and the frigid woman (see Foucault, 1979). The power and influence
of these sexological writings in the years before the First World War
must not be over-emphasised; their impact on ideas about sexuality
did not come into full effect until the 1920s and 1930s. This new 'science' (which incidentally fought long and hard to be recognised as a
'science' at all), had marginal status within the British medical establishment, and the work was often very difficult to obtain, frequently
being subjected to various systems of censorship.[8] Yet where the texts
were available, they clearly made it easier for women to think and
talk about issues which were formerly taboo. Sexology contributed to
the opening up of a space for women to discuss sex. Readers did not
need to accept the work wholesale, indeed many feminists made *selective* use of these writings. But these concepts did not, of course, start
from women's experience. As Caroll Smith-Rosenberg points out:
'Women's assumption of men's symbolic constructs [the language of
sexology] involved women in a fundamental act of alienation' (Smith-
Rosenberg, 1985, pp. 265–6). What this meant in practice will become
apparent.
    So what did these sexologists have to say about women's sexuality?
In pre-war Britain, the most influential of these 'sex psychologists',
as they were called at the time, were Iwan Bloch, August Forel and
Britain's Havelock Ellis.[9] Sexual theorists were not an homogeneous
grouping and there was no unanimity, but one view which has becoming prominent at the time of the *Freewoman* journal was that women,
whether heterosexual or lesbian, were, and should be, sexual beings.
The crucial factor in relation to married women was the legitimisation
of their heterosexual desire – so long as it was passive and responsive
rather than initiating. The other side of such legitimising was the assumption that married women who were not sexually 'reponsive' were

'frigid', and thereby pathological. As for relations between women, these were now sexualised and the 'romantic friendship' discredited, but the effects cannot be seen to have been always wholly negative. Although women who loved other women became defined as unnatural, many were simultaneously empowered through their ability to name themselves and their feelings, and through the help that 'naming' gave them in identifying other lesbians.[10]

FREEWOMAN DEBATE

The *Freewoman* first appeared in November 1911 and ran weekly up until October 1912, when it closed through lack of funds. Its insolvency had been exacerbated by W. H. Smith withdrawing the paper from its shops the previous month – ostensibly because of the paper's discussion of sex, although Dora Marsden, the editor, thought the ban politically motivated. The paper reappeared in June 1913 as the *New Freewoman*, now irrevocably a literary journal, but it again folded at the end of the year. In its third and last incarnation the following year, it took the name the *Egoist*; by this time under the control of Ezra Pound, its original feminist concerns were nowhere in sight (see Garner, 1990, pp. 71–2). The *Freewoman*'s circulation was always small, but its influence upon feminists and sexual radicals in Britain and the United States was far greater than its low print-run might suggest. Years later, Rebecca West's verdict was that the *Freewoman* had had 'an immense effect on its time' (West, (1926), reprinted in Spender (1984), p. 63).

Dora Marsden, born in 1882, was the main force behind the original paper. She came from an impoverished middle-class one-parent family (her father having deserted his wife and five children when Dora was eight). She had become a pupil teacher at thirteen, a university student in Manchester at eighteen, and later the head of a teacher-training college (see Garner, 1990). She had been a suffragette, indeed a paid organiser of the WSPU, but at the paper's opening she saw herself as an anarchist individualist. Contributors of articles and letters included many types of feminist, socialist and anarchist, such as socialist and radical suffragist Ada Neild Chew,[11] another ex-WSPU paid organiser Teresa Billington Greig, Rebecca West (writing book reviews for the paper aged nineteen),[12] Fabian novelist H. G. Wells, anarchist socialist and homosexual activist Edward Carpenter, socialist feminist Stella

Browne, and anarchists Guy Aldred and Rose Witcop.
The journal published various articles on women's waged work, housework, motherhood, the suffrage movement and theories of art and literature, but it was soon devoting more and more space, especially in its lengthy correspondence, to the discussion of sex, morality and marriage. The advent of the *Freewoman* might have been 'phenomenal' (to quote Dora Marsden) in relation to the discussion of sex, but the nature of debate was a mixture of old and new, rooted in past feminist concerns and explanations but developing new ideas and formulations. Sex as 'naturally' heterosexual was still implicitly assumed. Contributors continued to raise many of the same problems that had concerned feminists over the past forty years: birth-control, prostitution, problems with the present marriage system, the demand for male purity. Most contributors agreed that, ideally, sex was not an uncontrollable physical urge, indiscriminate in its object; most were opposed to promiscuity. All upheld a woman's right to control her body and fertility.

Many *Freewoman* contributors, concerned for sexual relationships to become more spiritual and more *meaningful*, sought to understand the 'true' purpose of human sexuality. This inevitably included a consideration of the relationship of sex to reproduction. Some assumed that the sexual instinct for *both* sexes was a 'reproductive instinct', and that any other deployment of sex was unnatural and immoral. This position was rooted, of course, in the Judaeo-Christian formulation that sex must be 'purposive': for procreation alone. Yet this view was presented with a new dimension, namely as an argument against the imposition of male sexual demands on women other than when they both desired a child. It was also a view which sanctified sex as sacred and consensual.[13] To many of the *Freewoman* feminists, however, sex was more than simply reproductive (although this did not prompt a discussion of sex between women; lesbianism was barely mentioned in the *Freewoman*). To Isabel Leatham, for example, sex needed to be *conceptually* separated from reproduction:

> I certainly hope that Freewomen will not enter upon their sex relationship for any such conscious purpose as that of reproduction, but rather that they will find in passionate love between man and woman, even if that be transient, the only sanction for sex intimacy.
> (*Freewoman*, 11 January 1912, p. 151)

'A grandmother' elaborated upon this conceptual separation, differentiating the human 'love problem' from the animal 'parenthood problem'.

She warned: 'Let us beware of allowing [the] more prosaic animal side of the sex-relationship to eclipse the other, which is human and spiritual' (*Freewoman*, 22 February 1912, p. 270). Thus in stark contrast to those who saw the reproductive aspect of sex as its only moral (as well as natural) function, she characterised it as the 'animal' and baser side of sex.

CONSTRUCTING A LANGUAGE

Feminists had for a long time perceived that one of the difficulties in talking about sex, indeed in *understanding* sex, was the lack of an adequate language. Stella Browne felt that a lack of language was a greater problem for women:

> The realities of women's sexual life have been greatly obscured by the lack of any sexual vocabulary. While her brother has often learned all the slang of the street before adolescence, the conventionally "decently brought-up" girl, of the upper and middle classes, has no terms to define many of her sensations and experiences. (Browne (1915), reprinted in Rowbotham (1977), pp. 103–4)

Dora Marsden pointed to another difficulty: even with the inadequate language available to discuss sex, there was disagreement over meanings. To Nora Kiernan, differences of meaning were contingent upon one's sex. Rather than discuss religion (which had been the 'utterly irrelevant' issue brought up at the Freewoman discussion circle she had just attended):

> We need to discuss . . . questions that we, as men and women, are as yet at variance, such as, for instance, the questions of love, passion and sex, which so many of us women do not conceive of in the same sense as men do. (*Freewoman*, 20 June 1912, p. 99)

That Nora Kiernan noted variance on the question of sex did not relate simply to a gender difference, but also to a broader linguistic confusion. An examination of various kinds of writing by feminists, sexologists and others, which touched on sexuality in the period 1885–1918, indicates that the meaning of sex as 'sexual intercourse'/'penetration' was only just starting to be used. Indeed, the early twentieth

century equivalent of the *Oxford English Dictionary* (Murray (ed.),
1884–1933, the volume for Q–Sh having been compiled in 1912–14),
does not register 'sexual intercourse' as one of the meanings of sex,
the primary meaning being the distinction between males and females.
I would suggest that the exploration of sex as something other than
simply physical and reproductive was easier before the *fixing* in popular speech of 'sex' as 'sexual intercourse' (and 'sexual intercourse' as
'penetration'). Logically, sex as other than heterosexual should also
have been conceivable, but for many feminists, this does not seem to
have been the case. Interestingly, the term 'heterosexuality', and of
course 'homosexuality', had only relatively recently entered the language,
both invented in 1869.[14] But the term 'heterosexuality' was simply not
used in popular speech before the First World War. This did not mean,
however, that it was any the less assumed.
   The different meanings of the word 'passion' may also have helped
in thinking about sex as non-physical. Nora Kiernan gave the *Freewoman*
an example of the different meanings given to the word:

> As a child I learnt of the "passion" of Jesus Christ, and nearly in
> the same breadth was told my "passions" would lead me to hell. . . .
> I have heard men describe themselves as "passionate", meaning thereby
> that they were susceptible to the solicitations of the average prosti-
> tute. Another man . . . described "passion" as the feeling he would
> have for a woman with whom he was in perfect agreement – men-
> tally and physically. (*Freewoman*, 20 June 1912, p. 99)

Murray's dictionary confirms that there were many different and contrasting meanings to the noun 'passion', including: 'the sufferings of
Jesus Christ on the Cross'; 'a vehement, commanding or overpower-
ing emotion'; 'amorous feeling; strong sexual affection; love'; 'sexual
desire or impulse' (Murray (ed.) 1909, vol. VII, p. 102). I would suggest
that although the dictionary definitions today are almost identical, passion
as 'sexual desire' is in far greater everyday usage than it was in the
early twentieth century. Indeed some feminists saw the concept 'passion' as standing in opposition to 'sexual desire', or at least in opposition to lust and sensuality. Thus Dora Marsden, for example, saw
passion as largely a spiritual experience, not the:

> bare counterfeit of passion [which] betrays passion – sensuality, lust,
> the tippling with sensation, the snacking at sex, the dreary, monot-
> onous sound of one note in sex.

She clearly disliked the Bacchanalian connotations of sexual 'tippling' and 'snacking'! Passion was nothing to do with promiscuity, and '[t]o anyone who had ever got anything out of sexual passion, the aggravated emphasis . . . bestowed on physical sexual intercourse is more absurd than wicked' (*Freewoman*, 28 December 1911, p. 102).

Most feminists held a positive definition of passion.[15] They tended to use the concept and its ambiguity of meaning to talk about ideal feelings and experiences which were 'above' the purely physical. Slippage between meanings facilitated the exploration of new ideas concerning sex – new possibilities and imaginings. Feminists used the concept of 'passion' to explore the potential for other states of being – states of *pleasure* – which were not inevitably rooted in *physical* sensation.

Dora Marsden's definition of 'passion' was not only primarily non-physical, but it also included the non-sexual. She described the experiences of 'a feminist rebel' (herself?) imprisoned for her beliefs, (Dora was herself imprisoned when a member of the WSPU):

Shut up for the night in the cell, suffering acute physical pain, with the quiet came an extraordinary sense of "spirit" expansion. . . . The whole was suffused with the consciousness of calm, radiant, *abiding* joy. The entire experience *lasted*, how long cannot be stated, but it was extended enough to appear "long". . . . The incident described, although arising from passion inspired by a Cause, is not in our opinion in any essential feature different from what might be inspired by human "love". It has, indeed, features which immediately suggest similarities with the exaltation of momentary semi-physical sex-experience. The chief difference would lie in the prolongation of time length of the experience given, as compared with that of sex. (*Freewoman*, 9 May 1912, p. 482)

A correspondent to the *Freewoman* signing herself 'M.S.', and declaring that she had been in a very happy free union for the past seventeen years, described a similar experience, although with her it was 'inspired by passionate love – not sexual, though tinged with sexual desire.' She continued:

I was in rather a nervous condition, having been unable to take food or to sleep for several days, when one night. . . . I flung myself across my bed and . . . the expansion suddenly began. I not only *saw* the vibration of the atmosphere, but, in it, the ethereal form of the beloved.

offers to lend their copies (often in the original German) to anyone interested. They frequently had difficulties in getting hold of these works, but in their keenness to discuss sex, its role and potential, many *Freewoman* contributors appear to have read as much sexology as they were able to lay their hands on. It was the only current discourse offering a set of ideas with which women could explore the possibility of being sexual *agents* as opposed to eternal victims. They may not have agreed with all they read, but many of them were determined to take from it anything which appeared useful in their pursuit of sexual self-expression. As we shall see, this could unfortunately be at the expense of other feminists.

CHASTITY, SELF-CONTROL AND 'ARTIFICIAL STERILISATION'

Although there was no straight-forward feminist polarity amongst *Freewoman* contributors, there were certainly one or two issues which radically divided them. The issues arose in relation to what constituted the desired feminist morality. Dora Marsden declared herself an advocate of the 'New Morality' as opposed to the 'Old Morality' of 'Indissoluble Monogamy'. The 'New Morality' of a 'freewoman' favoured 'limited monogamy' and 'free unions': monogamous relationships that could be freely entered and freely left. The 'Indissoluble Monogamy' of current marriage had 'maintained itself by means of the support of men's hypocrisy, the spinster's dumb resignation, the prostitute's unsightly degradation and the married woman's monopoly and satisfaction' (*Freewoman*, 4 January 1912, p. 121). No contributor to the journal favoured the 'Old Morality', but many disagreed on the definition of a 'freewoman', the implications of 'limited monogamy' and the negative portrayal conveyed in Dora's mention of the 'spinster's dumb resignation'. They also disagreed on the acceptability of birth control. These issues of dispute related in essence to the question of the desirability of *physical* relations and their frequency on the one hand, and the exercise of sexual self-control on the other.

Possibly one of the greatest disagreements between feminist contributors to the *Freewoman* related to the evaluation of chastity. As in the late nineteenth century, the debate over chastity in the *Freewoman* was frequently linked to reflections – positive and negative – on the spinster and her sexual status: a joust between viewing her chaste state as morally superior versus viewing it as sexually deficient. The journal's first issue contained a savage, ironic and anonymous attack: '"The Spinster" by One':

> I write of the High Priestess of Society. Not of the mothers of sons, but of her barren sister, the withered tree, the acidulous vestal under whose pale shadow we chill and whiten, of the spinster I write.

The writer went on to introduce the familar spectre of the sexually frustrated and sickening celibate:

> the Spinster does not overcome Sex as a saint overcomes Sin. . . . Driven inward, denied its rightful, ordained fulfilment, the instinct becomes defused. . . . If prurience has slain its thousands, chastity has slain its tens of thousands. (*Freewoman*, 23 November 1911, p. 10)

By the following week the article had elicted two indignant responses, but the debate on chastity only got truly underway (and was to continue weekly over a period of three months), when the American socialist Upton Sinclair asserted that it was amongst celibate women 'that modern psychologists discover the greatest proportion of nervous disorders, anaemics and insanities' (*Freewoman*, 18 January 1912, p. 165). In response, women wrote of the value of sexual self-control. E. M. Watson, unlike many advocates of celibacy, did not assume women to be less sexual than men – merely better at controlling their desires, but she questioned the 'suffering' of male celibates; to her it was simply an argument to force married women to 'sacrifice themselves . . . daily' (*Freewoman*, 8 February 1912, p. 231). Miss Kathlyn Oliver, suffragist and ex-Secretary of the Domestic Workers Union, declared: 'I am neither a prude nor a Puritan, but I am an apostle of self restraint in sex matters. What is it that raises us above the brute level but the exercise of self-restraint?' She wrote that she was nearly 30, unmarried, had always practiced abstinence and, challenging the health aspect, said she enjoyed the best of health; 'my married women friends, on the contrary, have always some complaint' (*Freewoman*, 15 February 1912, p. 252).

In the next issue of the *Freewoman*, E. M. Watson and Kathlyn Oliver were sharply rebuked by 'a New Subscriber', adamant that they should not 'make their temperamental coldness into a rigid standard for others' (*Freewoman*, 22 February 1912, p. 270). Kathlyn Oliver was indignant; wrongly assuming 'a New Subscriber' to be male (she

later revealed herself to be Stella Browne), Kathlyn claimed to speak
for most women in declaring that:

> until they love, the idea of the sexual relationship seldom enters
> their thoughts. Personally, I never desired the sex relationship until
> I "fell in love" at about 20.... We couldn't marry and from then
> till now I have had to crush and subdue the sex feeling. (*Freewoman*,
> 29 February 1912, p. 290)

'A New Subscriber' dismissively replied: 'It will be an unspeakable
catastrophe if our richly complex Feminist Movement . . . falls under
the domination of sexually deficient and disappointed women' (*Freewoman*, 7 March 1912, p. 313). Kathlyn replied in fury, but 'A New
Subscriber' finally silenced her by an accusation of cowardice:

> Let those women who . . . will not try to enjoy their elemental hu-
> man rights, refrain from unmeasured public attacks on the others
> who have the courage of their desires as well as their convictions.
> (*Freewoman*, 18 April 1912, p. 437)

The struggle over the moral status of the spinster being waged in the
Freewoman reflected a wider feminist debate. On the one hand there
were those such as Christabel Pankhurst (see Pankhurst, 1913) and
Cecily Hamilton (see Hamilton, 1909) for whom the chaste spinster,
seen as superior in health and morals to her married counterpart, was
the key to women's liberation. On the other hand, in opposition to this
claim of superiority was mobilised the view of the spinster as 'sexually deficient and disappointed'. Stella Browne and others deployed
sexological ideas to assert their right to be sexual, or rather heterosexual, but they did so via the condemnation of those women who wished
to disavow such a right.

While the concept of self-control was central to the defence of chastity,
it was also applied to the discussion of ideal marital relations. Self-
control within marriage was referred to as 'continence': infrequent sexual
intercourse with lengthy periods of abstinence. Unsurprisingly, those
who advocated chastity for single people tended to advocate continence for the married. To quote E. M. Watson:

> The free woman . . . will seek to teach the man the restraint that
> Nature has taught her to impose upon herself.... To this end she
> will seek to tame in herself as well as her lover the mere mating

instinct ... she will seek to raise marriage to the standard of a spiritual and intellectual as well as a physical union. (*Freewoman*, 8 February 1912, p. 231)

If the 'freewoman' was defined by Dora Marsden as a feminist in favour of limited monogamy and free unions, there were many who took issue with this definition and claimed her as an advocate of self-control. For example, E. M. Watson assumed that teaching man 'restraint' was central to what being a 'freewoman' meant, and Kathlyn Oliver, in asking rhetorically 'How can we possibly be Free Women if, like the majority of men, we become the slaves of our lower appetites?' (*Freewoman*, 15 February 1912, p. 252), clearly saw the *freedom* of the 'freewoman' as a freedom not only from unsolicited sexual advances, but also from the 'bestial' lower instinct of sexual excess – freedom from the 'beast in man'. There were other feminist contributors who thought likewise.[18]

Self-control in marriage was also seen as a 'natural' method of birth control: infrequent sexual intercourse except when a child was desired. Many women, including feminists, were opposed to 'unnatural' or 'artificial' methods, referred to as 'preventive checks', 'artificial sterilisation' or 'Malthusian appliances' (today's contraceptives). Their opposition related to a fear that the use of such appliances reduced a woman to the status of a prostitute, was possibly harmful (which is what most doctors claimed) and, as Mrs Sherwen informed the *Freewoman*, facilitated 'the indulgence of uncontrolled passions unfortunately *outside* ... marriage ... as well as inside' (*Freewoman*, 25 January 1912, p. 192). 'I cannot believe that such sterilisation will ever be the ideal of the freewoman, or that her freedom will take the form of a loose licence' announced E. M. Watson (*Freewoman*, 8 February 1912, p. 231). Even Isabel Leatham, so insistent that reproduction should not be the aim of sexual relations, was opposed to contraception: 'common Malthusian practices are ... a gross outrage on the aesthetic sensibilities of women and the final mark of their sexual degradation' (*Freewoman*, 7 December 1911, pp. 51–2).

In addition to total abstinence, 'natural' methods of fertility control included partial abstinence, in the sense of intercourse only during the so-called safe period (wrongly calculated as mid-month). Although there was disagreement as to whether *coitus interruptus* – the man withdrawing before orgasm – and *coitus reservatus* – intercourse without ejaculation – were 'natural' methods, there was one kind of *coitus reservatus* which was declared a spiritualised form of sexual intercourse entailing heightened self-control. A technique developed by John Humphrey Noyes at his nineteenth-century American Oneida Colony, the method involved the man, through will-power, supposedly redirecting the sperm back into the urethra, thereby retaining the 'vital fluid' (see Gordon, 1977, p. 85). American feminist physican and spiritualist Alice B. Stockham called her own version of this technique 'Karezza', and wrote a book on the subject in 1896. She argued that this method was of special benefit to women in that it both avoided unwanted pregnancy, and, through the prolonging of intercourse and its experience at a *spiritual* plane, it satisfied women's sexual and emotional needs. In contrast, the 'ordinary' method of sexual intercourse was hasty and spasmodic and left the woman unsatisfied. (Stockham, 1896).[19]

'Free union' couple Mary and Stanley Randolph wrote enthusiastically to the *Freewoman* about this technique (*Freewoman*, 13 June 1912, p. 79, and 27 June 1912, p. 118). The method was widely publicised in the United States, but it is impossible to know how many people actually attempted it either there or in Britain. As Linda Gordon caustically observes, whatever the obvious advantages for the woman, a technique which 'demanded a suppression of gratification by the male would not seem destined for great popularity' (Gordon, 1977, p. 62). This method was possibly used by the *Freewoman* feminist correspondent E. M. Watson however, whose references to 'self-control' may have referred not simply to abstinence, but also to the practice of Karezza. It all depends on whether or not E. M. Watson (who as I have noted, declared herself a woman) was in fact Edith M. Watson. When Edith, a member of the Women's Freedom League, wrote for the *Vote* and other papers, she signed herself 'Edith M. Watson', or 'E.M.W.'. I have no direct evidence of her familiarity with the *Freewoman*, but she was a close friend of Nina Boyle's, who certainly knew the *Freewoman* because she sent it a letter on one occasion; Edith was also an acquaintance of Rebecca West, a regular contributor to the paper. Edith married Ernest Watson, a socialist, on 1 February 1912 (the date, incidentally, of E. M. Watson's first letter to the *Freewoman*) but had been living with him beforehand. In her unpublished autobiography, she reflects back on their early sex life, referring to Ernest as 'Eustace':

> Eustace's lovemaking was as lengthy as many of his arguments. Indeed. . . . I was still, at 22, [she was 23 when E. M. Watson's first letter appeared in the *Freewoman*] ignorant of the exact nature of the sex act and the feelings it could engender, of its ordinary course

and completion. I had no idea that Eustace's long lovemaking without any culmination was anything but what he said it was, self-control. He prided himself on keeping his feelings under control – a Yogi had nothing on him.

It does sound as if Ernest/Eustace had been engaging in the Karezza practice, although she gives no name to his method of birth control. She continued: 'One reason he gave for this self-control was that we could not have children, not being married, and that in any case he was not going to bring a child INTO THE WORLD [*sic*] to be cannon fodder for the next war.' (He conceded on the child issue, marrying Edith and having one child, Bernard.) The 'prolonged loveplay' made her 'blissfully happy', but in the end it wore her out: 'I lost my health and had no energy.'[20]

THE PLACE OF PHYSICAL SEX

While what one might call the 'old school' of feminism prioritised freedom *from* undesired sex, and from lustfulness in both men and themselves as women, the 'new school' – those embracing the idea of the 'new morality' – was more concerned to gain women's freedom *to have* sexual relations, for women to develop their sexual potential. While both schools tended to hold spiritualised sex as the ideal, the place of *physical* sex was more controversial. However, the new moralists' position on physical sex varied. Dora Marsden's own views, for example, seem inconsistent. In one article she argued for the importance for women of satisfying 'the hunger of the body'. She bemoaned the pressure of cultural etiquette which forced denial in 'respectable women' and engendered self-renunciation: 'Whereas with men sex is an appetite which demands food, with respectable women sex as a need seeking its own satisfaction has to be ignored' (*New Freewoman*, 1 August 1913, p. 64). She was optimistic that things were changing, however:

> many women are coming to realise their own psychology, and are abandoning their long mistrust of life, with its impulses and pleasures. They are beginning to realise that capacity for sense experience is the sap of life. (*Freewoman*, 28 December 1911, p. 102)

Dora's position on the need for physical sex was not as straightforward as this quote might imply. When she referred to 'sense experience' elsewhere, it is clear that she was not seeing it as primarily a physical matter. 'The physical is a prison to sense' she wrote:

> it is the prolongation of the mental experience which is desired . . . the physical desire . . . was the whole of sex in the sub-human sphere, and . . . will be eliminated in the super-human . . . we have it only in the form of a remnant in the human. (*Freewoman*, 9 May 1912, p. 482)

In her description of the imprisoned feminist whose 'acute physical pain' turned to 'calm, radiant, *abiding* joy', she suggests that the sensation was essentially the *same* as that inspired by human love. Despite her growing hostility towards militant suffragism, she did not deny that bodily sacrifice in the form of the suffragette's hunger strike could be a rewarding, 'spiritual' experience. Neither did she reduce the experience to being simply sexual. On the contrary, she pointed to similarity not equivalence. She was as yet uncertain as to how sex was to be defined, let alone experienced. She did, however, believe in variation, for although claiming that 'with passion sex-satisfaction is primarily mental', she added that it 'depends upon opportunity and temperament' as to whether it is also physical (*Freewoman*, 2 May 1912, p. 461).

Even Stella Browne was not as clear-cut on the need for *physical* sex as her attack on the spinster suggests. She did not write about sex as 'spiritual' but she did see it as 'largely mental and imaginative'. She validated the role of fantasy over actual physical contact:

> Any direct external stimulation is much rarer among young girls than among boys. . . . But day-dreaming, the production of a higher degree of enjoyment, by means of vague yet delightful imaginings, is the most exquisite pleasure, and deepest secret of many imaginative and sensitive girls. (Browne (1915), reprinted in Rowbotham (1977), p. 101)

Yet this was about *girls*; of older women she had this to say: 'after twenty-five, the woman who has neither husband nor lover . . . is suffering mentally and bodily' (*Freewoman*, 21 March 1912, p. 354). More than Dora Marsden she insisted on a woman's right to *be sexual*: 'the sexual experience is the right of every human being not hopelessly afflicted in mind or body' (*Freewoman*, 21 March 1912, p. 354). Three years later she was demanding: 'Let [women] set their own requirements, and boldly claim a share of life and erotic experience, as perfectly consistent with their own self-respect' (Browne (1915), reprinted in Rowbotham (1977), p. 96).

In the nineteenth century the chief ideological polarity between women had been between the married woman and prostitute – the respectable and the despised. Now a new and additional configuration was being advanced between the *sexualised* married woman and the *sexless* spinster. It was a configuration instigated by sexology, medicine and the heightened concern with 'breeding', but in their attempt to claim a new identity, it was also drawn upon by some of the 'new moralist' feminists. That these feminists appeared only able to claim their right to be sexual through distancing themselves from – even condemning – that which they were not (the 'sexless' spinster), constituted part of the 'act of alienation' mentioned by Carroll Smith-Rosenberg in her analysis of the effects of using sexological ideas.

This brief moment in which a space was opened up for feminists to discuss sex was soon to evaporate with the increasing eugenical emphasis on 'fit' motherhood[21] and the tightening up of the definition of 'sex'. In the early twentieth century and into the inter-war years, while sexologists (including Freudians) *extended* the definition of the 'sexual', the definition of 'sex' itself was narrowed down into 'penetration' (and 'normal sex' into 'heterosexual penetration'). This emphasis on penetration related centrally to the stress on *reproductive* sex, itself in part the product of the fears in circulation about the declining birth-rate (an anxiety which continued in Britain right up until the Second World War).[22] Non-penetrative sexual activity was simply not 'real' sex.

Despite the advent of second-wave feminism, the gay movement and queer politics, the common-sense assumption still circulates today that lesbians cannot be having 'real' sex unless some kind of penetration is involved, and that non-penetrative sex between men and women is simply 'foreplay' to the 'real thing'. While hindsight permits us to see the limitations of the *Freewoman*'s views on sexuality, we need to recognise current contraints, not least a lack of the fluidity of sexual language available to feminists at the turn of the century.

NOTES

1. A greatly extended version of this article appears as Chapter 7 of Bland (1995).

Many thanks to Judy Greenway, Frank Mort, Helen Crowley and Martin Durham for their helpful comments and to Hilary Frances for sharing some of her research on Edith Watson.

2. Writing in 1926, Rebecca West reflected back on how there had certainly been 'a need for someone to stand aside and ponder on the profounder aspects of Feminism'. But she had thought that Dora Marsden 'was wrong in formulating this feeling as an accusation against the Pankhursts and suffragettes in general, because they were simply doing their job, and it was certainly a whole-time job' (West (1926), reprinted in Spender (1984), p. 64).

3. See S. Skelhorn, *Freewoman*, 28 March 1912, p. 376; R. C. Fletcher Woods, *Freewoman*, 4 July 1912, p. 132; C. Boord, *Freewoman*, 14 March 1912, p. 331.

4. In 1885 Karl Pearson coined the word 'sexualogy', meaning the science of sexual relations, but the word did not catch on. J. A. Simpson and E. S. C. Weiner (1989) cite 'sexology' as first used in 1902, but I would argue that it was barely in use in Britain before the First World War; the preferred term was 'sex psychology'. I have found a reference to 'sexology' in *The Adult* for 1897, but the meaning differs from what became the accepted meaning: 'It appears to me that the ban should be taken away from non-conformists in sexology . . .' (Leighton Pagan, 1897, *The Adult*, 1(4): p. 59).

5. There is evidence, of course, that there were women who did enjoy sexual intercourse; see Gay (1984) and Mason (1994).

6. I am indebted in Judy Greenway for enlightening me on the relationship between feminism and anarchism.

7. See Kent (1987), Gordon (1977, pp. 75, 109) and Bland (1995).

8. Havelock Ellis's *Sexual Inversion*, for example, was banned in 1898, only shortly after its publication; see Rowbotham and Weeks (1977). Many sexological works in bookshops and libraries were only available to members of the medical and legal professions.

9. For differences between these sexologists see Bland (1995, Chapter 7).

10. See Stanley (1992, Chapter 8), Hennegan (1982, pp. ix–x) and Smith-Rosenberg (1985).

11. See Chew (1982); and see A. Nield Chew to the *Freewoman*, 13 April and 18 April 1912, reprinted in Chew (1982, pp. 235–8). Realising that 'The *Freewoman* is too poor to pay', she offered her work for free (Garner, 1990, p. 76).

12. See Glendinning (1987) and Marcus (1982).

13. See Jane Craig, *Freewoman*, 25 January 1912, p. 192. In the same issue of the paper, Mrs Sherwen reflected that 'surely the ideal should be that sex relationship and sex organs should be held absolutely sacred to the production of children, and never be degraded to minister to a lustful pleasure' (*Freewoman*, 25 January 1912, p. 192).

14. Karl Kertbeny coined the terms; see Katz (1990).

15. Margaret Shurmer Sibthorp, editor of *Shafts*, was one of the relatively few feminists to see passion in a purely negative light, equating it with sensuality as opposed to love: 'It is not love but passion . . . which has made man ever resolve to hold dominion over woman. . . . [W]ith the

death of passion will cease all desire on the part of man to dominate over woman' (*Shafts*, November 1897) Also see Grand (1898, p. 386): 'Passion is the desire of the flesh for self-indulgence.'

16. And see E. Noel Morgan, *Freewoman*, 8 August 1912, p. 234, and 'Hibernian' *Freewoman*, 7 May 1912, p. 313, for other examples of 'passion' being defined non-physically.

17. Havelock Ellis meant more by 'auto-eroticism' than masturbation, namely 'the sexual energy of a person automatically generated throughout life and manifesting itself without any definite external stimulation' (Weeks, 1981, p. 149). In Stella Browne's discussion in The *Freewoman*, however, she seems to be restricting the term to masturbation.

18. For example, see Isabel Leatham, *Freewoman*, 11 January 1912, p. 151 and Jane Craig, *Freewoman*, 25 January 1912, p. 192.

19. And see G. N. Miller (1891, 1896). Edward Carpenter recommended Karezza's provision of 'a more complete *soul union*, a strange and intoxicating exchange of life and transmutation of elements' (Carpenter, 1906, pp. 173–4). Stockham's book was highly recommended by the Canadian Women's Christian Temperance Union's Purity Superintendent in 1897 (Valverde, 1991, p. 70). See Smith-Rosenberg, 1985, for a discussion of the technique.

20. Unpublished autobiography of Edith Watson, in private hands. I am indebted to Hilary Frances' generosity in sharing this and other details of Edith Watson's life.

21. See Davin (1978) and Bland (1995, Chapter 6).

22. See Soloway (1982).

REFERENCES

Bland, L. (1995) *Banishing the Beast: English Feminism and Sexual Morality, 1885–1914* (London: Penguin).

Browne, S. (1915) 'The Sexual Variety and Variability among Women and their Bearing upon Social Reconstruction'; reprinted in S. Rowbotham (1977) *A New World for Women: Stella Browne – Socialist Feminist* (London: Pluto Press), pp. 91–105.

Carpenter, E. (1906) *Love's Coming of Age*, 5th edn (enlarged) (London: Swan Sonnenschein).

Chew, D. N. (1982) *The Life and Writings of Ada Nield Chew* (London: Virago).

Cronwright-Schreiner, S. C. (ed.) (1924) *The Letters of Olive Schreiner 1876–1920* (Boston, MA: Little, Brown).

Davin, A. (1978) 'Imperialism and Motherhood', *History Workshop Journal*, 5: pp. 9–15.

Foucault, M. (1979) *The History of Sexuality, Volume 1: An Introduction* (London: Allen Lane).

Garner, L. (1990) *A Brave and Beautiful Spirit: Dora Marsden, 1882–1960* (Aldershot: Avebury).

Gay, P. (1984) *The Bourgeois Experience, Vol 1: Education of the Senses* (Oxford: Oxford University Press).

Glendinning, V. (1987) *Rebecca West: A Life* (London: Weidenfeld & Nicolson).

Gordon, L. (1977) *Woman's Body, Woman's Right* (London: Penguin).

Gordon, L. and DuBois, E. (1983) 'Seeking Ecstasy on the Battlefield: Danger and Pleasure in Nineteenth-Century Feminist Sexual Thought', *Feminist Review*, **13** (Spring): pp. 42–54.

Grand, S. (1898) 'Marriage Questions in Fiction: The Standpoint of a Typical Modern Woman', *The Fortnightly Review*, n.s., **63**: pp. 378–89.

Hamilton, C. (1909, 1981) *Marriage as a Trade* (London: The Women's Press).

Hennegan, A. (1982) Introduction to R. Hall 1982, *The Well of Loneliness* (London: Virago).

Jeffreys, S. (1985) *The Spinster and her Enemies* (London: Pandora).

Katz, J. (1990) 'The Invention of Heterosexuality', *Socialist Review*, **21**: p. 1.

Kent, S. K. (1987) *Sex and Suffrage in Britain, 1860–1914* (New Jersey: Princeton University Press).

Marcus, J. (1982) *The Young Rebecca* (London: Macmillan).

Mason, M. (1994) *The Making of Victorian Sexuality* (Oxford: Oxford University Press).

Miller, G. N. (1896) *After the Strike of a Sex, or Zugassent's Discovery* (London: William Reeves).

Miller, G. N. (1891) *The Strike of a Sex: A Novel* (London: W.H. Reynold).

Murray, J. A. H. (ed.) (1884–1933) *A New English Dictionary on Historical Principles* (Oxford: Clarendon Press).

Pankhurst, C. (1913) *The Great Scourge and How to End It* (London: E. Pankhurst).

Rowbotham, S. and Weeks, J. (1977) *Socialism and the New Life: The Personal and Sexual Politics of Edward Carpenter and Havelock Ellis* (London: Pluto Press).

Simpson, J. A. and Weiner, E. S. C. (1989) *The Oxford English Dictionary*, 2nd edn (Oxford: Clarendon Press).

Smith-Rosenberg, C. (1985) 'The New Woman as Androgyne: Social Disorder and Gender Crisis, 1870–1936', in C. Smith-Rosenberg, *Disorderly Conduct: Visions of Gender in Victorian America* (Oxford: Oxford University Press).

Soloway, R. (1982) *Birth Control and the Population Question in England, 1877–1930* (Chapel Hill and London: University of Carolina Press).

Stanley, L. (1992) *The Auto/Biographical I* (Manchester: Manchester University Press).

Stockham, A. B. (1896) *Karezza: Ethics of Marriage* (Chicago: Alice B. Stockham).

Strachey, R. (1931) *Millicent Garrett Fawcett* (London: John Murray).

Valverde, M. (1991) *The Age of Light, Soap and Water: Moral Reform in English Canada, 1885–1925* (Ontario: McClelland & Stewart).

Vicinus, M. (1985) *Independent Women* (London: Virago).

Weeks, J. (1981) *Sex, Politics and Society* (Harlow: Longman).

West, R. (1926) 'The Freewoman', *Time and Tide*, 16 July; reprinted in D. Spender (ed.) (1984) *Time and Tide Wait for No Man* (London: Pandora), pp. 63–8.

5 Mass Observation's 'Little Kinsey' and the British Sex Survey Tradition

LIZ STANLEY

INTRODUCTION

When I was 20 I didn't know a thing, and I went to see our parson. . . . He . . . said 'Do you grow marrows, George? . . . Well, you've got to pollenize marrows . . .', and he showed me how it was done.

some can go through a full life and never think nothing about sex, but they're very very few. I have done.

you can see women that's never been happy, and men that's never had a woman. And they look as if they're going seedy, they have that green and mouldy look.

Sex isn't very nice. . . . Yes, it can be harmful, it can ruin a woman's inside as easy as pie, ruin any girl's innards, intercourse can.

I am very satisfied. I have been very clever or very lucky in my choice of partner.

if only he had made love to me instead of using me like a chamber pot.

I shouldn't think they're [homosexuals] human. . . . I mean animals don't do that.

'Little Kinsey', from which these quotations derive, was Britain's first national random sample survey of sexual attitudes and sexual behaviour. It thus has considerable historical importance for understanding the development of random sampling and the associated post-war development in Britain of a 'sex survey tradition', something which is discussed in detail in Stanley (1995). However, 'Little Kinsey' also has importance in its own right, as the source of information about sexual behaviour, sexual attitude and sexual change in Britain in this crucial post-war period, as a still-fascinating piece of writing, and as research carried out at the cusp of great change in the organisation which carried it out, and this is the concern of this present discussion.

'Little Kinsey' was carried out in 1949 by Mass-Observation, which had been founded in 1937 to carry out radical popular sociology engaging the mass of 'ordinary' people. Mass-Observation was active as such until 1949, in part through frequent use of the work of a 'national panel' of Mass-Observers, in part through its many one-off projects exploring a very wide variety of topics, in part through its long-term research presence in 'Worktown', the Mass-Observation name for Bolton (Calder and Sheridan, 1984; Calder, 1985). 'Little Kinsey' was carried out as a British response to the 1948-published Kinsey study of American male sexual behaviour (Kinsey, 1948). Originally it was intended to be a typically 'Mass-Observation' piece of research, carried out through 'follows', 'overheards' and observation, and concerned with what people actually *did*, rather than questioning them about their *attitudes*, which might or might not correspond with actual behaviour. However, the planned research went through rapid changes, which were closely linked to methodological, epistemological and organisational changes occurring within Mass-Observation. These led during the course of 1949 to its transformation into a commercial market research organisation, still in existence, 'Mass-Observation Ltd' (Calder, 1985; Stanley, 1990).

These changes moved 'Little Kinsey' from a comparative observational study of sexual behaviour in 'Churchtown' (Worcester) and 'Steeltown' (Middlesborough) to a national random sample survey of attitudes. Contemporary reports of the research, particularly the articles using 'Little Kinsey' material published in the *Sunday Pictorial*,[1] referred to the survey data alone. Analytic difficulties in interpreting and using the two different kinds of data produced different versions of a planned book. The most complete manuscript was submitted to a publisher, Allen & Unwin, in 1949, but was not published at the time (see Stanley, 1995). 'Problems' with the manuscript were referred to in various internal correspondence; these are also referred to in letters between Mass-Observation researchers and the external 'assessors' who worked with them on the 'Little Kinsey' project.[2] These issues are discussed in the first section of this chapter.

'Little Kinsey' contains a coherent, albeit largely implicit, attempt to theorise, as well as to research, people's own constructions of sexuality.

It is this which forms the focus of the second section of the chapter, which looks at the understandings of 'sex' articulated by different sections of the sample, and also that which underpins the analytic stance taken by the writer/analyst of 'Little Kinsey'. 'Little Kinsey's' approach to researching, theorising and understanding sex is interestingly set against that of now better known post-war British sex surveys, and a discussion of these later surveys forms the concluding section of the chapter.

TEXTUAL VOICES AND RHETORICAL STRATEGIES

The chapters composing the final version of the 'Little Kinsey' manuscript[3] are concerned with how and when people found out 'the facts of life', their views on sex education, their knowledge and use of birth control, their approach to marriage and feelings about divorce, their views about extra-marital sex and specifically about prostitution, how and in what ways they think of sex as 'natural', and their views about changes in sex morality. The manuscript is completed by a look at the sexual attitudes and behaviours of the 'national panel' of Mass-Observers and an appendix on male homosexuality.

The research that became central to 'Little Kinsey' is composed of three related surveys. The first is a 'street sample' survey of over 2000 people selected by random sampling methods carried out in a wide cross-section of cities, towns and villages in Britain. The second is a postal survey of around 1000 each of three groups of 'opinion leaders': clergymen, teachers and doctors. The third is formed by the results of a 'directive' (a set of interrelated questions written in a Mass-Observation house style) and a follow-up directive sent to members of Mass-Observation's national panel and responded to by more than 450 of them. These related surveys are reported upon in tabular form (usually in whole percentage terms – 'out of every hundred, X responded . . .'), at a number of points within the text. These numerical statements are embedded in an extended argument developed around the topic that each chapter focuses on, and they are surrounded by extensive quotations which were written verbatim by the interviewers as they worked through the questionnaire with members of the 'street sample'.

Cross-cutting the quantitative and the qualitative material from the three surveys is an earlier Mass-Observation textual 'voice'. This is formed by extensive quotation from reports by Mass-Observation researchers who had worked in the 'Churchtown' and 'Steeltown' phase of the research (in the chapters dealing with prostitution and sexual morality in particular); by Mass-Observation researchers who had worked in the late 1930s in 'Seatown' (Blackpool) in a considerably earlier project (there is a long quotation from this in the chapter concerned with sexual morality); and by a Mass-Observation investigator who wrote about his research on/involvement in a 'homosexual group'. This 'voice' constitutes different kinds of rhetorical strategy within the text, and its presence has the effect of subordinating the 'quantitative' to the 'qualitative', but still with the dominant rhetorical strategy being that of the Mass-Observation analyst/writer of the text. This was Len England, a man with a long-term involvement in Mass-Observation, and then later in Mass-Observation Ltd.[4]

Thus, three competing rhetorical strategies characterise 'Little Kinsey' which in a sense speak past each other about different kinds of data and 'facts' about sexual habit and opinion, and they are articulated using, firstly, quantitative data from the three surveys, secondly, qualitative data collected alongside the street survey and, thirdly, observational reports from the 'other' Mass-Observation projects. Surrounding these is an argumentative structure which articulates these in a fourth strategy, that of the *sotto voce* analyst/writer himself, apparently absent, without gender or class, without a 'point of view'. This textual complexity and diversity constitutes what is almost a signature for Mass-Observation writing over the period from 1937 to 1949, a signature which signs away a single authoritative authorial identity in favour of a polyphonous and multi-layered set of textual strategies, which, by their very diversity, signal that no one of these is to be seen as *'the* voice'. There is 'authority', but at the same time authority is rhetorically dispersed.

This dispersal of authorial authority in 'Little Kinsey' is given additional emphasis by the way the survey data is used. Only infrequently are categorical conclusions drawn about 'people and sex', for the methodological treatment given to 'the numbers' interrogates these around multiplicities of difference: through comparisons of differences between the three different survey groups, and through statements about differences within each survey group by age, education, income, sex, by whether people lived in villages, towns or cities, and were churchgoers or not. The result is that almost every statement of 'this' has alongside it an alternative one concerning 'that', both being presented as 'fact' and 'true' for different groups and individuals.

Read this way, 'Little Kinsey' can be seen as a memorial to the failures of data triangulation.[5] This is triangulation seen as strangulation, the mass of resultant data choking away the ability to state 'the facts' with clarity. Almost every piece of numerical analysis can be used to produce a multiplicity of 'ends', fracturing broader categorical statements in order to represent numerically actual variability within the research population. However, producing untidy 'ends' of data, small and apparently 'insignificant' groups of numbers, is something which contemporary survey practice has turned its face away from in favour of the categorical, the analysis and representation of only dominant trends and thus research clarity. Such a scientific denial of untidy life to produce neat research does not appear in 'Little Kinsey', and its 'failure' in this regard actually constitutes an extremely interesting attempt to grapple with the very real complexities involved in investigating the social and the sexual.

'Little Kinsey', however, can be read in another equally plausible way, as an epistemological murder rather than a methodological suicide, as the murder of 'the facts' and any notion that these 'speak for themselves'. The text of 'Little Kinsey' at a number of points states that the facts must be allowed to do precisely this, speak for themselves, but then, ironically, it goes on to provide *alternative* facts, depending on social people's location: their class, age, sex, religious affiliation, locality and whether they were surveyed, interviewed or observed. The movement of Mass-Observation, from being an organisation concerned with methodological eclecticism within an observational framework focusing on actual behaviour, to becoming a market research organisation concerned with surveying and tabulating attitudes, was not achieved without difficulty. The text of 'Little Kinsey' is testimony to this, for it demonstrates the epistemological, not merely methodological, divide between the two approaches, and that these different data actually construct different phenomena which in the final analysis are irreconcilable. That 'Little Kinsey' was not published contemporaneously is closely related to this: its analyst/writer was unable to achieve a form for the text which achieved closure over the different kinds of data, and, relatedly, such a closure and so authority was increasingly seen as necessary by not only Mass-Observation's researchers but also by the wider research community in Britain.[6]

THEORISING SEX THE MASS-OBSERVATION WAY

'Little Kinsey' theorises sex, albeit in a largely implicit way, doing so around elaborative contrasts built up from an initial distinction between sexual 'habit', Mass-Observation's term for repeated behaviour, and sexual attitudes. These interconnected contrastive themes have a wider remit than 'sex' conceived narrowly, for they provide a guide to understanding social life, social structure and social action more widely. 'Little Kinsey' starts with a Preface which compares the Kinsey study of sex and the human male with Mass-Observation's work. On one level the Preface rejects the notion that 'Little Kinsey' is in any sense an appropriate title, emphasising that Kinsey's research involved considerably larger numbers and employed a more resolutely statistical stance. However, there is considerable irony here, for overtly rejecting the name 'Little Kinsey' actually brings this title, catchy and easily memorable, to public attention and closely associates it with this research. The Preface is equally double-edged in emphasising that Mass-Observation's research is both less and more than Kinsey's and making a virtue of both – the 'less' is a virtue because there are fewer tables and 'science' and, relatedly, the 'more' is also a virtue because there is more of the 'actuality' of 'the real life' provided by Mass-Observation's approach. By this latter the Preface means its extensive use of interview and observational material, insisting that no known method can produce total accuracy and that those which approach this lose the 'human' element by distancing themselves from what real people do in all its complexity.

The main text continues this approach, in particular through the distinction introduced in the first few chapters between 'habit' and 'attitude'. This distinction is seen to involve the relationship between truth and experience, with experience and behaviour being that which gives the 'true picture'. 'Little Kinsey' strongly argues that, the nearer to people's own lives, the more they will speak from experience instead of using 'other people' as their reference point. 'Attitude' is thus seen to exist when experience is lacking, and to be largely the views of 'opinion leaders' of different kinds.

'Little Kinsey' discerns a 'faint unease' about sex among its sample members, an ambivalent movement between sexual desire and fear, especially by women, who are described as finding sex more distasteful than men. 'Little Kinsey' notes people's considerably greater ease in being questioned about sex, women as much as men, than had been expected. However, it resolutely interprets women's frequent articulation of dislike and boredom with (hetero)sex, and their resentment of men's patronage of prostitutes and involvement in other extra-marital sex, as 'sexual conservatism'. This results in a textual inability to 'hear' what many women, and a good few men, actually say. Thus the fact that women are more in favour of early sex education than men is explained away as women 'really' wanting this because of needing to tell girls about menstruation. Similarly, women's fear of unwanted pregnancy is seen as 'really' a fear of sex, and women's anger about prostitution is recast as 'really' envy and jealousy. Indeed, when men are quoted expressing similar views, this is treated in exactly the same way, as the product of outdated conservatism. Such an essentialist stance, seeing 'sex' as the leitmotif of all social life, as a 'drive', an inner and determined impulse which propels social and sexual behaviour, was becoming fairly common through the conjunction of popularised Freudian ideas with those of social avant guardism: if 'they' think sex is bad, then 'we' think it good; if 'they' think it should be peripheral, then 'we' think it must be central; 'they' don't want social and economic change, and 'we' do. The effect in 'Little Kinsey' is to deny, by explaining away as 'really' something else, the commonsensical constructionist approach taken to sex that characterises a good deal of quoted responses, presenting this as an 'anti-sex' conservatism, rather than people's understanding that sex could and should be different and better.

This contrast between sexual conservatism and sexual progressivism is continued, for (moral) approval and disapproval of sex, particularly in relation to sex education, is discussed in 'Little Kinsey' around a number of sets of overlaying contrasts. One such is between the 'educated' and the 'church-going', with what is 'progressive' being associated with the former and what is 'conservative' with the latter, with women again characterised as more conservative and morally censorious than men. A more general – and stereotypically Freudian – approach to sexual progressivism and sexual conservatism is then developed through attempting to correlate the sex 'habits' of sample members with three aspects of parenting: whether their mothers were 'clean and tidy'; their parents' sex attitudes; and whether they experienced conflict with their parents. Although no statistical correlation of adult behaviour with these childhood factors exists, the text proposes that significant relationships may still exist because the statistical can mask and hide the behavioural – indeed, this argumentative thread about statistics masking life runs throughout the text.

This is a wider argument than the sexual alone, for the text associates the 'progressive' more generally with whatever is most 'pro-sex' (an approach, of course, not unknown amongst self-styled sexual vanguards today), and this in turn leads to the dismissal, denial or ignoring of any questioning of the assumption that sex is *the* centrally important feature of human life. Such questioning comes predominantly but not exclusively from women, from those who reject the idea that sex (i.e. sexual happiness) is necessary for happiness more generally; this is an important point, for it belies the emphasis in much later sex research that sex is so important that sexual unhappiness or dissatisfaction will *necessarily* affect the totality of a relationship and a life, and I return to it later. People's questioning and rejection is not least of the essentialist and masculinist assumption that sex is really 'sex (*for men*)' which characterises many male sample members' responses and also, although more ambivalently, in the stance taken by the analyst/writer.

The assumption of heterosexuality in 'Little Kinsey', along with the associated assumption that 'sex' is synonymous with penetration, occurs less through overt statement, more through the weight of the content of the successive chapters on the 'facts of life', sex education and birth control. The street-sample questionnaires certainly included questions on non-penetrative behaviours, including 'petting' and masturbation, as well as homosexuality, but nothing of this beyond one brief mention appears in the 'Little Kinsey' text. (Hetero)sexuality appears not only as a male phenomenon, but one which is also a 'drive' and thus the determined product of 'nature'. It is because of this that the necessity of sex outside marriage is conceded, because 'men are human': prostitution is seen as 'demand-led' by men's sexual 'needs' rather than 'supply-led' by women's economic necessity, and is condoned because of '*masculine* human nature'.[7] However, there remains an ambivalence, a hint and perhaps more than a hint of irony in an accompanying statement about the supposedly 'uncontrollable male'. Still, the overall implication is that 'sex'/heterosexuality is fairly much a male affair, not least because discussions of the street sample are frequently invoked through statements about 'the man in the street', repeated references to what the male part of the sample said, while 'the woman in the street' simply vanishes.

Sexual knowledge and sexual ignorance are most fully discussed in relation to 'birth control', with the text conjecturing whether there is a problem of terminology or a problem of ignorance on the part of sample members. This occurs around what is described as sample members' 'confusion' of birth control with controls over the birth process, and also with abstention and coitus interruptus, rather than with what the writer sees as its 'proper' meaning of a variety of (mechanical and chemical) contraceptives. This raises a wider issue, noted also by the sex surveys after 'Little Kinsey', concerning the language used in sex research, when neither formal nor 'everyday' terms may be appropriate or even familiar to many if not most people, for sexual behaviour may be typically not spoken about at all, even within long-term marital and sexual relationships.

What is invoked by 'Little Kinsey' as 'natural' is crucial to the perceived relationship between sex, marriage and children: 'sex' is that which produces babies, and it is this that constitutes 'the facts of life' which are the subject of sex education and birth control and are the substance of what marriage is all about. However, the perceived 'naturalness' of what is 'normal' is both seen as socially constructed *and* as having limits: the un/naturalness of sex occurs around the boundaries set by its nature and its frequency. Sex as biologically constituted and 'natural' occurs within marriage and produces children. However, sample members recognise that 'natural sex' can become 'unnatural' where there is sublimation and repression: if taken 'too far' in some unspecified way it can become uncontrollable and so unnatural. Similarly, the frequency of sexual behaviour is seen to traverse the boundaries between the natural and unnatural; and again notions of the possible uncontrollability of unfettered sexual habit are referred to here.

At various key junctures, women's patent dissatisfaction with 'sex' is expressed in the text. In one woman's graphic phrase, she had been 'used as a chamber pot' by a husband who, in terms of 'habit' at least, divorced sex and emotion and saw 'sex' as an entirely penetrational act. These dissatisfactions are so clearly articulated to today's ear, accustomed by successive researches and public discussion and debate of sexual behaviours and trends, that it seems incredible that their presence in the text can be treated as almost transparent by the analyst/writer of 'Little Kinsey'. And yet, such statements of women's longing, boredom, distaste, certainly are in the text; and, just as certainly, there they are 'unheard'.

One way to explain this is to draw a temporal (and gendered) distance, and say the time had not yet arrived when such statements could be 'heard' and understood, at least by a male author. However, there is another and in my view more plausible explanation that proceeds from Mass-Observation's earlier research on Britain's falling birth-rate, *Britain and Her Birth-Rate* (Mass-Observation, 1945), which centred women's dissatisfactions and their refusal to live lives like their mothers', and which related sexual change to changes in perceptions of relationships and in the social and economic possibilities, that is, to a wider pattern of dissatisfaction rather than specifically to sexual dissatisfaction. The different rhetorical strategies outlined earlier are crucial to understanding the successes and failures of 'Little Kinsey' here. In Mass-Observation's *Britain and Her Birth-Rate* a textual closure had operated because the entirety of the research had been concerned with representing one point of view, women's. Here marriage and child-birth (and, presumptively, (hetero)sex) were seen from a single textual viewpoint, that of the women who were giving birth to fewer children more widely spaced. 'Little Kinsey's' writer/analyst had a considerably more difficult task: how textually to represent a multiplicity of different and competing 'voices', only one of which is that of 'the women', speaking anger, sadness, rarely complete satisfaction, while representing these within a framework which has abandoned the 'female-as-norm' stance of *Britain and Her Birth-Rate* for one written in apparently ungendered terms, but which actually accepts the 'male-as-norm'. This analytic failure is not that of the writer/analyst in any simple or personal sense; it is rather something which derives from the theorisation of 'sex' which underpins 'Little Kinsey', the textual acceptance that 'sex' (penetrational, heterosexual, done by men to women) is normative and innate and so natural as to be effectively unquestionable. The problem for the analyst/writer was thus how to satisfactorily represent difference, the difference and questioning of women, while also writing from an almost unquestionable 'male' point of view. This assumption affects the analytic treatment of other behavioural departures from 'sex' conceived normatively. Thus the gulf between the frequency with which male homosexuality and masturbation occur and people's surprised outrage about these behaviours is noted in the text, although this is taken no further in an analytic sense, and nor is the distaste for the narrowly penetrational and 'animal' form that (hetero)sex takes which is expressed by many men as well as women.

The normality and naturalness of 'sex' as penetrational heterosexuality is, then, perceived by sample members as normatively inviolate but also, in behavioural practice, shaky and dependent on normative judgements of self against other and, even more seditiously with regard to women, of experience against expectation. However, such views are located in an analytic framework which centres only the normative naturalness of 'sex'. It is by no means surprising, then, that 'Little Kinsey's' author could not solve what was, in this formulation, unsolvable; what is of great interest is that he came so close to succeeding, to representing difference, complexity and fragmentation within a coherent textual strategy. Certainly the text of 'Little Kinsey' contains many articulations of women's dissatisfactions, but what is absent is the recognition that, through its relationship to other dissatisfaction, this constitutes a motor force for change, a recognition which startlingly marks Mass-Observation's research on Britain's falling birthrate. 'Little Kinsey' notes that sexual change has occurred and is still occurring, but what it does not 'hear', and so cannot bring together analytically, is the importance of women's *general* dissatisfaction with the kind of life their mothers led, and how this might connect with their *specific* sexual and emotional dissatisfactions. Both are present in the text, but hostages to the role assigned to 'progressive' views about sex, which lead the writer to assign women's dissatisfactions to sexual conservatism against the assumed norm of men's sexual progressiveness. 'Little Kinsey's' central rhetorical positioning of a 'male-as-the-norm' stance derives from its implicit theorisation of sex as not only normative but also *causative*; and it is this that prevents it from analytically coming to grips with the very sources of change it had set out to investigate. Interestingly, this is very close to Shere Hite's (1976, 1981, 1987, 1993) later sex research, which also assumes the causative centrality of the sexual and sees women's desire for social and economic change stemming from sexual dissatisfactions. My own interpretation of the evidence, however, is that of *Britain and Her Birth-Rate*: it is women's wider social and economic dissatisfactions which underpin the sexual ones.

'LITTLE KINSEY' IN THE BRITISH SEX SURVEY TRADITION

A number of well-known British sex surveys were carried out after 'Little Kinsey', with Eliot Slater and Moira Woodside's (1951) *Patterns of Marriage*, Eustace Chesser's (1965) *The Sexual, Marital and Family Relationships of the English Woman*, Michael Schofield's (1965) *The Sexual Behaviour of Young People*, Geoffrey Gorer's (1971) *Sex and Marriage in England Today*, and the Wellcome Trust's National Survey of Sexual Attitudes and Lifestyles (Johnson *et al.*, 1993; Wellings *et al.*, 1993), being the most substantial of these. Apart from the National Survey, these surveys were carried out with some specific purpose in mind, rather than the more general one, shared by 'Little Kinsey' and the National Survey, of 'mapping' sexual attitude and sexual behaviour. Thus Slater and Woodside's study was concerned with male 'neuroticism' and its effects on marital and other relations, while Chesser's focus was concerned with all aspects of women's emotional attitudes, not just those associated with sexual relationships; Schofield's concern was a more policy-oriented one, of trying to establish whether claims of post-war teenage 'promiscuity' were borne out by factual evidence, while Gorer's purpose was to look at change in sexual habits and attitudes among the under 45-year-olds.

In looking at the research tradition in which 'Little Kinsey' was located, I focus on large-scale random-sample-based surveys of sexual attitudes and sexual behaviours. However, it needs to be taken into account that these surveys were by no means the only public pronouncements of 'the facts' about sex through this period. From the 1940s on, Royal Commissions, popular textbooks, newspaper, magazine and radio discussions, dealt with sex education, the birth-rate, venereal disease, promiscuity, adultery, teenage sexuality, women's sexual 'problems' and more. In addition, a wide range of other research-based investigations of sexual conduct have been carried out, smaller-scale studies including ethnographic research on sex and social structure, laboratory investigations of physiological 'sexual response' and, latterly, interview studies of sexual beliefs and practices. Also, a very large number of 'popular' surveys have been sponsored and published by newspapers and magazines, and a smaller number of academic surveys of particular sub-sections of the population have been carried out. Thus the national random-sample survey tradition discussed here represents only one, albeit important, strand within a wider, immensely complex and often contradictory discourse about 'the sexual' in all its aspects.

These British sex surveys are apparently entirely empirical and descriptive in approach, but they actually articulate a coherent set of ideas about sexuality and its relationship to other aspects of social life. There are, of course, differences of approach and emphasis between them. None the less, their frameworks of ideas share a number of distinctive features, which bring them considerably closer to the views and understandings of the people who are the objects of their researches than the authors would have been eager to recognise. In particular, and with the apparent exception of the National Survey, such surveys operate in a context characterised by the taken-for-grantedness of what 'sex' is: everyone is assumed to know and agree about the 'what', 'when' and 'who' of sex, to the extent that the basic behaviours with which these surveys are concerned are not looked at in any detail. The gloss of 'sex' defined as 'intercourse' is more often than not used as though there can be no variant behaviour involved beneath this visible and easily investigated tip. This is linked to their additional assumption that 'what people do' is governed, indeed determined, by 'the natural', by some kind of innate biological urge or imperative which is universally experienced and enacted. However, it is clear from the various 'problems' discussed by these studies that what was considered to be 'natural' underwent some fairly wide-reaching changes over the half-century between the 1940s and the 1990s, and also that such changes considerably impinged on the research carried out.

Thus Slater and Woodside note that younger women compared with older not only expected more of marriage but tended to relate marital problems to difficult material circumstances; and they also note that the women interviewed frequently had no idea of what was meant by 'an orgasm', and were equally uncomprehending of some of the other terms used. Similarly, while Chesser fails to look in any detail at what 'intercourse' and 'petting' consist of, his research does pinpoint the changes that had occurred regarding women's increased sexual experience both before and outside marriage. Schofield's investigation of young people's sexual behaviour begins to deconstruct the monolith of 'sex', looking at a range of constituent behaviours, but many of which are then relegated to the glossing term 'petting' and thereby treated as different from 'real' sex. Here, of course, Schofield adopts a commonsensical viewpoint, although his purpose was neither to analyse commonsensical constructions of what 'sex' is, nor to discuss the different constructions of 'sex' held by men and women that Slater and Woodside's research hints at and Gorer's work centres on. For Gorer, the existence of a 'sexual double standard' constitutes the major way of understanding sexual behaviour, with women seen as having different understandings and behaviours from men. There are similarities here with Chesser's research, which at a number of points implies both that women's orgasmic functioning and sexual desire is different from men's, and also that it thereby constitutes a 'difficulty' that needs to be 'overcome'. The National Survey certainly asked people about a much wider variety of behaviours, the vaginal, oral and anal and 'other genital forms of sex', but, interestingly, it still fails to investigate how these genital sexual behaviours interlink with other erotic and sexual but non-genital behaviour, and nor does it investigate whether and in what ways these 'patterns' might differ with a change of partners, or on different occasions. Thus even at the level of describing the behavioural, the National Survey research is surprisingly limited, while it explicitly excludes meaning altogether and unaccountably eschews analysis except at the most basic of levels.

Behind such taken-for-grantedness about what 'sex' is and how its constituent behaviours articulate lies the even more fundamental assumption of heterosexuality as axiomatically 'the norm', as 'what is natural' in sexual terms because seen as entirely innate. In Slater and Woodside's and Chesser's researches there is no mention of any homosexual behaviour or partners at all, and while Schofield notes that a significant proportion of both boys and girls knew others involved in homosexual sexual experiences, with a smaller group being so involved themselves, this is not explored in his research, which focuses instead on 'sex' – that is, heterosex. Gorer's *Exploring English Character* notes that most of those people who were 'not interested in sex' were actually homosexually involved (and thus *were* 'interested in sex', although not of a heterosexual kind), but his later *Sex and Marriage* completely ignores the existence of homosexual behaviour and the overlapping of homosexual and heterosexual experiences and feelings in a large number of people's lives. Only the National Survey does not proceed from the assumption that the 'sex' that is being inquired about is necessarily heterosexual. However, it too ends by relegating everything else to an implicit 'and also' status, through its concern with fixing people to 'lifestyles' which are conceived as heterosexual or, for a supposedly tiny minority, gay male.[8]

The taken-for-grantedness of (heterosexual) sex links to a further related assumption, that of the synonymity of heterosexuality and specifically *penetrational* forms of sex. Thus Slater and Woodside are concerned almost exclusively with 'intercourse', looking at modes of its 'performance' on a weekly basis and people's assumption of a norm in its performance and their own claimed adherence to such a norm. Similarly, Chesser discusses mainly intercourse within marriage; and although women's perception of the absence or insufficiency of 'petting' behaviours – that is, non-penetrational forms of love-making – provides one of the key reasons they give for sexual dissatisfaction, this is ignored by him. In some contrast and perhaps because he was concerned particularly with teenagers, Schofield does note the different behaviours and stages of 'petting' activities, but then still conceptualises these as falling short of 'sex', that is, penetration. Gorer construes the point at which people first 'had sex' as synonymous with first having intercourse, while his discussion of 'rates of intercourse' is precisely that, not rates of sexual behaviour as such but instead rates of penetration. Again, the National Survey asks about a wider range of activities – vaginal, oral and anal sex and other genital contact – although it remains concerned with what is 'high risk', the specifically genital rather than 'sexual experience' or 'sexual contact' defined more widely.

The assumption of a 'natural' sexual division of labour which assigns different 'roles' in sexual encounters between men and women, a division which can be summarised in stereotypical ideas about male sexual 'activity' and female 'passivity', appears widely in these surveys, along with the accompanying supposition that the different sexual responses of men and women to penetrational sex are the product of constitutional differences. Thus Slater and Woodside propose that women are less successful in their adaptation to 'sex' than men, evidenced in their lower rates of orgasm and their generally greater levels of dissatisfaction with sex in marriage; and here Slater and Woodside apparently discern some common unchanging 'it' which both men and women experience (or ought to) which is somehow independent of the particular relationship and the particular ways that each couple do 'it' together. Chesser proposes something similar, seeing any orgasmic failure in women as the product of changing physiological capacity rather than of the specificities of their experience of sex or of their partners' in/abilities and concerns as a lover. Similarly, Schofield's research notes a number of differences between the sexes: that the sexually active girls most often are so within the context of a sustained relationship, while the sexually active boys are more likely to be involved in a variety of casual relationships; and that more girls than boys do not enjoy their first or even repeated sexual experiences. Gorer's research centres on a 'sexual double standard', seeing women as different in sexual behaviour and even more so in attitude from men, and thereby, of course, treating them as different from an assumed norm which is actually set by *male* behaviour and *male* attitude. Again, the National Survey takes a different approach to sexual divisions of labour, in the sense of asking respondents both 'what they did' and also 'what partners did to them'. None the less, the actually reciprocal nature of many heterosexual sexual practices is glossed by use of behavioural terms that conventionally assign 'passivity' to women and 'activity' to men, and this is particularly so regarding the range of penetrational activities the National Survey is especially concerned with.

These different surveys refer to changes in expectations concerning sexual behaviour and sexual pleasure occurring over time. The most obvious example is Chesser's discussion of changes across different age cohorts, although Schofield's research is premised on exploring the apparently different behaviour of young people in the 1960s as compared with earlier generations, while Gorer's work notes the increase in the numbers of women thinking that sex is important when evaluating their marital happiness. However, and with the partial exception of Chesser's work, all of these surveys – including, astonishingly, the National Survey, with its central concern with sexual change, transmission and control – *assume* rather than investigate change over time. The surveys see sexual change starting from relatively repressed and anti-pleasure ideas about sex in a relatively 'safe' context, and moving in the direction of more liberated and pleasure-based views, but in a relatively 'unsafe' context, either morally, or with regard to health, or both. However, in spite of their 'eye on the times' stance, the major change that occurred in sexual attitudes and sexual behaviour over the time-period that these surveys were carried out in is hardly recognised by them. This is the change that 'Little Kinsey' and also Mass-Observation's earlier work on the birth-rate both focused upon: changes regarding women's sexual expectations and women's marital behaviours. The earlier surveys all contain either ignored or undertheorised findings in this regard, while the National Survey excludes such information apart from with regard to birth control.

For the present-day reader what is perhaps most surprising is the almost complete failure in these surveys to subject to detailed investigation precisely what 'sex' consists of and how and in what kind of sexual/erotic circumstances the genital articulates with the non-genital. It is this failure to research what people were/are doing and not doing and the meanings that this had/has for them which prevents these surveys from coming to grips with social and sexual change.[9] However, while 'Little Kinsey' too fails to problematise 'sex', none the less it highlights in interesting ways Mass-Observation's more general and, by 1949, long-standing perception of a change in women's attitudes and behaviours, a change that encompassed the expectations that women had about their lives, their marriages and children, and of the part to be played by sex and sexual pleasure within this. In this regard 'Little Kinsey' certainly recognises social change and the part played by women's changing ideas within this, although, as I earlier commented, unlike Mass-Observation's work on the birth-rate it assigns an overcausative role to the sexual within social and economic life.

Whatever the faults and failures of 'Little Kinsey', there is clearly much in it that contemporary researchers can still learn from, methodologically even more than substantively. Its methodological importance lies in two things. One is that 'Little Kinsey' was indeed the first

British national random sample survey concerned with sex. This in itself gives it importance, not least because it has been an until recently 'lost' part of the history of the British sex survey tradition. The second is that it was carried out at precisely the point in time when Mass-Observation moved from one research tradition to another, from observing to surveying; and, relatedly, this was also the point at which mainstream British social science itself began to move, firmly but ultimately not decisively, into a survey mode. Had it been published in 1949 as intended, it is likely that the shape of the British sex survey tradition would have been very different, for it would have proceeded from the analytic and methodological point that the National Survey has only now reached: that of recognising and trying to represent sexual variability and difference. 'Little Kinsey's' greatest contribution is, however, one stage further on from this, for it moved considerably further in the direction of explaining wider social change and its links to changes in sexual and marital relationships and experiences than any of the later British sex surveys. Its methodological approach, and the resultant competing rhetorical strategies that characterise the text of 'Little Kinsey', which represented failure for its writer/analyst and contributed to its non-publication, are precisely what enable it to show with considerable success the diversity and complexity of people's lives, attitudes and behaviour, and to demonstrate the correspondingly complex methodological and textual means that are necessary to come to analytic grips with this.

NOTES

1. *Sunday Pictorial*, 3 July 1949, 10 July 1949, 17 July 1949, 24 July 1949, 31 July 1949.
2. This is discussed in detail in Stanley (1995).
3. The complete final manuscript of 'Little Kinsey' is contained in Stanley (1995).
4. As discussed with Len England in a personal interview, Len England/Liz Stanley, 22 August 1990. The manuscript report on 'Little Kinsey' was written over 45 years ago; not surprisingly, Len England does not recollect the details of its writing.
5. That is, the use of three different kinds of data generated by different methods: ethnographic, interview and survey data, for instance. The assumption is that these data simply provide three different 'angles' on the same social phenomenon. However, an epistemologically more informed view proposes that these data are ultimately unreconcilable because the

perspectival or epistemological frame that each is located within actually constructs the 'same' social phenomenon differently.

6. Both the internal correspondence here, and also the changing mood within the wider social research community, are discussed in Stanley (1995).
7. Stanley (1995), p. 152; emphasis in the original.
8. Johnson *et al.* and Wellings *et al.* both continually slide from 'homosexuality' to 'gay men', with the authors apparently not even noticing that they do this.
9. In Stanley (1995) I discuss this concern with change and how, methodologically and substantively, these surveys deal with it. I also compare 'Little Kinsey' with the work of Shere Hite with regard to explaining social change.

REFERENCES

Calder, A. (1985) 'Mass-Observation 1937–1949', in M. Bulmer (ed.), *Essays on the History of British Sociological Research* (Cambridge: Cambridge University Press), pp. 121–36.

Calder, A. and Sheridan, D. (eds) (1984) *Speak For Yourself: A Mass-Observation Anthology* (London: Jonathan Cape).

Chesser, E. (1965) *The Sexual, Marital and Family Relationships of the English Woman* (London: Hutchinson).

Gorer, G. (1971) *Sex and Marriage in England Today* (London: Nelson).

Hite, S. (1976) *The Hite Report on Female Sexuality* (New York: Macmillan).

Hite, S. (1981) *The Hite Report on Male Sexuality* (New York: Alfred Knopf).

Hite, S. (1987) *Women and Love* (New York: Alfred Knopf).

Hite, S. (1993) *Women As Revolutionary Agents of Change* (London: Sceptre).

Johnson, A., Wadsworth, J., Wellings, K. and Field, J. (1993) *Sexual Attitudes and Lifestyles* (Oxford: Blackwell Scientific).

Kinsey, A. (1948) *Sexual Behaviour in the Human Male* (New York: W.B. Saunders).

Mass-Observation (1945) *Britain and Her Birth-Rate* (London: Advertising Standards Guild).

Masters, W. and Johnson, V. (1966) *Human Sexual Response* (Boston, MA: Little, Brown).

Schofield, M. (1965) *The Sexual Behaviour of Young People* (Harmondsworth: Penguin).

Slater, E. and Woodside, M. (1951), *Patterns of Marriage: A Study of Marital Relationships in the Urban Working Class* (London: Cassell).

Stanley, L. (1990) 'The Archaeology of a 1930s Mass-Observation Project' (Manchester: University of Manchester Occasional Papers in Sociology no. 27).

Stanley, L. (1995) *Sex Surveyed, 1949 to 1994: From Mass-Observation's 'Little Kinsey' to the National Survey and the Hite Reports* (London: Taylor & Francis).

Wellings, K., Field, J., Johnson, A. and Wadsworth, J. (1993) *Sexual Behaviour in Britain* (Harmondsworth: Penguin).

6 From 'Immorality' to 'Underclass': The Current and Historical Context of Illegitimacy
ANDREW BLAIKIE

INTRODUCTION

A spectre is haunting North Atlantic family policy and it comes in the shape of 'Back to Basics', the Child Support Agency, 'workfare' and the 'feminisation of welfare'. With national bastardy ratios of 32 per cent (Central Statistical Office, 1994, p. 40) and 30 per cent (*The Economist*, 1994, p. 23) respectively, UK and US governments have moved to stem the 'rising tide of illegitimacy', and the 'subdued moral panic' of the mid-1980s has given way to a noisier rhetoric of condemnation. Accordingly, new folk devils have emerged in expiation of our economic ills: 'It is widely believed that young single women are likely to produce delinquent children and, since their numbers are assumed to be rapidly increasing, they are responsible for sending society in a fast spin towards moral degeneracy and social chaos' (Coote, 1990, p. 36). The inherent sexism of such thinking has been challenged by Bea Campbell who remarks that debates about the meaning of the 1991 riots repeatedly evoked the 'problem family' : 'Implicitly, if not explicitly, the mothers, but not the men, were scapegoated. No political commentators alluded to the resilience and ingenuity of single parents, or to the capricious and often cruel nature of the men who abandoned and harassed them' (Campbell, 1994, p. 10).

'Epidemics' of teenage pregnancy and 'amazing rises' in illegitimacy reflect a recurrent social fear about the implications of sexual nonconformity (Hartley, 1966; Vinovskis, 1988; Minkler and Roe, 1993). Simultaneously, major social investigations, such as the National Survey of Sexual Attitudes and Lifestyles (Wellings *et al.*, 1994), attempt to provide empirical assessments of actual sexual behaviour, although both this British Survey and a recent University of Chicago report on US national trends have been criticised for their sampling techniques which have produced, *inter alia*, unrepresentatively low incidences of homosexuality (O'Connell Davidson and Layder, 1994, pp. 93–4; Cockburn, 1994, p. 23). Such methodological failure to capture the country in microcosm is exacerbated by the often remarkable discrepancy between the images created by the Press and politicians and the experiences of their subjects. This chapter considers two issues: first, the ways in which moral concern is manipulated in the political interests of distancing a purportedly deviant group from the rest of society; secondly, the degree to which, in contrast to such supposition, members of this group fail to conform to the imposed stereotype. Detailed examination of an historical community indicates a mismatch similar to that recognisable in the study of contemporary unmarried motherhood. What observers wrote and what people were actually doing suggest rather different interpretations, and the underlying reasons can be read from differing vocabularies of motive: that is, the logics employed by conflicting social groups to justify their actions (Mills, 1940).

NEW STRATEGIES FOR BLAMING OLD VICTIMS?

> There is no concealing failure in American society: at best it can be translated into weakness and deployed in the manner of the weak – a female art, and typically a woman's lot.　(Moynihan, 1968, p. 27)

The origins of the North American War on Poverty can be traced to the early 1960s and President Kennedy's call for welfare reform to place the 'integrity and preservation of the family unit' at the head of the agenda (Murray, 1984, p. 124). Subsequently, Senator Moynihan's report *The Negro Family: The Case for National Action* (1965) argued that deprivation in the ghetto was caused by a cycle of disadvantage perpetuated by a dysfunctional family structure. On the other side of the Atlantic, overt racism was absent from Sir Keith Joseph's notion of transmitted deprivation, but the implication of inherited pathological traits was equally evident. And over the past century the 'submerged tenth', 'social problem group', and latterly 'the underclass' have preoccupied British scholars wishing to label and thus contain a deviant subculture (Macnicol, 1987). In the United States, doyen of the Right, Charles Murray, cites sharp demographic variations as direct indicators of ethnic variation. He contends that: 'The black–white difference in illegitimacy (black illegitimacy ratio, 66 per cent; white, 22 per cent) goes back to the earliest post-Civil War data. No scholar has ever succeeded in explaining away this racial difference with any combination of economic, social, or educational control variables. The residual difference is astonishingly large' (Murray, 1994, p. 23). 'Residual' can only be read as expressing 'otherness', a culture that 'tolerates illegitimacy'. The same methodology is used to explain variations between white trash welfare families and an ideologically and statistically normative social structure (Murray, 1986). And Britain, he asserts, 'has a growing population of working-aged, healthy people who live in a different world from other Britons, who are raising their children to live in it, and whose values are now contaminating the life of entire neighbourhoods' (Murray, 1989, p. 27).

In America, 'welfare' is synonymous with Aid to Familes with Dependent Children (AFDC). Since the early 1970s the real value of a welfare cheque has fallen. However, the number of single-parent families has doubled, prompting a new political consensus that AFDC needs to become transitional by discouraging illegitimacy and making the poor self-sufficient. Based on research indicating that over half of continuous poverty spells last less than three years (Bane and Ellwood, 1994), the present regime wants to 'make work pay' by providing training and job placements while subsidising low-income work and child care provision but withholding wages from 'deadbeat dads' failing to pay maintenance. It differs from 'workfare' in that 'with workfare, a mother who does not work can be "sanctioned" and so lose part of her AFDC cheque. With the Clinton plan, after two years there are no more AFDC cheques – only pay cheques. If you do not work, you get nothing' (*The Economist*, 1994, p. 24). The British Right has also watched keenly the New Jersey experiment of capping benefits rather than assisting return to work, specifically the denial of welfare to single mothers in respect of second children, while advocating an increased burden of obligation be placed upon grandparents (Blaikie, 1994a).

There is little new in such proposals: in England the 1834 Poor Law Report recommended that 'a bastard should be what providence appears to have ordained that it should be, a burden on its mother and where she cannot maintain it on her parents' and, in theory at least, most Boards of Guardians prohibited outdoor relief to any woman with an illegitimate child (Thane, 1978, p. 32, p. 41). In Victorian Scotland, two-thirds of the birth certificates of bastard children failed to record the father's name and it was suggested that 'it should be made compulsory for the mother of an illegitimate child, at the registration

of its birth, to report the supposed father. . . . The oath of the mother
should always be accepted as proof of guilt, unless an alibi can be
established' (Seton, 1888, p. 234). Although poor law authorities did
pursue fathers for maintenance, fatherhood was rarely to the fore: in
the absence of genetic fingerprinting, '"father" is a hypothesis but
"mother" is a fact' (Carter, 1992, p. 223), and it is so much easier to
deal with the latter. While some texts, such as Gilder's *Visible Man*,
codify conservative anxieties over the sexuality of the Black ghetto
male, illegitimacy nevertheless remains one of the few areas where
men, not women, are hidden from history (Gilder, 1978).

By 1990 an estimated 70 per cent of single mothers in Britain were
not receiving regular maintenance payments from the fathers of their
children, and only 10 per cent obtained 'adequate' alimonies (Miles,
1990, p. 4). The setting up of the Child Support Agency in April 1993
and the publicity given to Dennis and Erdos's influential *Families Without
Fatherhood* (1992) may be seen as attempts to rectify this gender imbalance. This, however, was not the case. The view that rising crime
has been caused by the breakdown of the 'traditional' family does highlight the anti-social behaviour of disaffected male youth. However, the
finger is not pointed at unemployment and social deprivation, but on
the decline of 'respectable working class' values: men avoid their responsibilities because of 'the weakening of the link between sex, procreation, child-care, child-rearing, and loyalty' which has left them
'suddenly denuded of the internalised tasks of a quasi-sacred duty to
their sexual partner', whereas women 'are the beneficiaries of the sexual revolution and the weakening of the bonds of kinship' (Dennis and
Erdos, 1992, pp. 118, 70, xx). According to this logic, irresponsible
masculinity leading to violent crime – and by extension social anarchy
– is caused by divorce, separation, illegitimacy, childminding, nursery
provision and women's paid work. This persistent invective against
mothers is summarised in Murray's words: 'as Moynihan said first and
best, a community that allows a large number of young men to grow
up without fathers "asks for and gets chaos". I believe it is not hyper-
bole but sober fact that the current levels of illegitimacy already threaten
the institutions necessary to sustain a free society' (Murray, 1994, p.18).
Unmarried motherhood, not unemployment, it is argued, is the root of
the underclass problem. Abolish welfare and it will wither on the vine.

Unfortunately for this interpretation, increased single parenthood does
not appear to have been due to welfare: between 1972 and 1988, as
the number of illegitimate births per annum in the USA rose by over
260 per cent, the proportion of single mothers on AFDC fell by almost

20 per cent. The increase in illegitimacy was due to a decline in the marriage rate and falling marital fertility: fewer women married, and they they were having fewer children. Meanwhile, more single parents supported their families by working. Thus although illegitimacy ratios soared, the component composed of mothers and children on welfare decreased (Macnicol, 1993). In addition, across Northern Europe, ascending rates of cohabitation and divorce (highly correlated with the proportion of births outside marriage) have begun to augment marriage as the conventional framework for child rearing. By the late 1970s, in Sweden it was more common to have a child in a consensual union than to marry before having a child (Central Statistical Office, 1992, pp. 43–4; Duncan, 1994, p. 18).

While such broad social trends suggest unmarried parenthood to be far from solely a poverty-related phenomenon, analysis has nevertheless concentrated on mothers on benefits. Two distinct patterns are recognisable: first, long-term acute poverty is increasingly concentrated in particular geographical areas; secondly, a large variety of social groups are treated as though they were one cultural problem. When the two are conflated, as they generally are, confusion arises over whether underclass is a behavioural definition or a measure of the local density of claimants for income support. The disease metaphor is then invoked, for not only can a distribution be plotted by means of statistical surrogates, but within these locales its symptomatology can be impressionistically delineated by investigative journalism and TV documentaries. An article by Murray in *The Sunday Times Magazine* is illustrated by a cover picture of a woman and her family together in their living room. The accompanying caption reads: 'Kathy Saggers is bringing up five children alone on £87.38 a week. She lives in a Britain you wouldn't recognise.' The text goes on to enumerate the horrors of the North Peckham Estate – 'zoological tenements' similar to those 'discovered' in the USA where, 'merry and salacious' junkie moms, or 'Brigette, who is nineteen . . . a thin blond with a mop of frizzy hair . . . and a chipped front tooth' putter about the garbage in housecoats and curlers (White, 1965; Sheehan, 1977, p. 2; Auletta, 1980, pp. 74, 78; Murray, 1989). In Los Angeles single grandmothers in their late twenties suffer from role conflict (Burton and Bengston, 1985) while on 98th Street, Manhattan, a girl has borne two sets of triplets and twins by age 13 (Auletta, 1980, p. 78). In Britain, the self-styled 'sociologist of the respectable working class' throws up his hands in horror at ram-raiding and burglary in Tyneside's Meadow Well, and an Oxford professor asks: 'How do you stop single, teenage mothers from breeding up tomorrow's football hooligans?' (Stone, 1989; Dennis and Erdos, 1992). Such is the 'tangle of pathology' (Clark, 1965).

Cultural deprivation offers an omnibus explanation: 'the "multiproblem" poor suffer from the psychological effects of impoverishment, a deviant value system . . . consequently, though unwittingly, they cause their own problems. . . . The proposed remedy for the problem is to work on the victim [her] self . . . never to change the surrounding circumstances' (Ryan, 1976, pp. 5–8). Ryan anatomises victim-blaming as follows: identify the social problem as 'a problem only to those outside the boundaries of what we have defined as the problem'; find out how those affected are different from the rest of us; then define these differences as the cause (we might add that it is a common strategy to make global generalisations on the basis of uniquely local cases). Hence high illegitimacy ratios can be explained by dint of an imputed pattern of sexual behaviour which reflects promiscuity, a fatalistic desire for instant gratification, and cultural acceptance on the grounds that the welfare system will manage the consequences (Ryan, 1976, Chapters 1, 4). This analysis was forged in the 1960s as a critique of Moynihan's argument that the welfare problems of black America were caused by the absence of conventional (white) family norms and values. However, there are some striking parallels with other seemingly unlikely contexts and from these we might draw abiding generalisations.

'THE MAP OF VICE IN SCOTLAND', 1855–1900

Moral panics have often used the language of epidemics to equate social ills with a medical vocabulary of causation and a moral vocabulary of motive. Thus throughout nineteenth-century Europe 'questions of public health and public morality were closely intertwined as objects of state policy and of medical expertise . . . [via] a common concern with lower-class sexual comportment [that] bolstered their devotion to middle-class decorum with a medical rationale' (Engelstein, 1987, p. 177). The nuclear family was the healthy body and all else represented disease.

In Calvinist Scotland the advent of civil registration of births, marriages and deaths in 1855 meant accepting new and startling facts, facts so stark that whole new ideologies had to be invented to accommodate them. The national illegitimacy ratio was 7.8 per cent while England's was only 6.4 per cent. Worse was to follow when the Registrar General enumerated bastardy totals by counties indicating alarmingly high levels in stable rural areas but only modest quotas in the modernising Central Belt. The situation was similar to that almost a century later when Kinsey's reports on sexual behaviour caused a furore precisely because they revealed a shocking disparity between what North Americans were thought to be doing and what was actually happening (Kinsey *et al.*, 1948, 1953). For bastardy was seen to be associated with the heartland of peasant virtue rather than the supposed hotbeds of urban vice. Most scandalous of all were the inland farming parishes of the Northeast where bastardy ratios rose to over 40 per cent.

In the 1820s, the Scottish evangelical reformer Thomas Chalmers had associated 'improvident marriages' and 'illicit unions' among the working classes with the deterimental effects of industry and the expansion of city life (Smout, 1980, p.199). His Glasgow Experiment was an attempt to end pauperism and 'vice' by recreating the *Gemeinschaft* of small rural communities in an urban setting. By 1860 such a vision was no longer tenable and explanations for rural illegitimacy were sought in illiteracy, intemperance, hiring markets, imbalanced sex ratios, race, religion and even rainfall. None of these theories was borne out by the Registrar General's figures (Smout, 1980). New reasoning was required, and it came via the concept of 'immorality'.

Like the 'underclass' argument, 'immorality' accentuated cultural difference. The construction of an inherited malady peculiar to a particular social group is evident in the focus on farm and domestic servants whose divergent sexual behaviour strengthened the middle-class assumption that they were a 'race' apart. The pronounced concentration of the 'vice' among those in their teens and twenties suggested an emerging 'youth problem', whilst in 1859 Dr Strachan, a country GP with a large midwifery practice, recognised in clandestine 'stolen interviews' and 'midnight assignations' a pattern of courtship widely different from the open chaperonage of the respectable stereotype (Strachan, 1859).

The Registration Examiner proclaimed 'Scotia is sick. Already have her physicians, diplomatised and undiplomatised, written off no end of prescriptions' (List, 1861, p. 3). In keeping with Sontag's characterisation of sexually transmitted illness, the imagery of 'immorality' was that of invasion, and the ideology offered in response was one of containment (Sontag, 1989). If the parental hearth, divinely appointed, was the bulwark of social order, then any departure represented an index of disarray: 'Now at this rate of 10, 000 bastards a year, we shall in ten years have nearly 100, 000 bastards, or a population of them equal to that of one of our largest cities; a result sufficiently startling, and well-fitted to alarm all classes of moral and social reformers' (Boyd, 1980, p. 33). Compare this with a comment from the 13th Annual Report of the President's National Advisory Council on Equal Opportunity (Washington, September 1981): 'All other things being equal, if the proportion of poor in female-householder families were to increase at the same rate as it did from 1967 to 1978, the poverty population would be composed solely of women and their children before the year 2000.'

Statistics played a key role in locating pockets of contagion, particularly in northeast Scotland, literally a 'black spot' on the map containing adjacent parishes with bastardy ratios exceeding 23 per cent. In villages such as Aberchirder which contained upwards of 40 unmarried mothers with five to six bastards each living in just two or three streets, 'the very air seem[ed] impregnated with the germs of immorality' ('C.', 1887). In the city, a similar logic prevailed. Valentine's analysis of the residences registered for unmarried mothers in Aberdeen showing 'very distinctly that in the districts where the lower class of houses are situated, there does illegitimacy most prevail. No case is reported to have occurred in Union St., King St., Crown St., Dee St., Bon Accord St., Bon Accord Tce., Albyn Place, Victoria St., Union Tce., or Skene St' (Valentine, 1859, p. 225). All the desirable districts were free from blight, and, unlike cholera, illegitimacy could be quarantined via a cordon sanitaire whereby domestics employed in the fashionable districts were forced to leave their situations when pregnancy was discovered. The Prison Board typified the moral career of the illegitimate as a cycle of poverty, inadequate education, migration to the city, unemployment, prostitution and unmarried motherhood, lamenting that 'illegitimate children furnish more than their numerical proportion of the inmates of our prisons and poor houses. Daughters are also very apt to follow the evil example of their mothers ... licentiousness is hereditary' (Report, 1860, p. 8). Following research down among the soup kitchens Sheriff Watson offered a simpler explanation – 'vice' was the result of factory lay-offs by which unemployed females were 'driven by dire necessity to prostitution and gave birth to illegitimate children' (Watson, 1877, pp. 11–12). The trouble with this argument was that, in a free-market economy, it could offer no solutions save a recourse to better welfare arrangements, and, by extension, more official subsidy. Notwithstanding a few voluntary hand-outs, *laissez-faire* capitalism remained sacrosanct, as did the ideal of the economically self-sustaining family unit that looked after its own without becoming a burden on the collective purse.

Such rural philanthropy as was practised was faced with insurmountable obstacles. Thus a maternalistic outfit like Lady Aberdeen's Onward and Upward Association, whose magazine recruited farmers' wives to train their servants in the virtues of housewifery, was forced to shift its focus from mobile single women to the young wife who was less likely to leave the district. With rhetoric like 'the work of the home [which] must always be women's first mission' (*Onward and Upward*, 1894, p. 212) it could scarcely be expected to appeal to youngsters lodging in stable lofts and it quickly restyled itself as 'a mother's magazine'.

The old arrangement whereby the farmer ate and slept under the same roof with servants had been superseded by systems whereby 'promiscuous assemblages' of workers boarded in bothies (huts) and chaumers (rooms) away from the moral purview of the farmer and his wife. This clearly represented a perversion of the idea of the extended family, and behind such slogans as 'bothies cause bastards' reformers had lambasted the emerging social relations of capitalist agrarian production. Pre-marital conceptions were not a concern if they were later regularised through marriage, but frequently the unavailability of accommodation for married servants or intending crofters meant that this did not happen. Thus the evangelist Rev. Dr James Begg maintained the need to 'put an end to roving and unstable habits by giving [farm servants] a stake in the country' (Begg, 1871). However, his advocacy of a 'property-owning peasant democracy' worried a Free Church eager to establish that respectable morality was not simply a matter of universal home-ownership (Boyd, 1980, p. 32; Blaikie, 1991, p. 86). Although his reasoning had not been entirely illogical, given the housing shortages enumerated repeatedly in the Blue Books, it comes as no surprise that the social solutions advocated in lieu of his dangerously socialistic suggestion were patently unworkable. In particular, pleas that employers should boycott known fornicators or be fined for not providing 'proper sleeping apartments' (Cramond, 1888, p. 69; Seton, 1888, p. 234) could not expect to be implemented since they might interfere with the smooth operation of the labour market. The failure to effect change lay not so much in the inability to comprehend the 'problem' as in the material impossibility of grafting a middle-class family ideal onto the social relations of service.

It was, however, more than simply a matter of targeting a single issue. When William Cramond surveyed all Banffshire in 1888, 125 clergymen, proprietors, lawyers, public officials and others responded to his questionnaire on the causes of bastardy, leading him to place the absence of dwelling-house accommodation for married servants and for the servants inclined to marry' and the 'low moral tone' prevalent in the county at the head of the agenda for reform. While he suggested that providing suitable housing might indirectly improve morals, he added that 'of course, even with a good deal of house accommodation . . . you are liable to have no abatement' (Cramond, 1892, p. 585). As a local schoolmaster he was well aware that in a village like Aberchirder, the presence of no less than five religious denominations had a minimal effect on the large numbers of unmarried mothers who congregated there, that, indeed, church elders were themselves by no means free of the 'contagious taint' of illegitimacy, and that Poor Law inspectors were no saints either – in one parish, for instance, the inspector had sixteen children, the first of whom was conceived well before marriage (Blaikie, 1993, pp. 198, 205–8, 223). In short, the 'low moral tone' was a measure of an overall 'other morality' in the region.

Such distancing was effected through the use of a language that equated undesirable sexualities with 'disgusting moral disease' and 'moral leprosy', hence the conflation of social fear with medical epidemics. Thus during the closing decades of the nineteenth century, when the impact of agrarian depression became evident in an exodus of young women into domestic employment in the towns and young men into the army and police force, outmigration from rural districts prompted fears of racial deterioration. One Banffshire clergyman commented:

> Many who are now in service – indeed the great majority of them – are those who by training, physique, character or education are unable to do anything else – not fit for trades, shops, &c; indeed they are the illegitimates of the country. (Cramond, 1888, p. 43)

In line with the pathological pattern, those left on the land were seen to form a pool of degenerates, the folk devils of their time. Nevertheless, explaining cultural difference entails more than simply illustrating how a middle-class ideology developed.

UNCERTAIN PROSPECTS: DOWN AMONG THE SINNERS

'Immorality' was a culturally convenient myth through which to maintain a safe distance between classes: it created the fiction of a racially distinctive sub-group, habitually 'incontinent' and politically threatening to the nuclear family as the mainstay of national stability. But it failed signally to explain the motivations of unmarried mothers. The comments of philanthropists and religious reformers clearly reflect a class-based agenda and we would be foolish to grant them undue credence for, ultimately, they tell us far more about their own suppositions than about the real behaviour of the subjects they purported to be investigating. However, in the absence of oral recall, exploring the lived experiences of unmarried mothers before the twentieth century necessarily involves making inferences from the written record. Perhaps the least inaccurate way of doing this is to reconstruct patterns of sexual behaviour, family formation and dissolution using data linkage across a range of demographic and welfare sources.

Reconstitution studies of a rural area of North-east Scotland reveal that many women bore illegitimate children, often several by different fathers, and by the 1880s four-fifths of all first births among the women who married were conceived before marriage (Blaikie, 1993, Chapter 4). Such popular patterns do not indicate dysfunction; on the contrary, those who conceived and bore their first child after marriage were the nonconformists.

The majority of young adults were in service on local farms and every six months they would either be re-engaged for another term or be hired by a different farmer, often several miles away. Most aimed to leave service by their late twenties, the men by becoming tenant farmers, the women by marrying such men and bearing children, who would, in their turn, enter service when they reached adolesecence. This cycle had persisted for generations, as had an attendant pattern of pre-marital sexual liaisons and consequent bridal pregnancy – given the dependence on family labour it made sense for the intending peasant couple to test their fertility before setting up home. Crucially, however, farm engrossment and the demolition of cottages after the 1840s brought a shortage of leasehold accommodation as smallholdings were swallowed up by larger capitalist concerns. As the crisis deepened, servants found it increasingly difficult to find accommodation should they wish to marry: some left the land for the city and others emigrated, but many continued in service locally. In the last case, this meant either that marriage ensued with the man living and and working on the farm while his wife and children were boarded separately in a nearby village, or, failing this, the partners delayed marriage (but not having children), often losing contact with one another until the relationship dissolved and the woman was left to seek shelter for her offspring (Gray, 1976, pp. 96–101). A courtship convention that saw no harm in sex before marriage was potentially disruptive of social arrangements if marriage no longer ensued. Thus when holdings were plentiful pregnancy was soon followed by marriage, but as opportunities became increasingly attenuated so first, then second and third children were born outside wedlock.

Similarly, since both male and female servants moved between farms and districts twice each year, it cannot have been easy to maintain liaisons over longer periods. As the research indicates, periods of courtship shortened and women began to bear children by several suitors whether or not they eventually married (Blaikie, 1993, pp. 111–15). Correspondingly, contemporary evidence suggests that men were willing to marry women who had already borne children by others, the obstacle being lack of housing not lack of chastity. Indeed, in such unbinding cirumstances, neither sex saw any sin in unmarried motherhood (Cramond, 1888, pp. 45–9). It is insufficient, however, to argue that illegitimacy was merely an unfortunate outcome of structural transformations in agriculture. If marriage lost its practicability or desirability, then some measure of birth control might reasonably have been expected, via abortion, or more probably abstinence and delayed first births. That these did not occur indicates that alternative arrangements for child-rearing must have been provided, either through extended family support or the collective welfare system.

The institution of hired service saw an increasing separation between home and work that allowed casual, fleeting and unsupervised sexual liaisons to occur. By the mid-nineteenth century, the proportion of fathers present to register their children's births had fallen to one in three. The churches found increasing difficulty in bringing to book young men who moved regularly from one district to another, and Poor Law records indicate that absconding became prevalent as the pull of the cities and the Colonies and the push of land hunger exerted their influence. Cohabitation was almost non-existent, yet there is little evidence of unmarried women living alone with their children for long periods or of ghettoised single-parent subcultures. Although nearly 90 per cent of legitimate children lived in nuclear families consisting of simply themselves and their parents, 70 per cent of illegitimate children lived with one or both of their grandparents.

The investigation of household structures in both North-east and South-west Scotland demonstrates that grandparents indeed provided a crucial prop, often allowing mothers to remain in service elsewhere while they brought up the children (Paddock, 1990; Blaikie, 1994b). For example, examination of consecutive census enumerators' books for the Banffshire parish of Rothiemay between 1851 and 1891 reveals that 93 mothers were present with their children, while at least 78 were not. Of those present, 65 (69.9 per cent) lived with parents with another 14 in other arrangements involving kin. Only 14 (15 per cent) were lone parents, and significantly these women were on average ten years older (40.3) than all other unmarried mothers. While there was no difference in age between absent and present mothers, those with young children, especially infants under one year, were far more likely to be recorded as living with parents than those whose children were slightly older: amongst co-resident mothers in 1881 the mean age of the youngest child per household was 2.4 years whereas for absent mothers this age rose to 5.1 years. The ages and number of children were the important variables. Thus while unmarried mothers were often absent from the household in the earlier stages of their childbearing careers, they were more likely to remain as part of a three-generational unit as they bore more children. As they grew older – and fewer in number as marriage intervened for some – so parents died and younger siblings left home, leaving them as lone parents.

As in the industrialising cities of the north of England, the extended family unit provided a vital support mechanism when collective welfare provision was limited (cf. Anderson, 1971). It represented an adaptation to a changing agrarian economy in which the peasant mode of production was increasingly difficult to sustain and, as such, can be regarded as a safety net ensuring the survival of both younger and older generations in a situation where one or both of the parents were often forced to live and work elsewhere.

In tandem with such findings, recent research on single parenthood in contemporary Britain by McRobbie and others 'shows that almost everything, including the health and welfare of mother and child depends on the goodwill and financial support of the baby's grandparents' (McRobbie, 1991, p. 221). In particular, teenage mothers demonstrate a marked tendency to live with their parents. Such a supportive relationship prompts one to ask what benefits accrue to the grandparents. Sharpe suggests that babies are doubly welcome to some grandmothers who are confronted with redundancy and the prospect of old age because they provide 'something to do' while filling the vacuum left by unemployment (Sharpe, 1987). Also, it might plausibly be assumed that in the Scots Victorian countryside a grandchild would reciprocate the care invested in its upbringing by labouring on the family croft as the older children left for service and, as the grandparents aged, catering for some of their domestic and financial needs. Nevertheless, in neither instance can instrumental calculations of the availability of domestic support be imputed to the mother, since there is no clear evidence of family planning taking place prior to conception.

Longitudinal studies have established that in contemporary America the behavioural effects of poverty are fourfold: 'the preponderance of short-term usage of the welfare system, the substantial extent to which receipt of welfare income alternates or is mixed with income from other sources, the importance of demographic events in affecting entries into and exits from welfare, and the absence of an intergenerational transmission of welfare-status' (Duncan and Hoffman, 1986, p. 45). Similarly, Poor Law folios indicate a complex web of domestic interdependence further complicated by relief supplements. Consider this example. William Mitchel and Anne Hay married in Rothiemay in 1827 having already had a bastard two years earlier when she lived on a small farm in the parish but he was a servant in nearby Grange. They went on to have a total of 13 children whilst at the farm of Backdykes. Two of the children sired and bore bastards and subsequently married, although not to the same respective partners, whilst two other sisters also bore illegitimate children. The 1851 census shows eight children in the household plus one very young grandchild, who was daughter Jane's illegitimate daughter. By 1871, the household had dwindled in size to five. William and Anne, working still but now into their sixties and seventies, again provided shelter for a daughter, this time Elizabeth, who had been a domestic servant, but was now partially reliant upon out-relief to aid in supporting (financially) her two bastards, each sired by a different man. Meanwhile, her sister Anne had given birth to three bastards between 1864 and 1867, the Register of Poor noting in November 1870 that: 'This Pauper's child, Elizabeth Anne (whose father is now dead) is boarded with her maternal aunt, Widow Simpson, who receives direct from the Inspector 2s. 6d. weekly. . . . The mother is in service and pays for the upkeep of the child Jane. The other is kept by the paternal grandfather in the parish of Skene – the father is now in America.'

Household units tended to dissolve through the desertion of the father (in this case death and desertion together explain its dispersal) and female claimants – widows, deserted wives and unmarried mothers – greatly outweighed men. Older lone mothers eked out a subsistence from a combination of part-time labouring and out-relief, and remarks such as 'No available means – earns a little by knitting' are common in the records (Blaikie, 1993, Chapter 6). There is evidence to suggest that in regions of high illegitimacy in the past, considerable local variations existed in the interpretation of national policy strictures, and in both East Anglia and North-east Scotland there is some suggestion of lenient welfare arrangements in selected areas (Digby, 1978; Blaikie, 1993). However, means-testing was always imposed and women and children moved on and off the poor roll as their household and employment circumstances changed. Only when kin were themselves impoverished would temporary aid be forthcoming from the parish purse. And in both regions, particularly after the 1870s, unmarried mothers were routinely offered the poorhouse with the sanction that if they refused relief would be summarily terminated. It would be stretching a point to suggest that the welfare system of itself ever provided anything more than a conditional minimum subsistence. The language of deservingness revealed in inspectors' remarks echoes the imputations of contemporary journalists, with the added proviso that degrees of improvidence, ignorance and insubordination, as well as economic necessity, affected the chances of receiving relief as did dressing 'gaudily', or smelling of alcohol. 'Fecklessness' and 'irresponsibility' have a lineage too.

CULTURES OF POVERTY OR RELATIVE DEPRIVATION?

Ryan's concept of 'blaming the victim' has some explanatory force for both historical and contemporary analyses. First, 'concerned reporters' isolate a social problem group by describing its members' sociosexual behaviour as fundamentally at odds with the accepted social norm; 'otherness' is then posited as the cause of the problem (Ryan, 1976). Thus nineteenth-century philanthropists focused on the comportment and conditions of farm and domestic servants whereas since the 1960s academics have conjured up an 'underclass' from statistical and sub-anthropological observations of inner urban decay. Both have used medical analogies to label sexual deviance as disease, hence Victorian references to bastardy and prostitution as parasitic 'moral leprosy' and the latter-day condemnation of AIDS as a 'gay plague' (Sontag, 1989; Blaikie, 1991). Cultural assumptions disguise economic hard facts and the blame for behavioural difference shifts from causes which lie with structural inequalities in access to education, jobs and housing to the symptoms that are visible in the supposed moral shortcomings of the victims.

Meanwhile, the lifestyles and living arrangements of absent fathers remain unresearched, and the ineffectiveness of the Child Support Agency of the early 1990s in tracking down maintenance defaulters only parallels that of equivalent bodies in earlier times.

As in the cities now, so in the Victorian countryside a double standard clearly existed when it came to the differing gender experiences: while mothers were subjected to inquisition by the churches (who saw in pregnancy the proof *sine qua non* of their guilt) and Poor Law inspectors, putative fathers generally escaped scot-free.

In the absence of traceable male partners, transferring the financial obligations of parenthood from the state to other family members has long been regarded as politically desirable. And given the historical prevalence of such forms of support it is scarcely surprising that both President Clinton in the USA and Peter Lilley, the Social Security Secretary in Britain, have accented the need to get teenage mothers off welfare and into the moral and financial care of their parents (Blaikie, 1994a). The motives of the mothers themselves are less easily explained. Nevertheless, historical studies fail to bear out Murray's contention that the economic feasibility of having a baby without a father has changed because a threshold has been reached where it is manageable, whereas in the past a punitive welfare system denied such an option. It would be no more justifiable to project present-day arguments onto past circumstances. For instance, to borrow the argument that wagelessness 'disrupts the whole life-cycle from adolescence to adulthood. It jeopardises the dream of a home of one's own and creates instead a "new social state"' (McRobbie, 1991, p. 223) would be unsatisfactory with reference to nineteenth-century rural Scotland, where wages for both young men and women were relatively good and unemployment was not a major issue. The problems lay with other vicissitudes of capitalist social relations, not least the difficulty of acquiring suitable accommodation in which to rear a family in a countryside where leases were becoming scarcer as peasant family farms were swallowed up by larger capitalist estates.

Against the view that unmarried mothers represent the unfortunate, passive victims of male infidelity, their coping strategies suggest that many are active agents capable of transforming their own lives. The notion that motherhood was and is the most fulfilling possibility achievable in the circumstances appears to be applicable to a range of different contexts and is perhaps connected to the belief that child bearing, but not necessarily child rearing, involves a 'natural' female role. Thus, if unemployed teenagers in London or Birmingham are today propelled towards a 'precocious maturity' by 'only bringing forward what, if

they had been at work and if their partners had a good job, they would
have done in two or three years time' (McRobbie, 1991, pp. 227, 230),
it is equally tenable to argue that young domestic servants in Victorian
Scotland could continue in hired work for good money rates while
parents and, indeed, the Poor Law supported their children. In both
cases staying single arguably confers a degree of domestic freedom
denied them by marriage – as Hilary Graham eloquently notes, 'the
feminisation of poverty felt better than the poverty of marriage' (Graham
cited in McRobbie, 1991, p. 236). Yet in neither case are the perceived disadvantages of wedlock – in one case the additional burden
of looking after an unemployed couch-potato, in the other that of hanging
on in service for years simply then to succumb to a mercilessly hard
round of physical toil on an economically squeezed smallholding –
outweighed by the advantages of single parenthood. Welfare dependency has never been a desirable option and ultimately (short of having
a child taken into care) there is little opportunity to escape parental
obligations, be it as an older mother or as a grandmother. Indeed, there
is scant evidence that most women would wish to disregard child-rearing over the longer term. None the less, when it comes to weighing up
whether having a baby or getting married is the better route to adult
self-esteem it appears that some women in certain circumstances may
opt for the former.

Twenty years ago Askham studied the family size preferences of
married women in different social classes. She concluded that the poorest
social groups showed the highest fertility levels because 'a variety of
situational factors, such as economic insecurity, poverty, low status
and powerlessness, combine to [create] a group which has poor chances
of controlling its environment and has norms which arise out of these
relatively poor life chances' (Askham, 1975, p. 10). The strategy was
thus one of adaptation to circumstances. Unmarried mothers face similar
obstacles, except that by dint of not being with a partner continuously
for several years their period fertility is often lower than would be the
case if they were married. Against such reasoning three other approaches
dismissed or qualified by Askham remain ideologically powerful. The
'culture of poverty' model asssumes a separate subculture with its own
values and norms, a demonstrable lack of integration with rest of society and a fatalistic attitude towards family formation. This approach
has a long pedigree, stretching from the 'low moral tone' cited by
Cramond, via Oscar Lewis, to the 'underclass' arguments of Murray *et
al.* Secondly, a situational approach emphasising the lack of material
resources – income, education, housing, and occupational opportunities

– is equally pervasive, from Cramond's other main factor 'want of accommodation' and Onward and Upward's stress on training in domestic tasks to current feminist pleas for appropriate job training and childcare provision. Finally, the 'personal inadequacy' model criticising the deviant attributes of the individual is all-too-evident in the populist caricaturing of racially unfit 'illegitimates of the country' or today's 'teenage welfare mothers'. These modes of interpretation are frequently compounded, resulting in such illogicalities as claiming that young women become pregnant due to ignorance about birth control and have babies in order to obtain council housing and benefits. As Phoenix points out they cannot simultaneously be both ignorant and unfortunate *and* scheming and manipulative (Phoenix, 1991).

Murray himself admits that 'the map linking welfare and illegitimacy still has big gaps', and his contention that 'single young women get pregnant because sex is fun and babies are endearing' can hardly be said to fill any of them (Murray, 1994, p. 30; 1989, p. 43). Indeed, the fact that the conservative position he espouses uses both 'rational choice' and culture of poverty arguments, depending on the case in point, suggests an underlying ambiguity. Meanwhile, although ethnographic researchers have revealed the disparity between official ideology and lived realities, their lack of influence with policymakers, who are far more ready to listen to 'ethical socialists' like Dennis and Halsey adopting a moralistic stance close to the New Right, forces a pessimistic conclusion (Blaikie, 1994a). As MacNicol (1993) remarks, moral panics have a lot to do with deflecting criticism over impending budget deficits, whilst 'one function of the recently-revived underclass concept is to establish an agenda of pessimism and inaction, so that we thereby tolerate mass unemployment'.

In codifying popular morality the media have generally reinforced government attitudes. None the less, such ideological hegemony is not impervious to scrutiny. In 1994 the Broadcasting Complaints Commission upheld a decision in favour of the National Council for One Parent Families (NCOPF) against BBC Television, whose *Panorama* programme 'Babies on Benefits' was adjudicated to have 'unfairly used unrepresentative examples to portray young single mothers as typically feckless' and given 'a misleading and unfair impression of the proportion of young single mothers compared to other lone parents, such as the widowed and divorced' (Broadcasting Complaints Commission, 1994). In aiming to 'examine the cost to the tax payer of young single women raising families on welfare benefits', the programme had deliberately compared the Tory flagship London Borough of Wandsworth, where abandonment of the right of an unmarried mother to a place on the council's housing waiting list had been initiated, with the St Mellons estate in Cardiff where it had been claimed – inaccurately – that over half of the families consisted of lone parents and their children. Rather coyly the Commission noted in parenthesis that the source of the latter assertion had been a speech by John Redwood, the Secretary of State for Wales. While NCOPF may have drawn a crumb of comfort from the verdict, the disclosure that the Welsh Secretary had been cooking the books did not damage the ship of state: ironically, the credos of 'Victorian Values' and 'Back to Basics' which helped to keep successive British governments afloat through the 1980s and early 1990s were sunk by the scandal of past sexual indiscretions returning to haunt those in power. It would not be the first nor the last time that the contagion of 'immorality' caught up with the body politic. A subsequent High Court decision based on the technicality that the Complaints Commission had acted beyond its powers, since NCOPF did not have a 'direct interest' in the programme, comes as no surprise either (Williams, 1995).

NOTE

I wish to record my thanks to John MacNicol for his helpful critical comments, and for stimulating and sustaining my interest in the 'underclass' debate. I am also grateful to an audience at the BSA annual conference (1994) for raising some pertinent questions concerning an earlier draft of this paper.

REFERENCES

Anderson, M. (1971) *Family Structure in Nineteenth-Century Lancashire* (Cambridge: Cambridge University Press).

Askham, J. (1975) *Fertility and Deprivation: A Study of Differential Fertility Amongst Working-Class Families in Aberdeen* (Cambridge: Cambridge University Press).

Auletta, K. (1982) *The Underclass* (New York: Random House).

Bane, M. J. and Ellwood, D. T. (1994) *Welfare Realities: From Rhetoric to Reform* (Cambridge, MA: Harvard University Press).

Begg, J. (1871) *The Ecclesiastical and Social Evils of Scotland and How to Remedy Them* (Edinburgh: Church of Scotland).

Blaikie, A. (1991) 'The Country and the City: Sexuality and Social Class in Victorian Scotland', in G. Kearns and C. W. J. Withers (eds), *Urbanising*

Britain: Essays on Class and Community in the Nineteenth Century (Cambridge: Cambridge University Press), pp. 80–102.

Blaikie, A. (1993) *Illegitimacy, Sex, and Society: Northeast Scotland, 1750–1900* (Oxford: Clarendon Press).

Blaikie, A. (1994a) 'Family Fall-Out', *The Times Higher Education Supplement*, 4 March, p. 18.

Blaikie, A. (1994b) 'A Kind of Loving: Illegitimacy, Grandparents and the Rural Economy of Northeast Scotland, 1750–1900', *Scottish Economic and Social History*, 14: pp. 41–57.

Boyd, K. (1980) *Scottish Church Attitudes to Sex, Marriage and the Family, 1850–1914* (Edinburgh: John Donald).

Broadcasting Complaints Commission (1994) *Complaint from the National Council for One Parent Families – Adjudication* (London: Broadcasting Complaints Commission).

Burton, L. M. and Bengston, V. L. (1985) 'Black Grandmothers: Issues of Timing and Continuity of Roles', in V. L. Bengston and J. F. Roberston (eds), *Grandparenthood* (London: Sage), pp. 61–77.

'C.' [W. Cramond] (1887) 'Illegitimacy in Banffshire', *The Scotsman*, 13 March.

Campbell, B. (1994) 'Riots of Passage', *New Statesman & Society* ('Bite the Ballot' supplement), 29 April, pp. 9–11.

Carter, A. (1992) *Wise Children* (London: Vintage).

Central Statistical Office (1992) *Social Trends 1992*, no. 22 (London: HMSO).

Central Statistical Office (1994) *Social Trends 1994*, no. 24 (London: HMSO).

Clark, K. (1965) *Dark Ghetto: Dilemmas of Social Power* (New York: Harper & Row).

Cockburn, A. (1994) 'Poor Politics', *New Statesman & Society*, 4 November, pp. 22–3.

Coote, A. (1990) 'Birth Rights' (review of Phoenix 1991), *New Statesman & Society*, 14 December, p. 36.

Cramond, W. (1888) *Illegitimacy in Banffshire: Facts, Figures and Opinions* (Banff: Banffshire Journals).

Cramond, W. (1892) 'Illegitimacy in Banffshire', *Poor Law Magazine*, new ser., 2: pp. 571–90.

Dennis, N. and Erdos, G. (1992) *Families Without Fatherhood* (London: Institute of Economic Affairs Health and Welfare Unit).

Digby, A. (1978) *Pauper Palaces* (London: Routledge & Kegan Paul).

Duncan, G. J. and Hoffman, S. D. (1986) 'Welfare Dynamics and the Nature of Need', *Cato Journal*, 6(1): pp. 31–54.

Duncan, S. (1994) 'Gender Inequality and the European Regions', *ESF Communications*, pp. 18–19.

The Economist (1994) 'Welfare Reform in America', 18 June, pp. 23–6.

Engelstein, L. (1987) 'Morality and the Wooden Spoon: Russian Doctors View Syphilis, Social Class, and Sexual Behavior, 1890–1905', in C. Gallagher and T. Laqueur (eds), *The Making of the Modern Body: Sexuality and Society in the Nineteenth Century* (London: University of California Press), pp. 169–208.

Gilder, G. (1978) *Visible Man: A True Story of Post-Racist America* (New York: Basic Books).

Graham, H. (1987) 'Being Poor: Perceptions and Coping Strategies of Lone Mothers', in J. Brannen and G. Wilson (eds), *Give and Take in Families* (London: Allen & Unwin).

Gray, M. (1976) 'North-East Agriculture and the Labour Force', in A. A. MacLaren (ed.), *Social Class in Scotland: Past and Present* (Edinburgh: John Donald), pp. 86–104.

Hartley, S. F. (1966) 'The Amazing Rise of Illegitimacy in Great Britain', *Social Forces*, 44(4): pp. 533–45.

Kinsey, A. C. *et al.* (1948) *Sexual Behaviour in the Human Male* (Philadelphia and London: W. B. Saunders).

Kinsey, A. C. *et al.* (1953) *Sexual Behaviour in the Human Female* (Philadelphia and London: W. B. Saunders).

List, A. C. C. (1861) *The Two Phases of the Social Evil*, 2nd edn (Edinburgh: Ogle & Murray).

MacNicol, J. (1987) 'In Pursuit of the Underclass', *Journal of Social Policy*, 16(3): pp. 293–318.

MacNicol, J. (1993) 'Is there an "Underclass"? The Lessons from America', paper presented to Employment Service/Policy Studies Institute Conference 'Unemployment in Focus', 23 November.

McRobbie, A. (1991) 'Teenage Mothers: A New Social State?, in A. McRobbie (ed.), *Feminism and Youth Culture: From Jackie to Just Seventeen* (London: Macmillan), pp. 220–42.

Miles, J. (1990) 'Single Mothers to Name Father or Risk Benefits', *The Observer*, 5 August, p. 4.

Mills, C. W. (1940) 'Situated Actions and Vocabularies of Motive', *American Sociological Review*, 5(6): pp. 904–13.

Minkler, M. and Roe, K. M. (1993) *Grandmothers as Caregivers: Raising Children of the Crack Cocaine Epidemic* (London: Sage).

Moynihan, D. P. (1965) *The Negro Family: The Case for National Action* (Washington, DC: US Department of Labor, Office of Planning and Research).

Moynihan, D. P. (1968) 'The Professors and the Poor', in D. P. Moynihan (ed.), *On Understanding Poverty: Perspectives from the Social Sciences* (New York: Basic Books), pp. 3–35.

Murray, C. (1984) *Losing Ground: American Social Policy, 1950–1980* (New York: Basic Books).

Murray, C. (1986) 'White Welfare Families, "White Trash"', *National Review*, 28 March, pp. 30–4.

Murray, C. (1989) 'Underclass: A Disaster in the Making', *The Sunday Times Magazine*, 26 November, pp. 26–46.

Murray, C. (1994) 'Does Welfare Bring More Babies?', *The Public Interest*, 115: pp. 17–30.

O'Connell Davidson, J. and Layder, D. (1994) *Methods, Sex and Madness* (London: Routledge).

Onward and Upward (1894) 4: p. 9.

Paddock, R. (1990) 'Aspects of Illegitimacy in Victorian Dumfriesshire', unpublished PhD thesis, University of Edinburgh.

Phoenix, A. (1991) *Young Mothers?* (Oxford: Polity Press).

Report by a Committee of the Prison Board of Aberdeenshire on the Repression of Prostitution (1860) (Aberdeen: Smith).

Ryan, W. (1976) *Blaming the Victim* (New York: Random House).

Seton, G. (1888) 'Illegitimacy in the Parish of Marnoch', *Proceedings of the Royal Society of Edinburgh*, 19 March, pp. 227–34.

Sharpe, S. (1987) *Falling for Love: Teenage Mothers Talk* (London: Virago).

Sheehan, S. (1977) *A Welfare Mother* (New York: Mentor).

Smout, C. (1980) 'Aspects of Sexual Behaviour in Nineteenth-Century Scotland', in P. Laslett, K. Oosterveen and R. M. Smith (eds), *Bastardy and Its Comparative History* (London: Edward Arnold), pp. 192–216.

Sontag, S. (1989) *AIDS and its Metaphors* (London: Allen Lane).

Stone, N. (1989) 'The Gas Chamber Mentality', *The Guardian*, 14 December, cited in Coote (1990), p. 36.

Strachan, J. M. (1859) *Address upon Illegitimacy to the Working Men of Scotland* (Edinburgh: Religious Tract and Book Society of Scotland).

Thane, P. (1978) 'Women and the Poor Law in Victorian and Edwardian England', *History Workshop Journal*, 6: pp. 29–51.

Valentine, J. (1859) 'Illegitimacy in Aberdeen and Other Large Towns of Scotland', *Report of the British Association for the Advancement of Science*, pp. 224–6.

Vinovskis, M. (1988) *An 'Epidemic' of Adolescent Pregnancy?: Some Historical and Policy Considerations* (New York: Oxford University Press).

Watson, W. (1877) *Pauperism, Vagrancy, Crime and Industrial Education in Aberdeenshire, 1840–1875* (Edinburgh: Blackwood).

Wellings, K., Field, J., Johnson, A. M. and Wadsworth, J. (1994) *Sexual Behaviour in Britain: The National Survey of Sexual Attitudes and Lifestyles* (Harmondsworth: Penguin).

White, T. (1965) *The Making of the President* (London: Jonathan Cape).

Williams, R. (1995) 'Judge backs BBC over "Babies on Benefit" Report', *The Independent*, 23 February, p. 6.

Part III

Identities, Communities and Control

7 Medicalisation and Identity Formation: Identity and Strategy in the Context of AIDS and HIV

BRIAN HEAPHY

INTRODUCTION

Over recent years we have witnessed a remarkable increase within the social sciences in the publication of work concerned with identity. Indeed it appears, as Kobena Mercer (1990, p. 43) suggests, that now everybody wants to talk about identity. The extent to which questions of identity and subjectivity have come to be seen as important and influential within various social scientific disciplines may understandably lead one to ask why this should be so. While some suggest that identity has become a watchword of our times as it provides a much needed vocabulary in terms of how we define our loyalties and commitments (Shotter, 1993), others suggest that identity only becomes an issue when it is in crisis. In this sense the crisis of identity occurs, as Mercer suggests, when something we assumed to be fixed, coherent and stable is displaced by the experience of doubt and uncertainty.

Within much of the recent social-scientific work on the topic, the notion of identity as fixed, neutral and unproblematic has been questioned. As Kitzinger (1989) suggests, rather than viewing identities as freely created products of introspection, or the reflections of some unproblematic inner self, they are more accurately understood as being profoundly political, both in their origins and implications.

Much of the recent concern with identity and subjectivity can be seen to focus on two areas. Firstly, debates have focused on the possibility of viewing identities in terms of agency and strategies for radical change. Secondly, recent work has also been concerned with the processes through which modern identities are shaped and created. Both concerns, of course, are not unrelated. How one understands and makes sense of the processes through which identities come into being and are worked upon has important implications for how they can be viewed and theorised in terms of their radical potential and in terms of agency.

In terms of the relationship between AIDS and identity, Thomas Yingling suggests:

> We must think AIDS not only as a public issue of ideology, apparatus, and representation but also *as it is internalised and expressed* by those infected and effected . . . because 'AIDS' as a signifier lodges in deep subliminal zones . . . that in the end are among the most crucial sites on which disciplinarity is inscribed and therefore potentially disrupted. (Yingling, 1991, p. 303)

In this chapter I would like to argue that it is possible to do this by viewing AIDS/HIV in terms of theories of identity and identity formation. To adopt such an approach is to question the ways in which the identities of people with AIDS/HIV are shaped and formed through dominant discourses on the virus and syndrome and is further to question the extent to which those most closely effected can actively participate in the creation of their own identities.

In what follows, I would like to address these questions by drawing on the experience of some people living with AIDS/HIV and in providing an account of how the meaning of AIDS/HIV can be seen to be negotiated by some of those most closely effected. This account is based on the interpretation of data gathered through interviews or 'conversations' with people with AIDS/HIV.[1] It is not intended to be an account of the 'truth' about the various ways in which AIDS knowledge is mediated and negotiated. Rather, it is constructed in certain ways so as to allow for a discussion of the usefulness of particular theoretical approaches to identity and identity formation in the context of AIDS and HIV. The early work of Foucault (1979a, b) and the more recent work of Giddens (1991) are considered in this context.

While the early work of Foucault can be seen to focus on the domination of individuals through social institutions, discourses and practices, I would like to suggest here that we can also draw on Foucault to explore the extent to which 'strategies of resistance' have a part to play in providing resources through which the meaning of AIDS/HIV can be understood. I would also like to suggest that in attempting to explore the extent to which the person with AIDS/HIV actively participates in the shaping and moulding of their own identities, the recent work of Anthony Giddens can provide important and useful insights.

However, it is further argued that both approaches are not without limitations.

FOUCAULT: IDENTITY AND DISCIPLINARY SOCIETY

From the early work of Foucault (1979a, b) we have come to see that identity is bound up with the workings of power. Indeed, Foucault's work can be seen as a fecund source for much recent work on identity and subjectivity. In particular, it is the relationship between discourse, power, knowledge and subjectivity drawn out in his work that has attracted much attention. Through his concern with the emergence of new technologies of power during the eighteenth century, we are, it would appear, presented with a picture of the domination of individuals through social institutions, discourses and practices. We are also presented with a picture of subjectivities as they are shaped by disciplinary power.

However, for Foucault power must not be understood purely in negative terms, but also in terms of its productive nature. Hence, in *Discipline and Punish* (Foucault, 1979a) we are presented with a study of the 'micro physics' of power as it operates within the institutions of prisons, schools and hospitals. Here, power exercised on the body is conceived not as a property, but as a *strategy*, a power exercised rather than possessed, a power that is productive of knowledge and subjectivity.

Importantly, in this scheme it is not the activity of the subject of knowledge that produces a corpus of knowledge, useful or resistant to power. Rather, it is power–knowledge that determines the forms and possible domains of knowledge. Discipline is identified in this work as one of the primary techniques that serves as a relay route and support for power–knowledge relations that invest human bodies and subjugate them by turning them into objects of knowledge.

Through discipline, as it is linked with normalisation strategies, the individual is not merely observed and regulated but 'carefully fabricated'. Discipline, as it is tied up with normalisation strategies, has as its ultimate goal the elimination of all social and psychological irregularities and the production of useful docile bodies and minds. Here, the individual is not only a discursive construct but also an effect of political technologies through which its very identity, desires, body and 'soul' are constituted:

But it should not be forgotten that there existed ... a technique for constituting individuals as correlative elements of power and knowledge. The individual is in no doubt the fictitious atom of an 'ideological' representation of society; but he is also a reality fabricated by this specific technology of power that I have called 'discipline'. We must cease once and for all to describe the effects of power in negative terms. ... In fact, power produces; it produces reality; it produces domains of objects and rituals of truth. The individual and the knowledge that may be gained of him belong to this production. (Foucault, 1979a, p. 194)

This theme is further considered in the first volume of *The History of Sexuality* (Foucault, 1979b), where again the modern individual is both the object and subject of knowledge. Here again the productive nature of power is emphasised, while power relations and their technologies are viewed as open strategies. In this scheme the individual is not repressed, but is shaped and formed within matrices of scientific-disciplinary mechanisms. As Best and Kellner (1991) point out, drawing from Dews' (1987) analysis, the subject here has a double meaning: subject to someone else by control and dependence, and tied to their own identity by a conscience or self-knowledge. Self-knowledge in this sense is a strategy and effect of power, whereby one internalises self control or monitoring. The subject as characterised here is far from pregiven, neutral, unified and unchanging.

Foucault's earlier work, then, as outlined above, can be seen, in part, to be concerned with posing a challenge to the notion of identities as pregiven, neutral, unified and fixed. Indeed, as Best and Kellner (1991) suggest, a key assumption in Foucault's work is that micrological strategies, in terms of resistance, would have to attempt to destroy the prisons of received identities and challenge hegemonic discourses to encourage the proliferation of differences of all kinds in countering normalising strategies of power.

In what ways can the theoretical framework above be employed to make sense of how people with AIDS or HIV (PWA/HIV) negotiate the meanings of the virus and syndrome? How can we account for identity formation in the context of AIDS and HIV? I would like to suggest that it may be productive to view the topic in terms of the following questions: what resources are available for the PWA/HIV to draw upon in making personal sense of infection and diagnosis?; how do people with AIDS/HIV come to understand what it means to be HIV positive or a person with AIDS? As medical discourses serve as the master discourse that informs all others on AIDS/HIV (Patton, 1990), and given that medical discourses have long been associated and critiqued as having a role to play in the workings of power (Plummer, 1988), is the PWA/HIV produced in discourse, and is the reality of the experience structured by disciplinary discourses and practices?

The Clinic: Knowledge, Power, Discipline

As Triechler (1988) suggests, the meaning of AIDS is constructed through language, and particularly through the language of medicine and science. It is further suggested by Patton (1990) that medical and scientific discourses on AIDS and HIV serve as the master discourses through which AIDS and HIV are given meaning. If, following from Foucault, discourse is power, because the rules determining discourse enforces norms of what is rational, sane and true, medical scientific discourses on AIDS/HIV can also be seen in terms of power as they, in the main, determine what is rational, sane and true in the contexts of AIDS/HIV.

Indeed, in the context of the clinic, and in the relationship between 'expert' and 'patient', medical knowledge is often initially approached as if it can or does know the truth about AIDS/HIV, particularly in relation to what a positive diagnosis means:

Then I asked them certain questions that got very quick answers, and not explained properly enough I felt. And, I kept trying to get truthful answers out of them, i.e. what does it really mean as far as they're concerned? What are the time factors on this? Could they be more specific? (Nigel)

I sat there with this vile doctor saying 'I don't know what to say'. I mean he's getting paid to tell me about it. I asked him how long I'd got, I wanted to know the truth and he just sat there looking at me. (Joan)

Further, when asking PWA/HIV what they know about AIDS/HIV it would appear that 'knowing about' AIDS/HIV is often in the first instance knowing what medicine knows:

I'd say I was pretty ignorant . . . for instance I only found out about two months ago that HIV only infected one part of your immunity, about one in ten cells, and I always thought that T-cells were a major part of your immunity. . . . I'd say being well informed would be knowing everything about it. How it works.   (Nigel)

For many PWA/HIV the clinic serves as the primary source of medical knowledge on the virus and syndrome. However, medical knowledge is not limited to clinical aspects of AIDS. Indeed, in the context of the clinic, medical experts and therapists can also be seen as a resource of non-clinical meanings of AIDS/HIV. This is particularly the case in terms of how one should approach living with HIV infection:

> It was either that doctor or another doctor that said there's not much we can do. And, you know, he said carry on with the things you want to do and don't let it interfere with your life, but you know, don't live excessively, be careful.   (Mark)

> He told me not to worry about it, and if I need to discuss it, if I need to know anything about AIDS or the virus or whatever . . . he would like to discuss it with me . . . and he said the important thing is to tell the people you know who will accept the fact that you're HIV positive, but don't go and tell anyone you don't know, be very careful of who you tell and I said yeah. . . . He said there were people out there who don't understand the virus.   (Linford)

The clinic and the practitioner, then, is not merely the source of 'expert' knowledge on the clinical aspects of AIDS/HIV, but can also be the source of more 'common-sense' knowledge on how to approach infection or illness. However, beyond clinical and common-sense knowledge, the expert, as the medical practitioner or counsellor, in the context of the clinic, can also be seen as a moral resource. This can be clearly seen in a quotation from Henderson (1991), where she suggests that women with HIV or AIDS are often seen in terms of their reproductive roles or very particular notions of 'normal' female sexuality:

> For instance, some so-called post-test counselling sessions were comprised of being advised to 'ask God's forgiveness for being so wicked' . . . or of being informed of the test result by means of a request to 'promise you won't get pregnant in the next six months before I see you again'.   (Henderson, 1991, p. 266)

However, attempts to intervene in the sexual autonomy of 'patients', and influence moral decisions, are often more subtle. These can take

the form of constant enquiry with regard to the number of sexual partners clients have had and with respect to what sexual acts have been
engaged in, or can involve 'advice' with regard to particular sex acts:

> every time they ask me how many people I've slept with, and I tell
> them, they ask me what I do with those people, was I passive or
> active, whether I use condoms or not. (Daniel)

> then he said are you still going to penetrate, and I said no, he said
> 'that's good, I just wanted to know'. Then he asked me how many
> people I slept with.... He said carry on like you have a normal
> life, but be aware that you are HIV positive, and just be safe. And,
> he said, be careful of other people, and not to get penetrated....
> and I realised what he was saying and I thought yeah, I'm not going
> to penetrate. (Linford)

The emphasis placed by practitioners and counsellors on the need for
discipline and control in relation to sex is a constant theme in accounts of the how clinics are experienced. The need for the regulation
of particular practices is framed both in terms of safer sex and the
need to avoid 'further' infection. However, accounts such as the above
illustrate that often there is a shift from safer sex as protected sex, to
safer sex as non-penetrative sex.[2]

The extent to which 'experts' talk and think about HIV infection
primarily as a sexually transmitted disease is evident from accounts
where the discussion of 'patients' sexual habits and practices appear
to be central to the concerns of many practitioners and counsellors.
This would seem to be particularly the case when AIDS/HIV medical
services are located in STD clinics. While the construction of particular infections as STDs can work to produce, as Patton (1985, p. 9)
suggests, social and psychological penalties of 'getting caught', or reveal the individuals infected as having engaged in illicit sexual activity, the construction of HIV as an STD can also work to legitimate
the role of the medical practitioner in policing the sexual activity of
people with AIDS/HIV *to* people with AIDS/HIV:

> I think the problem is with it being V.D. doctors that they are too
> aware of how it's caught, their emphasis is always on what you
> have done recently, has anyone come into contact with you, are you
> aware of safe sex. Their emphasis is all about whether you're spreading
> it or not ... to the point where they can't help thinking of how it's

caught basically, which is fair enough, that's part of their job, to make sure it doesn't spread . . . [non-VD doctors] can see it as a disease that anyone could catch, whereas I think V.D. doctors associate it very much with an us and them situation. (Nigel)

Indeed, this emphasis on the need to know what acts are committed, it appears, is often a concern with *what* the 'patient' is:

The kinds of questions they ask are . . . was it sex between men only or was it, was I bisexual, and was it safe sex. And then various things like do you have a monogamous relationship, and . . . the usual kinds of questions . . . at the time I thought it was for statistics, I never felt really annoyed that they were asking. (Warren)

For many practitioners, HIV/AIDS is intrinsically bound up with particular acts and identities. Emphasis is often shifted from knowledge of the virus/syndrome to knowledge of particular acts, and from here to knowledge of particular actors. Indeed, while medical knowledge of the illness, it appears, must often include knowledge of *who* is ill, the management of the psychological aspects of AIDS/HIV are also often dependent on this knowledge:

it seemed that sort of, all the counsellor was doing was sort of, I don't know, trying to find out all about me. She wasn't really interested in how I felt or whatever, she just wanted to know for her own sort of thing. (Dave)

It appears, then, that the 'experts' in the clinic are to a large extent concerned with who or what people with AIDS/HIV *are*. Assessment, diagnosis and prognosis are made, it appears, not only in terms of the infection and illness, but also in terms concerning the individual's habits, practices and identity:

They were useless at telling me, they wouldn't look at me, and *all* they wanted to know was how I'd got it, that was their only interest. . . . And they went on and on about drug abuse. . . . I think it's purely for statistics, and particularly with women they do like to know. . . . I mean it was a constant question, every time the doctor came round they would say 'do you think you could tell us how you think you got it' and I would just say no. (Maya)

The judges of normality, according to Foucault, are everywhere: 'We are in the society of the teacher-judge, the doctor-judge, the educator judge, the "social worker"-judge; it is on them that the universal reign of the normative is based' (Foucault, 1979a, p. 304). Indeed, while the need to know about routes of transmission is most often framed in terms of 'statistics' and 'prevention', it can also be understood in terms of categories of normality:

> They like to feel that ordinary people do not go around getting HIV, you *have* to have done something that falls into what they call risk categories . . . and they just want to feel that it's being contained, em, and that it isn't suddenly breaking into the 'straight' community. I really do think that that's their agenda, that they want to see where it is . . . they were just interested to know what I was doing basically so that they could slip me into one of their categories.   (Maya)

Within the clinic, then, knowledge is not only dispensed to the person with AIDS/HIV but is gained *of* the PWA/HIV. Also, as we have seen, medical knowledge, as it is dispensed within the context of the clinic, is not confined to 'expert' clinical knowledge. Rather, the clinical practitioner and counsellor can also be the sources of commonsense and moral knowledge on AIDS and HIV. Further, in some cases, the role of 'experts' within the clinic can be seen to go beyond the dispensing of information and the management of the physical and psychological aspects of HIV infection, to include roles as judges of who or what people with AIDS/HIV are, teachers of self-discipline with regard to sexual activity, and to police moral issues in terms sexual practices and reproduction.

In light of the above, we may question the extent to which medical knowledge and practice in relation to AIDS and HIV, as it is found to exist within the clinic, can be seen to be neutral and beneficent. In terms of providing resources through which the experience of AIDS/HIV can be understood and be given meaning we are presented with a rather pessimistic picture.

Beyond the Clinic: Multiplicity of AIDS/HIV Knowledges

However, knowledge on AIDS/HIV is not confined to the clinic, and is not confined to medical discourses. While the history of AIDS/HIV can be seen, in part, as a history of discourses, it is also a history of dominant discourses and reverse discourses. While medico-scientific and medico-moral discourses tend to dominate our thinking on the virus and syndrome, these meanings have been consistently challenged from various positions. Indeed, the ever-expanding mass of publications and knowledges on AIDS/HIV is an indication of the extent to which the meaning of AIDS is continuously propounded and disputed. It also indicates that what AIDS means is still, in some senses, up for grabs.

People with AIDS/HIV are faced with a multiplicity of meanings with regard to the virus and syndrome, and bring to the clinic 'other' knowledges of what AIDS is:

> Most of what I knew, I suppose, was from the gay press, and from T.V. documentaries. And, I suppose, from talking to friends. I did make an effort to know. The first time I came across it was probably as a gay concern. . . . I remember I read in the gay press that it was a plot to stop us having sex. (Daniel)

Indeed, while for many women and non-gay men the popular media appear to provide initial information on AIDS, for many gay men knowledge on the virus and syndrome is primarily mediated through the gay press and gay friends. This can particularly be seen to be the case in the early days of the epidemic:

> of course I did come across it because of things like the gay press, and just because my friends were talking about it, quite a lot about it at that point. You know 'have you heard about it', 'what do you think about it'. . . . I suppose we thought it was some kind of mysterious disease which nobody really understood, which was uniformly fatal, which effected homosexuals in the great part. (Mark)

While discourses on AIDS/HIV are now more widespread, and while AIDS has in some senses been 'degayed', for many gay men living with AIDS/HIV, gay orientated services and gay community contacts, continue to be important sources of information with regard to the virus and syndrome. Importantly, while the degaying of AIDS has allowed, as King (1993) suggests, the channelling of resources *away* from the communities most effected, these communities continue to be a primary source of information and support for many:

> Well, I find out from friends, because I'm gay, so I have a lot of gay friends as well. I find out from them. . . . I read pamphlets about

it, you know, you get pamphlets in good gay clubs, and generally talk to friends about it . . . and I'm a person who goes out a lot to gay clubs, and I read the gay news, and it's all written in the gay news and things like that.   (Linford)

Furthermore, many PWA/HIV actively seek out 'other' knowledges and meanings in various and different ways. Holistic approaches, for example, are adopted by some as:

the power of the mind is given much more range, it's given much more scope. You know, a lot more importance is placed on that, on the way that your thinking, and your attitude to the whole thing, and it's putting yourself in control of your own body.   (Rob)

The personal experience of others, too, is often sought out and considered more 'authentic' knowledge:

I certainly knew as much about it before, except that now I know more about people's personal accounts, people that have actually been effected by it. Whereas before I didn't know anyone, but I made a point of finding out more . . . which is more of the realistic information you're going to get really.   (Nigel)

Further, networks, both official and unofficial, can be seen as an important source of medical and 'other' knowledges:

there is a kind of underground network of what to do. And I, especially with my close friends, we talk quite a lot. You know the subject comes up of HIV and things that are going on and things that we've read and whatever.   (Rob)

I tend to keep up on the research, I keep an eye on what's going on. . . . I read all the Body Positive leaflets or reports, anything I can get my hands on I read it.   (Warren)

I do keep an eye on what is happening. Like with ACT-UP or Body Positive, just to make sure that I'm aware of everything, like drug trials and things.   (Joan)

Medical and 'other' knowledges about AIDS/HIV are mediated in various ways, through the gay press, alternative medical manuals, and self-help groups, which approach dominant perceptions of AIDS/HIV in ways that are not uncritical.

Indeed, while I suggested earlier that PWA/HIV can often approach medical knowledge as if it can or does know the truth about AIDS/HIV, this is by no means always the case:

> Well, I thought, and I still think, that they don't really know very much what they're talking about. And, you know, they're always telling people that they're about to drop dead. . . . I've got a friend who was told that he had two years to live and that was five years ago, and you know they don't know anything about it. No one knows. But they set themselves up to know everything, and of course what they know is not enough. They can't set themselves up like this, like you know, to know all sorts of things. Because they don't know anything. They don't know enough about it and they shouldn't profess to know.   (Joan)

Further, while many may initially approach medical knowledge as if it can provide the meaning or the truth about AIDS/HIV, this faith is often problematised through contacts with other PWA/HIV and through contact with other ways of seeing the virus and syndrome:

> I mean I did have faith in them to begin with, you know, where else are you going to have faith! I thought the medical profession! Medicine!!. . . But I met more people who are HIV and, you know, I learnt more about other kinds of approaches. I mean, you know, holistic medicine and all that, homeopathic and all those things.   (Rob)

Drawing from the above, then, it is possible to suggest that while the clinic may serve, for some, as a primary source of information (medical, common-sense and moral) regarding AIDS and HIV, the clinic is far from the only source of information available to people with AIDS/HIV. Further, dominant medical discourses on AIDS/HIV are continuously challenged and contested, both by other health discourses and activist discourses, which compete to establish different meanings of AIDS/HIV. Finally, many people with AIDS/HIV do not accept dominant meanings uncritically and draw on various resources in making personal sense of infection and illness.

In terms of the work of Foucault, how is it possible to account for the negotiation of the meaning of AIDS/HIV as outlined above? How can we work the experience of PWA/HIV into his account which has attempted to shed light on the ways in which identities are shaped and worked upon? How can power be seen to be implicated in the formation and creation of PWA/HIV identities.

In *Discipline and Punish* (1979a), Foucault provided an account of a disciplinary society that functions through an incitement to regulation, that works by investing individuals with a distinct sense of place, function and atribution, and further operates according to binary divisions of mad/sane, normal/abnormal and sick/healthy. We are further provided, as I suggested earlier, with a picture of the disciplined and self-disciplining subject. In considering this account in the context of AIDS/HIV, we can ask the following questions: to what extent can we see 'the automatic functioning of power' where individuals regulate themselves and their behaviour? to what extent can the 'self-knowledge' of the person with AIDS/HIV be seen as a strategy and effect of power?

Perhaps it is possible to see evidence of the workings of power in Nigel's account of the way he sees himself and his relations with others:

It was a point a doctor made, that HIV doesn't equal AIDS, but that HIV itself is an illness. It's the same thing, there's no distinction, and it's relevant to the way I feel now. It doesn't matter what you think, you can not live or think the same, you can't be normal. No matter what you do you will have the notion of illness.

I don't have a lot of sex anymore.... I also find myself in a situation, like I said before, in a situation where.... I don't feel confident enough to go out there, because I can't perceive myself fucking them, if the condom broke I'd feel horrified.... I mean I've heard people, even when it comes down to kissing worrying about whether they can catch it. And I feel like, I feel bad doing that with them. Even though that's a thing they should face up to themselves.

I think I'm constantly aware of it, without even wanting to be, no matter what situation I'm in I am constantly aware of it, which is ridiculous, you shouldn't be.... I'm constantly aware of it in that kind of family thing and constantly aware of it with young healthy crowds.... I find myself standing in a situation where I presume that most people are healthy, and I feel completely unhealthy and dead, and old. And they're the same age as me! Probably because I have this thing (HIV) and they haven't. (Nigel)

While physical illness can be productive of disablement for people with AIDS/HIV, the experience of being a person with AIDS/HIV can also be productive of a sense of 'difference' and 'abnormality'. This self-knowledge, of being different or abnormal, can in Foucauldian terms, be interpreted as a strategy and effect of power. From the above we can also see that the experience can work to provide a sense of place within binary oppositions that are characteristic of disciplinary society.

Yet, testing for HIV and living with AIDS/HIV can also be productive in other ways. Productive of a sense of control, or indeed a sense of value and even a sense of empowerment:

I had the test because.... I thought that I had an unhealthy lifestyle socially, as far as drugs, cigarettes and alcohol and em ... so I thought if I find out about it that then, maybe, I will be. And, secondly, I think I needed something to jolt me into, em, changing certain things in my life. That I knew I was running into a kind of dormant phase, and I knew that knowing that would maybe help, 'cause that's how it can effect you, which is strange really. (Nigel)

I went along to the test as I wanted something to, because I needed to be induced into changing things, and induced into safe sex. (Rob)

I'm much more in control of my health.... I tend to eat healthily ... and I check myself, and if I feel ill I will relax. If I have a headache, I know why I have it, I haven't eaten properly or I've been working too hard, so I know why my headaches start. Yes, I'm in control of my health, much better that anyone else I think! (Linford)

Well I think it makes me appreciate every day, which doesn't mean I go water ski-ing one day and ballet dancing the next. But, it does mean that, I don't know how to put it, not 'happy' that's quite narrow, but I find satisfaction in all sorts of things. It's not *things*, it's your state of mind really. It's about looking at your state of mind and not forcing yourself to do things. (Joan)

For many then, the experience of being HIV positive, or of living with AIDS, can be productive of a 'new' or 'different' sense of self or self-understanding. However, as we have seen, while the accounts of PWA/HIV may provide evidence of the production of 'disciplined' selves, they also appear to provide evidence of 'empowered' selves.

In providing a theoretical framework which can account for the productive nature of power, the early work of Foucault, I have suggested, can enable us to get a sense of the extent which power may be implicated in the self-knowledge of PWA/HIV. Further, if we consider Foucault's proposition that while power is omnipresent it is not omnipotent, we can see that there exists in his work a means of accounting for the possibility of resistance in the context of AIDS/HIV. While people with AIDS/HIV are, in some senses, subject to dominant medicomoral and medico-scientific discourses on AIDS and HIV, they *do* draw on counter-discourses in making personal sense of the virus and syndrome, and do not accept dominant meanings uncritically.

Yet, in attempting to account for the complex ways in which PWA/HIV actively take part in the fabrication of their own identities, the framework offered by Foucault's work must also be seen to have its limitations. While Foucault talks of power in terms of open strategies, in his early work the emphasis remains largely placed on domination, and while the possibility of resistance is acknowledged, it remains largely under-theorised. Importantly, if we are to account for the extent to which the experience of living with AIDS/HIV can be productive of a sense of empowerment, it is necessary to move beyond a narrow focus on domination/resistance to provide a more dynamic account of agency.

Indeed, while it is in terms of providing a limited account of agency that Foucault's work has been most widely criticised, there have, as Best and Kellner (1991) suggest, been other important criticisms of his work. Particularly, his work is seen to be over-focused on the repressive nature of modernity and not to account for its progressive aspects. Further, his work has been criticised as it does not directly address present political issues and is limited in its focus on powers such as the state and capitalism. For many sociologists, the recent work of Anthony Giddens (1991) is important as it precisely these issues that his work addresses.

GIDDENS: IDENTITY AND REFLEXIVITY

As outlined above, the early work of Foucault can be seen to consider subjectivity and identity in terms of strategies of normalisation and in terms of discourse politics as a strategy of resistance. In Giddens' *Modernity and Self Identity* (1991) strategy is linked to identity and subjectivity in terms of reflexivity and in terms of humans' essential needs for ontological security.

Self-identity, as understood by Giddens, is a reflexively organised project, sculpted from the complex plurality of choices offered by high modernity. Identities, in this scheme, are formed through the asking of questions and continual reordering of narratives:

> The reflexive project of the self, which consists in the sustaining of coherent, yet continuously revised, biographical narratives, takes place in the context of multiple choice as filtered through abstract systems. (Giddens, 1991, p. 5)

Here, self-identity has to be routinely created and sustained in the reflexive activities of the individual. What to be? How to act? Who to be? are questions we must all address in late modernity, either discursively or through day-to-day behaviour, but they are problematic. However, Giddens suggests, while modernity confronts us with many choices, we are offered little guidance regarding which choices should be taken. Of the various consequences that follow from this, there are particular implications for lifestyle:

> Yet because of the 'openness' of social life today, the pluralisation of contexts of action and the diversity of 'authorities', lifestyle choice is increasingly important in the constitution of self-identity and daily activity. Reflexively organised life-planning, which normally presumes consideration of risks as filtered through contact with expert knowledge, becomes a central feature of the structuring of self-identity. (Giddens, 1991, p. 5)

The more that tradition loses its ability to provide a secure and stable sense of identity or self, Giddens suggests, the more individuals have to negotiate lifestyle choices and attach importance to these choices. Indeed, the more post-traditional the setting in which the individual moves, the more issues of lifestyle concern the very core of self identity. Lifestyle, in these terms, is directly linked to individuals' needs to establish a meaningful and reliable sense of self in late modernity, in an era where personal meaninglessness is a fundamental psychic problem. Yet, concern with lifestyle can be thrown into radical doubt by 'fateful moments':

> Fateful moments are times when events come together in such a

way that an individuals stands, as it were, at a crossroads in his existence; or where a person learns of information with fateful consequences. (Giddens, 1991, p. 113)

At fateful moments the individual, according to Giddens, is likely to recognise that he or she is faced with an altered 'set of risks and possibilities' (1991, p. 131). In such circumstances the individual is called on to question routinised habits of relevant kinds, even sometimes those most closely integrated with self-identity.

Fateful moments, Giddens suggests, are threatening for the 'protective cocoon' which defends individuals against ontological insecurity. However, while during these moments individuals may choose to have recourse to more traditional authorities, and seek refuge in pre-established beliefs, they can also mark periods of 'reskilling' and empowerment. For empowerment is routinely available to lay people as part of the reflexivity of modernity:

Coupled to disembedding, the expansion of abstract systems creates increasing quanta of power – the power of human beings to alter the material world and transform the conditions of their own actions.... In any given situation, provided that the resources of time and other requisites are available, the individual has the possibility of a partial or more full-blown reskilling in respect of specific decisions or contemplated courses of action. (Giddens, 1991, pp. 138–9)

For Giddens, then, during fateful moments the individual must 'sit up and take notice of new demands as well as possibilities' (Giddens, 1991, p. 143). At these times, when life has to begin anew, endeavours at reskilling are likely to be particularly important and intensely pursued. Fateful moments, Giddens stresses, are transition points which have major implications for the individuals future conduct *and* self-identity.

In what ways can Giddens' work on identity formation processes in late modernity be of use in consideration of PWA/HIV identities? I would like to argue that as Giddens is concerned with the ways in which the conditions of high modernity make modern individuals' confrontation with death particularly diffiicult, consideration of his work in terms of AIDS/HIV would seem appropriate.

In terms of the identities of PWA/HIV, it is possible to see the diagnosis of infection or the experiences of related illness as 'fateful moments'. As we have seen, while diagnosis of HIV or AIDS can mark an important transition point in an individuals' life and self-understanding, at such moments the individual can choose from a multiplicity of knowledges in making personal sense of infection or illness. Indeed, the accounts of the negotiation of the meaning of AIDS/HIV, outlined earlier, can be understood in terms of 'reskilling'. This reskilling can be seen to be influenced by where the individuals have pre-positioned themselves in terms of the various 'expert' knowledges. Further, the consequential decisions taken with regard to reskilling will, once taken, reshape the reflexive project of identity of the PWA/HIV through the lifestyle consequences that ensue:

> I mean I have made great lifestyle changes, I've stopped partying and I do sometimes wonder is my life better now or was it then. When I think of the gay scene now . . . it seems to be totally drug orientated and I don't participate anymore. I don't go to many gay places now, I don't relate to the whole gay thing at all . . . because I'm sitting on the fence and looking after my health, and that to me is very important. (Michael)

From the accounts outlined earlier, it would appear that reskilling is indeed a task undertaken by most PWA/HIV. Further, that fateful moments, and the ensuing period of reskilling, may be marked by a sense of positive change can be seen from some of the accounts above and the following:

> Yeah, life's changed a lot, I mean I tend to give more time to my friends, I tend to be more happier, I tend to be more considerate to other people. . . . I'm more generous to people. . . . I respect life, because before I was diagnosed I used to be like, you know, I never cared a shit. (Linford)

> I just decided to enjoy life more, which is what I do. The other thing I've done is to shrug off that awful Catholic guilt, I now, whenever I catch myself feeling guilty, I stop myself and, you know, think 'you haven't got time for this'. And it works! Yes, it seems to work. Yeah, I have changed, I think I've changed my attitude quite radically in many ways. (Paul)

Giddens, to some extent, allows us to account for the active role played by people with AIDS/HIV in the creation of their own identities through the 'reskilling' that is part of the reflexive process of self-identity.

Even further, in this scheme, the PWA/HIV can be 'empowered' with the help of 'expert systems':

> Hence it is not surprising that at fateful moments individuals are today likely to encounter expert systems which precisely focus on the reconstruction of self-identity: counselling or therapy. A decision to enter therapy can generate empowerment.   (Giddens, 1991, p. 143)

Part of sense of empowerment can be a sense of gaining a 'new' understanding of self not only in terms of HIV infection but in other respects:

> I mean I understand a lot more about myself through therapy, I've seen my psychotherapist around why I actually did start using drugs, what I was running away from. I understand quite a bit actually. Whereas when I was using I didn't care. . . . Acupuncture and homeopathy help too, and with psychotherapy as well, to change patterns that I've had in my life, and to change behaviour as well, or to understand behaviour.   (Michael)

Within the framework provided by Giddens, then, diagnosis of HIV infection or AIDS, as a 'fateful moment', can threaten to overwhelm the PWA/HIV with anxieties concerning the meaningfulness and reality of themselves and the world around them. However, reskilling, expert systems and theraputic resources can be used to maintain the identity of the PWA/HIV in the face of ontological security. Through an employment of this framework we can, it would appear, go beyond the early work of Foucault which had as it's primary focus the domination of individuals, to an account that can allow for agency in the context of processes of identity formation.

The Limits of Reflexivity

While Giddens' work can be seen as important in that it provides insights into identity formation processes in high modernity, there have also been important criticisms of this work. Shilling (1993), for instance, points out that Giddens' analysis of ontological security seems based on the view that humans have a fundamental and unchanging need for a secure sense of themselves and the world around them. Lash (1993), in a critique of Giddens, provides a more detailed account of the *limits* of reflexivity.

For Lash, modern subjectivity should be understood as only capable of subsuming a limited amount of content under the reflexive self. Contradiction and contingency, he suggests, are far more characteristic of contemporary self than Giddens as a theorist of reflexivity will allow. Lash reminds us that what Foucault has characterised as disciplinary discourses that discipline and normalise individuals, Giddens sees as 'expert systems' that ward off contingency. Where Giddens wants expert systems to impose order in the face of chaos, Lash suggests, Foucault is on the side of flux, difference and opposed to the ordering properties of discourse. Importantly, Lash points out that what appears as freedom of agency for the theory of reflexivity is just another means of control for Foucault, as the direct operation of power on the body has been displaced by its mediated operation on the body through the 'soul'.[3]

Indeed, in the context of AIDS and HIV, there are limits of reflexivity to be considered. These can be seen in terms of both the limits of choice and the limits of reskilling. In western societies people with AIDS/HIV have, it is suggested by Giddens' analysis, no choice but to choose. However, while Giddens acknowledges some of the restraints placed on choice and reskilling, in terms of the cultural and economic resources available to individuals, these are somewhat underemphasised. In attempting to account for the possibility of agency in the context of AIDS and HIV, these restraints, I would suggest, must be understood as being *central* in dictating the extent to which choices can be made, and the extent to which it is possible to reskill.

Further, while people with AIDS/HIV are confronted with a multiplicity of knowledges with regard to the meaning of infection, we should not underestimate the effectiveness of the rarely questioned proposition that AIDS is primarily medical. While dominant medico-scientific discourses may be challenged from various positions, they retain a privileged position in defining what is rational, sane and true with regard to the virus and the syndrome. Beyond this, it must be acknowledged that while the multiplication of expert systems that mediate different AIDS/HIV knowledges may appear to open up choice, this multiplication may also be indicative of both the expansion of judges of normality and the extension of disciplining discourses.

Importantly, to overemphasise reflexivity also underplays the extent to which identities in the context of AIDS/HIV are marked by difference and complexity. Any questioning of identity in this context must account for different experiences of people living with AIDS/HIV in terms of various cultural and social positionings, such as gender, race and sexuality. Further, it is also important to acknowledge that while these categories help to structure the experience of AIDS/HIV, they themselves are fluid. To consider AIDS/HIV identities in terms of difference and complexity is not only to see differences *between* particular accounts of how the virus and syndrome are experienced, but differences *within* particular accounts. In this sense, we need to account for experiences where AIDS/HIV can appear both to empower *and* discipline individuals.

CONCLUSION

Both the early work of Foucault and the recent work of Giddens can be seen to be useful in providing a theoretical approach to questions of identity and identity formation in the context of AIDS and HIV. However, as suggested above, both have their limitations, particularly in respect of Foucault's overemphasis on domination and in Giddens' overemphasis on reflexivity. While we may wish to account for agency, we must, as Lash suggests, consider the limits of reflexivity.

Foucault and Giddens provide important theoretical frameworks through which it is possible to explore the extent to which strategies of power are implicated in the creation and moulding of the identities of people with AIDS/HIV. Drawing on this work we can begin to account for both domination *and* agency in relation to AIDS and HIV. Yet the usefulness of the frameworks and tools provided is dependant, in this context, on the extent to which they refer to the lived experience of those infected and effected. For it is only through this experience that we can account for the strategies employed by people living with AIDS/HIV in both negotiating personal meanings of the virus and syndrome and in actively participating in the formation of their own identities.

NOTES

1. The quotations in this chapter come from semi-structured interviews with men and women living with AIDS or HIV. The interviews were conducted in the Bristol/Avon area and the Greater London area.
2. The importance of distinguishing between 'safe sex', which aims for the total elimination of all risk, and 'safer sex', which aims for a drastic reduction of risk, is considered by King (1993, pp. 85–134). In the context

of HIV prevention campaigns aimed at gay men, King suggests, initiatives should be geared towards encouraging safer, rather than safe sex. It is argued that while this approach is likely to be more successful and effective, such an approach is also necessary in shifting the focus from deterring gay men from anal sex to enabling gay men to make their own informed decisions about risk reduction.

3. Lash is referring here to Foucault's use of the term 'soul':

> it is the element in which are articulated the effects of a certain type of power and the reference of a certain type of knowledge, the machinery by which the power relations give rise to a possible corpus of knowledge, and knowledge extends and reinforces the effects of this power. On this reality-reference, various concepts have been constructed and domains of analysis carved out: psyche, subjectivity, personality, consciousness, etc. (Foucault, 1979a, pp. 29–30)

REFERENCES

Best, S. and Kellner, D. (1991) *Postmodern Theory: Critical Interrogations* (London: Macmillan).

Dews, P. (1987) *Logics of Disintegration* (London: Verso).

Foucault, M. (1979a) *Discipline and Punish* (Harmondsworth: Penguin).

Foucault, M. (1979b) *The History of Sexuality*, vol. 1 (Harmondsworth: Penguin).

Giddens, A. (1991) *Modernity and Self Identity* (Cambridge: Polity).

Henderson, S. (1991) 'Care: What's in it for Her?', in P. Aggleton, G. Hart and P. Davies (eds), *AIDS: Responses, Interventions and Care* (London: Falmer Press).

King, E. (1993) *Safety in Numbers* (London: Cassell).

Kitzinger, C. (1989) 'The Regulation of Lesbian Identities', in J. Shotter and K. J. Gergen (eds), *Texts of Identity* (London: Sage).

Lash, S. (1993) 'Reflexive Modernisation: The Aesthetic Dimension', *Theory, Culture and Society*, 10: pp. 1–23.

Mercer, K. (1990) 'Welcome to the Jungle: Identity and Diversity in Postmodern Politics', in J. Rutherford (ed.), *Identity: Community, Culture, Difference* (London: Lawerence & Wishart).

Patton, C. (1985) *Sex and Germs: The Politics of AIDS* (Boston, MA: South End Press).

Patton, C. (1990) *Inventing AIDS* (London: Routledge).

Plummer, K. (1988) 'Organising AIDS', in P. Aggleton and H. Homans (eds), *Social Aspects of AIDS* (London: Falmer).

Shilling, C. (1993) *The Body and Social Theory* (London: Sage).

Shotter, J. (1993) *Cultural Politics of Everyday Life* (Buckingham: Open University Press).

Triechler, P. (1988) 'AIDS, Homophobia and Biomedical Discourse', in D. Crimp (ed.), *AIDS: Cultural Analysis, Cultural Activism* (London: MIT Press).

Yingling, T. (1991) 'AIDS in America: Postmodern Governance, Identity, and Experience', in D. Fuss (ed.), *Inside/Out* (London: Routledge).

8 Community Responses to HIV and AIDS: The 'De-Gaying' and 'Re-Gaying' of AIDS

JEFFREY WEEKS, PETER AGGLETON,
CHRIS MCKEVITT, KAY PARKINSON
and AUSTIN TAYLOR-LAYBOURN

The health authorities haven't really done much for the gay communities. Maybe because they've been scared. Maybe because the funding they get restricts them. Maybe because they don't give a damn. You can't tie it down to one factor. The fact is . . . a gay man in the UK is tested positive about once every six hours . . . but . . . they don't want to address these issues. Other organisations besides the health authorities . . . started de-gaying the epidemic for their own particular reasons . . . they started to reduce what they were doing for the gay community, till nobody seemed to do anything. And I think it is very important that the gay community, that is the largest community that is affected, should know. . . . In the early days when the epidemic first came around it was the gay community that fought back for their own survival. . . . Maybe if they hadn't been so quick to mobilise themselves they wouldn't have been left to themselves.

Volunteer, Gay Men Fighting AIDS

The term 'community' has a resonant tone. This resonance is evoked in a variety of ways, suggesting something more than the individual (though it is composed of individuals), less than the state (though the state can embody a sense of community) – a vital intermediary body, or rather series of bodies, between both. Hardly anyone, unless they are prepared to deny altogether that society is something more than individuals and their families, is against the notion of community. The difficulty lies in the fact that this evocative term means different things to different people.

When we speak of a community-based response to HIV and AIDS we are actually referring to particular types of communities, often those constructed by and for highly marginalised groups of people. The first community responses – indeed in many places, the first responses at all – to the emergence of the HIV/AIDS epidemic, came from those most affected by the spread of sickness and death, in the gay male and lesbian communities. Later other communities, of Black people, of women affected by HIV, of people with haemophilia and so on, developed their own particular responses. But they did so while the wider (that is to say heterosexual) 'community', with notable individual exceptions, displayed a range of unhelpful responses, ranging from panic to indifference, being stirred into managerial action only when contagion seemed in danger of seeping from the marginal communities into what became known as the 'general population'. Now we have a government social policy which stresses 'care in the community', and which is likely to have significant effects for the community-based response to HIV and AIDS; a policy whose ideological roots lie in the professed belief that care for the sick and needy is better and more 'cost effective' when left to individuals and their families, living in diverse communities.

Here we have at least three types of meanings of community: community as a focus of identity and resistance against a backdrop of marginalisation and discrimination; community as a euphemism for 'everyone else', that is the 'normal' population; and community as a metaphor for a greater stress on self-help in welfare provision. A term that is so powerful but elastic obviously has its uses in social policy and cultural rhetoric. But in attempting to understand social responses to the HIV and AIDS crisis in Britain, it is vital to grasp that the use of the term can obscure as much as it can clarify, unless it is used with proper attentiveness to an important but often obscured history.

Two central arguments underpin this chapter. The first is a recognition that the vital initial social response to HIV and AIDS came from within the group most affected by, and still most at risk from, the British epidemic – the gay male population. Gay men were not alone in that response. Many women, lesbian and heterosexual, and some heterosexual men, worked alongside them; and the informal alliance between early AIDS activists, physicians and others working in genitourinary medicine (GUM) clinics, and public health officials was to play a central part in shaping the policy agenda that a reluctant British government was eventually to accept (Weeks, 1993). The point is that gay men, shaped by a strong sense of identification with a political, cultural and sexual community whose achievements of the previous decade now seemed at risk because of a deadly threat of epidemic, took the lead in resistance to it. We can see this both in a community stress on the need to change sexual practices in the direction of safer sex, and in the development of direct services to those who were ill or dying. To say that is not to deny the vital contribution of other individuals or groups, then or since. It is simply to recognise a temporal and moral priority.

The second argument is that community-based activity took the form of a powerful voluntary response, both in terms of volunteering in a range of organisations, statutory as well as voluntary, and in the establishment of a range of specialised HIV and AIDS voluntary organisations, from large service organisations such as the Terrence Higgins Trust to local self-help groups, from high-profile care facilities such as the London Lighthouse to a huge variety of national, regional and local help and information lines (Aggleton *et al.*, 1993). A high percentage of the volunteers were, and continue to be, gay men or lesbians. Indeed, the majority of the earliest HIV/AIDS-specific voluntary organisations were founded by, and staffed by, gay people. They were responding to a crisis that particularly affected gay men, and a crisis which, in most of Britain anyway, still largely affects gay men. Yet, as we will see, when the community group Gay Men Fighting AIDS (GMFA) was founded in 1992, it could claim with some justification that it was the first HIV/AIDS organisation in the UK specifically directed at the needs of gay men (King, 1993).

There is a major paradox here which it is the aim of this chapter to explore. The data we use comes from the first major national study of the HIV and AIDS voluntary sector. Funded by the Economic and Social Research Council (Grant R 000233669), the project entitled 'Voluntary Sector Responses to HIV and AIDS: Policies, Principles, Practices' began work in 1992 with a survey of some 550 voluntary agencies working on HIV/AIDS issues. These included both HIV/AIDS-specific organisations, founded with the aim of responding to this particular issue, and generalist organisations which had more recently started work in this area. Subsequently, a series of case studies was conducted in a range of individual voluntary organisations; these are the source of the quotations used in this chapter.

FROM THE PAST TO THE PRESENT

The early voluntary groupings, such as the Terrence Higgins Trust (founded in 1983), were established because of the absence of a coordinated national response in the early stages of the crisis. Voluntary services had to develop, because outside the hospitals and GUM clinics caring for people with HIV and AIDS, there was nothing else. The reasons for this have been documented elsewhere (see Berridge, 1993), but lie in the fact that HIV and AIDS first appeared amongst a highly stigmatised group of people, gay men, at a uniquely unfavourable political conjuncture. It was a period when the political impetus of the initial wave of lesbian and gay politics seemed to be weakening, and a New-Right-influenced government had an economic agenda which favoured cutbacks in welfare expenditure and a moral agenda which strongly disapproved of an assertive homosexual politics.

The initial success of this community effort was remarkable, in two senses. First, there was a widespread adoption of safer-sex activities amongst gay men, as they responded to community-based health promotion rooted in a strong awareness of community norms and values (Watney, 1994). Second, embryonic services were established: helplines, self-help groups for people with HIV and AIDS, buddying services, support networks and so on. These were almost entirely supported by voluntary sources of funding (Weeks *et al.*, 1994a).

But there was success of another kind too. A crucial part of the voluntary sector strategy was to campaign for the statutory sector to provide much-needed services. At first, the new sector saw itself as a substitute for absent services, an advocate for better services which it was assumed could and should be provided through the community at large. However, after a change in government policy announced at the end of 1986, there was a more sustained statutory response, directed at limiting the spread of the epidemic. This took the form both of a generalised health education campaign, and the rapid development of a variety of services funded either directly by central government, or through local and health authorities. In fact between 1985/6 and 1992, central government granted £8.9 million through Section 64 funding to voluntary organisations in the HIV/AIDS field; and over £500 million was made available to statutory bodies for 'prevention, treatment and care', some of which found its way to voluntary bodies (Department of Health, 1992). A consequence of this new government policy was rapid expansion of the voluntary sector.

The origins, and subsequent histories, of the organisations which came into being in this period were diverse. Some developed in response to grass roots initiatives: of people with AIDS (e.g. Frontliners), of women (e.g. Positively Women), of minority ethnic communities (e.g. Blackliners, Black HIV/AIDS Network), and of injecting drug users (e.g. Mainliners). Others did so as a result, in effect, of partnerships between statutory and voluntary effort (e.g. The Landmark in south-east London). Many started and remained largely informal networks, with few, if any, paid workers. A large number, however, became significant service delivery agencies.

Though the main stimulus behind the origins of such organisations was a growing recognition of the needs of different populations at risk, in the process of development several tendencies have been widely observed. As the HIV/AIDS sector has developed, so has the expertise, and 'professionalisation' of the staff. As the size and range of activities of individual organisations have increased, so has the division of labour between management committees, senior managers, paid workers and volunteers. As some of the organisations have acquired formal trust status, and become integrated into a network of interagency activities, especially into joint planning with statutory bodies, so have difficult questions emerged about the relation between advocacy, campaigning and service provision. In consequence, and despite their frequent origins in communities of need and at risk, many voluntary agencies have found that their links with their origins are becoming increasingly tenuous.

One sign of this is the clear shift in the populations targeted by the organisations we surveyed. The largest grouping of organisations (44 per cent), stressed that they gave the highest priority to the needs of the 'general HIV constituency'. Some 30 per cent emphasised priority to 'gay/bisexual men', 27 per cent to injecting drug users, 23 per cent to women, 20 per cent to children and young people, 9 per cent to people from minority ethnic communities, and 5 per cent to people with haemophilia. By way of contrast, the reported modes of transmission for diagnosed cases of AIDS between 1982 and 1993 were: 74 per cent through sexual intercourse between men, 7.3 per cent were cases of women through various sources, 4.8 per cent were amongst injecting drug users, and 4.8 per cent among people infected through contaminated blood products.

Such evidence tends to confirm the picture that the early HIV/AIDS voluntary agencies, despite the pattern of the epidemic, were not especially gay-oriented organisations. On the contrary, there is evidence to suggest that those organisations that did have their origins in the lesbian and gay community went out of their way to emphasise that they were generic AIDS Service Organisations (ASOs). It is this set of circumstances that has given rise to the issue of 'de-gaying'. Briefly, de-gaying has been defined as:

> the denial or downplaying of the involvement of gay men in the HIV epidemic, even when gay men continue to constitute the group most severely affected, and when the lesbian and gay community continues to play a pioneering role in non-governmental (and some-times) governmental responses, such as the development of policy or the provision of services to people living with HIV.   (King, 1993, p. 169)

This raises three types of question: (1) the extent to which it is accu-rate to talk about 'de-gaying' as having taken place within the HIV/ AIDS voluntary sector; (2) the extent to which such an analysis ignores or downplays the needs of other groups at risk of HIV and AIDS; and (3) the extent to which contemporary social policy actually addresses the needs and specific experiences of those people most at risk.

THE DE-GAYING AND RE-GAYING OF AIDS

In Britain, the concept of de-gaying has informed the work of a number of gay writers and others long active in the field of HIV and AIDS, for example, Simon Watney (1994), Edward King (1993) and Peter Scott (1993). However, understanding the development of responses to AIDS in terms of de-gaying is not limited to Britain. Cindy Patton, for example, has used the term to account for the links between homophobia and the way in which AIDS has been conceptualised, as well as offering a critique of the way in which voluntary-sector organ-isations such as Gay Men's Health Crisis (New York) have been trans-formed from a radical grass roots origin to professionalised bureaucratic agencies (Patton, 1990; see also Altman, 1993).

As has been amply documented (e.g. Weeks, 1993), AIDS in Brit-ain and most other Western countries was originally thought of as a disease which affected gay men only. Since gay men were, in Britain, the first to die of AIDS-related illnesses, there evolved an almost metonymic link between the two 'diseases' – homosexuality and AIDS. At the same time, gay men began to organise to meet the need for information and support of those who were already infected, and to educate others about how to avoid infection. Thus in terms of the epidemiology, and the social responses to that, AIDS rapidly acquired the status of a 'gay disease' – a disease with a corresponding socio-sexuality which served to contain the danger, apparently limiting it to a deviant outsider category of persons.

By the mid-1980s, fears that the epidemic was also likely to affect 'normal' people began to be voiced. In Britain and the United States, government officials predicted that the epidemic could spread into the general population, and parallels were drawn with the African epidemic. An attempt was made to shift the emphasis from categories of person who were (or were not) at risk, to types of behaviour which were (or were not) risky.

Organisations formed to assist people with HIV infection were also being transformed both in terms of the dominant discourses they used, and in terms of their relationships with funding agencies. Thus voluntary-sector organisations began to emphasise that they were not gay organisations as such, but offered their services to anyone affected by HIV. Simultaneously, they began to rely more on funds from state agencies which led to an increased professionalisation of personnel, whereby gay identity became secondary to professional identity, and to an increased conformity to statutory models of organisation, including the adoption of equal opportunities policies, a desire for 'respectability', and fear that failure to conform would mean discontinuation of funds.

This 'de-gaying' of voluntary-sector organisations was acutely felt in the area of HIV prevention work. Gay men who had been involved in initial community-based efforts to educate other gay men about safer sex practices began to experience difficulty in continuing such work through voluntary-sector organisations keen to reiterate the message that anyone could be affected by AIDS, and concerned that state funders might object to explicit safer sex education for gay men. At the same time, statutory-sector agencies had begun to undertake generic HIV prevention work, and work targeting a range of specific constituencies such as women, young people and people from minority ethnic communities.

In the light of these developments, research was conducted in 1992 which sought to confirm the assertion that HIV prevention work with gay men was not being carried out. King *et al.* (1992) surveyed 226 agencies – health authorities, local authorities and voluntary organisations – to find out what HIV prevention initiatives targeting gay and bisexual men were being undertaken. Their study found that there was an 'alarmingly low level' of such work, even though gay and bisexual men continued to be the group most at risk (King *et al.*, 1992, p. 1). Respondents gave various reasons why this might be, such as difficulties associated with contacting gay men (including the belief that there were no gay men in the area); having elected to work with other – or no specific – target groups; believing that work with gay men was too sensitive or illegal; and believing that HIV prevention with gay men was already being carried out by other agencies (cf. King *et al.*, 1992, pp. 12–14).

The establishment in 1992 of GMFA as a new voluntary agency can be linked directly to the frustration of certain gay men long active in the field of HIV and AIDS with the politics and effects of what they would come to describe as de-gaying. The formation of GMFA was, therefore, an attempt to redress the imbalances some saw, and to initiate the process of 're-gaying' AIDS. One of the founding members describes the origins of GMFA thus:

> there'd been a invisible college of a number of gay men working in the field who were extremely dissatisfied and distressed at the response to the epidemic as it affected them throughout the sectors, and we'd been talking for something like two years about the need to set up a specific organisation which refocused upon gay men's needs because nobody else seemed to be . . . doing it. (Founding member, Gay Men Fighting AIDS)

A more explicitly gay form of campaigning was seen as essential if GMFA were to begin to influence how resources are allocated. Through articles and advertisements in the gay press, posters, postcards and concerted efforts to recruit gay male volunteers to the organisation, the group quickly sought to make itself and its position known. GMFA argued strongly in favour of re-allocating resources to meet the need, now well documented through epidemiological data and the demonstrated paucity of HIV prevention work targeting gay and bisexual men.

At the same time, GMFA volunteers began to devise and implement small, local-level HIV prevention initiatives. These were part of a training process for volunteers and a demonstration that ordinary gay men were capable of doing such work (as they had done, it was argued, in the early days of the epidemic). Both were seen as necessary as GMFA leaders began to negotiate with statutory bodies for funds to carry out larger-scale work. What was being sought was the power to influence resource allocation, and the power to devise prevention strategies un-encumbered by the ethos of statutory agencies, or voluntary-sector agencies perceived to have been de-gayed. Underlying such an approach were two key assumptions: first, that underpinning the de-gaying process was an 'institutionalised homophobia'; and, second, that a strategy of health promotion based on 'community mobilisation' had been successful in the early stages of the epidemic, but was in danger of being lost because of de-gaying.

The authors of the 1992 survey of gay men's HIV prevention initiatives remarked that 'underlying all of the reasons given for failing to do work with gay and bisexual men we may detect varieties of homophobia, whether passive or active, frank or implicit, institutional or individual' (King *et al.*, 992, p. 5). Institutions failed to meet the needs of gay men, to resource health education/promotion specifically for them because their primary concern was not for the lives of gay men, but to ensure that infection did not 'enter' the heterosexual pool. They also failed to meet the needs of gay men because there have been no real precedents for acknowledging and funding the real needs of gay men.

Against this is counterposed a model of health promotion which prioritises community mobilisation. The existence, it is argued, of a 'moral community' of gay men in the early 1980s provided the basis for a process of health awareness and perception of risk which led to a rapid development of techniques of 'safer sex'. GMFA, for example, claims that the early days of the epidemic saw a reduction in HIV infection because gay men themselves 'passed on the word' about how to have safer sex, on how to avoid infection. The methodology employed by GMFA – community mobilisation – seeks to create the conditions whereby that 'naturally occurring' safer sex movement will be repeated. This strategy requires that there be a 'community' to mobilise, and so it is argued HIV prevention work should begin in the nucleus of gay communities that already exist, most obviously, among men with a confident gay identity who use gay structures, venues and community groups. When questioned about the role of GMFA, one volunteer replied:

> to be very basic it's there for the survival of the gay community. Without organisations like GMFA, the gay community will die or be driven underground. . . . The amount of gay men that are coming out and amount of gay men that are dying will soon overtake each other because HIV and AIDS is not limited to age barriers . . . so

unless there are organisations such as GMFA to educate people . . .
not just about sex but about gay sex, gay way of life, the age of
consent, issues regarding couples and council houses and not being
able to leave it to your partner, unless people know about discrimination such as that it won't change. (Volunteer, Gay Men Fighting
AIDS)

Such an analysis marks a striking change of emphasis from the early
days of the epidemic when AIDS activists emphasised the importance
of making the distinction between 'risk groups' and 'risk activities'. It
was the latter, it was argued, that should be targeted, because everyone was potentially at risk unless they modified behaviour which could
transmit the virus. To target the former would be to remain complicit
with a discourse which blamed gay men for the epidemic.

There are, however, some problems with the above analysis. First,
it assumes that 'de-gaying' had taken place across the board, whereas
it may be more appropriate to suggest that most HIV and AIDS voluntary organisations were not in a position to be de-gayed because
they were never explicitly gay to start with. As part of our study of
voluntary-sector responses, we have looked closely at two non-Lon-
don organisations in areas of relatively low HIV prevalence. The first,
a local volunteer-led community group, has one part-time paid worker
and between 30 and 40 volunteers. Although the group was originally
formed by a core of individuals, predominantly gay men, who were
dissatisfied with the then existing Body Positive local group, members
are keen to stress they have never been a gay-oriented organisation.
The group's constitution for example states that one of their primary
aims is 'To promote the benefit of the inhabitants (of the local community) living with HIV and AIDS without distinction of sex, sexual
orientation, race or of political, religious or other opinions' However,
the vast majority of support for the group, particularly with regard
to fundraising, comes from the local gay community. As one member
put it:

This group isn't just for gay people, it's for heterosexual people,
men, women, children, haemophiliacs, drug addicts . . . It's for everyone. . . . I could never stand any group anywhere and being part of
it and saying its only for gay people. . . . Talking about the gay
community, the group is very much on the gay scene, very, very
well known and in every gay pub and club we have our leaflets,
our posters.

The other agency, a significant regional one founded in the mid-1980s, again had a strong lesbian and gay membership and staffing, and most people in the area affected by HIV were gay men, but it has always seen itself as a generic agency. Indeed, it is only in the past few years, with statutory funding, that it has been able to support explicitly gay outreach work. This in turn has led to tensions within the organisation over the priority that should be given to this sort of activity, and its weakening effect on other, broader-based activities. It is an ironic fact that statutory funding for gay health promotion has been seen as undermining the generic ambitions of a gay founded and run service agency.

Both of these examples illustrate the point that while staff and volunteers might be lesbian and gay, and specific work (fundraising, outreach) may be targeted at the gay community, beyond large centres like London there may be no alternative but for voluntary agencies to be generalist in their work. This contrast does not in itself invalidate the arguments of GMFA, but it highlights the difficulties of developing a community-based model of HIV/AIDS health promotion that would be straightforwardly applicable throughout the country.

THE BROADENING CONSTITUENCY OF AIDS

The recognition of different populations at risk, and of their diverse needs, has posed difficult questions about the sensitivity and appropriateness of existing services. The articulation of new needs, or existing needs that are unmet within current service provision, coupled with the release of public funds, stimulated the emergence of a whole range of HIV/AIDS groups during the 1980s. To exemplify the diversity of the response, such groups included Positively Women, founded in 1987 by a small group of women in response to the lack of appropriate support services available at that time to women living with HIV; Positively Irish Action on AIDS, founded in 1989 by a group of Irish HIV and drug workers and Irish gay men who were increasingly concerned about the number of Irish people with drug and HIV problems; the NAZ project, formed in 1991 by a group of concerned and affected people who felt that the needs of South Asian, Turkish, Irani and Arab communities were not being adequately addressed by the statutory and voluntary sectors; Blackliners, which came into being as a telephone helpline in 1989 out of concern that people of African, Asian and Caribbean descent living with or affected by HIV/AIDS did not have the much-needed sources of information and advice; and the Black HIV/AIDS Network (BHAN), formed in 1988 to offer self-help and provide services to Asian and African–Caribbean people living with and affected by HIV and AIDS.

The emergence of these new community-based groups was made easier because of a conscious policy reaction by some local authorities. Influenced by the notion of general risk, these authorities applied an equal opportunities framework to their resource distribution, targeting their funding at specific communities in response to a new recognition of identity. Some, within minority communities, have been highly critical of the resulting 'category policies':

> While great progressive social changes have resulted from self or-
> ganised communities that are based in a collective identification,
> this is not the same as the identity politics that is dominant in parts
> of the voluntary sector and in some local authorities and which in-
> forms a great deal of work around race, gender, sexuality, disability
> and HIV disease. (BHAN, 1991, p. 9)

The danger of such a critical response, however, is that it suggests that the flourishing of these new community-based groups was the result of a top-down decision. Our own research suggests that organis-ations such as Blackliners did not simply arise because there was money available, but were born out of the sense of exclusion and the identi-fication of real need by the people themselves. However, this devel-opment coincided with efforts to decouple AIDS from homosexual identity. As noted above, the need to stress that 'AIDS is everyone's problem' led to a shift in the nature of much HIV/AIDS health promo-tion activity. The coupled effects of the shift in understanding from high-risk groups to high-risk activity, and the homophobic responses to AIDS as the gay plague, led to attempts to unravel the 'natural' association of AIDS with a gay identity/lifestyle. It is precisely this juncture in the late 1980s – the identification of unmet need; the re-sulting, and sometimes inflexible application of an equal opportunities response; a lack of adequate understanding of the epidemiology of the disease; and a movement within gay/AIDS activists to delink practices and identity – that led to the development of 'diverse' needs-led com-munity based organisations.

In America, Cindy Patton (1990) has documented the rise of the new HIV/AIDS groups which addressed the needs of African American, Latino, Haitian and Asian communities. She argues that these newly emergent group developed for two reasons, out of existing multi-service agencies and cultural affirmation projects, and as projects with a more liberationist ethos. Pointing to the fact that 'government planners, the media and funders often failed to recognise how communities of colour organise around AIDS by extending church or community programmes' (Patton, 1990, p.11), she argues that the planning of service provision had not taken into account the diversity of social formations and the different philosophies of particular communities that would impact on appropriate HIV/AIDS provision. In some respects, the British experience has closely followed the American situation:

> We know of many Black people who have been made clearly unwelcome in some voluntary sector organisations, particularly if they are heterosexual or women, or go with their family, even though the services are clearly intended for all people living with HIV and AIDS. The low use of support services established by well known voluntary organisations extends even to many Black gay men living with HIV. There have also been some serious incidents of racial harassment and abuse of black people with AIDS attending voluntary organisations. (BHAN, 1991, p. 40)

The argument suggests that within a few years of their inception many of the existing organisations were not meeting the needs of the Black communities. While Black people facing HIV/AIDS will share some of the same needs as white people, others will be specific to their race and ethnic experience (e.g. poorer housing conditions, a greater likelihood of unemployment, racial discrimination in health care and in housing allocation, racial violence and harassment). Their medical condition is thus only one of many problems they may face.

This justification for specialist services is in part a critique of existing services, but also a demand for greater choice in health care – people are more comfortable with services which address their particular needs. This has led to changes in some organisations targeting the Black population. Blackliners, for example, in its short history has shifted many of its priorities. As already stated, it began as a helpline managed by volunteers from diverse backgrounds. In the early days, many of the calls received were from Black gay men. Five years after its foundation it continues to provide services for gay men and other men who have sex with men, but also offers services for single women, women with children and other groups in need. Blackliners believe that it is important they acknowledge the diversity within their own client groups, as well as the more subtle workings of culture:

> There's your Afro-Caribbeans, Africans, Asians, even within different Asian communities, the people operate differently and culture is to do with lots of things, it's not just to do with your colour.... It's not about all this lumping of people together, it doesn't work. (Management Committee Member, Blackliners)

The existence of organisations such as Blackliners and BHAN is not only a response to existing service provision, or lack of services, it is also bound up with the history of the epidemic, and media representations of HIV and AIDS. For many Black people, AIDS has been presented not only as a gay disease, but also as an African disease. Such media sensationalism stigmatised people living with HIV and AIDS, and acted as a pressure to hide HIV/AIDS in Black communities.

The situation becomes even more complex when looking at individual social and sexual experiences. Many Black men who have sex with men do not identify as gay, and many Black lesbians' and gay men's activities are separate from the 'white' scene. In daily life, therefore, there are important practical questions about where to go for services, be they from the gay community, the Black community or the wider social relations of the family.

In other words, different minority communities can and do make the same claims for specialist directed services as gay activists around AIDS. As King (1993, p. 271) states, 'it would be unthinkable to attack an organisation such as Positively Women ... because it does not provide services for men; or to criticise the Black HIV/AIDS Network ... for not working with white people. These organisations are properly recognised as being not separatist, but specialist.' In fact, it is precisely the need for specialist groups that offers support to recent demands for a re-gaying of AIDS. If specialisation is the best way to get an appropriate model of provision, then gay men need their own specialist groups.

However, this attempt to re-prioritise gay men's needs has not gone without comment. In a polemical article in Mainliners' newsletter, Nicola Field has argued strongly against the existence of organisations such as GMFA:

> Fighting solely on one issue and from one corner, GMFA does nothing to challenge the system and undermines the gradual moves towards

unity that have been growing since the mid-1980s. (Field, 1993, p. 20)

She sees AIDS as a 'crisis of poverty, homophobia, racism and misogyny' (Field, 1993, p. 20), and accuses GMFA of 'ducking issues' which link struggles. Although it is easy to write off her views as 'queer bashing', her thoughts probably echo wider reservations voiced elsewhere within the voluntary sector about specialist gay organisations. Our own research suggests, however, that such a view is misguided. It would be absurd to argue that all groups regarded as at risk need specialist and targeted services, except for gay men. Gay men are still the group most affected by HIV, and it is clear that the gay community requires culturally sensitive services and targeted health promotion as much as any other group. On the other hand, in most parts of Britain, there is no scope or opportunity for specialist agencies addressing the needs of a specific community. The best that can be expected is targeted services within more generalist organisations. Within such organisations, a community mobilisation model might well be an appropriate one by which to address the needs of the gay population. It is not, however, the only available health promotion model. What our analysis suggests is that services, statutory as well as voluntary, need to be acutely sensitive to the differences of particular communities at risk – their histories, their communal norms and traditions, and their assessed needs.

TARGETING

The evolution of the HIV/AIDS voluntary sector illustrates the need for services and wider social policies to be targeted to the needs of specific communities. The difficulty, however, lies in the fact that this has to happen in a cultural climate influenced by several contradictory factors. First, as we have seen, a number of early AIDS service organisations which were rooted in the gay community have achieved a certain legitimacy by stressing that they are not specifically gay organisations, but meet the needs of all at risk. This hard-won credibility is unlikely to be readily abandoned. Second, the emergence of organisations to articulate the needs of other groups at risk has diversified the HIV/AIDS voluntary sector, and created potentially competitive interests and diverging emphasis in relation to targeting. Third, all of this is occurring in a climate where there is a developing funding crisis (Hopper, 1992), and where government emphasis on targeting may have different implications from those of the community based agencies themselves (Weeks *et al.*, 1994a).

Shifts in government policy, in fact, provide the crucial context for understanding recent developments in the HIV/AIDS voluntary sector. The National Health Service and Community Care Act 1990 resulted in a 'shifting climate' for both the voluntary and statutory sectors characterised by a sharp demarcation between the statutory sector as the 'purchasers' of services, and the voluntary sector as 'providers'. While there might be some potential benefits in such a system, in providing 'quality' and 'choice' of services to clients, while ensuring the targeting of resources to areas of greatest need, commentators have also focused on the complex contracting arrangements and increased bureaucratic procedures that have ensued.

The extent to which AIDS community-based groups have entered into the arena of service contracts depends largely on their own relationship with the statutory sector, and their ability to attract puchasers. This, in turn, is influenced by a range of factors including the group's own organisational culture, their style and structure of management, and the extent to which funders see them as a 'professional' organisation (Weeks *et al.*, 1994a). These important criteria are viewed by funders as a means of gauging how able a group is in coping with more explicit criteria for funding. However, funders may also rely on their own political sensibilities and discretion when entering into funding negotiations with potential voluntary-sector providers.

Although government rhetoric seems to advocate the targeting of resources to those populations most affected, recent cuts in Section 64 funding and the ending of ring-fenced money will directly affect HIV voluntary organisations who may be 'better placed than statutory bodies to reach those populations most at risk' (Rudd, 1993, p. 8). This may, however, lead to HIV/AIDS voluntary organisations having to compete with other voluntary organisations who cater for more 'popular' constituencies; the loss of HIV-specific posts; a breakdown in collaboration between the voluntary sector and statutory sector particularly in the area of HIV prevention for marginalised groups such as gay men; the loss of intersectoral developmental strategies; and a reduction in the range and quality of specialist HIV/AIDS services in favour of more mainstream activities.

The implications of such far-reaching cuts in community-based initiatives are many. In some parts of the country, for example, HIV-related prevention and care is provided solely by voluntary organisations via the deployment of statutory funding. This has raised fears that, with the amount of money available to statutory agencies shrinking, contracts may not be offered to voluntary agencies that are too 'political' or deemed to represent 'unpopular' or 'marginalised' groups such as gay men.

In a recent workshop attended by a range of national and local HIV voluntary organisations (Weeks *et al.*, 1994b), Trisha Plummer of Blackliners suggested that the advent of a contracting culture and increasing restraints on resources would necessitate painful choices being made over prioritisation, equal opportunities, and specialisation versus generic services. The integration of HIV/AIDS services into more generalist provision, she suggested, is proceeding alongside the targeting of resources and services, and has obvious advantages both in addressing HIV/AIDS and in combating the continued stigmatisation and marginalisation of those particular populations most affected and most at risk.

For many agencies, however, not only does the ending of ring-fencing and the gathering pace of 'mainstreaming' mean that purchasers are now at liberty to 'select' the type of voluntary-sector providers they fund, regardless of the local epidemiology, but also that purchasers are at liberty to determine the level of local HIV-specific services they provide. The move towards generalised HIV education and funding seems only to further marginalise the needs of those most at risk.

Targeting, therefore, has a dual implication. If intended as the necessary channelling of inevitably limited resources to those most at risk, it opens opportunities for meeting the criticisms of groups like GMFA. If, on the other hand, it means targeting resources to those organisations which are least challenging or controversial, least 'political', it can have the effect of magnifying the impact of the epidemic within the communities most at risk, among those who tend still to be the most marginal and least 'popular' parts of the population.

This returns us to the discussion of the concept of community with which we opened this chapter. It is clear that without the mobilising energy provided by communities at risk, the response to HIV/AIDS would have been severely retarded. Yet at the same time, voluntary action on its own has neither the scope nor resources to combat the growing magnitude of the challenge posed by the epidemic. Diverse communities are a reality. They are also a model ideal, offering a stance from what could be achieved through which we can see the limitations of what has been achieved. The communities struggling to articulate need are offering an image of what is both necessary and desirable.

Governments, on the other hand, have a responsibility to choose between often conflicting priorities in a context of limited resources. Not all needs can be met. But if government ignores the voices of those at risk, then the dimensions of the crisis are likely to grow as scarce resources are misdirected. Particular communities can articulate need, campaign, provide support and care for those falling ill or dying, but without the properly targeted support of the community as a whole, as represented in statutory agencies, they cannot hope to cope with all the dimensions of the epidemic. This is why community-based organisations have been essential and necessary elements in combating HIV and AIDS, but on their own their actions can never be sufficient. A successful voluntary sector still requires an activist and compassionate state.

REFERENCES

Aggleton, P., Weeks, J. and Taylor-Laybourn, A. (1993) 'Voluntary Sector Responses to HIV and AIDS: A Framework for Analysis', in P. Aggleton, P. Davies and G. Hart (eds), *AIDS: Facing the Second Decade* (London: Falmer Press).
Altman, D. (1993) 'Expertise, Legitimacy and the Centrality of Community', in P. Aggleton, P. Davies and G. Hart (eds), *AIDS: Facing the Second Decade* (London: Falmer Press).
Berridge, V. (1993) 'Introduction', in V. Berridge and P. Strong (eds), *AIDS and Contemporary History* (Cambridge: Cambridge University Press).
BHAN (Black HIV and AIDS Network) (1991) *AIDS and the Black Communities* (London: Grosvenor).
Department of Health (1992) *HIV Infection: The Working Interface Between Voluntary Organisations and Social Services Departments* (London: Social Services Inspectorate/The AIDS Unit).
Field, N. (1993) *Mainliners Newsletter*, reprinted in *Rouge*, 12: pp. 20–1.
Hopper, C. (1992) 'The Role of the Voluntary Sector', in *HIV and AIDS in the Community*, Occasional Paper no. 2 (London: All Party Parliamentary Group on AIDS).
King, E. (1993) *Safety in Numbers* (London: Cassell).
King, E., Rooney, M. and Scott, P. (1992) *HIV Prevention for Gay Men: A Summary of Initiatives in the UK* (London: North West Thames Regional Health Authority).
Patton, C. (1990) *Inventing AIDS* (New York: Routledge).
Rudd, L. (1993) 'Analysis', *AIDS Matters*, 13: p. 18.
Scott, P. (1993) 'Appendix 1: Gay and Bisexual Men or Men who have Sex with Men?', in B. Evans, S. Sandberg and S. Watson (eds), *Healthy Alliances in HIV Prevention* (London: Health Education Authority).

Watney, S. (1994) *Practices of Freedom: Selected Writings on HIV/AIDS* (London: Rivers Oram Press).

Weeks, J. (1993) 'AIDS and the Regulation of Sexuality', in V. Berridge and P. Strong (eds), *AIDS and Contemporary History* (Cambridge: Cambridge University Press).

Weeks, J., Taylor-Laybourn A. and Aggleton, P. (1994a) 'An Anatomy of the HIV Voluntary Sector in Britain', in P. Aggleton, P. Davies and G. Hart (eds), *AIDS, Foundations for the Future* (London: Taylor & Francis).

Weeks, J., Aggleton, P., McKevitt, C., Parkison, K., Taylor-Laybourn, A. and Whitty, G. (1994b) *Maintaining Momentum: Voluntary Sector Responses to HIV and AIDS* (London: HERU, Institute of Education, University of London).

9 Prostitution and the Contours of Control

JULIA O'CONNELL DAVIDSON

Feminist thinkers have long been concerned to explore parallels between marriage, prostitution, slavery and wage labour, as well as the sexual, political and economic relations that underpin these institutions (see Jackson, 1994). For those radical feminists who foreground the sexual domination and political subordination of women by men in their analyses of gender inequality, prostitution is the unambiguous embodiment of male oppression. It reduces women to bought objects, it allows men temporary, but direct, control over the prostitute, and increases their existing social control over all women by affirming their masculinity and patriarchal rights of access to women's bodies (Barry, 1979, 1984; Dworkin, 1987; Pateman, 1988). Prostitution is, for such commentators, a form of slavery: 'Free prostitution does not exist . . . prostitution of women [is] always by force . . . it is a violation of human rights and an outrage to the dignity of women' (Barry, 1991, quoted in Van der Gaag, 1994, p. 6). Since no person willingly volunteers to have their human rights and dignity violated, it follows from radical feminist analyses that the decision to exchange sex for money is always and necessarily forced and irrational. The logic of such arguments, combined with the liberal use of military metaphors, produces self-contradictory, but equally unpleasant and patronising, visions of the prostitute woman. One moment she is a tragic, front-line casualty, the next she is a self-serving collaborator betraying her sisters.

Although critics of this school of thought certainly do not speak as one, many academics and researchers as well as prostitute organisations and most groups campaigning for prostitute's rights make a strong distinction between what is termed 'free choice' prostitution by adults and all forms of forced and child prostitution (see Delacoste and Alexander, 1988; Brussa, 1991; Mr A. de Graaf Foundation, 1994). Whilst the latter is to be outlawed and resisted, the former is held to be a type of paid work, a job like any other. In this 'sex work' camp, there are liberals who view 'free choice' prostitution in the same way that they view the capitalist employment relation, namely, as a mutual voluntary exchange.

Where the voluntary, contractual character of the prostitute–client exchange is emphasised, a view of prostitution is constructed which diametrically opposes that produced by radical feminists. It is argued that, unlike wives whose legal right to refuse sexual access to their husbands was only even formally established in Britain in 1991, prostitutes actually exercise a great deal of power and control over their sexuality. It has even been asserted that, in contracting out their sexual services, women prostitutes are *resisting* patriarchy by refusing to allow any one man ownership of their bodies. Roberts (1992, p. 355), for example, insists that 'implicit in the demand that women have control over their own bodies is that they also have the right to sell their sexual services', and that because of her financial and sexual autonomy, the 'whore is dangerously free'. In the same way that seventeenth-century political philosophers provided a justification for wage labour by insisting that a person's labour is property that can be freely alienated, the idea is that by exchanging their sexual services across a market prostitutes can secure freedom from the yoke of patriarchal ownership.

Although there is very little reliable data on the socio-economic background of British prostitutes, existing empirical data from North America and a number of European countries (see Bowker, 1978; Bracey, 1979; Jarvinen, 1993) suggests that it is primarily 'women from the working class and the lumpenproletariat who are recruited into prostitution' (Hoigard and Finstad, 1992, p. 15), and there is also evidence to suggest that women of colour, who experience multiple oppressions in 'racist' societies (see hooks, 1981; Hill Collins, 1991; Mama, 1992), are over-represented in prostitution. In the USA, it is estimated that approximately 40 per cent of street prostitutes are women of colour (Alexander, 1988, p. 197), and in Amsterdam's red light district, the Mr A. de Graaf Foundation, a research organisation campaigning for the legalisation of prostitution, estimates that over 50 per cent of street and window prostitutes are of African, Latino or South-East Asian descent. Preliminary analysis of British contact magazines by this author suggests that women of African Caribbean descent are hugely over-represented in this form of work, constituting around 18 per cent of prostitutes using this advertising medium.

This chapter draws on an ethnographic study of a successful and independent white British prostitute (who will be referred to as Desiree), her receptionists and her clients.[1] Desiree is, therefore, probably at best representative of only a very small elite of prostitutes. Despite her atypicality, however, an examination of the transactions she enters into with clients does usefully highlight a number of theoretical problems.

In particular, her experience suggests that issues of power, control and consent in prostitution are rather more complex than either the radical feminist or the liberal sex-work model imply. At a more general level, the material presented in this chapter suggests that because the phenomenon of prostitution refuses to fit neatly into existing empirical and theoretical categories such as 'slavery' or 'wage labour', it represents an important challenge for contemporary social theory.

DESIREE'S BUSINESS

Desiree owns a house in a residential area of a Midlands town from which she operates what is, effectively, a small business selling sexual services. She advertises in the classified section of a national tabloid and in contact magazines, she employs a receptionist to deal with enquiries and bookings and, on average, sees between six and ten clients daily. In Britain, it is the activities associated with prostitution (loitering, soliciting, running a 'house of ill-repute', benefiting from 'immoral earnings' and so on) which are illegal, not the actual act of exchanging sex for money. Because Desiree does not solicit from the streets and is the only sex worker on her premises, she does not attract unwanted attention from the vice squad.[2]

The market for heterosexual prostitution, like that for homosexual prostitution (see West 1992), appears to be segmented, with street workers catering primarily to men who want cheap 'quickies', and women like Desiree catering to men who are better off and/or more cautious or inexperienced, as well as to men who have more demanding requirements in terms of skill, equipment and props. Where local street prostitutes charge between £20 and £25 for penetrative sex, and men visiting massage parlours will pay about £35 for the same service, Desiree's rate is £70. Prices for hand, breast and oral 'relief' are also significantly higher from self-employed prostitutes like Desiree. Domination clients, meanwhile, are willing to pay upwards of £80 a session and, increasingly, Desiree is specialising as a dominatrix. She has turned one room into a fully equipped 'dungeon' and invested in an extensive range of PVC and leather garments. She has also read widely and devoted a great deal of thought to developing specialist skills. In short, Desiree serves what could be described as a high-priced, niche market. Running her business in this way, Desiree reaps substantial financial rewards from self employed prostitution. She regularly turns over between £1000 and £2000 per week and, after four years in the business full time, she has saved around £30,000 in cash, owns two properties, a BMW and another small business. For a more detailed account of her business, see O'Connell Davidson (1995).

POWER AND CONTROL IN THE PROSTITUTE–CLIENT TRANSACTION

Desiree designs and plans all aspects of her business: where and how to advertise, who to employ and what tasks to assign to them, the pricing system, what services are and are not on offer, the hours and days of business. In this sense, she exercises more control over her working life than do a majority of workers. It would also be over-simplistic to describe her as powerless in relation to the individual client. To begin with, Desiree actually has far more experience of prostitute–client encounters than does any punter. Many clients are (deliciously) anxious about visiting a prostitute, and they are diffident and uncertain as they approach the house and knock on the front door. As one client explained: 'You don't know the set up, you don't know who'll be behind the door. It might be a con. You might get robbed or anything'.

Providing that Desiree is not already with a client, she unchains and opens the door herself, standing half hidden behind the door, wearing a low cut shirt, a barely visible lycra skirt, suspenders, stockings and very high-heeled shoes. As soon as the man steps over the threshold, she shuts the door behind him, beams and says 'Hi, how are you? Would you like to come up?' and walks him up the stairs to the massage room. Apart from the dungeon, the house is decorated entirely in pink and grey. It is scrupulously clean and neat and somehow reminiscent of a fashionable private dentist's surgery. The massage room has a grey tiled floor and a medical feel to it. There is a trolley stocked with oils, creams, surgical gloves, tissues and condoms, and a couch of black plastic and tubular steel, covered by a paper sheet of the type used by doctors and dentists. Here, Desiree tells the client to take off his clothes and lie down, whereupon she gives him a brief and spurious massage. During this, the more confident or experienced client will generally tell her the kind of services he requires, but with the inexperienced client, it is Desiree who has to lead the conversation and discover whether he wants hand relief or penetrative sex, with or without a uniform, etc.

If the client wants penetrative sex, Desiree leads him from the massage room to another room which is similarly impersonal in ambience, but equipped with a double bed. A range of uniforms and outfits hang in view of the client, as do a selection of whips, crops, restraints and chains, so that he can see what is on offer and ask for any 'extras' he happens to fancy. Tape-recordings of sessions with nervous, inexperienced clients suggest that Desiree is very much in control of the situation here as well. The following extracts from one tape show how Desiree guides the client through the various stages of the transaction:

Stage 1: Settling him in

Desiree: Can I just move these things out of the way, is that all right?
Client: Yes, yes, thank you.
Desiree: I'll put your clothes over here so they don't get whatever all over them . . .
Client: Thank you. Thank you.
Desiree: Right, you make yourself comfortable over there, I'll just get some creams. . . . OK. Would you like to move along for me?
Client: Sorry.
[Desiree picks up her vibrator.]
Desiree: Have you played with one of these before?
Client: No, I haven't [nervous laughter].

Stage 2: Getting him going

Desiree: OK, you hold it a moment. Do you want me to do it for you? Put that in. Yes. I think we're getting some reaction now [referring to the fact that client is by now beginning to achieve an erection].
Client: Yes. Sorry it's taking a bit long. . . . It's a bit small. Sorry.
Desiree: No, it's not. You're fine. It's perfectly formed, [laughs] it's fine.

Stage 3: Getting him to 'Shoot his Load'

[Desiree is on top of the client, he is lying still.]
Desiree: Do you like this?
Client: Yes.
Desiree: Oh yes, oh yes [starts gasping, heavy breathing, less than 60 seconds pass until he laughs].
Client: That was it.

Stage 4: Reassuring him

Desiree: There, it wasn't as bad as you thought was it? . . . You seemed ever so nervous. I wondered what you were expecting.
Client: I've never done it before so I was, I didn't know what to expect.
Desiree: Well, I hope it was nicer than you thought.
Client: Yes, thank you.

Stage 5: Normalising and getting him out

Desiree: The shower's through there and there's plenty of hot water.
Client: Thank you. Do you want the money before I go through?
Desiree: Yes, that'll be fine.
Client: £70?
Desiree: Yes, that's right, that's lovely.
Client: Thank you very much, thank you.
Desiree: OK. What are you doing for the rest of the day? Anything exciting planned?

[Desiree then makes polite and very impersonal conversation as he gets dressed and shows him out.]

This kind of client relies on Desiree to script the encounter and she can get such men in and out of the house in fifteen minutes. But even when dealing with punters who regularly visit prostitutes, who are confident and who know exactly what they want, Desiree's far greater sexual skill and knowledge allows her to exert some control over how much of her sexual labour she provides in exchange for a set fee. She is highly skilled at getting clients to come (and therefore to go) very quickly. Though the receptionists tell prospective customers over the phone that the £70 fee for a 'full personal service' entitles them to an hour of Desiree's time, and though many men fondly imagine themselves to be such studs that an hour will not suffice, in practice it is rare for any non-domination client to stay more than half an hour, and that includes time spent in the massage room, showering and getting dressed.

Even when clients arrive with a clear idea of the script that they want her to follow (some specify in advance the order of events that are to take place, the exact insults she is to hurl at them, the terminology she is to use to refer to body parts), Desiree still dictates the limits and terms of their interaction. She will not perform acts that she believes endanger her own health and she will not agree to practices which she personally finds too repulsive (like giving enemas), too intimate (like kissing), too hostile (like ejaculating in her face) or too risky (being restrained herself). If, having asked for hand relief, the client decides half way through that he would also like penetrative sex, Desiree will charge him for both. Although clients occasionally grumble, few attempt to insist or even ask for a refund. They do not know who else is in the building, their knowledge of the laws surrounding prostitution is usually minimal, and they are often fearful of blackmail or embarrassment.

Almost by definition, there is a level at which domination clients make themselves powerless in relation to Desiree. Again, this affords her some control over what she provides in exchange for a set fee. For instance, recently one of her regular domination clients expressed a desire to be shackled and beaten before penetrating her. 'It had been a long day and I just wasn't in the mood for it' she told me, so she flayed his penis, rather than his buttocks, and did so for so long and with such violence that it was impossible for him to go on to penetrate her. However, Desiree could only get away with doing this and keep his custom because she knew the client well enough to be certain that he would find this experience equally satisfying. Tape-recordings of sessions with unknown domination clients show that they do retain control at another level. They will interrupt her performance to ask for poppers (amyl nitrate, a legal drug used by some to enhance sexual pleasure) or to tell her that they have had enough.

There is also a sense in which domination clients, like all submissive parties in sado-masochistic sex, could be said to exercise control by relinquishing it (see Stoller, 1991) and certainly these clients are more emotionally demanding and time consuming than 'straight' punters who want penetrative sex or hand relief. Desiree is a highly skilled and versatile dominatrix, she does not simply beat these men, but crafts an immense variety of roles and scripts to meet their individual desires. One of Desiree's regulars, for example, wants her to role-play a strict school mistress. He brings along a schoolboy's outfit, a diary in which he has noted down his imaginary misdemeanours, and several pages of lines set by Desiree on the previous visit. Desiree spends a good fifteen minutes reading through and marking the material he has brought with him (promising one stroke for every mistake she finds), and because he once found her performance too convincing (he did not visit her for several months and when he returned said he had been upset because he thought that she was *really* angry with him), she takes care to inject a good deal of humour into the role-play that precedes his beating. Other domination clients are different, but equally exacting in their requirements, as the following extract from a letter to Desiree shows:

> I need twenty minutes or so of severe physical and sexual abuse; followed by a fairly "formal" beating. . . . I will have shackles attached to my wrists, ankles and genitals. Put the collar and lead on my neck. . . . Then lead me on my hands and knees to your 'salon'. Make me lie and roll around on the floor; stand over me . . . and generally abuse me as a body slave and sex-object. If I do not respond to my instructions quickly enough, or if I do the slightest thing wrongly, help me to be completely obedient with the cane or the crop.

He then goes on to provide a further page of detailed instructions on precisely how she is to dominate him and six rules which Desiree must not break, the first of which is 'You must NEVER chuckle, snigger or try to make me feel foolish.' To lead someone around on a dog leash, make them lie and roll around on the floor and so on without making them feel foolish clearly calls for quite staggering thespian skills on the part of a person who, like Desiree, has no personal interest in bondage and discipline sex play.

Two points need to be made about all this. First, it highlights a problem with the radical feminist insistence that prostitution reduces women to bought *objects*. As both dominatrix and 'straight' prostitute, Desiree performs intensive and highly skilled emotional labour in exchange for the client's money. She is far from simply the 'passive, inert, and open' object conjured up by, for example, Dworkin's (1987, pp. 181–2) feverish rhetoric. Second, it points to the limitations of those analyses which reduce the client's motivation to a simple and universal wish to exert and experience male power. Pateman, for example, holds that in buying the use of a woman's body, punters are simply securing an opportunity to exercise their patriarchal rights of access to women and thereby positively affirming their masculine identity. This forces her to deny that the commercial acts of a dominatrix can 'appropriately be called prostitution', tautologically defining prostitution as involving only those activities which constitute or are associated with 'the sex act' in order to sustain the argument that 'the institution of prostitution ensures that men can buy "the sex act" and so exercise their patriarchal right' (Pateman, 1988, p. 199).

There are, without doubt, clients whose sexual excitement is primarily and directly linked to the exercise of power over a woman whom they consider to be degraded and worthless,[3] but punters are not an entirely homogeneous group. To insist that the same ambition to affirm masculinity and male power drives both the nervous man featured in the transcript material above and the domination client whose letter to Desiree was quoted, for example, would be so sweeping and generalised as to be analytically redundant.

This section has attempted to show that the prostitute is not always, necessarily or inevitably powerless within the prostitute – client exchange. The remainder of this chapter seeks to show that if the question of what exactly is being purchased by the client (and thus of what exactly is being commodified by the prostitute) is examined more closely, issues of power and control begin to look so complex that they cannot be adequately accommodated within the analytical frameworks employed by radical feminists or liberals (or indeed many Marxists) as they stand. For, as is argued below, within prostitute – client exchange, the prostitute becomes a person who is not a person, a slave who is not a slave, and a wage worker who is not a wage worker.

A PERSON WHO IS NOT A PERSON

There is enormous diversity in terms of clients' demands and desires, yet clients do share something in common. All pay to step outside the complex web of rules, meanings, obligations and conventions which govern non-commercial sexuality. Because the prostitute enters into the transaction for economic reasons, she is indiscriminate about punters in terms of their age, physical appearance, 'racialised' identity, personality and so on. This means that, first, the client is freed from cultural definitions of what is and is not sexually attractive. It is not necessary to be socially or sexually skilled, charming, handsome, athletic or confident to 'pull' a prostitute. It also means that the client can transgress rules about the social identities of sexual partners, for instance those which dictate the 'proper' age difference between them, or those which insist on a shared 'racialised' identity. Moreover, no desire is too 'perverse', too insulting or too disgusting to be confessed to a prostitute (although, of course, some requests are refused). Prostitution thus enables the client to escape from the constraints and contradictions of his own gender, age, class and 'racialised' identity as well as from the social conventions governing sexuality.

In stepping outside this web of rules, the client is effectively securing access to a sort of twilight sexual realm wherein a man can have sex with a real, live, flesh and blood person and yet evade all the social obligations that go along with sexual relations between real, live people. For some clients, this represents freedom from the obligation to engage in what they consider to be 'normal' sex. Many of Desiree's domination and transvestite clients tell her that they are married (as a large proportion of all prostitutes' clients appear to be – see McLeod, 1982; Kinnell, 1989), but would not dream of telling their wives or indulging their tastes with any 'respectable' woman. Clients who pay for 'straight' sex often want both physical and psychic pleasures which they could not permit themselves in non-commercial sexual encounters – to have objects inserted in their anuses, to have the prostitute dressed as a schoolgirl, to call her a 'bitch' or a 'whore' as they approach climax. Others actually want to simulate a romantic attachment. They go to elaborate lengths to conceal the commercial aspect of the transaction, hide the cash payments, send valentine cards, bring chocolates and flowers, and generally enjoy the pleasures of a 'romance' without any real threat of intimacy. Whether he is submissive, flattering or abusive, the client's treatment of the prostitute represents a denial of her subjectivity and humanity, and this process of denial both draws upon and reinforces profoundly misogynistic images of women.

The author's preliminary research[4] suggests that 'racialised' barriers can also be temporarily evaded, suspended or reconstructed in this marginal sexual world. For example, prostitution removes many of the 'racialised' barriers which normally obstruct Asian men's sexual access to white women, and, more significantly, prostitution can divest certain 'racisms' of their power to impede white men's sexual access to Black women. hooks (1992, p. 27) has remarked on the white west's 'romantic fantasy of the "primitive" and ... concrete search for a real primitive paradise, whether that location be a country or a body, a dark continent or dark flesh', and white men who would not dream of 'dating' or marrying a Black woman can indulge a 'racialised' sexual fascination by purchasing temporary sexual access to the Black Other. The 'racist sexist fantasies' which 'set the ideological terrain for interactions between Black women and non-Blacks (as well as in relationships with Black men)' (Small, 1994, pp. 99–100) can be briefly enacted with a prostitute, enabling some white men to simultaneously express and transgress their own 'racisms', again without fear of any real intimacy.

Preliminary research also indicates that even in this marginal and transgressive world, the 'racialised' barrier between Black men and white women often remains intact. It is not uncommon for street walkers' pimps and sauna owners to tell 'their girls' to turn down Black punters on the basis of the 'racist' assumption that all Black men are pimps and thus potential competitors.

In short, prostitution typically allows the client to transgress the rules which he believes apply to sexual relationships and variously frees him from the confines of his masculinity (whether that be the 'burden' of machismo or the 'burden' of being a protector), from the restrictions that go along with his 'racialised' identity (securing him access to Otherness, whether idealised, denigrated or forbidden), and/or from the social meanings attached to his age (giving him license to have sexual contact with women who are either much younger or much older than himself). The client is thus liberated from the codes and conventions that tyrannise his non-commercial sexual encounters. Men who 'suffer' from erection 'problems' or 'premature' ejaculation, men with very small penises, fat men, shy men, lonely men, bald men, old men, masochistic men, sexually passive men, transvestite men, 'racist' white men, can all simply purchase 'time out' of those facets of 'racialised', gender and sexual ideologies which they find oppressive.

The corollary of this is that the prostitute must be, in an almost literal sense, all things to all men. She must become whatever the client wants her to be – variously nothing but a 'cunt', a voraciously hypersexual 'bitch', his own beloved paramour, the firm Mistress waiting to discipline him, the 'working girl' who has never been fucked by a real man before, even his lesbian lover. Indeed, the prostitute's skill and art lies in her ability to completely conceal all genuine feelings, beliefs, desires, preferences and personality (in short, her self) and appear as nothing more than the living embodiment of the client's fantasies. As Desiree puts it, 'I'm just a role, a fantasy for them. I don't exist for them as a person.' As well as paying for the sexual pleasure, physical labour and/or the making available of body parts, this means that the client is effectively paying the prostitute to be a person who is not a person. No matter how much control and discretion the prostitute exercises over the details of each exchange, the essence of the transaction is that she is an object, not a subject, within it. Does this mean, as some feminist commentators suggest, that prostitution is a form of slavery?

THE SLAVE WHO IS NOT A SLAVE

Some prostitutes in Britain are literally coerced into slave-like relationships with brothel owners or pimps, either by their status as illegal migrants (and given Britain's current immigration policies, it seems likely that women of colour will be most at risk of this), or by the use of force. But there are also some parallels between the experience of a successful, self-employed prostitute like Desiree and that of a slave. For no matter what her legal status, the prostitute becomes what Patterson (1982) might term 'socially dead' for the duration of each transaction, that is, a person without power, natality or honour. Patterson holds that the slave is not distinguished by the fact that others exercise property rights over him or her, for these rights are also exercised over people who are not enslaved (husbands, wives and children, for example), but by the fact s/he cannot exercise claims, rights and powers over things or other persons. Likewise, the prostitute cannot be distinguished from other sexual partners by the fact that clients make claims over her or demands within the sexual encounter (people do this in non-commercial relationships as well) but only by the fact that she is not entitled to make claims over or demands of the client. The prostitute is without natality in the sense that her real identity and personal history is invariably concealed from the client, who has no real interest in it, and she is without honour in the sense that the degraded status of the 'whore' dissolves her entitlement to the protection and respect accorded to non-prostitute women.

What is it that leads the self-employed prostitute to embrace these transitory but serial experiences of social death? Some prostitutes are physically coerced by a third party, but no man (client or pimp) exerts direct, personalistic power over a woman like Desiree. The idiom of the client's power over her is not personalistic nor indeed primarily sexual, but economic. Unlike the slave owner, then, the client can only draw Desiree into this liminal world with his money and only his money frees him from the codes and conventions which shackle him in his non-commercial sexual encounters. Marx's comments on money as a procurer are particularly apposite:

> Money's properties are my – the possessor's properties and essential powers. Thus what I *am* and *am capable* of is by no means determined by my individuality. I *am* ugly, but I can buy for myself the *most beautiful* of women. Therefore I am not *ugly*, for the effect of ugliness, its deterrent power – is nullified by money. (1977, p. 122; original emphasis)

In Britain, all prostitutes are non-persons in the sense that the laws surrounding prostitution restrict their civil rights, and it has also been argued that even successful, independent prostitutes like Desiree must become non-persons in each individual transaction. However, unlike the slave, Desiree is not the legal property of any man. She enters into a series of one-off contracts with numerous men, and, again unlike the slave, these are contracts from which she can freely retract. If Desiree feels that a punter is wasting her time or 'messing her about' in any way, she will tell him to leave (and generally refuses to refund any advance payment that has been made).[5] There are thus similarities and dissimilarities between slavery and prostitution. Desiree is both a person who is not a person, and a slave who is not a slave.

A WAGE LABOURER WHO IS NOT A WAGE LABOURER

Both wage labour and prostitution represent a form of economic survival for those who have no alternative means of subsistence. Like a wage worker, Desiree renders herself temporarily unfree in relation to her own body when she exchanges her 'services' for cash. She can impose limits on which parts of it can be used and how, just as certain groups of waged workers can set constraints on how and how much of their labour power an employer can use. But unless Desiree allows clients to exploit some part of her body as a resource for their own ends, whether that be her vagina, her hands, her breasts or whatever, the deal is off. The essence of the deal is that the client obtains certain rights and claims over her body. It makes no sense to say that she is not contracting out her body, only her 'services', because these services, like human labour power, are embedded in and cannot be detached from the body (Pateman, 1988, pp. 202–3, actually makes this point very clearly). The 'freedom' to alienate property in the person is thus a freedom to surrender certain freedoms.

One obvious difference between a self-employed prostitute like Desiree and a wage worker is that the self-employed prostitute does not enter into a relationship with one employer. She is not dependent upon any individual client, and does not make her living by transferring rights of command over her person to anyone or any firm in particular. However, the fact that the prostitute 'hires out' her 'services' to numerous different clients does not make her somehow more free than the wage worker who 'hires out' her 'labour' to one employer. For in order to make a living from prostitution, it is actually imperative that Desiree sees clients not as a series of separate individuals, but as one unified, collective body. Desiree cannot use her own desire as a criterion for entering into transactions, volunteering only to engage in acts which bring her pleasure or only to entertain only those clients she finds attractive. If she did, her income would plummet to next to nothing. She would no longer be making a living from providing 'sexual services' in exchange for cash, but merely indulging a personal taste for anonymous sexual encounters involving the exchange of cash. To make a living from prostitution, it is necessary to surrender control over whom to have sex with, and how and when, just as it is necessary to surrender control over who directs your labour power and to what ends when you enter employment. The prostitute–client exchange is thus 'voluntary' only in the extremely limited, abstract and theoretical sense that the capitalist employment relation is a 'voluntary' one.

There are, then, continuities between prostitution and wage labour. Yet there are also discontinuities. In particular, it is important to note that the prostitute exchanges across a market something that is not fully or universally commodified in this society and hence has no meaningful or measurable exchange-value. Sayer (1991, pp. 25–6) observes that, for Marx:

> In the process of exchange ... all commodities are routinely compared and equated to one another: they have in addition to a use value, an exchange value.... The exchange value of all commodities, relative to one another, are expressed in quantities of a single equivalent, money. The price-tag on a given commodity tells us in what proportions it can exchange for every other commodity: how many units of commodity x would have to be sold in order to purchase commodity y or z.

The concept of value presupposes exchange, and sexual services, unlike human labour power, are not generally exchanged across a market. In capitalist societies, it is the norm to sell labour power and people are not dishonoured by temporarily 'contracting out' this form of 'property' in their person. But sexual acts are not typically viewed as commodities, and sexuality is not regulated by the ideology of the market. Instead, a complex set of pre-capitalist and non-market ideas – including honour, shame, love, pleasure, loyalty – generally govern people's sexual interaction. Prostitutes and clients alike are socialised in a world where particular meanings are attached to human sexuality (meanings which underpin the codes and conventions governing sexual interaction), a world in which it is widely held that the only legitimate sex is between people who love each other and that 'money can't buy you love'. In buying access to the 'sexual property' that a prostitute has in her person, the client thus draws the prostitute into a marginal social world where 'sexual services' are assumed to have an exchange value and where the 'normal' codes and conventions regulating the interaction between sexual partners do not apply. The working life of the prostitute thus takes place in a space between two worlds, incompletely dominated by the ideology of the free market and yet detached from pre-market values and codes.

The client exchanges money (the universal medium for the expression of the exchange values of *commodities*) for something which is *not* universally recognised as a commodity. Unlike other parties to commodity exchange in capitalist societies (see Sayer, 1991, pp. 58–9), then, prostitute and client are not socially equated through their transaction. The client parts with something that is alienable, permeated by his will, a mere commodity. The prostitute parts with something that is socially constructed as an integral part of her identity, her honour, her position in society. She is not posited and confirmed as the client's equal through the exchange, but stigmatised as his, and everyone else's, social inferior. To a majority of people, often even the woman herself, the prostitute, unlike the wage labourer, is genuinely and irrevocably dishonoured through the contracts she enters into with clients. Even substantial sums of money will not necessarily buy a woman an escape from this stigma and its social and psychological consequences.

SOME CONCLUSIONS

Those who take patriarchal domination, the political subjugation of women and parallels between prostitution and marriage as a starting point for their analyses deflect attention from the very real differences between the lived experience not just of prostitutes and wives, but also between prostitutes working in different settings (and countries), and encourage a tendency to privilege patriarchy over class and 'racialisation' in explanations of oppression and exploitation. But to insist that prostitution differs from other forms of paid work *only* in that it is stigmatised and often criminalised is equally problematic, for there are significant differences between the prostitute–client exchange and that between employer and employee in capitalist societies. Such an approach is equally likely to obscure links between prostitution and 'racialisation', downplay the extent to which prostitution, unlike many other forms of paid work, is underpinned by an especially virulent form of misogyny, and imply that, if only prostitution were de-stigmatised, women would be able to achieve autonomy through it.

Prostitute organisations around the world have convincingly argued that campaigns to abolish laws which criminalise prostitutes, to ensure that prostitutes are accorded full civil rights, and to publicise the hypocrisy and misogyny which underpins the 'whore's' stigma, are of utmost urgence and vital importance (see Jaget, 1980; Delacoste and Alexander, 1988). However, there is no logical connection between an opposition to blatantly sexist, obscenely iniquitous laws and sexual ideologies, and an acceptance of the liberal fiction of property in the person. People only elect to 'hire out' any kind of 'property' in their person in the absence of any better alternative means of subsisting, and any 'freedom' involved in prostitution could only ever have the same abstract and ephemeral character as the wage worker's 'freedom'. At present, inequalities structured along lines of class, gender and 'racialised' identity mean that the people for whom prostitution (like other jobs that are equally 'caring', menial and hazardous, calling for intensive and depleting emotional labour) becomes a rational economic 'choice' are predominantly working-class women and within this, disproportionately women of colour. There is no reason to assume that, even without the stigma, women workers within a 'service' industry as gendered and as 'racialised' as the sex industry would be well placed to acquire meaningful economic, social or political power.

It might be objected that Desiree is living proof of the prostitute's *potential* for financial and emotional autonomy of a kind that is not normally achieved by wage workers. Certainly she herself believes that prostitution will afford her a kind of control over her life that she could not hope to attain by any other means. She plans to work another four years, save £250,000 and then retire:

> I don't ever again want to think that I have to keep a man happy just to keep the roof over my head. I don't want to feel obligated to any man, and I never ever will. I will get the money I want and then I will live exactly as I want. That's what I think women should be entitled to in life, it's just it takes money to do it. . . . I want to be in control of my own destiny. . . . I've got a friend who has to

ask her husband for money, even 'Can I have some money to buy some tampax?' That's so degrading. It's horrible. I don't want that shit. . . . It all comes back to money. You have to have money to make choices.

Money, then, appears to Desiree also as a '*distorting* power both against the individual and against the bonds of society' (Marx, 1977, p. 124), something that will transform all her 'incapacities into their contrary' (Marx, 1977, p. 122), freeing her of all threat of male control and abuse. Unlike most prostitutes, Desiree is in a position to decide for herself whether £250,000 is enough to compensate for the physical, emotional and psychic toll of her work and to secure for her the freedom she desires. But in pursuit of this end, like other prostitutes, she must repeatedly transform herself into an object who is not an object, a person who is not a person, a slave who is not a slave and a wage labourer who is not a wage labourer. It seems a high price to pay for the kind of liberty that is supposedly the birthright of each juridical subject in a capitalist democracy.

ACKNOWLEDGEMENTS

This chapter builds on arguments that have already appeared in an article in *Gender, Work and Organisation* (O'Connell Davidson, 1995), and I am grateful to the editors for permission to reproduce this material. I am also indebted to John Hoffman and to Stephen Small for detailed and extremely helpful comments on earlier drafts of this paper.

NOTES

1. The research has been in progress since May 1993, and forms part of a wider, on-going study of prostitution and sex tourism. The research with Desiree has employed a number of techniques: interviews and informal conversations with Desiree, her receptionists and clients; observations of clients arriving, leaving and waiting at her premises; tape-recordings of Desiree's sessions with clients; questionnaires on client requirements completed by Desiree after clients leave; and participant observation as a receptionist. The ethical and methodological issues posed by the research are discussed at length in O'Connell Davidson and Layder (1994).
2. The complex and wide-ranging effects of the laws surrounding prostitution on prostitutes' businesses, work and lives are considered in some detail in Kennedy (1993), Delacoste and Alexander (1988) and Jaget (1980).

3. Interviews with street-walking prostitutes suggest that some punters seek out and prefer vulnerable and/or abused women as their sexual 'objects' – they tell of 'bag ladies' in their fifties doing brisk trade, of women 'doing business' after having been so badly beaten that their faces are swollen and bruised, or during the late stages of pregnancy.

4. The relationship between prostitution and 'racialised' ideologies is being investigated through research on British sex tourists (see O'Connell Davidson, 1994) as well as in my on-going research on street and sauna prostitution in Britain.

5. Her power to do this rests upon her relative economic success and independence, however. Women working in saunas and massage parlours generally have to pay the owner both a session fee and a punter fee, and are therefore not always in a position to turn away even the most obnoxious client. A streetwalker in a punter's car may also be less able to retract for fear of violence, either from the punter or a pimp.

REFERENCES

Alexander, P. (1988) 'Prostitution: A Difficult Issue for Feminists', in F. Delacoste and P. Alexander (eds), *Sex Work: Writings by Women in the Sex Industry* (London: Virago).

Barry, K. (1979) *Female Sexual Slavery* (Englewood Cliffs, NJ: Prentice Hall).

Barry, K. (ed.) (1984) *International Feminism: Networking Against Female Sexual Slavery* (New York: International Women's Tribune Center).

Bowker, L. (1978) *Women, Crime and the Criminal Justice System* (Toronto: Lexington Books).

Bracey, D. (1979) *Baby-Pros* (New York: John Jay Press).

Brussa, L. (1991) 'Survey on Prostitution, Migration and Traffic in Women: History and Current Situation', Seminar on Action Against Traffic in Women and Forced Prostitution as Violations of Human Rights and Human Dignity, Council of Europe, Strasbourg, 25–27 September.

Delacoste, F. and Alexander, P. (eds) (1988) *Sex Work: Writings by Women in the Sex Industry* (London: Virago).

Dworkin, A. (1987) *Intercourse* (London: Secker & Warburg).

Collins, P. Hill (1991), *Black Feminist Thought: Knowledge, Consciousness and the Politics of Empowerment* (London: Routledge).

hooks, b. (1981) *Ain't I a Woman?: Black Women and Feminism* (Boston, MA: South End Press).

hooks, b. (1992) *Black Looks: Race and Representation* (London: Turnaround Press).

Jackson, M. (1994) *The Real Facts of Life: Feminism and the Politics of Sexuality, c. 1850–1940* (London: Taylor & Francis).

Jaget, C. (1980) *Prostitutes: Our Lives* (Bristol: Falling Wall Press).

Jarvinen, M. (1993) *Of Vice and Women: Shades of Prostitution* (Oslo: Scandinavian University Press).

Kennedy, H. (1993) *Eve was Framed: Women and British Justice* (London: Virago).

Kinnell, H. (1989) *Prostitutes, Their Clients and Risks of HIV* (Birmingham University: Department of Public Health Medicine).

Mackinnon, C. (1982) 'Feminism, Marxism, Method and the State: An Agenda for Theory', in N. Keohane *et al.*, (eds), *Feminist Theory: A Critique of Ideology* (Brighton: Harvester Press).

McLeod E. (1982) *Women Working: Prostitution Now* (London: Croom Helm).

Mama, A. (1992) 'Black Women and the British State: Race, Class and Gender Analysis for the 1990s', in P. Braham, A. Rattansi and R. Skellington (eds), *Racism and Antiracism: Inequalities, Opportunities and Policies* (London: Sage).

Marx, K. (1977) *Economic and Philosophic Manuscripts of 1844* (London: Lawrence & Wishart).

Mr A. de Graaf Foundation (1994) 'Prostitution in the Netherlands: The Current State of Affairs', Westermarkt 4, 1016 DK Amsterdam.

O'Connell Davidson, J. (1994) 'British Sex Tourists in Thailand', paper presented to the Women's Study Network Annual Conference, Portsmouth, 8–10 July.

O'Connell Davidson, J. (1995) 'The Anatomy of "Free Choice" Prostitution', *Gender Work and Organisation*, 2(1).

O'Connell Davidson, J. and Layder, D. (1994) *Methods, Sex and Madness* (London: Routledge).

Pateman, C. (1988) *The Sexual Contract* (Cambridge: Polity Press).

Patterson, O. (1982) *Slavery and Social Death* (Cambridge, MA: Harvard University Press).

Roberts, N. (1992) *Whores in History* (London: Grafton).

Sayer, D. (1991) *Capitalism and Modernity* (London: Routledge).

Small, S. (1994), *Racialised Barriers: The Black Experience in the United States and England in the 1980s* (London: Routledge).

Stoller, R. (1991) *Pain and Passion: A Psychoanalyst Explores the World of S&M* (New York: Plenum Press).

Van der Gaag, N. (1994) 'Prostitution: Soliciting for Change', *The New Internationalist*, **252** (February): pp. 4–7.

West, D. J. (1992) *Male Prostitution* (London: Duckworth).

Part IV

Intimacy

10 Intimacy, Altruism and the Loneliness of Moral Choice: The Case of HIV Positive Health Workers
NEIL SMALL

INTRODUCTION

In the spring of 1993 the UK succumbed to a new variation in the recurring scenario of 'AIDS panics'. This panic related to the risk to their patients from HIV positive health workers. The panic was manifest in five settings – the media, the public, the professional, the political and finally in the lives of some individuals. In this paper I will introduce some details associated with this panic and specifically with the way it appeared to be understood by the various parties concerned.

One of the responses to the panic was a modification of guidance issued by the Department of Health on the way that health-care workers, their physicians and their employers, should respond to health workers who believe they might be infected with the HIV virus. Specifically, new guidelines stated that health authorities had a duty to inform patients who may have been at risk of infection from doctors and other medical staff with the HIV virus (Department of Health, 1991, 1993). In prefacing these changes, Secretary of State for Health Virginia Bottomley told Parliament that 'health workers have a paramount responsibility to their patients' (*Hansard*, 12 March 1993). This paramount responsibility would have an impact on other apparent defining values characteristic of health provision, notably confidentiality. I will explore the possible impacts of such a change in emphasis but will be more concerned to use this panic, and the details of the reaction, to help illuminate a number of theoretical debates current within sociology.

Any discussion about responsibility, and about the assumption that a Secretary of State can readjust the relative position of those aspects of ethical systems that infuse the practice of health care, can be enriched by looking to the picture of postmodern ethics being developed by Zygmunt Bauman. It is also a scenario that can locate, in the specifics of an empirical example, some of the discussion about risk present in Beck's much quoted book (1992) and allows an examination of Giddens' argument that a transformation of intimacy holds out the possibility of a radical democratisation of the personal and public spheres (Giddens, 1992). I will argue that the case of HIV positive health workers is best understood as representing an encroachment on intimacy and an expansion of a dictatorial public sphere into the personal.

'RISK SOCIETY'

The idea of risk has infused the whole debate about HIV and AIDS. However, the way that risk has been used and (mis)understood in the debate means that it is difficult to assess what paradigm of risk and risk behaviour we are responding to. Risk of becoming infected, or the risks if infected, risk reduction, risk management, the percentage risk of encountering someone who is infected in a situation of high risk of virus transmission, the risk in such a situation of virus transmission, the everyday risks, the risks to society, the risks of encountering foreigners, the risks of bisexuals, the risks from the secretly infected. Risk infuses this debate. It does include a construction of risk that uses a 'scientific' paradigm – the possibility of physical harm understood in such a way as to imply a technical or mechanistic response, if we do this then that will or will not result. But there is also a reflexive incorporation of risk into personal identity which contributes to a sense of felt vulnerability or invulnerability. Negotiating between, or within, these paradigms can be problematic. For example, there are gaps between the messages of risk (say from health educators), the statistics of risk presented as scientific data, and the felt experience of risk – how it is incorporated into the *weltanschauung* of individuals and social groups. We might get health educators saying that heterosexuals can get AIDS, that it's everybody's business; statistics on transmission say that in the UK the number of people infected via heterosexual routes with partners from the UK was perhaps thirty-seven in 1991,[1] public opinion is that AIDS is a homosexual and drug-takers problem and so many don't see the need to change sexual behaviour in the ways advised by health educators. The aim of health educators appears to be to break through the barriers of personally constructed risk identities and so insert the scientific into the reflexive. But the reflexive is well protected.

The complexities of risk as a concept, and as something applied to HIV and AIDS, have been well developed (see, for example, Douglas, 1986; Bellaby, 1990) and I have explored the details of health education, risk and behaviour change elsewhere (Small, 1993). Here I want to move on from identifying complexity to consider how it fits with Beck's theory. Or is Giddens on reflexive modernity closer to the emerging picture of risk and AIDS?

Beck argues that industrial society is characterised by the 'axial principle' of the distribution of goods, and inevitably is structured around the dimension of social class. Risk society, its successor, is structured through the distribution of 'bads', or dangers, and is individualised. Beck also sees this shift as one from a dominant cultural form of scientism, where culturally imposed constraints claim rationality as their justification, to reflexive modernisation in the private sphere. This results in an individualisation of social agents who construct their own biographies. Health workers who are HIV positive, I will argue, sit on the cusp of this change. They can be cited as evidence of an intrusion of the scientific into the reflexive, as living with a damaged personal risk identity. This arises from the interface of help and harm that they encompass. Their claim to a private world, to a realm of the intimate, is negated by their societally imposed risk identity.

Anthony Giddens (1991) considers similar areas to Beck when he identifies the form reflexivity takes in modernity. Risk assessment is fundamental to colonising the future, and so the monitoring of risk is a key aspect of modernitys' reflexivity. Giddens cites the impact medical statistics of mortality have upon the avoidance of health risks as an example of the interaction between expert systems and lay behaviour in relation to risk. But there are limits to reflexivity. Lash (1992) points to:

> the lack of identity, and even coordination, between the subjective capacity to reflect and the immunity of the world to the practical measures which reflection may suggest. (quoted in Bauman, 1993, p. 202)

Interaction between expert systems and individuals incorporating them into their futures occurs in an environment in which risks, often collectively generated, become privatised when solutions are offered:

Risks are pre-selected and pre-processed in such a way that the awareness of dangers comes together with the intimation of the individual's blame for continuing risk exposure and individual responsibility for risk avoidance. (Bauman, 1993, p. 202)

As well as the difficulties in operationalising ones own risk choices, and the tendency to diffuse collective cause into individual blame, there is a defense against reflexivity built up by institutions who argue that *they* are trustworthy and credible. The incidence of radiation-linked cancer may be higher than average in areas near nuclear power stations but the 'trustworthy' scientists say it is an anomaly unrelated to nuclear power. Cancer in these areas is to do with a series of individual cause scenarios. People living nearby are not simplistically duped by the scientists, they create their own risk scenarios which include a reading of the scientific, a sense of the problems inherent in acting upon fears and perhaps losing their jobs and having to move home and area, and a sense of the operation of fate – if we are going to get cancer then there is nothing we can do about it. The 'my Granny lived to 101 and she smoked sixty a day' approach to life and to risk underlines the problem in trying to leave behind the residues of folk belief which sit alongside the scientific as we make choices.

There is a psychology of risk as well as a sociology. That psychology appears layered with 'primitive' and 'modern' views coalescing into a shifting, vulnerable, construction of the self in relation to risk. It may be that this presents evidence of the postmodern as we see the development of a plurality of mutually autonomous contexts in which life is constructed. Considering risk serves to remind us that the individual in each of those contexts carries with them a legacy of a complex psychology which may manifest different features in different places at different times. Risk exists as a fissure running through these layers and exposing them to the glare of the immediate. Further there is a collective social psychology that, in some circumstances, manifests an 'epidemic' form. Strong (1990) invokes a medical version of the Hobbesian nightmare – the war of all against all:

Societies are caught up in an extraordinary emotional maelstrom which seems, at least for a time, to be beyond anyones' immediate control. (Strong, 1990, p. 249)

The result is not only a limitation on the *de facto* capacity to be reflexive but also a recognition that neither the classic, Weberian, construction of the modern as a separation of spheres of activity, nor Beck's claim for a new modernity, survive the maelstrom.

AN EXAMPLE OF 'PANIC'

In March 1993, four cases involving HIV positive health workers emerged into the public view in quick succession. Dr Yarab Almahawi, a Bolton GP, had died age 33 in May 1992. He had been diagnosed HIV positive in 1990. The health authority in Northern Ireland, whose area he then worked within, had been informed and had moved him from areas of work that involved invasive surgical procedures. He had subsequently moved to Bolton and, as well as working in general practice, had done a very short period of work, forty-nine hours in all, in the casualty department of the town's Royal Infirmary. He had not informed the hospital of his HIV status, something the guidelines then operative required because of the possibility of involvement in invasive procedures in casualty.

The Chief Medical Officer for Northern Ireland, Dr James McKenna, said that the health authorities Dr Almahawi worked for when diagnosed:

> had not been secretive about the doctor. It was normal practice not to broadcast details of a patient's condition, whether he was a health worker or not. (*The Guardian*, 16 March 1993)

In the same week that the HIV status of the late Dr Almahawi became publicly known details of the death from AIDS of Dr Leonard Taitz, a 56-year-old paediatrician from Sheffield, were published. Again the health authority knew of his HIV status. Dr Paul Snell, director of public health summed up the policy:

> where there is absolutely no risk, as in the case of Dr Taiz, there is no reason to alert the public. (*The Guardian*, 18 March 1993)[2]

Also in March and April 1993 the deaths of Kent gynaecologist, Terence Shuttleworth, and Welsh junior hospital doctor Peter Clayton were reported. Mr Shuttleworth was said to have stopped invasive surgery when he was diagnosed. Dr Clayton had contracted HIV two years before his death and had not informed his health authority. His previous health status only became known at his death.

The state of scientific knowledge at this point was that it was possible to transmit HIV from doctor to patient, and vice versa, during
invasive interventions. But there was no known case where an HIV-
infected health worker had passed the virus to a patient.[3] It is possible, in principle, to screen health workers. But in practice it would
need to be done regularly and the chance of an individual becoming
infected between tests would rule out its complete reliability. As to
cost, Kennelly and Tolley (1993) estimate that routine testing of all
hospital doctors, nurses, midwives and dentists would have cost £65.2
million in 1993. In an NHS with a fixed budget that money would
have to come from somewhere else in the health service and so impact
on the availability, or the quality, of care for others.

If this, then, is the detail of the presenting problem, the next stage
is to consider the reaction. I have commented above on the governmental
reaction – changing guidelines in such a way as to seek to redefine
the relationship between confidentiality as a patient and responsibility
as a service provider. The other main locations of response were in the
reactions of health authorities, individual politicians, the media and those
individuals who came to believe that they might have been at risk.

We have seen how first reactions of health authority representatives
were strongly supportive of established procedure, the assertion of
confidentiality for patients even if patients were also staff, and the
attempt to separate theoretical risk from evidential risk. However, when
the status of their infected worker entered the public domain the reaction was much more active. Characteristically, health authorities contacted patients who had been treated by the infected worker and set up
help-lines and counselling services for the worried. Bolton Health
Authority wrote to the 260 patients they identified as having been
treated by Dr Almahawi in his hospital practice. They opened a local
helpline and received 220 calls in the first few days. A similar procedure was followed in Northern Ireland. Officials from Medway Health
Authority in Kent sought to contact 17 000 former patients of Dr
Shuttleworth. They set up a bank of forty telephone lines and brought
in a hundred trained counsellors. Senior health personnel reiterated the
low risk to patients. Dr Kenneth Calman, the Chief Medical Officer,
argued that the potential problem of HIV positive health workers should
be responded to according to the strict observance by health care workers
of their professional and ethical responsibilities. The practical difficulties of doing widespread testing were noted. Rosemary Jenkins, Director of Professional Affairs at the Royal College of Midwives,
introduced the likelihood of a perverse effect whereby a greater degree

of institutional openness, in terms of disclosing the names of infected health workers, might generate greater individual secrecy. Dr Fleur Fisher, head of ethics at the British Medical Association, added another dimension in pointing out that:

> There is no case known in the world where a doctor or nurse has infected somebody. In the world, we have I think, 148 documented cases of health care workers getting the virus from patients. (*The Guardian*, 6 April 1993)[4]

Politicians with constituency interest wanted more activity. More intervention at diagnosis and a central registry that doctors and nurses who were HIV positive would have to inform were two ideas. The media response varied between talking up a crisis and seeking to assert the values of confidentiality and the recognition that this was a public anxiety problem not an AIDS problem (see Editorial in *The Daily Telegraph*, 11 March 1993).[5]

The discovery of HIV positive health workers in March and April 1993 did not prompt an orthodox panic that reverberates through society. Nor did it constitute a moral panic in the terminology of Cohen (1972) and of Hall and colleagues (1978). But it did produce a reaction that included panic in some sectors and it did indicate the lack of any mature and measured response to HIV and AIDS, the sort of response that might have been hoped for in the second decade of the epidemic. Moral panics occur when a person, or group of persons, emerge to become identified as a threat to societal values and interests. Socially accredited experts pronounce their diagnosis and solutions. Sometimes the panic is passed over and forgotten quickly, sometimes it has long-lasting repercussions and might produce change in law, in social policy or in the way that society conceives itself (Cohen, 1972, p. 28). Cohen was writing about 'mods and rockers' and Hall *et al.* were looking at the arrival of 'mugging' as a cause of panic in 1972–3.[6] But the overall critique of the social history of a moral panic is applicable to many varied scenarios. One feature of the discourse of moral panic is that there is some sort of generalised response that includes professional, political and public opinion, fuelled by the media. But what we have described above in relation to HIV positive health workers, while a panic in some peoples eyes, does not show the sort of generalised reorganisation within hegemonic configurations that was characteristic of 1970s' moral panics. Different domains are able to maintain different responses. This is a postmodern panic.

RIGHTS TO PRIVACY AND RIGHTS TO KNOW

Marshall (1963) saw different forms of rights developing sequentially, civil rights forming the basis upon which political rights were exercised in the pursuit of social rights. Taylor-Gooby (1991) identifies both the interdependence and instability of these rights in democratic welfare capitalist society. A further dimension of rights has been presented via the argument that there are 'body rights' (Shaver, 1992). These rest on a claim that an individual has rights secure from the interference of the state. It is a position that has been argued specifically in relation to abortion. It has echoes also in debates around euthanasia, about withholding or withdrawing critical care. Consider John Dawson, a former head of the Professional, Scientific and International Affairs Division of the British Medical Association:

> In the case of AIDS, for example, refusal to help people suffering from AIDS to die in their own way at a time of their own choosing may simply perpetuate the isolation and rejection that as a society we may have inflicted upon them through the course of their illness. (Dawson, 1992, p. 82)

Decisions are made on an *ad hoc* basis about withholding, or withdrawing, critical care. But there is at least the beginnings of discussion about ethical frameworks that 'balances hopeful science with dignified death' (Sanders and Raffin, 1993, p. 175).

What is emerging here is a picture of rights as non-sequential and contested. If one does not abrogate rights in areas of the treatment of illness to medicine then there is a need to enter into a discussion that balances and assesses conflicting claims. It may be that for HIV positive health workers we are seeing a conflict between civil rights and body rights on the one hand – the right to confidentiality about how one uses knowledge concerning ones body – and social rights, defined in terms of risk and protection of the public and operationalised via a call for the right to know about the HIV status of health workers. These are mediated via the intrusion of political judgements which, in effect, are shifting to a position where they are acting on behalf of social rights and denying civil rights – the opposite process to the one described by Marshall and, paradoxically, at odds with the rhetorical stance of the Conservative government in the UK.[7]

But at this point the political judgements are not acting according to a construct of rights. Rather we are in a situation where the dimension of power is crucial. The mediating force between the social and the civil is a set of codes and laws that are contingent and are designed to be livable for the many or the powerful, even if they are oppressive of the few or the powerless. They are not law as a manifestation of values but of discourse defined from the top. The shape of this discourse is influenced by the paradigm of risk, discussed above.

If the resulting terrain is discourse-dependent, as opposed to dependent on the interplay of rights, then the postmodern recognition that one cannot equate the good and the true is sustained (see Squires, 1993). Rights are not the way to move us on in understanding the position of HIV positive health workers. Perhaps the ethics surrounding individual decisions and societal reactions are an alternative way to locate the problem of HIV positive health workers.

THE ETHICS OF THE GROUP AND THE MORALITY OF THE INDIVIDUAL

The intrusion of the societal on the intimate, via the exercise of political power, is evident in many of those areas in which a claim for 'body rights' can also exist. In obstetrics, for example, the development of technology appears to have contributed to a view of the pregnant woman as a foetal container. Increasingly her voice is ignored as the foetus is given the status of an individual, with society as its putative protector.[8] Recent case experience in the USA and the UK includes situations where doctors have carried out vaginal examinations and Caesarian sections against the wish of the mother, and their actions have been supported in the Courts, contributing to what has been described as a situation in which 'The rights of women over bodily integrity are being slowly and subtly eroded' (Miller, 1993, p. 98).

The potential for a clash between the need to respond to the suffering of individuals and to further the development of science is evident in the history of Laura Davies, the Manchester five-year-old born with gastroschesis and given the world's most extensive organ transplant in the USA. Laura died shortly after the operation. Two controversies surrounded her death. First, had she been denied care that should have been available in the UK? Second, were the repeated treatments she underwent essentially concerned with her chances of life or were they, at the end of her life, contributing to a more optimistic future for others who would suffer similar conditions in times to come? Laura's parents, and her US doctor, emphasised the treatment rather than the research rationale. Others, for example Catherine Arkley, director of the Childrens' Liver Disease Foundation, pointed to the way that knowledge of both the technique of surgery and the post-operative management of very sick children would be enhanced (*The Guardian*, 12 November 1993). Here there is some reluctance to accept that to act altruistically may also have claims to legitimacy, the exercise of intimate rights contributing to social good. It is perhaps because in making decisions involving children we believe that the best we can achieve is proxy altruism, parents deciding on behalf of children. Proxy altruism is discarded as a legitimate rationale by Laura's parents and doctor in favour of the pursuit of the specific welfare of this individual child. But it is implicitly claimed on behalf of Laura by Catherine Arkley. I will return to the complexities of altruism in a subsequent section.

A leading expert in vaccines, Dr Stanley Plotkin, managing director of Pasteur Merieux, the French–American pharmaceutical giant, spoke frankly about what he called the moral dilemmas of developing and testing an AIDS vaccine. Field trials of any vaccine would be carried out on volunteers from high-risk groups in target countries such as Zambia, Uganda and Brazil as well as the South Bronx in New York. Some people would be given the test vaccine, others would get a placebo. Two years later follow up studies would be carried out to determine infection rates in the two groups. Plotkin's dilemma was that 'we just cannot vaccinate volunteers and leave them. We will be morally obliged to educate them about AIDS.' His scientific dilemma was that after educating people they might change their behaviour, and although individuals will then have a greater chance of avoiding ill health and premature death, this would not do a lot for *his* science. Plotkin continues:

> We have to see if the vaccine can protect HIV-challenges, but if people start being sensible, we will not be able to do that. It's a real dilemma. We might be tempted to neglect to tell people the risks and let a few hundred die so we can develop a vaccine quickly, but the world would not accept this. (*The Observer*, 12 September 1993)

It is emerging, I hope, that in any situation in which we do not give ourselves as individuals and as societies into the hands of others, the realm of body rights will be one rife with contesting claims of preference and jurisdiction. Indeed we can see the shortcomings of a modernist construction of the possibility, however difficult, of finding an

ethical code that reflects both individual and collective interest, where collective interest is defined from above. It is the disbelief in such a possibility that is postmodern. A non-ambivalent morality, free from contradictions, an ethics that is universal and objectively founded, is a practical impossibility, perhaps a contradiction in terms (Bauman, 1993, p. 10).
Bauman argues that:

> the novelty of the postmodern approach to ethics means not abandoning moral concerns but rejecting the modern way of going about its moral problems. (Bauman, 1993, p. 3)

That modern way includes responding to moral challenges with coercive normative regulation. Such regulation is often present in political practice. The modern way also involves the philosophical search for absolutes, universals and foundations in theory. It is not that great issues of ethics have disappeared. Postmodernism does not mean that we must ignore questions of human rights or the synchronisation of individual conduct and collective welfare. But we do need to contemplate the moral condition in a postmodern way. We move from the dominance of ethical pretensions, conflated with the globalising tendencies of the domain of political powers, to a new sort of morality.

Bauman identifies seven features of the moral condition as contemplated from the postmodern perspective. Such a condition is without ethical codes; it is non-rational; it recognises that contradiction cannot be overcome; it does not contain precepts that are universalisable; it cannot be socially managed; it is not about denying aspects of the self; and it seeks the emancipation of the autonomous self (Bauman, 1993, pp. 10–14).

Ethics, according to this postmodern critique, moves morality from the realm of personal autonomy into that of power-assisted heteronomy. Morality, in contrast, accepts that few choices are unambiguously good. The majority of moral choices are made between contradictory impulses. Moral impulses can lead to immoral consequences, the wish to care for someone, for example, can lead to a denial of their autonomy. Most critically, in terms of the argument relevant to the position of HIV positive health workers, is the analysis of the relationship between the individual and the social.

Bauman argues that being for the other, before one can be with the other, is the first reality of the self. This is a starting point rather than a product of society. Conventionally morality is seen as being about abrogating some aspect of self interest whereas moral responsibility is, in fact, precisely the act of self-constitution:

> The surrender, if any, occurs on the road leading from the moral to the social self, from being for to being 'merely' with. (Bauman, 1993, p. 14)

In practice, such a distinction is exemplified in the development of market principles in the welfare state. In its initial principles the welfare state represented a tangible bond between the private and the public via the institutionalised communality of fate it implies. Now, market principles mean there is an institutional diversity of fate in which the taxpayers' privations are balanced against the benefit recipients' gains (Bauman, 1993, p. 243).

Postmodernism is not doing away with the moral but is ending a recourse to the certainties of ethical systems. Morality is not about doing what one is told one should do, it is not about acting in accord with the dictates of science, authority, power or religion. But morality is not lessened by this, 'the frustration of certainty is moralities' gain' (Bauman, 1993, p. 223). Now:

> Moral responsibility is the most personal and inalienable of human possessions, and the most precious of human rights. It cannot be taken away, shared, ceded, pawned, or deposited for safe keeping. Moral responsibility is unconditional and infinite, and it manifests itself in the constant anguish of not manifesting itself enough. (Bauman, 1993, p. 250)

The loneliness of uncertainty and the anguish of the lack of reconciliation between the individual and the social might be the moral condition for most of us most of the time. Using the terminology, introduced above, we now can properly put the civil before the social but recognise that the civil is constituted by the imperative of being 'for'. Before asking specifically what that means for our subject, the HIV positive health worker, two situations in which we might, quintessentially, be viewed as being 'for', altruism and intimacy, will be considered.

ALTRUISM AND GIFT-GIVING REVISITED

From blood to care, the sociological debate about altruism touches many points revisited in the history of AIDS. Richard Titmuss (1970) developed a picture of the gift of blood, through blood transfusion, as illustrating that when a gift is safe, that is non-injurious to the recipient, it has to be freely given. Land and Rose (1985) argue that this is even more true in 'the complex and enduring task of caring for another person' (p. 93). They identify that many women are subject to 'compulsory altruism'. The presence of available alternatives to their own labour of caring is what is required to separate subjugation from what would be an altruistic society. Gift-giving more generally is assumed to be 'a means through which individuals communicate the values which they assign to their significant others' (Cheal, 1987, p. 150). But it is a value mediated by society. The autonomy to structure gift-giving in a way other than that socially, or commercially, defined is severely restricted (see Land and Rose, 1985, p. 80).

In the world of AIDS we have to tread carefully between two different mythological constructions, one of which emphasises selfishness and the other altruism. The first is of the promiscuous and irresponsible individual. This reaches its apogee in publicity about those HIV positive individuals who deliberately seek out hapless victims to seduce and infect. The second construction is of the now selfless, dedicated and responsible person whose actions have been transformed by the awareness of AIDS. It would appear that a few of the former exist, the history of AIDS is peopled by many who approximate to the latter. People living with AIDS, or intimately connected with those who are – including many members of the gay community who feel the context of their lives is touched by AIDS, committed medical staff, researchers and activists, all have come together to care *about* and to care *for* people with AIDS in a way that, while not unique in the history of responses to ill health, is broader in its self-defined remit than any previous movement around a disease and the social reaction to that disease (see for example Kayal, 1993, on the USA's 'Gay Men's Health Crisis').[9] Self-help groups have been set up, political lobbying carried out, medical research protocols challenged, prejudice confronted. All this has been done while at the same time many of the most active have been confronting illness and imminent death.[10]

We know now, in the world of AIDS, that even the most altruistic of gifts can carry secret harm. Blood and semen, as the stuff of life and the gift of death, mean that we must rethink the connection between intimate gifts and altruistic intention. But we also know that AIDS has reminded us that individuals can both be with the other and be for the other, they can care for and care about. We also see how the bereaved mother in Robert Frost's poem is wrong when she says:

> The nearest friends can go
> With anyone to death, comes so far short
> They might as well not try to go at all.
> No, from the time when one is sick to death,
> One is alone, and he dies more alone.

> (from *Home Burial*, 1914,
> in Frost, 1973, pp. 62–3)

It may be that it is the confluence of the two spheres of the intimate, sex and death, that explain the capacity, evident in many involved in this epidemic, to empathise and to act altruistically. It may be the sense of proximity – a feeling that you care *for* today but may *need* care tomorrow. All of us know when we care for the sick and dying that we also, one day, may be sick and will die. But the ontological encounter with death through AIDS is more immediate when one knows that the intimacy which underpins the care is also a reason why you may need care.

Giddens describes what he calls the emergence of 'plastic sexuality' (perhaps in the age of the ubiquitous condom he might have better used 'rubber sexuality'). This is decentred sexuality, freed from the needs of reproduction. It is also a sexuality that:

> can be moulded as a trait of personality and thus is intrinsically bound up with the self. At the same time – in principle – it frees sexuality from the rule of the phallus, from the overweening importance of male sexual experience.   (Giddens, 1992, p. 2)

It is crucial to the development of what he terms the pure relationship, a relationship of sexual and emotional equality. Such a relationship implies a wholesale democratising of the interpersonal domain. As such it might be a subversive influence on modern institutions as a whole. Giddens is locating a democratising of the intimate with the pursuit of democracy in the public sphere and suggesting the former could help contribute to the latter.

In developing this argument he has to take issue with Foucault. Not with the Foucault who shows us that discourse becomes constitutive of the social reality it portrays. Nor with his idea of the intrusion of 'power-knowledge' into social organisation (Foucault, 1981). Where Giddens parts company with him is that he would wish, while acknowledging the dimension of power, to see the institutional reflexivity that is constantly in motion around sexuality. The intimate, transformed, becomes a sphere in which one can act 'for' and in acting for can act 'upon' the social. That there is also a reciprocal reflexivity is clear.

Three things can be contested in Giddens' scenario. First, is there a general move in the direction of the achievement of plastic sexuality? Second, what other changes in sexuality are occurring and how do they contribute to, or detract from, plastic sexuality? Third, what evidence is there that if there is a transformation of the personal it can impact on the political, and what current changes are occurring in the political that impact upon the personal? Many of the issues raised benefit from being located in empirical enquiry. HIV, AIDS and the reactions to them can provide the context.

THE SOCIAL GOOD

In a part of his remarkable novel *The Runaway Soul* Harold Brodkey considers the impact of the Second World War on those newly conscripted to the army. He describes how they march with a collective step but live with a solitary fear (Brodkey, 1992, p. 367). To be part of a collective might shape one's apparent stance in the world, but what is manifest in the reaction to risk, and evident when we encounter death or the prospect of death, is loneliness. This is the same feeling that we encounter in a world where we have to make choices. That we seek certainties, or devices to avoid choice, is not surprising. The route to the avoidance of the loneliness of choice most often taken is to locate authority in something or someone 'higher' than the self. A good thing too, some argue. The Catholic encyclical *Veritas Splendor* (Pope John Paul 2nd, 1994) sees freedom of individual conscience as something that has been abused by making it the only criterion for moral judgement. It argues that the authority and tradition of the church should be looked to.

Where we have contesting claims as to what the right course of action is, looking to authority provides one way to solve our problem.

But it is a superficial solution. HIV positive health workers had been instructed to sacrifice confidentiality on the grounds of furthering the social good. Such instructions were consistent with the ascendency of the social over the individual in areas of body rights. The claims of the social are strengthened by evoking risk. HIV positive health workers will be forced to 'act altruistically'.

Just as this was flawed altruism so it was bad risk management. To punish people for their HIV status by making that status public is to risk the furtive world of secrets and uncertainties. People will not seek knowledge of their HIV status and will not change their behaviour. More people will be put at risk when fear replaces even that measure of safety that now exists. It is the intimate that, although for many equating with the route of infection, offers the way forward. From the intimate can grow acting for, acting altruistically, consistent with a morality that belongs with the self and not with the ethics of the powerful.[11]

NOTES

1. Department of Health, 29 January 1992, Press Release. Figures for AIDS and HIV include a category of people infected via heterosexual intercourse with people not included in the following categories: bisexuals, injecting drug users, people from abroad, those infected by contaminated blood. Rates of HIV infection in this group increased by 30 per cent in 1991. In this group, newly identified as HIV positive in 1991, were fifteen men and twenty two women (another fifty men and thirty-five women were still under investigation to ascertain which category they should be included in).

2. Dr Almahawi was born in Saudi Arabia, Dr Taitz worked in South Africa and the USA. These aspects of their biography featured in news reports. They do not seem integral to the point at issue but do reflect a tendency to equate AIDS with the 'foreign' that is present in much AIDS discourse.

3. It is generally cited that, world-wide, one case shows such transmission. But the details of this are sufficiently opaque to make a clear association problematic.

4. In the USA there is considerable attention given to the danger to health care workers who come into contact with HIV positive patients, see Landau-Stanton and Clements (1993, pp. 97–132).

5. The guidelines issued by the Department of Health, on the recommendations of the Expert Advisory Group on AIDS, were modified in March 1994 (Department of Health, 1994). The new guidelines represent an attempt to reconstruct the balance between protecting patients, retaining public

confidence and providing safeguards for the confidentiality and employment rights of HIV-infected health care workers. They reflect the active lobbying against the 1993 guidelines by, amongst others, eminent doctors such as Professor Pinching (1994). In theory, the new guidelines offer some protection to the confidentiality of HIV positive health workers. In December 1994, Greater Glasgow Health Board made it known that a surgeon, working in Glasgow, had been found to be HIV positive. They gave no details of his identity, where he worked or how he was thought to have contracted the virus. The Health Board stressed the absence of any cases of doctor-to-patient infection. After a working group had scrutinised cases the surgeon had worked on, any people perceived to be at even the remotest risk would be contacted and offered counselling (*The Guardian*, 24 December 1994). Within days we saw such apparent protection as the new guidelines provided being undermined by the press and TV who published the name of the doctor alongside the sorts of stories that alarmed large numbers of people. A help line was set up and former patients contacted and offered counselling. In short, the overall response was much as before (see Richard Ingrams' column in *The Observer*, 1 January 1995).

6. The choice of metaphor in Hall *et al.* is perhaps indicative of the way that health risks, in particular, might constitute the most potent form of moral panic. Writing about mugging they talk of a 'new strain of crime'. 'The police, reacting to these events, spurred on by a vigilant press, by public anxiety and professional duty, took rapid steps to isolate the "virus" and bring the fever under control. The courts administered a strong inoculating dose of medicine' (Hall *et al.*, 1978. p. 17).

7. Of course, the rhetorical stance is not simple – the British government's 'back to basics' policy of 1993–4 implied some imposition of societal values, even if those values were about individual responsibility. The Conservative hegemonic project does not go away simply because the rhetoric talks of less government! Michael Portillo, then Chief Secretary to the Treasury, provided an illustration of one side of the government's stance when he said that, 'It's hard to be neighbourly if we are told the state should look after our neighbours. Good should not be done by proxy or by the State' (*The Guardian*, 16 September 1993). Changing guidelines on individual responsibility and behaviour in regard to HIV are illustrative of the other side.

8. After a child is born the rhetoric of the political and moral Right asserts that it is the parents' responsibility, not the state's, to care and provide.

9. The death of Derek Jarman on 19 February 1994, two days before Parliament declined to lower the age of consent for homosexuals to sixteen, provides a vivid image of the juxtaposition of the personal and the political. Jarman had written, in 1991, 'On December 22, 1986, finding I was body positive, I set myself a target: I would disclose my secret and survive Margaret Thatcher. I did. Now I have set my sights on the millennium and a world where we are all equal before the law' (quoted in *The Guardian*, 3 March 1994).

10. In writing about the Miners' Strike of 1984, Dave Hill (1994) discusses engagement and solidarity in ways that are resonant of some of the things

that can be said about the self-help response to HIV and AIDS: 'It is not only touching but essential that the strike should be so keenly remembered. This is not because every participant was an unblemished socialist saint. It is because, when the balance sheet is totalled, the striking miners, their families and friends represented a version of British life that is a thousand times more generous than that preferred by those who set out to destroy them. And the more that version of Britain is cherished, the better the prospect that, in some new form or other, it will flourish once again.'

11. Fox presents the concept of 'arche-health'. In so doing he is developing an approach evident in earlier work by Derrida (see, for example, Derrida, 1976). Fox argues that this is a state of becoming which resists being created discursively by medicine or sociology. It is facilitated when one's responsibility to act is guided by the responsibility to otherness, by becoming. Arche-health, in its ethics and politics, involves engagement, 'always on the side of the nomad thought, of responsibility to difference and Otherness, against identity, and in support of generosity against mastery' (Fox, 1993, p. 141).

REFERENCES

Bauman, Z. (1993) *Postmodern Ethics* (Oxford: Blackwell).

Beck, U. (1992) *Risk Society: Towards a New Modernity* (London: Sage).

Bellaby, P. (1990) '"To Risk or not to Risk": Uses and Limitations of Mary Douglas on Risk-Acceptability for Understanding Health and Safety at Work and Road Accidents', *Sociological Review*, **38**(3): pp. 465–83.

Brodkey, H. (1992) *The Runaway Soul* (New York: Harper).

Cheal, D. (1987) '"Showing them you love them": Gift Giving and the Dialectic of Intimacy', *Sociological Review*, **35**(1): pp. 150–69.

Cohen, S. (1972) *Folk Devils and Moral Panics: the Creation of the Mods and Rockers* (London: MacGibbon & Kee).

Dawson, J. (1992) 'Last Rites and Wrongs – Euthanasia: Autonomy and Responsibility', *Cambridge Quarterly of Healthcare Ethics*, 1: pp. 81–3.

Department of Health (1991, revised 1993) *AIDS/HIV-Infected Health Care Workers. Occupational Guidance for Health Care Workers, their Physicians and Employers*, Recommendations of the Expert Advisory Group on AIDS (London: HMSO).

Department of Health (1994) *AIDS/HIV-infected Health Care Workers: Guidance on the Management of Infected Health Care Workers*, Recommendations of the Expert Advisory Group on AIDS (London: HMSO).

Derrida, J. (1976) *Of Grammatology* (Baltimore, MD: Johns Hopkins University Press).

Douglas, M. (1986) *Risk Acceptability According to the Social Sciences* (London: Routledge & Kegan Paul).

Foucault, M. (1981) *The History of Sexuality*, vol. 1 (Harmondsworth: Pelican).

Fox, N. (1993) *Postmodernism, Sociology and Health* (Buckingham: Open University Press).

Frost, R. (1973) *Selected Poems* (Harmondsworth: Penguin).

Giddens, A. (1991) *Modernity and Self-Identity in the Late Modern Age* (Cambridge: Polity Press).

Giddens, A. (1992) *The Transformation of Intimacy* (Cambridge: Polity Press).

Hall, S., Critcher, C., Jefferson, T., Clarke, J. and Roberts, B. (1978) *Policing the Crisis. Mugging, the State and Law and Order* (London: Macmillan).

Hill, D. (1994) 'A Fight to the Death', *The Guardian Weekend*, 5 March, pp. 6–9.

Kayal, P. M. (1993) *Bearing Witness. Gay Mens Health Crisis and the Politics of AIDS* (Oxford: Westview Press).

Kennelly, J. and Tolley, K. (1993) 'Screen Test', *Health Service Journal*, I (July): p. 31.

Land, H. and Rose, H. (1985) 'Compulsory Altruism for some or an Altruistic Society for all?', in P. Bean, J. Ferris and D. Whynes (eds), *In Defence of Welfare* (London: Tavistock).

Landau-Stanton, J. and Clements, C. D. (1993) *AIDS, Health and Mental Health* (New York: Brunner / Mazel).

Lash, S. (1992) 'Asthetische Dimensionen reflexiver Modernisierung', *Soziale Welt*, 3: pp. 261–77.

Marshall, T. H. (1963) 'Citizenship and Social Class', in T. H. Marshall (ed.) *Sociology at the Crossroads* (London: Heinemann).

Miller, L. (1993) 'Two Patients or One? Problems of Consent in Obstetrics', *Medical Law International*, 1: pp. 97–112.

Pinching, A. J. (1994) 'HIV/AIDS: Ethical and Social Dimensions', paper presented at a conference on AIDS' Impact, Brighton, UK, 7–10 July.

Pope John Paul 2nd (1994) *Veritas Splendor* (Dublin: Catholic Truth Society).

Sanders, L. M. and Raffin, T. A. (1993) 'The Ethics of Withholding and Withdrawing Critical Care', *Cambridge Quarterly of Healthcare Ethics*, 2: pp. 175–84.

Shaver, S. (1992) 'Body Rights, Social Rights and the Liberal Welfare State', paper presented at Workshop in Comparative Welfare State Development, University of Bremen Centre for Social Policy Research, 2–5 September.

Small, N. (1993) *AIDS: The Challenge. Understanding, Education and Care* (Aldershot: Avebury).

Strong, P. (1990) 'Epidemic Psychology: A Model', *Sociology of Health and Illness*, **12** (3): pp. 249–59.

Squires, J. (ed.) (1993) *Principled Positions: Postmodernism and the Rediscovery of Value* (London: Lawrence & Wishart).

Taylor-Gooby, P. (1991) 'Welfare State Regimes and Welfare Citizenship', *Journal of European Social Policy*, **1** (2): pp. 93–105.

Titmuss, R. (1970) *The Gift Relationship* (London: Allen and Unwin).

11 Whose Orgasm is this Anyway? 'Sex Work' in Long-term Heterosexual Couple Relationships
JEAN DUNCOMBE and DENNIS MARSDEN

For we live now with a new sexual dogma that allows as little deviation as the old one did. . . . And sex has become another issue that needs time and attention, another obstacle to be overcome, instead of a time out for gratification and pleasure.

(Rubin, 1991, p. 189)

The growing instability of heterosexual couple relationships has deep roots in socio-economic change. Yet it also stems from the increased media emphasis on 'the pure relationship' as the ultimate source of emotional and sexual fulfilment: according to Giddens, pressures from women for 'the transformation of intimacy' clash with men's dominative sexuality and fear of intimate emotion (Giddens, 1992); and Rubin identifies deep contradictions in the search for *self*-fulfilment through *another* person:

we are left [by media images] with an extraordinarily heightened set of expectations about the possibilities in human relationships that lives side by side with disillusion that, for many, borders on despair. (Rubin, 1991, p. 160)

In this chapter we ask how heterosexual couples in long-term relationships come to terms with any disparity between such heightened expectations and their actual sex lives. And we ask whether individuals may be viewed as performing a kind of 'sex work' – analogous to 'emotion work (Hochschild, 1983) – to bring their sexual feelings more into line with how they suspect sex 'ought to be' experienced.

In earlier papers we have discussed the nature of women's complaints concerning men's reluctance to express intimate emotion in close relationships (Duncombe and Marsden, 1993a, b). And we have suggested that to sustain the sense of intimacy in long-term relationships, women often undertake 'emotion work' on their partners and *on themselves* by insisting that 'we're ever so happy really' and putting up defences against evidence to the contrary. This process may be described as 'living the family myth' (Hochschild, 1990) or, as we would say, 'playing the couple game'. Over time, relationships may pass through various phases as change or decay proceeds at a different pace for each partner (Vaughan, 1987; Duncombe and Marsden, 1995a, b). Individuals (usually women) may initially 'deep act' away doubt, then 'shallow act' to conceal growing suspicion (Hochschild, 1983), and later 'leak' criticisms to the partner or a close friend – while still acting 'the happy couple' for outsiders – before finally talking openly. By then, men may make belated efforts to 'restage' earlier romance but women sceptically resist, no longer able to perform emotion work for this particular partner.

By analogy with emotion work, in doing 'sex work' individuals would 'manage' their emotions according to 'feeling rules' of how sex *ought* to be experienced (Hochschild, 1983), to try to attain or simulate (for themselves and/or their partners) a sexual fulfilment they would not feel 'spontaneously': for example, to endure sex, Victorian brides-to-be were exhorted to 'lie back and think of England'; and, more recently, women admit they sometimes fake orgasms, and couples (or women) are advised to 'work' on their fading relationships by restaging romance.

Currently, the new media emphasis on relationships conflicts with various feminist prescriptions of how heterosexual relationships should be enacted and experienced. In this paper we want to argue that it is essentially an empirical question how far such 'discourses of heterosex' actually become the guide-lines by which people seek to manage their sexual behaviour and emotions. But before we turn to the empirical evidence, we will first discuss the concept of sex work a little further.

SEX WORK, DISCOURSE AND POWER

The term 'sex work' has been used to refer to prostitution – contrasting paid with consensual relationships – but some feminists have denied the distinction by asserting that marital sex is essentially a form of alienated work – 'sex work' (Delphy and Leonard, 1992). While usefully stressing the hierarchical and exploitative institutionalisation of the 'male'/'female' relationship, this structuralist perspective tends to deny the relevance of individual subjective experience of sex. And, similarly, Foucault's perspective that sexual discourse shapes the way that individuals perceive sex, has not yet been extended to explore how individuals actually experience sex (Foucault, 1981; Kitzinger and Wilkinson, 1993).

Yet, as Segal insists, 'Our experiences do not simply mirror social meanings, though they are inevitably filtered through them' (Segal, 1990, p. 209); and individuals may be seen as actively 'locating themselves' within a conflicting range of discourses (Haug *et al.*, 1987; Jackson, 1990). We would suggest that these processes can be seen as the continual confirmation or reconstruction of gender and sexual identity, through the *individual* 'management' of sexual emotion in accordance with *societal* discourses which embody 'sexual scripts' (Gagnon and Simon, 1975; Hochschild, 1983; West and Zimmerman, 1991).[1]

In our later discussion of the empirical evidence, we will attempt to chart this process by examining how the creation of personal narratives taps into broader discourses, cultural narratives or 'sexual stories' (Plummer, 1994; Duncombe and Marsden, 1995a). However, a weakness of cultural studies literature is its neglect of power and the failure to locate such narratives in particular social contexts. We would argue that *societally* institutionalised gender inequalities of power ensure that most emotion (and by analogy sex) work will be performed by women, with men lacking the necessary emotional empathy and skills (Hochschild, 1983; James, 1989; Duncombe and Marsden, 1995b). While at the level of *individual* couple relationships, sex work takes place in the context of an interpersonal balance of power that derives from the unequal exchange of a range of resources, where one partner possesses what the other 'wants' or 'needs' or 'stands in awe (or fear) of' (Eichler, 1981; Duncombe and Marsden, 1995b). Such resources may include money, physical strength, sexual attractiveness (Connell, 1987), and the capacity (and propensity) to feel and deploy love or anger, but also the traditional hierarchical heterosexual discourses which construct 'men' as superior, powerful, autonomous and rational, and 'women' as subordinate, weak, dependent and emotionally needy (Rubin, 1991).

Undoubtedly, the balance of power in such exchanges tends to be tilted towards men. Yet male actors do not invariably deploy their power, nor do women always defer: actual behaviour in heterosexual relationships will depend to some extent on how deeply individuals have been influenced by the changing discourses of heterosex, which we will now briefly explore.

SEX WORK, POWER, AND THE CHANGING DISCOURSES OF HETEROSEX

In fact, Giddens's version of the pure relationship – with open disclosure and (what he inappropriately terms) 'plastic' sexuality – mirrors the media ideal in being innocent of gender power and implying no need for sex work by either partner: feelings would spontaneously match the ideal. However, an obstacle to the attainment of this ideal is the persistence of traditional phallocentric sex, where the dominant male pays no attention to his partner's sexual needs (Hamblin, 1983; Seidler, 1989; Cohen, 1990; Jackson, 1990), and the only sex work is performed by dependent women upon themselves, in order to suppress their distaste or protect male self-esteem.

Second-wave feminism urged women to become sexual subjects and take the initiative in reaching orgasm *for themselves* (Koedt, 1971; Hite, 1976; Ehrenreich, 1987); but the recommended means was clitoral self-stimulation, which meant that the issue of women's attainment of sexual pleasure was detached from any consideration of possible heterosexual contexts or any need to perform sex work beyond the suppression of traditional inhibitions (Segal, 1983; Wilson, 1983; although see Segal, 1990).

Against this view, Hamblin (1983) argued that women's sexual pleasure depends on sexual empathy (or as we would say, a willingness by both parties to undertake sex work on behalf of the other) in a relationship with a non-traditional male. However, such a 'domesticated' view of heterosex has been challenged in several ways. As we have just seen, some radical feminists insist that heterosex *invariably* involves male domination (Dworkin, 1993), backed by the threat of male power and sanctioned by society: on this view, any sex work by women would be undertaken through false consciousness and serves only to reproduce their own subjection (Duncombe and Marsden, 1995b). Alternatively, Webster asks of Hamblin's ideal: 'Where is he erotic in all those bland images women are supposed to like?' (Vance, 1984), and claims that if women are to tell their lovers what they want, they must first confront and accept the true nature of their own desires –

or, in our terms, they must do sex work to free themselves not only from traditional inhibitions but also from the influence of recent domesticated discourses of heterosex. Hodgkinson, however, regards such feminist accounts of female desire as women simulating male levels of sex-drive which they do not spontaneously feel; and she argues that the only way to maintain any long-term relationship with men is to negotiate celibacy from a position of financial independence (Hodgkinson, 1986).

Recently, a small number of heterosexual feminist women and male writers on masculinity have tried to argue that their own individual subjective experiences contradict the prevailing feminist discourse which rejects penetrative sex with men on the grounds that heterosex is always male-dominated. Wendy Hollway says that she feels equal in sex if she feels equal in the wider relationship, and she actually feels *more* powerful where the man openly desires her: some men admit that their need for a particular woman makes them feel vulnerable and her appear powerful – although men try to conceal such vulnerability (Hollway, in Cartledge and Ryan, 1983). Indeed David Cohen is impatient with women who say that sex is always done 'to' or 'against' them, when he experiences sex 'with' women as equal: he resents being blamed as an oppressor by women who fail to communicate their needs and preferences, yet still expect him to initiate sex and bring them to orgasm (Cohen, 1990; see also, Seidler, 1989; Jackson, 1990).

However, while there is undoubtedly some truth in these individual subjective accounts, any attempt to generalise must take on board the whole complex range of dimensions of interpersonal power which we outlined above. Similarly, recent claims that men are 'victims' (Lyndon, 1992), fail to understand how gender inequalities of power remain institutionalised both in the wider society, and at the level of the basic discourses of sexual exchange which undermine women's ability and right to initiate or refuse sexual intercourse. However, the argument that men are sometimes pressured into having sex unwillingly has at least the merit that it problematises male sexual response, and suggests that men too may sometimes come under pressure to do sex work to simulate desire and suppress distaste.

The range and conflict among these various discourses underlines the need for empirical research, and also suggests how we may focus our interest in sex work. We can explore the influence of the discourses of heterosex upon people's behaviour and subjective experiences of sexual relationships by asking: which partner may be seen as doing sex work for whom, and under the influence of which particular discourse of how heterosex 'ought' to be?

EMPIRICAL FINDINGS FROM OTHER STUDIES

With this question in mind we will now describe some empirical find-ings from other recent research and from our own study of long-term heterosexual couple relationships.[2] We should, of course, warn that the way individuals play 'the couple game' means that exploration of the phenomena of sex work raises difficult methodological, ethical and philosophical questions, not only for the research process but in the evaluation of what individuals are prepared to reveal about this most intimate part of their lives (Duncombe and Marsden, 1995c).

Rubin's large US survey and Mansfield and Collard's study of 60 UK newly-weds both found that people tended to gauge the state of their relationships and emotions according to the media ideal, but they also found a large disparity between that ideal and couples' actual behaviour (Mansfield and Collard, 1989; Rubin 1991). For example, Rubin reported that although some men said they welcomed the 'new sexual assertiveness' in women's behaviour, others feared that it re-vealed wide experience with other men: in fact, men appeared to want a 'sexually-experienced virgin'! (Rubin, 1991, p. 151). Meanwhile women said they valued tenderness and sensitivity, yet they 'still wanted a man to be a man', not a 'wimp'. Similarly, Mansfield and Collard found that men wanted their wives to take the initiative more in sex – but not to 'take over'; while women wanted their husbands to be 'domi-nating but in a gentle sort of way'.

Both studies found that the goal of heterosexual sex had become the mutual orgasm, and Rubin reported a large decline in women admitting to faking; but women now saw their own orgasm as important for their husbands too, whereas men's orgasm was still seen as automatic and unproblematic. However, Mansfield and Collard found that mar-riage had quickly changed the balance of the couples' sex-lives: wives now found it more difficult to refuse sex in case their husbands felt rejected, but husbands were less likely to express the emotional inti-macy that wives felt they needed for sex to be fulfilling (husbands, however, interpreted any reduction in their wives' sexual interest as due to the pill rather than their own behaviour).

In fact, married couples generally experience a long-term decline in sexual activity,[3] which has been attributed to 'habituation', or the 'dis-tractions' of family life and work (Frank and Anderson, 1980; Rubin, 1991; Weiss, 1990). It has been suggested that a companionate 'ten-derness' may outweigh any sexual regrets (Frank and Anderson, 1980), but Rubin reports how many of her respondents in longer-term relationships 'mourn the passing of ... passion' (Rubin, 1991, pp. 166–71), and occasionally get nostalgic flashbacks and wonder, 'Why can't we make this happen all the time?' (Rubin, 1991, p. 186).

OUR STUDY OF CHANGE IN LONGER-TERM RELATIONSHIPS

Our respondents echoed this puzzlement that they could not recapture earlier passion and romance – apart from the occasional sense of déja vu with the aid of wine or the romantic setting of a holiday (Duncombe and Marsden, 1995a). But the decline of passion and tactile or sensual intimacy seemed somehow inevitable: one wife said, 'We don't have sex so much now, I mean I think you'd have to be pretty energetic to maintain that sort of.... Sometimes we have a long kiss but not so much now. Not every day.... We like being, I mean *I* like being close.'

However, it was surprisingly common for women now to 'confess' that they had *always 'at some level'* found their sexual relationships unfulfilling:

> He didn't really bother with foreplay. But somehow I was so into him that it didn't matter, and I never said anything. I sort of didn't notice, yet I sort of did. ... I think somehow it doesn't seem important, and you don't want to hurt their feelings. And somehow the sex seemed wonderful even when it went wrong.

Other wives commented on early doubts (about erection failures, or the shape or size of their husband's penis) about which they had reassured their husband or blamed themselves, but which they now consciously recognised *had* mattered 'at some level' even then, and had come to matter more later.

In contrast, men who acknowledged early problems tended to blame what they saw as their wives' low sex-drive:

> I really do ... *try*, but. ... I think she might be one of those women who just doesn't need sex.... I remember a very funny night, we went out to see some friends and the bloke had devised a chart.... There were three colours, one where his wife wanted it, one when he wanted it, and one when they both wanted it.... But I thought, I wouldn't need ... the one when Penny wanted it.... [But] if I'd sat down and said, 'Look Penny, we've got a problem in our sex

life, we need to talk about it', she would have gone off in a rage, so I just didn't bother.

However, several husbands had recognised their own deficiencies, again initially at some rather deep level:

> We kind of settled into a routine where I liked sex early in the morning ... but she was sleepy ... although she'd let me have it (I was a 'dawn raider'!). ... I can remember ... 'subliminally'. ... I was frightened of *letting* her get into it ... because I wouldn't know what to do with it. ... It made me feel a bit inadequate. ...[But] it's not all my fault because she never said – she sort of said she got pleasure even if she didn't come – and she would never participate much if I tried anything different.

Discussion was avoided because each partner did not want to hurt the other, but also men feared looking vulnerable while women feared men's anger:

> It was like he knew there had to be foreplay so – a couple of squeezes up here, then a quick rummage about down there and straight in. But he went *berserk* when I tried to say I'd like him to try more in the foreplay bit. ... I thought he'd hit me.

So couples tended to develop informal strategies and routines – restricting sex to particular nights, or giving coded messages like wearing sexy nighties or bathing at an unusual time – which indicated and regulated sexual availability (and incidentally avoided the need for woman openly to show desire).

THE DISRUPTIONS OF WORK, CHILDBIRTH AND FAMILY

We have discussed in more detail elsewhere (Duncombe and Marsden, 1993a, b, 1995b) how men's preoccupation with work, leading to a kind of 'psychic desertion' of their marriages, may strike at the roots of intimacy between the couple. As one man said:

> It's almost as if I 'climb into my head'. ... Sometimes when my wife comes in and fancies a cuddle, I just can't do it. ... I can go

through the motions ... but I know I'm not really there – and she senses it too. ... I'm even worse with actual sex. ... I just have to come clean with my wife and tell her I can't. ... She tries to understand; but it's one thing to understand once in a while, but it's another to have to put up with repeated disappointments.

The wife of another man attributed the major sexual difficulties in their relationship to her feeling that, 'He's not been married to me emotionally. ... When the chips were down, when I really needed him – not anybody else, just him – he couldn't be there for me.'

Another major change came with childbirth. The relatively unusual couples who had experienced little disruption said they had consciously 'worked at' their relationship:

The difficulty for quite a lot of the men is ... he feels very left out. ... She seems very bound up with [children], not fancying him any more. ... I think we recognised that it's actually important to have some time for ourselves ... make the effort – go out and have supper together, go to the theatre, dress up, go through the social sort of ritual of looking pretty or whatever.

In contrast, other couples said they had married to have children and seemed swallowed up in family life: one husband commented, 'Well, you don't get much time [for sex] do you. Well, I mean on the odd occasion ... [His wife put in meaningfully, '*Very* odd!'] But it's all right though. We'll have plenty of time when they're grown up.' In another couple, the wife said:

[Sex] was our greatest togetherness. It was very silly, very personal and very intimate. ... [Now] we have a problem of *biology*. ... We're late night people, but I have to get up in the morning with Rosie, but then by the time she goes to bed, [my husband's] just getting going.

Sometimes post-natal depression had cast a shadow that couples could still hardly bear to talk about. One wife recalled that for a long time after she had her first baby:

I couldn't do it [sex]. ... I was petrified and [my husband] got angry which made it worse. ... I'd got it into my head that there was something psychologically wrong with me and I was frigid. ... We didn't communicate much because he got madly into DIY. . . . I do remember now, being upset with no sex life, but as soon as I sort of thought, I pushed it away. . . . I was consumed with guilt. . . . I thought I was a failure. . . . And the funny thing is, people used to envy us, they thought we looked a really sexy couple. . . . As a couple we didn't have any sex but we were a really happy *family*.

Another wife described a similarly precarious 'tacit agreement':

Pete used to say, like, he didn't mind. . . . But every now and then, you know, 'the erection in your back'. . . . I used to feel it was my *duty* . . . and sex was horrible, I used to cry afterwards.

We suspect that such breakdowns and difficulties in sexual relations after childbirth may be much more common than is generally recognised (Saunders, 1983).

SEXUAL EXPERIMENTATION, PORNOGRAPHY AND MASTURBATION

To overcome boredom or sexual difficulties couples sometimes experimented with the use of pornography or changes of sexual techniques, or they had resorted to more frequent masturbation.[4] Our data suggest differences between the incorporation of pornography during the earlier passionate phase of a relationship, as compared with the attempt to liven up sex that had lost its passion. In either case men tended to be the initiators because they more readily found pornography arousing and hoped it would help overcome women's inhibitions (get them 'worked up'). But pornography was more acceptable to women early in the relationship (when they might also dress up in sexy undies) than later with a partner for whom they had lost their sense of intimacy, when they felt less able to 'allow' themselves to become (and admit to being) sexually aroused.

Some couples had agreed to experiment with the introduction of pornography later in their relationship: as one husband said, 'What else can you do if you've been married for twelve years and you don't want to endanger your relationship by having affairs?' However, this couple were uneasy at how maintaining the boost to their sex-life seemed to need more frequent changes and ever 'harder' porn. Then, it was women who began to find pornography distasteful and a 'turn-off'.

In our study, the husbands had often wanted their wives to give them oral sex, although it was not uncommon for wives to refuse even early on. And while a few who had complied, sensed a power over men's vulnerability, they sometimes admitted suppressing qualms about smell and taste. However, as intimacy decayed, such feelings increased as did the sense of coercion, until oral sex ceased.

As a relatively guilt-free and 'functional' safety-valve for their marriages, husbands began to resort to more frequent solitary masturbation – not uncommonly at work where pornography was available.

> You have to be quiet, it's funny really. Sometimes I wonder, afterwards, how many other blokes were wanking in the loo!

Although some wives felt released by this from pressures to have sex, over time husbands might become resentful:

> It would be no skin off her nose. . . . Sometimes I just want her to let me put it in and do it. . . . She's broken the contract. Sex is *part* of marriage, and I can't see that anything's changed enough to alter that.

One woman claimed she didn't mind her husband masturbating in the bathroom but she resented the way it joggled her about in bed; but the husband claimed that she aroused his desire, so she should help or at least let him do it in comfort! For a husband deliberately to let his wife know he masturbated could be a deliberate attempt to induce guilt.

A few men said they felt uneasy at how masturbation seemed to affect their view of women or their relationship. One had noticed:

> I seem to get into looking at *bits* of women's bodies, bums and tits and fannies! And then when my wife occasionally lets me do it . . . it's like what I call 'fanny wanking', just me going at this bum and this fanny, and not like doing it with a *person*.

Another worried that:

> By getting into the magazines I'm shifting my interest away from her, so I'm making it more difficult to get back together again. . . . [And] when I'm with her sometimes these magazine images come up into your head, you seem to *need* them sometimes to get that extra 'edge' so you can come.

Another man gave his definition of authentic sex: 'When the woman you're making love to, or at least the bits of her you're looking at, fit your ideal fantasy! Then it's *wonderful*. But if she's a long way off, it can be hell, you feel terrible doing it!'

Unlike men, women actually *preferred* to masturbate alone, out of greater shyness but also afraid their husbands would see their behaviour as an insult or a prelude to penetration. Women's masturbation might also be seen as 'functional' for marriage (giving them the orgasm their husband could not). However, (as with men) masturbation could bring the realisation of lack of fulfilment in their relationship; and discovering about orgasms (in one instance through contact with a women's group) could sometimes change women's lives more radically:

> I started to think [feeling frigid] wasn't my fault – which actually [my husband] had . . . let me believe. And I started to feel angry, . . . I read about [masturbation] so I decided to try it and it made me feel very powerful to learn about my own body.

This wife then discovered she could attain orgasm with other men, and the couple have now negotiated an open relationship.

THE 'BRICK WALL' OF RESENTMENT

With a degree of good-will and openness, sexual difficulties could be helped or contained, but in some relationships disappointment and resentment accumulated until – as described by the woman whose husband had 'not been married to her emotionally':

> Now I've got a sort of brick wall round my sexual feelings. . . . But it's been bad for a long time, and we've been papering over the cracks, or I have. . . . I look at him and I think, 'God, what's matter with me. He's a *good* man . . .' But there's no chemistry for me any more. . . . I can sort of work myself up into it if I've been out with friends. . . . I can almost transport myself back into how I felt then. Then I feel, 'It's OK! It's going to work'. Then it's almost as if, a day later, I think, 'Oh dear, I let too much of myself out'. I let the barriers go up again.

Another woman said she used to 'love her husband to death', but after years of his failure to support her and increasingly violent drunken behaviour she could no longer bear to sleep with him: 'I now feel steely-strong inside.'

Men too may build a wall around their feelings, but perhaps more often from this sense of the breach of some unspoken sexual 'contract',[5] and from injured pride of possession. Another man was (somewhat unjustifiably) enraged to find his wife was having an affair, but then she had tried to patch up a truce:

For the last three years . . . she's been the perfect wife, I can't fault her. But the trust has gone and the resentment has come. The awful thing is, I have this brick wall of resentment. I can't take it down even if I want to, it's as if I'm concreted in. . . . I can't bear to touch her.

Although the wall might be built only brick by brick, final completion and rupture of the relationship could come suddenly and finally indeed.

CELIBACY AND AFFAIRS

A sizeable proportion of couples had negotiated long or short periods of celibacy (sometimes rationalised as due to snoring or incompatible sleep patterns). But such negotiations were seldom equal or amicable because usually only one partner wanted to give up sex, and there could be the open or concealed influence of affairs.

One wife felt her husband had always dominated her, and he still continued to desire her although she found sex with him distasteful because she was now secretly in love with someone else. She had no means to gain her independence, but she managed to move to another room saying she needed her own space (an arrangement the husband respected). Now she still allowed him sex when she wanted a new dress or a day out. Another couple (after first presenting a happy front) confessed they had once negotiated celibacy after long conflict over the husband's failure to show intimacy. Even so, she had resisted his moving out, and when he became depressed she allowed him to negotiate to return – but on the basis that he must now at least simulate affection.

Where one partner was having an affair, the negotiated truce or stand-off seemed likely to prove unstable. One woman had resorted to affairs because she did not want to break up her family although she no longer loved her husband:

> I'd feel really miserable and think to myself, 'Is this all there is?' But then when I've got an affair, while I'm having sex with my husband I can think about sex with the other man, and that makes it bearable.

However, she had now fallen in love and wanted to spend her life with her lover. Similarly, thinking she was frigid, another of the women who described a 'brick wall' around their sexual feelings had got into an affair almost by accident, but it now threatened to end her marriage:

> It's frightened me. He [the lover] awoke those feelings. I felt, 'Gosh!... I can feel those feelings . . .' Meanwhile my husband thinks perhaps we'll go off for sex therapy . . . get the mechanics working again, that will cure everything . . . but it can't. It's all that other stuff that's gone before that's caused the situation.

In all these instances where couples had come to some kind of negotiated stand-off arrangements about sex, there was the ever-present danger that the marriage would be destabilised by one partner becoming involved in a passion that would highlight the inadequacies of the marriage.

EMPIRICAL EVIDENCE OF THE PERFORMANCE OF SEX WORK

We will now sum up the empirical evidence concerning the influence of ideologies or feeling rules of how sex 'ought' to be experienced, and whether we can see any shift of power between the sexes by looking at who does what sex work for whom.

Both Rubin's and Mansfield and Collard's data may be interpreted as women now needing to do less sex work to overcome their own inhibitions, and also being less inclined to do sex work ('faking') on behalf of men. However, although the 'new' woman now values her orgasm for herself, she also wants it *for* her man, and she still wants him to take the initiative – which in fact suits the 'new' man because he remains reluctant to allow power in sex to shift so far that he becomes the 'object' of women's desire. But, unfortunately, it seems to be only relatively briefly (before marriage!) that the 'new' man is prepared to do sex work for his partner, so the suspicion is that he welcomes women taking the sexual initiative only to the extent that this relieves him of doing the sex work necessary to make her come – although (now he knows women can reach orgasm) he needs this as evidence to validate his own sexual performance.

During the initial phase of 'falling in love' it is as if spontaneous desire wipes out doubt and feelings match the ideal, so no sex work may be 'necessary'. However, it also seems true in some relationships that initially individuals (particularly women) 'deep act' away any early doubts about sex, but later rewrite the narrative to acknowledge that they always knew 'at some level' that something was wrong.

As time passes, 'habituation' and loss of eroticism bring the need for sex work to restage romance to regain earlier feelings (*déjà vu*), but recapturing earlier passion in the context of everyday life becomes harder or impossible. Also, men become more unwilling to do emotion and sex work for their wives, and instead resort to *physical* experiment or pornography to arouse them (get them 'worked' up). However, faced with what they see as men's insensitivity, women too become less inclined to do sex work for their partner, to behave erotically, watch pornography or suppress any distaste for their husband's practices or body. For both partners, resort to solitary masturbation avoids the need for sex work on behalf of the other.

In some long-term relationships where there is poor communication and less goodwill, over time, men's emotional insensitivity and women's response of increasing reluctance to allow men sex may result in the disappointment of both partners. And there is a corresponding downward spiral into resentment which ends in the building of a 'brick wall' around sexual feelings for one or other, although usually the woman. A minority of wives, subject to the traditional discourses of duty, may become so cross-pressured that they feel 'frigid', but an affair may bring 'release' – perhaps from sex work *negatively directed* against the husband.

When relationships become stripped of their underpinnings of sex work – whether through resentment, one partner's attempt to negotiate celibacy, or the disruptions and stress of childbirth – the different dimensions of interpersonal power emerge more starkly and sex assumes in 'exchange value', now regulated by verbal, or more-explicit bodily negotiation rather than the earlier unspoken 'contracts' (Saunders, 1983).

Finally, for many (perhaps all) individuals, reaching orgasm involves fantasy – either fantasies coming unbidden or the auto-eroticism of fantasies more calculatedly evoked to attain orgasm during solitary masturbation or sex with a partner. Segal argues that this process too entails 'work': for women, not only the sex work of conjuring up the fantasies but also the work of coming to terms with their *content* and their effect upon sexual relationships (Segal, 1983, 1990; Kitzinger and Wilkinson, 1993).[6] With a commendably open (but rare) self-knowledge and frankness, Segal discloses that any gain in power from achieving her own orgasm is undermined because:

> I resent the content of my fantasies [of domination and degradation] and I resent the effort I have to make to produce them. . . . I don't want to have to do all that work for myself. [I also resent] the disconnection which occurs with lovers who are caring, gentle and as extensively physically stimulating as I could wish. (Segal, 1983, pp. 39, 44)

This sense of separation through masturbation was echoed (although less explicitly and sensitively) by several of our male respondents.

IN CONCLUSION: THE PURSUIT OF 'AUTHENTIC' SEX

Overall, we would argue that there is considerable empirical evidence of sex work, both where individuals reveal the influence of ideologies of how they believe sex 'ought' to be and, more explicitly, where they say they have to 'try' or 'work' or 'force' themselves to have sex. We cannot say how far sex work pervades sexual life, but we are not arguing that people live at a constant pitch of sexual disappointment or even desperation – only that we suspect that 'at some level' many long-term couples would recognise the difficulties described here.

In arguing that the performance of sex work is probably widespread (even among couples who get on well together), we risk implying that sex is normally difficult, distasteful or alienating. Yet, like 'work' itself, sex work may be either fulfilling or distasteful, depending upon the relational context in which it is performed: a woman may fake an orgasm under duress, to placate or flatter the self-esteem of someone powerful whom she dislikes; but alternatively she may do so to express sexual fulfilment with someone she loves but who does not sufficiently turn her on sexually.

We have finally to confess that we do not know where this exploration of sex work has taken us – or our respondents. In our more cynical moments we suspect that there is no 'authentic' sex, that individuals' (mainly women's) performance of emotion work and sex work serves merely to mask from participants in intimate heterosexual relationships the operation of basic imbalances of power, which then emerge when such work ceases to be done. And even when sex does not *feel* like work or oppression, this is merely because feelings match the feeling rules and: 'to feel free is to lie easy in one's chains'.

Perhaps in the pursuit of 'authenticity' we are asking impossible questions: to have feelings devoid of any reference to the cultural images of the societies in which we live as social beings, would be merely a world of polymorphous perversity. Or to put it another way, Arlie Hochschild's question: 'Am I acting now: how do I know?', may have no possibility of an answer, since the perspective of emotion work merely removes key questions to other levels of explanation (Hochschild, 1983, p. 45 and Appendix; Cohen and Taylor, 1992). Perhaps, after all, the concept of 'sex work' provides not an explanation of change in behaviour but merely an alternative description or metaphor.

Meanwhile, when we try to chart changes in power between the sexes by asking our respondents the very modern question: 'How was it for you?', we are left only with further levels of complexity. If men now want women to have orgasms but are not prepared to do enough sex work on (or 'for') them to make sure they come – and women want to have orgasms for themselves, but also want to have orgasms for men and for them to take the sexual initiative – but women are no longer prepared to fake – yet they may also do sex work through fantasy to make themselves come – although this act of fantasy may drive a wedge between the couple in what 'ought to be' a mutual orgasm. . . . We may well return to the question in the title of our paper: Whose orgasm *is* this anyway?

NOTES

1. The process of identity reconstruction should be seen as bounded by (possibly) biology and by early psychodynamic and socialisation experiences (Hochschild, 1983, Appendix; Rubin, 1991).

2. We gratefully acknowledge receipt of ESRC funding for this study (grant ROOO 23 2737). This working paper is based on a series of pilot and group interviews, along with a main core sample of 38 White couples, married 15 years, drawn from one locality and weighted for social class.
3. In the US and UK, sexual activity and marital satisfaction decline, the latter reaching a low point after 15 years although the pattern is by no means simple (Frank and Anderson, 1980; evidence summarised in Goodman, 1993; Wellings *et al.*, 1994).
4. Rubin gives some evidence on pornography and changes in sexual technique, e.g. oral sex is now practised by most younger couples – though not anal sex (Rubin, 1991). US surveys indicate that masturbation is relatively common in marriage, men more than women (Aldridge, 1983; Goodman, 1993).
5. One of Weiss's businessmen respondents complained: '[Sex] is not as important to me as it once was. We just agree to disagree. . . . But I guess I feel deprived. I agreed to a monogamous relationship, but somehow I'm not getting out of it what I think I should be getting out of it. . . . But I don't express [my] anger because I don't want to hurt my wife. . . . I look at the anger in a way as childish. Although I'm not sure it is' (Weiss, 1990, p. 226).
6. For further discussions of heterosex from the perspective of heterosexual feminism, see Jackson (1996, in this volume) and Segal (1994).

REFERENCES

Aldridge, R. G. (1983) 'Masturbation during Marriage', *Correctional and Social Psychology Journal*, 27: pp. 112–14.
Cartledge, S. and Ryan, J. (1983) *Sex and Love: New Thoughts on Old Contradictions* (London: The Women's Press).
Cohen, D. (1990) *Being a Man* (London: Routledge).
Cohen, S. and Taylor, L. (1992) *Escape Attempts* (London: Routledge).
Connell, R. W. (1987) *Gender and Power* (Oxford: Polity).
Delphy, C. and Leonard, D. (1992) *Familiar Exploitation* (Oxford: Polity).
Duncombe, J. and Marsden, D. (1993a) 'Gender Inequalities in the Performance of Emotion Work in the Private Sphere', in *Conference Proceedings of the 1992 Cambridge Stratification Research Seminar* (Cambridge: Social Research Group).
Duncombe, J. and Marsden, D. (1993b) 'Love and Intimacy: the Gender Division of Emotion and "Emotion Work"', *Sociology*, 27(2): pp. 221–41.
Duncombe, J. and Marsden, D. (1995a) 'Can Men Love? "Reading", "Staging" and "Resisting" the Romance', in L. Pearce and J. Stacey (eds), *Romance Revisited* (London: Lawrence & Wishart).
Duncombe, J. and Marsden, D. (1995b) '"Workaholics" and "Whingeing Women": Theorising Intimacy and Emotion Work – the Last Frontier of Gender Inequality?', *Sociological Review*, 43(1): pp. 150–69.
Duncombe, J. and Marsden, D. (1995c) 'Can We Research the Private?', paper presented to the BSA Conference, Essex 1993, in L. Morris and S. J. Lyon (eds), *Gender Relations in Public and Private* (London: Macmillan).

Dworkin, A. (1987) *Intercourse* (London: Arrow).

Ehrenreich, B. (1987) *Remaking Love* (London: Fontana Collins).

Eichler, M. (1981) 'Power, Dependency, Love and the Sexual Division of Labour', *Journal of Women's Studies Quarterly*, 4(2): pp. 201–19.

Frank, E. and Anderson, C. (1980) 'The Sexual Stages of Marriage', *Family Circle* February, p. 64.

Foucault, M. (1981) *The History of Sexuality* (Harmondsworth: Penguin).

Gagnon, J. and Simon, W. (1975) *The Sexual Scene* (Chicago, IL: Transaction Books).

Giddens, A. (1992) *The Transformation of Intimacy* (Oxford: Polity).

Goodman, N. (1993), *Marriage and the Family* (New York: Harper Collins).

Hamblin, A. (1983) in S. Cartledge and J. Ryan (1983).

Haug, F. *et al.* (1987) *Female Sexualization* (London: Verso).

Hite, S. (1976) *The Hite Report on Female Sexuality* (New York: Macmillan).

Hochschild, A. R. (1983) *The Managed Heart* (London: University of California Press).

Hochschild, A. R., with Maching, A. (1990) *The Second Shift* (London: Piarchus).

Hodgkinson, L. (1986) *Sex Is Not Compulsory* (London: Columbus Books).

Jackson, A. (1990) *Unmasking Masculinity* (London: Unwin Hyman).

James, N. (1989) 'Emotional Labour: Skill and Work in the Social Regulation of Feelings', *Sociological Review*, 37: pp. 15–42.

Kitzinger, C. and Wilkinson, S. (1993) *Heterosexuality* (London: Sage).

Koedt, A. (1971) 'The Myth of the Vaginal Orgasm', in V. Gomick and B. Moran (eds), *Women in Sexist Society* (New York: Basic Books).

Lyndon, N. (1992) *No More Sex War* (London: Sinclair Stephenson).

Mansfield, P. and Collard, J. (1989) *The Beginning of the Rest of Your Life?* (London: Macmillan).

Plummer, K. (1994) *Telling Sexual Stories* (London: Routledge).

Rubin, L. B. (1991) *Erotic Wars* (New York: Harper Row).

Saunders, J. (1983) in S. Cartledge and J. Ryan (1983).

Segal, L. (1983) in S. Cartledge and J. Ryan (1983).

Segal, L. (1990) *Slow Motion: Changing Masculinities, Changing Men* (London: Virago).

Segal, L. (1994) *Straight Sex: The Politics of Pleasure* (London: Virago).

Seidler, V. (1989) *Rediscovering Masculinity* (London: Routledge).

Vance, C. S. (1984) *Pleasure and Danger* (London: Routledge).

Vaughan, D. (1987) *Uncoupling* (London: Methuen).

Weiss, R. S. (1990) *Staying the Course* (New York: Fawcett Columbine).

Wellings, K., Field, J., Johnson, A. M. and Wadsworth, J. (1994) *Sexual Behaviour in Britain: The National Survey of Sexual Attitudes and Lifestyles* (London: Penguin).

West, C. and Zimmerman, D. (1991) 'Doing Gender', in T. Lorber and S. Farrell (eds), *The Social Construction of Gender* (London: Sage).

Wilson, E. (1983) in S. Cartledge and J. Ryan (1983).

12 Reputations: Journeying into Gendered Power Relations
JANET HOLLAND, CAROLINE RAMAZANOGLU, SUE SHARPE and RACHEL THOMSON

INTRODUCTION

In this chapter we reflect on some of the findings from two feminist research projects carried out between 1988 and 1992 in the UK. The Women, Risk and AIDS Project was based primarily on unstructured interviews with 150 young women in London and Manchester, and the Men, Risk and AIDS Project was a comparative study of 50 young men in London.[1]

These studies of young people aged 16–21 were conceived in the late 1980s at a time of escalating public fear and confusion about HIV/AIDS, and expressions of anxieties about sexual identities and the nature of heterosexual risk. In young people's accounts of their sexuality given in interviews, attention to sexual reputation appeared important to them. Men and women clearly had different sexual reputations, and were taken as standing in different relations to sexual responsibility.

COLLISION AND COLLUSION

Sexual reputations can regulate behaviour, knowledge and expectations, since they are constituted through very powerful normative conceptions of what it is to be masculine and feminine. In journeying into adult sexuality, young women appeared under pressure to safeguard their reputations, young men under pressure to demonstrate theirs. While individual young people gave varying accounts of responses to these pressures, the effects of sexual reputation were experienced as different for young men and young women.

As young people become heterosexually active, they have to engage with gendered relations of power, even though they may resist specific effects of power.[2] In accounts of sexual reputation in the interview transcripts, we find both clear expressions of a double standard of sexual behaviour for men and women, and also a much more hidden area of power in which the masculine dominates the feminine. It is the tension between this apparent dualism of masculine/feminine sexual reputation, and a feminist conception of male power, that is the focus of this chapter.

Our thinking about accounts of sexual reputations has been influenced by looking at the young men's data through our earlier experience of analysing the data on young women. We came to the conclusion in the first study, that the young women were under pressure to construct their sexuality in response to what we have called the 'male in the head' – the surveillance power of male-dominated heterosexuality.[3] Young women gave very clear accounts of the construction of heterosexual identities within a framework of acceptance of, or resistance to, femininity. To be feminine is to construct oneself in relation to the heterosexual male.

We were struck by the limits of pleasure and absence of female desire in the young women's accounts of their sexuality as well as the extent to which they produced their femininity as disembodied (Holland *et al.*, 1994a, b). This led us to reconsider the meaning of masculine and feminine sexual reputations as opposites – as cultural constructions in collision. Young men's accounts of their sexual reputations did not make sense simply as the other side of femininity.

We had already concluded that achieving femininity was an unsafe sexual strategy in that it is constructed in relation to masculine desire and 'needs' in ways that subvert women's control of their bodies. But when we looked at the accounts young men gave of their sexual expectations and first sexual experiences, we did not find that they embarked on their sexual careers under the surveillance of a 'female in the head' (a term we are not yet able to define for reasons we discuss below). Young men, like young women, generally responded to the 'male in the head', with their male peers as the primary audience for their first sexual experiences. While male and female sexual reputations clearly exist in relation to each other, we argue that there is no balanced binary opposition between them. Young people appear to be colluding in reproducing male power through regulation by the 'male in the head'.

Young people embarking on their first sexual encounters must travel into unknown territory, guided by what they have already absorbed (or resisted) of masculinity and femininity. We felt that as feminist sociologists studying sexuality we had to make a comparable journey since the exact nature of the gendered power relations which constitute heterosexual encounters could not be taken for granted. We suggest that young people's accounts of sexual reputation locate a critical area of collusion in the production and exercise of male power.

We have arrived, by a rather different route, at some of the questions which Judith Butler (1993) has explored and which she claims feminism is inadequate to answer. She asks how resistance to heterosexuality is possible, and argues that the heterosexual dualisms of masculine/feminine, male/female have to be disrupted in order to find answers. We aim to show that by conceptualising both the 'male in the head' and the parts young people play in producing male dominance, female heterosexual reputation can be opened up as one possible area for the political subversion of male-dominated heterosexuality.

We have approached this disruption by looking beyond the conceptual constraints of seeing masculine and feminine as a pair of opposites, as mirror images of each other, different but complementary. This male/female dualism resembles a trick with mirrors – what we see dissuades us from looking for what is there. When the impetus of our data analysis pushed us to look for the 'female in the head' in the young men's transcripts, and for feminine power and empowerment in the young women's, it pushed us, as it were through the mirror. But, like Alice in *Through the Looking Glass*, what we found on the other side was not a mirror image but a different way of looking at power and collusion, so that things never appear quite the same again.

In the rest of the chapter we consider the positioning of young people in heterosexual relationships by looking at the gendering of sexual reputations, and the efforts young people make around their reputations in their first sexual encounters. We reflect on young people's accounts with an eye on the wider problem of why masculine young men have power in ways in which feminine young women do not. We suggest that a feminist reading of these accounts offers some explanation of men's continuing success in exercising power over women. We have also analysed the accounts for suggestions of resistance (by both women and men) to the power exercised by the 'male in the head'.

SEXUAL REPUTATION AND GENDER: THE DOUBLE STANDARD

Not surprisingly, young people's accounts reproduced a broad consensus that the same sexual attitudes, desires and behaviour by men and by women resulted in different sexual reputations. One young woman captures it succinctly: 'If you sleep around you're a slag, if a bloke sleeps around he's lucky'. This double standard of sexual reputation was taken for granted by some, resisted or even ridiculed by others, but the interview transcripts give a very strong sense that it is there and it is powerful, and this is confirmed in other studies (Lees, 1986, 1993; Sharpe, 1987, 1994; contributors to Weiner and Arnot, 1987). Young people varied in the ways they perceived, accepted or confronted this power, but it was generally accepted that duality existed and had to be reckoned with.

The double standard can be conceived as a vigorous mechanism for regulating sexual expectations and practices, and so a point of reference for young people in establishing sexual relationships. One young woman picked up this point when she commented on a sense of being assessed by someone else's standards:

A: I'd like to know whose standards they're measuring by, because obviously it's a double standards thing. It's all right for the lads to go out and bonk all women in sight. (21 ESW MC)[4]

Another young women implies this imbalance as she comments on the way sexual reputation impresses conformity to normative femininity:

A: With girls you're brought up to be ladylike, because if you start being rampant you're called a slag or a slut or whatever, but with boys they can get away with anything, like they won't get called no major names, they just get called Casanova and things like that, but that's not really going to hurt them, like if a girl gets called a slag. (16 AC WC)

This use of 'rampant' did not occur in any other transcript, but it stands out because it is both evocative of unfettered female desire, and impossible in terms of normative femininity. The double standard rules out rampancy, since the rampant woman is constituted, and so subdued, in relation to the male. The actively desiring woman, the woman luxuriating in extravagant sexuality, the woman seeking out men for her own sexual pleasure is constituted as a wholly negative subject. What does the rampant woman do with her man? How engulfing is her sexuality? In bursting out of her femininity, she is profoundly threatening to the 'male in the head'.[5]

In the next section we illustrate the conventional differentiation of masculinity and femininity through the operation of the double standard. While young people respond to the constraints of sexual identities and reputations in a variety of ways, and with differing degrees of acceptance and resistance, both men and women are under the surveillance of the 'male in the head' as they journey into adult sexuality, and must take account of the double standard's existence.

Women want Love and Men want Sex

Conformity to the double standard was understandable to both women and men because of the assumption that 'women want love and men want sex'. Implicit more often than explicit in the transcripts was the message that women could not afford to want sex – being rampant was off the feminine agenda.

Young women who are under pressure to produce feminine sexual identities and disciplined bodies (hair, skin, girth, orgasms, menstruation, spots) are subjected to social pressures to treat their bodies and sexuality as essentially unruly and in need of control. Smart (1992, p. 7) usefully summarises the pressures on young women to conform to a feminine standard when she points to:

> the complex ways in which discourses of law, medicine and social science interweave to bring into being the problematic feminine subject who is constantly in need of surveillance and regulation. A key focus [of Smart's paper] is the dominant idea of disruption and unruliness which is seen to stem from the very biology of the body of Woman.

These are complex and negotiated processes to disrupt or resist, but to lose this control is to lose your reputation.

Women can experience sexual pressure from men, on a continuum from mild coaxing to the point of extreme violence (Kelly, 1988; Holland *et al.*, 1992b) but women can also regulate themselves under the surveillance of the 'male in the head'. It is not usually men who choose women's clothes, hairstyles and makeup, or decide how young women should get themselves up for a night out (although their responses may be influential). Women who do not present themselves as conventionally sexually attractive are threatened with the reputation (so frequently attributed to feminists and lesbians) of being unable to get a man. Girls are often under considerable pressure to lose their virginity, but to preserve their reputations.[6] Those who do not question heterosexuality have to learn how to negotiate and communicate the uncertain boundaries between sexual allure and unqualified availability. Men are also under pressure to produce themselves in relation to a dominant conception of acceptable masculinity and to maintain their own sexual reputations (Holland *et al.*, 1994c).

These common social pressures produce differing responses. Some young men expressed their awareness of the pressures on them to approach their early sexual encounters as physical conquests rather than loving relationships:

A: I thought to myself, I've got a right winner here, I've got something to tell my mates now – and you get really excited and everything because you go to your mates and say, 'yeah – I was sweet. Had a result.' (19 Other WC)

A: I just think men go out to give her one and that's it sort of thing, you know it doesn't matter to me, the fact that the woman could become pregnant – it's just the general male attitude – get as many as you can. (20 ESW WC)

Others slip between the general image of the male, and their own behaviour:

A: But you tend to get a lot of blokes who, you know what I mean, who always want to get laid basically, you know – when you go out to a club and you do the manly thing because it's a bit of a laugh really, you know
Q: what do you mean by the manly thing?
A: I mean just being stud, you know and going on the pull and who you can pull and that. (19 ESW WC)

Some defended this view through assuming an innate difference between the sexes:

A: When a bloke gets turned on, it takes a little while to calm down again doesn't it? And they might think, 'whilst I'm here I might as well go for it', where with a woman it takes a lot longer. It takes a girl a lot longer, doesn't it?

Q: So you think once men are sexually aroused right, once they have got an erection, they have to keep going, they can't stop?

A: They can stop, but they have to be told to stop. Say a boy can't stop, the girl will try and push him away, he [may] use force. He could rape her or something, because a woman's got no chance really against a bloke who forces himself on her.   (16 ESW WC)

Other young men did not feel the male standard had to be accepted but did assume it to be powerful and dominant.

A: I don't think it's anything innate that makes men and women very different to be honest, but I think you get roles thrust upon you and the women's movement has been very good in pointing out the roles – the stereotyped roles that women are forced into. But men are forced into stereotyped roles as well, and some them are more subtle, because it looks as if they are getting what they want and the roles that are pushed on men make it – it looks as if their power roles may be [the ones] they should want most, but they are not always. I don't particularly fit the stereotype of Arnold Schwarzenegger and I don't particularly want to. I am not – I'm not the strong silent type or anything like that. I don't see many roles that – I mean, looking back on it, when I was supposed to be looking for role models, there weren't that many that were terribly attractive of men, not many at all.   (21 ESW MC)

A: I think men are quite ashamed to admit that they want other things than just a fairly quick fuck and an orgasm and women are ashamed to admit that occasionally that might be what they want. I mean sometimes you want sex, you want fairly mechanical sex and a lot of women don't seem to be able to admit to that. A lot of men don't admit to it – it's the only thing they seem able to relate to at all.   (21 ESW MC)

Masculine sexual reputation can be enhanced in this way even in the context of a 'steady' relationship:

A: A man thinks he's a stud – 'I'm going to tell all my mates I lasted twenty minutes last night, because then they will look up to me', kind of thing – 'I've got a woman and she's there to be used, let me use her'.   (18 ESW WC)

A young women summed up this version of male sexual reputation in the phrase, 'lads don't care'. Another commented, 'most of the blokes I know are completely irresponsible'. Irresponsibility (especially in relation to contraception), and wanting 'one thing only', was very general in young women's perceptions of men and masculinity, even if they personally had relationships with men whom they considered to be different.

Young women identified the same conventional differentiation of masculine and feminine reputations as the young men. The following young woman does not deny female desire, but explicitly presents it as silenced:

A: The girl is not meant to want sex, even if she does, and she's not meant to say that she does, but I mean a boy, he's meant to be sort of more dominant, 'I want sex', you know, cave-man type of thing. (16 ESW WC)

Another young woman gave examples of masculine sexuality in terms of behaviour patterns which are too strong to be easily changed:

A: My brother, my eldest brother, he is a male chauvinist. He will go with what he can get. He is – I mean, he doesn't – he's not like it to me but that's because I'm his sister, but I mean, he womanises every single girl that he goes out with, which is disgusting, but I mean, what can I do? My sister's boyfriend, he was always Jack-the-lad. (19 AC MC)

Conformity to these patterns of behaviour was not necessarily seen as inevitable, but was taken to be very general:

A: Most boys, they've only got the intentions, if – they've got a girl-friend – they're going out with this girl – they just think about the sexual side of the relationship, they don't think about anything else. (16 AC WC)

While identifying male behaviour in this way, the same young woman specified that there are girls who are like men in some respects:

A: Some girls, they think just the same way the boys do, but most girls that I know of, they want to see the different side of it, the other side, the non-sexual side.

We could perhaps conceive 'thinking in the same way as boys', as being unruly in terms of normative femininity – letting the rampancy out. Young women in this position are not only subject to self-discipline and responses from men, but from girls too, as they attribute negative sexual reputations to each other:

A: But some girls, they bring it on themselves. If they're called a slag they bring it on themselves. The way – the way some of them behave.
Q: They invite it?
A: Yeah, yeah. So I can't really help you. But if I knew that you was getting – getting called a slag and you wasn't – not one, or behaving like one, then I'd really say, 'oh, that's not fair'. But if I knew that you was all bringing it on yourself I'd say, 'I can't help you, I'm sorry'. (16 African MC)

Recognition of a double standard of sexual reputation can be found in the transcripts in very conventional terms. But the transcripts also show, sometimes explicitly as in the excerpts above, that young women may not find conventional femininity easy, and are feeling the pressures on them to dampen down desire and focus on relationships rather than their own pleasure (a point we have developed in more detail elsewhere, Holland *et al.*, 1992a). The audience for their first sexual experience, however, is their male partner, in the shadow of the 'male in the head'.

For men, achieving a masculine reputation provides a sexual licence which is denied to women, but at the expense of gentleness, intimacy, passivity and dependence. It sets young men standards they can recognise, but which they may not want, and often fail to achieve. The audience for their first sexual experiences is not the tender, caring, desiring female, but the harsher gaze of the 'male in the head', particularly as it is constituted in the male peer group (Holland *et al.*, 1994c).

One young woman commented:

A: I got to the stage where I think 'Oh, well, all lads are the same.'
Q: In what way?
A: In what way? I'm not saying they're out for one thing, I mean a lot of them are but, I don't know. Do you know, that's really hard that! All lads are the same. (21 AC WC)

In this bleak conclusion, she seems to have some sense that there is more than the male standard, but is unable to get beyond this.

Some young men did object to the idea that they are 'all the same'. Just as there were girls who 'thought like boys', there were also some young men who had tried to think and behave in more caring and sensitive ways. They made explicit distinctions between the experience of sexual conquest, and that of falling in love with a sexual partner (Holland *et al.*, 1994c). This failure to conform raises questions about resistance to normative masculinity and femininity which we take up in the next section.

New Men and Wicked Women

In analysing the double standard, we have not meant to imply that young people simply conform in general ways to its dictates. If we look at the complexity and contradictions of young people's accounts of managing their sexual reputations, we can see them not only accepting the socially constructed 'truths' of heterosexuality, but also having to deal with real power structures and relationships. Wittingly or unwittingly they can make 'gender trouble' through resistance to hidden power relations.[7]

One way in which young people commented obliquely on current complexities was through observations that the double standard was altering. Men, more than women, suggested this change. Their sense that women's ability to acquire sexual knowledge and to express sexual desire was changing was seen in different ways. It could be a straightforward threat to a man:

Q: What do you think that women want from sex?
A: I think they want a lot more than they ever have done. With discussions with people like my parents, my Mum and Dad and that – he actually says, 'I don't know how you could be with a 19 year old in this day and age, with women knowing what they do about sex.' He said, 'it would a total embarrassment to me'. He said, 'in my time, you knew absolutely nothing about sex, but the best thing was that the girl knew even less than you – so you seemed quite knowledgeable about what you were doing'. (19 ESW WC)

While a few insisted that the double standard should stay, others recognised, and often welcomed, a move towards more equality, sometimes explicitly associated with feminism or changes in the law, which gave women more space for expression of their own desires. The young men who welcomed these changes did not see them as particularly threatening to themselves. Freer expression of women's desires was seen as making women more available to men without the need for men to conquer them. It also gave men access to closer relationships and more emotionally rewarding practices. It was the pressures to conform to a rigid masculinity that were perceived as threatening:

Q: What about women. What do you think they want out of sex, is it similar or . . .?

A: Yes. I think some women just want sex and some women want to make love. I think there is similarities. I think more so now than twenty or thirty years ago, or forty years ago. I think women's awareness of their own sexuality was like kept down a lot. . . . I think more men are now getting more aware of that sort of side of women's feelings. (20 African MC)

This sense of change included young women being more able to express interest in sex and even make the first move (within constraints) but the prevalence of a double standard is still assumed:

A: I think it's just something born out of like what people think should happen. Women probably feel they shouldn't really make the first move because the men are going to think something of them that they shouldn't do.

Q: You think they might think badly of them?

A: Yes, I think that happens quite a bit. Which is just a shame really, because its like the old thing that if the man kind of makes the first move he's just looked at in a different light, to what if a woman did the same thing, and that's just a shame because that situation never came about really. (19 ESW WC)

Some were explicit that any changes in men's behaviour were coming about because of greater sexual freedom for women:

Q: So you think things are changing then in sexual beliefs?

A: Yes, I think they have got this thing now where they are all talking about the new man kind of image all the time. I don't actually think there is such a thing as a new man, I think the woman he is with has changed, demanding different things from her man, which is changing it. I don't think men have changed at all. I think it's just women that have changed. . . . I think they are changing men which is a great idea. (19 ESW WC)

For those men who were not threatened by their perceptions of change, what was particularly welcome was the possibility of women making sexual advances to them. This relieved them of the pain of being rejected, and took them out of the peer-group competition for sexual conquest. One young woman commented on the problem of negative reputation still dogging changes in behaviour, and hints that it is love that makes negotiation possible for women making the first move:

A: Some say that it's always the men who should make the move, but I disagree with that, I think if you both want to do it, well then – Some men feel really intimidated, they think, oh God, you know, what's wrong with her, sort of thing. You're sex-mad or something. No, it's – it's just like it makes a change. I said, well, why should it always be the man that wants to do it? You know, it should be an equal thing, it's between two people, you don't make love to yourself. So – I don't know, some men can be really funny about it. (18 AC MC)

There were some young people, particularly students, who thought that, amongst their own friends at least, the double standard had faded away, or certainly they themselves did not think or act that way. Or perhaps they were even-handed in condemnation of male and female 'promiscuity' whilst the double standard might still operate elsewhere. But the majority felt that, unfair and undesirable though it may be, the double standard was active and powerful. A sexual reputation was a positive attribute for a man, but deeply negative for a woman.[8]

Other young people did not emphasise change, but took explicitly critical stands towards the pressures to conform. The following young woman tries to reject the positive image of male sexual reputation:

A: Yeah, the boys – there is double standards, because like I suppose there is – they say, 'oh, the man's a bit of a stud', you know, but – I mean, if it's true the guy's a bit of a stud, I'm more likely to think he was a bit of a prat really. (18 ESW WC)

And here are two young men both, in different ways, recognising gendered sexual strategies, and distancing themselves from conventional evaluations of them.

A: I couldn't spend my time in a room of men – the majority – I mean I hate sort of other people covering a blanket of, 'oh, men!', you know. But I know a lot of sort of male people that are I mean competitive. You know, it's sort of sex is this, you know, and you go out and pick someone up, and, you know – it seems sort of tedious to me. (18 ESW MC)

A: I don't go calling girls slags. I mean I've had more than one partner, so I could be called a slag or whatever as well – but it's
wrong. If blokes do it they're studs; if women do it they're slags.
Something ought to be done about it, it's not very nice.
Q: It's quite hard for women . . .
A: They want to enjoy themselves and they're slags then, well, they've
got to choose between – they shouldn't be called slags or anything, I think it's out of order. (16 ESW WC)

The young men who distanced themselves, and saw themselves as distanced from, the social pressures to conform to prevailing conceptions
of heterosexual masculinity, regarded themselves as different, and had
explicit explanations from personal experience for their difference, from
their perception of conventional masculinity and other men. Since heterosexual masculinity is socially constructed in opposition to femininity
and homosexuality, men cannot simply step out of social maleness
(Woodhouse, 1989). To be a man is to be not-woman, not-gay, not
absorbed back into a mother/son relationship. A man who rejects heterosexual conquest, who makes himself a willing wimp, may call himself a new man, but in the terms of the double standard he is a loser.
The femininity of the wimp could be said to produce unruliness within
the present frameworks of heterosexuality and so to require regulation. This process of regulation is not just a matter of discursive practices; it can be violent, making male resistance to masculinity physically
dangerous.

This process of regulation works in ways which young people can
be aware of, but do not necessarily see as regulation. The wimp can
come under pressure from women to stand up for himself and be a
'real man'. Men were very explicit about the pain of having to make
the first advance and risk rejection, and especially the pain of public
rejection. This was much more of an issue when men cared for a particular woman, rather than seeking sexual conquests. Negotiating a close
relationship is risky because it can give private space for women's
power.

When men want love and women want sex they can simply reverse
their conventional male/female roles, but they may instead begin to

deconstruct heterosexual dualisms and, in private at least, to negotiate other possibilities. Problems arise not only in the process of negotiation, but in moving negotiated relationships from private to public, or from one relationship to another. It is possible for men to negotiate types of relationship in private with a (male or female) sexual partner (or partners) which cannot easily be made public – on the streets, in the family, at school, at work; just as private violence between lesbians cannot easily be made public (Kelly, 1991).

The mirror trick of the double standard can be shown from the other side of the looking glass, when we see that the wimp's male model of sexual power has no female converse. The apparent dualism of the double standard excludes the possibility of an independent female desire. The sexually desiring female is constituted within the structures of heterosexuality as a wicked woman. The wicked woman is available as an object or means of men's desire, but is subordinated within masculine sexuality.

This may be clearer if we distinguish between social power and individual power. When it is claimed that women *do* have sexual power over men, this can refer to rejection experienced by men, or to power exercised by individual women in private. Women can dominate in the bedroom, but do not become socially powerful through femininity. Men have social power in the sense of access to male dominance through conventions of masculinity. As individuals, however, they need not choose it, or may fail to access it. Heterosexual masculinity is constructed so that only a minority can access it. It is a game of winners and losers. Young men can lack power in personal sexual relations (for example when a man is nervous about his performance, or wants emotional dependence and his female partner is experienced and confident). Personal power can become more important in later sexual relationships as people reflect critically on their experience, but this is not necessarily the case.

Ideas of women's pleasure, of rampant femininity, do not fit into the dualism of the double standard and so become shocking, as one young woman noted:

A: I was in the third year coming home on the bus. It was mainly girls for some reason that got on the bus. And these few lads were hell bent on embarrassing these girls by saying, 'do you masturbate?' The girls that knew what it was, most of them went scarlet, put their eyes down, their heads down and went 'shut up, shut up'. Girls aren't supposed to do it. Boys do it because it's their virility. They've got a willy so that's what they are supposed to do. But I don't think that a lot of men even realise that a lot of women do masturbate. They got to me and said 'do you masturbate?' I stood up and said 'yes I do, what about it?' The lads sat down and didn't say a single word until the end of term. They were horrified, very embarrassed.   (20 ESW WC)

Within the boundaries of 'compulsory heterosexuality' (Rich, 1983), female desire is undefined, underdeveloped and difficult to articulate.

Young women cannot change femininity without fundamentally affecting the 'male in the head'.[9] It is easier to disrupt male definitions of desire than to produce female desire itself. We have argued elsewhere (Holland *et al.*, 1994a, p. 35) that women's empowerment in confronting men's dominance begins with their ability to reclaim their own experience and claim their bodies as the site of their own desires. But, as one young man commented, it is more feminine to disparage the body than to speak its power:

A: if you're with a group of friends, suddenly your girlfriend walks in and says, 'my bum's huge, look at it!' That's normal, whereas if a man comes in and says, 'look at my willy, it's tiny!' that's, you know – everybody would say 'no, thank you' – I mean women are far more open about it.   (16 AC WC)

Comedian Ben Elton draws on this sense of shock when he contrasts male attitudes to penis size and performance with the inappropriateness of women's presentation of their genitals as powerful: 'you never hear a woman say, "beware my mighty muff!"'[10]

The threat of female rampancy in the reputation of the wicked woman is not necessarily a direct threat to individual men – who can be educated to enjoy it (Holland *et al.*, 1992a) – but to the power of the 'male in the head'. The unacknowledged wickedness of the wicked woman lies in visions of sexual relationships with or without men that include a female in the head or, indeed, no head at all.

THE ABSENCE OF THE 'FEMALE IN THE HEAD'

Our analysis of young people's accounts of sexual reputation shows individual young people accepting or resisting the pressures and skills to produce themselves as conventionally feminine or masculine in different, and often contradictory, ways. But neither women who resist conventional femininity nor men who resist masculinity have a 'female in the head' as the basis of their identity. Young women could, and some did, resist pressures on them to discipline their bodies into a docile femininity, but they did so with reference to constructions of bodies, sex and gender in which male needs, male bodies, and male desires were critically dominant. Where the 'female in the head' could be, we find no discourse, no existence, vacancy.

In the language of poststructuralism, the 'female in the head' seems to lie outside the 'truths' of heterosexuality that are defined in existing discourses of sexual identities. The ways in which sexual reputations are produced rules out the possibility of female power.[11] The limitation of seeing male and female reputations as two halves of a pair is shown not only by the absence of the 'female in the head', but by the absence in discourses of heterosexuality of any sense of what a 'female in the head' might be. How can an active female sexuality, positive female desire and performance, feminine prowess, power and empowerment be conceived when we have available only negative, deviant or subordinated conceptions of the desiring woman? This remains a central problem for feminism.

Some feminists have raised a comparable problem in situating lesbian existence in relation to the dominance of heterosexuality (Butler, 1990, 1993; Martin, 1992; Stanley, 1992). They have argued that the heterosexual dualism of masculine/feminine leaves absence, silence or exclusion where lesbians are. Diana Fuss (1989, p. 111) says:

> To the degree that sexual difference in poststructuralist feminist theory has long been anchored in the male/female binarism, the place accorded to homosexuality has more accurately been a no-place, or at least a no-place near the privileged source of 'difference' between male and female subjects.

These theorists, in different ways, see excluded lesbian existence as a political site from which the unthinkable can be thought, and so as a possible source of the disruption of heterosexual dominance. In Judith Butler's terms, this is making 'gender trouble' (Butler, 1990). We would argue that although conventional femininity falls within the realm of the heterosexually thinkable, women's resistance, in terms of, say, a feminist heterosexual femininity, remains unthinkable, outrageous, subversive.

A similar point, from a different perspective has been made about young women by Carol Gilligan (1993) who talks of women 'speaking' but not being 'heard'. She conceives empowerment as women moving out of objectification and into voice – beyond an internalised, cultural, feminine voice to a full human voice. While boys move into masculinity (or those who do so successfully) by holding onto their full human voice, adolescent girls are under pressure to lose theirs, as they move into adult femininity. Girls who struggle to keep their full voice – who say what they *know* – make trouble. Gilligan argues that feminine girls move into silence. If girls did keep their full human voice, the world would have to change.

Sandra Bem distinguishes between *looking through* the lenses of a culture – seeing as the culture permits us to see, and looking *at* the lenses themselves – at how cultural realities are discursively organised (Bem, 1993). We do need to see how the trick with mirrors is played in producing the male/female dualism of the double standard, but it is difficult to see the mirrors from the site in which we are being tricked. We have tried to illustrate that making the power of the 'male in the head' visible does push us *through* the looking glass, and this is different from *looking at* or through the mirror. Unruly women and unruly men (those who resist conventional femininity and masculinity) are subject to regulation through the discourses which constitute the 'male in the head', but the 'male in the head' is neither static, nor simply a discursive construction. Explaining sexual reputations in terms of the absence of the female in the head confronts us with the persistence of social, political and embodied relations of male domination.

We have argued that within the confines of sexual reputation it is not possible to be female, powerful and feminine. To be feminine and powerful is to be outrageous, and to threaten male power. There is little sense in the young women's transcripts of respect or value for an independent power – it is too much of a threat to hard-won femininity. It is only where young people had gained some feminist consciousness, that they had thought more independently about power.

Producing awareness of embodied, grounded and structured male power in, for example, the recognition of rape, marital rape, date rape, domestic violence, sexual harassment, has changed the ways the 'truths' of sexual reputations are known, but not without confusion and struggle. Feminism, because of its oppositional status, still grapples with the constraints of dualistic thinking. Conceptualising female power is uncomfortable for young people because it disturbs the available categories with which we think; it reaches into the realm of the personal and upsets people. If young women do access female power they usually have nowhere to go with it.

Thinking the unthinkable gives voice to a silenced, insubordinate femininity. Both knowledge of and the exercise of female power are possible, but they are challenging, disruptive, 'pathological'. A powerful woman cannot exist/be perceived as both feminine and powerful. Within the present framework of dualistic thinking, she can only be an unnatural woman. Some women can become powerful by accessing male power: exercising power like a man, being a masculine woman, joining a girl's gang. There are plenty of available stereotypes of female battle-axes, emasculating – possibly with an over-endowment of male hormones or high on HRT. A powerful woman unmans a man by depriving him of his position of binary opposition. Powerful young women, at least in London and Manchester, are socially contradictory because power is not feminine. There is no public language of independent femininity for them to draw on (except the insubordinate discourses of feminism).

CONCLUSION

We cannot give a clear voice to discourses of female power because this chapter is coming out of the silences we found in our data and have lived ourselves. We did find some expressions of female power, but these were almost entirely contained within a framework of male dominance. If we abandon the binary opposition of male-constituted-through-reason/female-constituted-as-body, we have no model for empowered female sexuality, although we may find accounts of resistance to the regulation of the feminine/masculine.

There is growing pressure in sociology to see heterosexuality in terms of discourses, rather than patriarchal structures and relationships. We have argued that the discourses of sexual reputation can be seen to have considerable regulatory power, but if we ask why young people do not simply resist regulation, heterosexuality appears more in the guise of a thundering juggernaut, than as multiplicity, choice or productive power. We have been impressed by the enormous power of heterosexuality as the exercise of male power, but also by the capacity for individuals to develop the kinds of critical consciousness of this power that enable them to challenge 'compulsory heterosexuality' in at least some personal encounters.

The mirror trick of the double standard appears to have regulated the 'female in the head' out of existence, but there is still resistance in the extra-discursive void: still possibilities for constructing identities, counter-discourses; still challenges to the 'male in the head'; other bases for living. Very few young people in the WRAP and MRAP studies explicitly articulated a critical consciousness; the majority accepted their gendered lives. But there are many hints of reflection, struggle and change, as we have tried to show in the excerpts above, as they try to negotiate sexual identities, practices and relationships in response to the surveillance of the 'male in the head'.

It is still not clear, though, how thinking the unthinkable translates into practical disruption of male dominance, nor what the dangers are. Collective political strategies for disrupting the male in the head, and thinking about feminine power, need more than counter-discourses. There is also the persistent problem of how a positive conception of feminine power can operate across the social divisions between women.

Alice, being the child of fantasy, could not remain through the looking glass, and returned to her cosy bourgeois, heterosexual certainties. Once we have exposed the trick with mirrors we need not be so constrained, we can keep working on the ways in which subversion can occur. But any transformation of heterosexual relations will require radical imagination to escape the forceful constraints of sexual reputations.

NOTES

1. The Women, Risk and AIDS Project was staffed by the authors and Sue Scott, University of Stirling, working collectively, and financed by a two-year grant from the ESRC. It also received grants from Goldsmiths' College Research Fund and the Department of Health. Valuable assistance was given by Jane Preston, Polly Radcliffe and Janet Ransom. WRAP used purposive samples to interview 150 young women aged 16–21 in London and Manchester in depth between 1988 and 1990. The Men Risk and AIDS Project was staffed by the authors and Tim Rhodes, and was given a grant by the Leverhulme Trust for a study of 50 young men in London 1991–2, and for comparison of the two studies. Information on publications from these studies is obtainable from The Tufnell Press, 47 Dalmeny Rd, London N7 ODY, UK.
2. In this paper we have not considered sexual reputation in relation to gay and lesbian identities, but lesbian critiques offer a relevant debate on disrupting the dualism of heterosexuality (see, for example, Fuss, 1989; Stanley, 1992; Butler, 1993).
3. There is some similarity between the 'male in the head' and Sandra Lee

Bartky's Foucauldian notion of femininity as a 'disciplinary project': 'In contemporary patriarchal culture, a panoptical male connoisseur resides within the consciousness of most women: They stand perpetually before his gaze and under his judgement' (Bartky, 1990, p. 72).

4. The speakers in the excerpts from transcripts are identified by age; classification of ethnic origin (African; African Caribbean (AC); Asian; English, Scottish or Welsh (ESW); Irish; Other; and categorisation as either working class (WC) or middle class (MC).

5. Halson (1993) in her study of sexual harassment of girls at school gives examples of the construction of the few girls who respond 'inappropriately' to negative reputation. Beating a boy who called her a slag gained one young woman a reputation among staff as 'fishwife material'.

6. Where young women are under pressure to remain virgins until they marry, the concern for guarding their reputations becomes the responsibility of parents, siblings and the wider community. They are under pressure to make their virginity their definitive identity.

7. Sexual reputations can be seen as constituted in discourses through which power is exercised over young people, and as 'truths' of masculinity and femininity in relation to which young people discipline themselves and their bodies. But feminist politics are grounded, in part, in areas of social life that might be termed extra-discursive and embodied. We do not have space to develop this point here (see Ramazanoglu and Holland, 1993; Cain, 1993). Michèle Barrett (1992, p. 209) usefully summarises Laclau and Mouffe's example of *how* the football is constituted as a football, to illustrate how knowledge is apprehended through discourse: 'The spherical object exists, but it has no significant *meaning* outside the systems of rules and conventions (discourse) by which it is constituted as a football.' This may well be so, but since feminism is hanging on to the problem of taking people's accounts of their experience seriously (Cain, 1993), feminists are also concerned with the extra-discursive life of the football, that is the possibilities of its existence outside the rules that define its meaning: *why* 'girls can't play'; the pain of the ball that erupts through your front window and so on.

8. This is more strongly recognised and emphasised in some subcultures than others (see Holland, 1993). See also Ford and Koetsawan (1991) for an interesting elaboration of the working of the double standard in another culture.

9. Margaret Jackson (1994, p. 179) has shown for Victorian and Edwardian England, how female sexuality was socially constructed as the eroticisation of oppression, so that any resistance to a notion of sexuality as female submission to male desire became not independence, but pathology.

10. *The Man From Auntie*, BBC TV, 10 February 1994.

11. This point was illustrated by a young man aged 16, who asked the authors if 'maniser' was a known term. He had been with a male and a female friend, walking through his sixth form college, with arms linked; the woman in the middle with a man on each arm. They felt the woman was attracting attention for having 'caught' two men. She suggested she should be seen as a 'maniser' – the female equivalent of a womaniser, but the men argued that the maniser was 'really' a slag or a slut.

REFERENCES

Bartky, S. (1990) *Femininity and Domination* (London: Routledge).

Barrett, M. (1992) 'Words and Things: Materialism and Method in Contemporary Feminist Analysis', in M. Barrett and A. Phillips (eds), *Destabilizing Theory: Contemporary Feminist Debates* (Cambridge: Polity Press).

Bem, S. (1993) *The Lenses of Gender* (New Haven, CT: Yale University Press).

Butler, J. (1990) *Gender Trouble: Feminism and the Subversion of Identity* (London: Routledge).

Butler, J. (1993) *Bodies That Matter: on the Discursive Limits of 'Sex'* (London: Routledge).

Cain, M. (1993) 'Foucault, Feminism and Feeling: What Foucault Can and Cannot Contribute to Feminist Epistemology', in C. Ramazanoglu (ed.), *Up Against Foucault: Explorations of Some Tensions between Foucault and Feminism* (London: Routledge, 1993).

Ford, N. and Koetsawan, S. (1991) 'The Socio-cultural Context of the Transmission of HIV in Thailand', *Social Science and Medicine*, 33(4): pp. 405–14.

Fuss, D. (1989) *Essentially Speaking: Feminism, Nature and Difference* (London: Routledge).

Gilligan, C. (1993) Lecture and Discussion, The Gender Institute, London School of Economics, 28 February.

Halson, J. (1993) 'Sexual Harassment, Oppression and Resistance: A Feminist Ethnography of Some Young People from Henry James School', PhD Thesis, University of Warwick.

Holland, J. (1993) 'The Sexual Knowledge and Practice of Young Women in the Context of HIV/AIDS with Particular Reference to Different Ethnic Groups', Report for the Department of Health.

Holland, J., Ramazanoglu, C., Scott, S., Sharpe, S. and Thomson, R. (1992a) 'Pressure, Resistance, Empowerment: Young Women and the Negotiation of Safer Sex', in P. Aggleton, P. Davies and G. Hart (eds), *AIDS: Rights, Risk and Reason* (London: Falmer Press, 1992).

Holland, J., Ramazanoglu, C., Sharpe, S. and Thomson, R. (1992b) 'Pleasure, Pressure and Power: Some Contradictions of Gendered Sexuality', *Sociological Review*, 40(4): pp. 645–674.

Holland, J., Ramazanoglu, C., Sharpe, S. and Thomson, R. (1994a) 'Power and Desire: The Embodiment of Female Sexuality', *Feminist Review*, 46: pp. 21–38.

Holland, J., Ramazanoglu, C., Scott, S. and Thomson, R. (1994b) 'Desire, Risk and Control: The Body as a Site of Contestation', in L. Doyal, J. Naidoo and T. Wilton (eds), *AIDS: Setting a Feminist Agenda* (London: Taylor & Francis, 1994).

Holland, J., Ramazanoglu, C., Sharpe, S. and Thomson, R. (1994c) 'Achieving Masculine Sexuality: Young Men's Strategies for Managing Vulnerability', in L. Doyal, J. Naidoo & T. Wilton (eds) *AIDS: Setting a Feminist Agenda* (London: Taylor & Francis, 1994).

Jackson, M. (1994) *The Real Facts of Life: Feminism and the Politics of Sexuality, c. 1850–1940* (London: Taylor & Francis).

Kelly, L. (1988) *Surviving Sexual Violence* (Cambridge: Polity Press).

Kelly, L. (1991) 'Unspeakable Acts: Women who Abuse', *Trouble and Strife*, **21**: pp. 13–20.

Lees, S. (1986) *Losing Out: Sexuality and Adolescent Girls* (London: Hutchinson).

Lees, S. (1993) *Sugar and Spice: Sexuality and Adolescent Girls* (London: Penguin).

Martin, B. (1992) 'Sexual Practice and Changing Lesbian Identities', in M. Barrett and A. Phillips (eds), *Destabilizing Theory: Contemporary Feminist Debates* (Cambridge: Polity Press, 1992).

Ramazanoglu, C. and Holland, J. (1993) 'Women's Sexuality and Men's Appropriation of Desire', in C. Ramazanoglu (eds), *Up Against Foucault: Explorations of Some Tensions between Foucault and Feminism* (London: Routledge, 1993).

Rich, A. (1983) 'Compulsory Heterosexuality and Lesbian Existence', in E. Abel and E. K. Abel (eds), *Women, Gender and Scholarship: The SIGNS Reader* (Chicago, IL: University of Chicago Press, 1983).

Sharpe, S. (1987) *Falling for Love: Teenage Mothers Talk* (London: Virago).

Sharpe, S. (1994) *Just Like A Girl*, 2nd edn (London: Penguin).

Smart, C. (1992) 'Disruptive Bodies and Unruly Sex' in C. Smart (ed.), *Regulating Womanhood: Historical Essays on Marriage, Motherhood and Sexuality* (London: Routledge, 1992).

Stanley, L. (1992) *Is There a Lesbian Epistemology?* (Manchester University Sociology Department: Feminist Praxis Monograph 34).

Weiner, G. and Arnot, M. (eds) (1987) *Gender Under Scrutiny: New Inquiries in Education* (London: Unwin Hyman).

Woodhouse, A. (1989) *Fantastic Women: Sex, Gender and Transvestism* (London: Macmillan).

13 The Conundrum of Sex and Death: Some Issues in Health Care Practice

DAVID CLARK and JULIA HIRST

In this paper we set out some ideas for exploring the inter-relatedness of sex and death from a sociological perspective. In order to do this we draw on a number of key texts, combined with observations from our own research and teaching. One of us (JH) has been engaged for several years in teaching programmes for health workers concerned with sexuality and HIV/AIDS. The other (DC) has, over the same time, developed an interest in palliative care and related issues. Our starting point has therefore been the potential linkages between these two broad areas of interest, which appear connected by some common threads, principally relating to the concepts of identity and of ageing. The purpose of the paper is to identify these connections and to illustrate ways in which they are represented in the particular context of health care and the work of professional carers.[1]

Taken individually, the themes of sex and death each pose major challenges for sociology. Although interest in the former has, at least very recently, been greater than in the latter, they nevertheless occupy increasingly identifiable positions within the sociological corpus. Sex, sexuality, sexual identity, mortality, dying, death – all of these provide territories on which sociological imaginations are brought to bear. Being sociological about either sex or death also requires the application of similar intellectual processes and frameworks. Each challenges us to identify the limits and constraints of biology and the opportunities and boundaries of the social, or even to move beyond such dualisms. Each requires us to make sense of aspects of social life which involve deep value systems and which are often constructed as 'taboo' areas. Sex and death appear to us to occupy overlapping social spaces.

It has often been observed that the Victorians sustained very public responses and ritual reactions to death and bereavement, whilst at the same time consigning sex to a private and secret world where it was rarely subjected to public gaze apart from judgmental speculation on

261

the sexual behaviours of others. The popular morality of the Victorians thus produced the celebration of death and the repression of sex. By contrast, in the late twentieth century, some commentators suggest that the reverse is true. Today sex has become a matter for open debate, exploration and promulgation, whereas death is hidden, stigmatised, banished to the margins. Interestingly, Gorer, an early commentator on death in modern Britain, used the phrase 'the pornography of death' (Gorer, 1965) to describe this process. In a sense then, features of the 'triple edict' which Foucault saw characterising Victorian sexuality, might also apply to death in the late twentieth century: 'taboo, non-existence and silence' (Foucault, 1984, p. 5). The ways in which we have come to know each have been through attempts at governance. Such assertions, needless to say, raise as many questions as they resolve.

One factor is that, as Weeks (1981) demonstrates so clearly, despite the public repression of sex in Victorian times, sexuality pervaded the social consciousness (Weeks, 1981, p. 19) and was a part of wide-ranging discussions relating to birth and death rates, public health, housing, factory work, birth control and prostitution. Sexuality had no place, however, within the Victorian middle class domestic ideal, which idealised motherhood and through the double standard created a division between public morality and private license. It was this same setting of the bourgeois family which did so much to create the Victorian way of death, the ostentatious displays of grief, the fine-grained detail of mourning ritual and the separation of widows from the wider society. Both speak of attempts to manage and govern aspects of human experience which are perceived as dangerous and taboo. Sex is turned into reproduction and death becomes a managed event, but sexual practices and the process of dying prove difficult to police and may escape the regulatory 'gaze'.

More recently, in the course of the late twentieth century both sex *and* death have been vehicles for particular social movements concerned with self-actualisation, personal discovery and the search for meaning in modern culture. We are thinking here of the rather contrasting examples of the gay liberation movement and the hospice movement. In the first a primary task has been to liberate areas of sexuality from the definitions of biology and medicine. Gay liberation challenged the reductionism of biology and sought to supplant it with an ideology of choice in which homosexuality ceases to be a disease and a crime and becomes a personal and political statement. Similarly, the hospice movement confronted the medical management of death, refused to see death as a failure and called for the adoption of holistic approaches to caring for dying people and those close to them. In other ways of course these two social 'movements', although co-terminous, have very little else in common, emerging from very different political and cultural settings and eliciting sharply contrasting public reactions. Gay liberation has been supported by the actions of individuals who challenge the dominant morality and question powerful norms and conventions relating to gender and 'family' relations, incurring a significant measure of public opprobrium as a result. The hospice movement, like the gay liberation movement, is characteristically white and middle-class but in contrast is also Christian and works chiefly within the mainstream of 'respectable' society, attracting popular support through charitable giving. Paradoxically, however, the epidemic of HIV/AIDS has created a point of contact between the two movements (Small, 1993). Some gay men with AIDS have been cared for in hospices (Andrew and Andrew, 1991; George, 1992) and, of course, gay men have been involved in creating their own systems of care for people affected by HIV and AIDS, drawing on the central concerns of hospice philosophy: the combination of physical, social, emotional and spiritual care. Examples of this within the UK include the care and support offered by organisations such as London Lighthouse and the Landmark Trust.

Images and experiences linking sexuality and death also gain wider expression in relation to the phenomena of *ageing* and generational change within modernity. Older people facing death today do so having lived through periods of huge transformation in public discourse about sexuality. To use our earlier analogy, sex appears to be moving in from the margins to occupy a more central role in the way individuals think about themselves and their needs. Changes in sexuality have therefore begun to make up an important strand in the ageing process so that sexual needs, feelings and preferences may well remain important considerations, even as death approaches. Similarly, dying and the onset of death are now increasingly faced in old age and sudden death from infectious diseases has become far less common than a century ago. Sexuality and death thus inter-connect through the experience of ageing and the changing trajectories of dying. As Jerrome puts it: 'Contrary to popular assumption, old people are sexual beings' (1993, p. 246).

Sex and death in the late twentieth century might increasingly be seen as inter-related and intertwined. The epidemic of HIV/AIDS is clearly the most graphic expression of this, constituting a powerful combination of forces linking desire and sexuality with disease, disfigurement and death. Indeed these inter-connections continue to have a major influence on the social and cultural construction of the epidemic. But it is also possible that these links extend further, into other social settings and groups. This indeed, is the main theme of our paper. In what ways are sexuality and death associated within the ageing process more generally; how might these relate to gender, age and generation; and how in particular are the associations shaped and determined through health care practice? Our starting point in addressing these questions lies in recent sociological writings on the body and identity.

MODERNITY, IDENTITY AND THE BODY

In the last few years the writings of Anthony Giddens have turned their attention to the relationship between 'high' or 'radical' modernity and the concept of identity. Giddens highlights a number of points which are relevant to our discussion here. He argues for three central characteristics which contribute to the dynamism of modernity: the separation of time and space; the disembedding of social systems; and the reflexive ordering and reordering of social relations (Giddens, 1990). It is this latter theme which Giddens has taken up in his most recent writings (Giddens, 1991, 1992), arguing for a notion of *the self* as a reflexive project, trading off rewards and satisfactions against a shifting array of risks and insecurities. A principle determinant of this reflexive self in modernity is the growth of 'abstract systems' (1990) which de-skill, alienate and fragment the self. We shall return to this in the following section which is concerned with the 'abstract system' of health care.

This concept of the self as a fragile project has of course been developed by other social theorists in recent decades, including Berger and associates (Berger and Luckmann, 1971; Berger, 1973; Berger *et al.*, 1973; Sennett, 1977; Lasch, 1980). The significant area of new development, however, is in the connection between these ideas and the current interest in the sociology of the body. There has been a marked turnaround from the situation of only a decade ago when Turner (1984) could draw attention to the 'missing body' within sociological concerns. Interest in the sociology of the body has increased dramatically in the interim (Frank, 1990; Turner, 1992; Scott and Morgan, 1993). As a result, possibilities now exist for the introduction of ideas about the body into a number of substantive areas of enquiry, not least

Turner's own twin concerns with the sociology of religion and the sociology of health and illness.

Giddens provides an important bridging point between sociologies of 'the self' and of 'the body'. Crucially, for Giddens, the reflexive self is also an *embodied* self. Within modernity the images, surfaces and experiences of the body become central to conceptions of the self. Most obviously in areas such as fashion, dieting and fitness, but most crucially in 'fateful moments' relating to death or sexuality, when the smooth workings of abstract systems are called into question. As a consequence, Giddens argues, sickness and death have become *sequestrated* in modern society, so that death is routinely hidden from view and medicalised. A parallel is drawn here with the removal of sex 'behind the scenes', which Giddens suggests is 'not so much a prurient concealment from view as a reconstituting of sexuality and its refocusing on an emerging sphere of intimacy' (1991, p. 164). In rather different ways, therefore, both sex and death become entwined in the reflexive project of the self and are in turn both present and absent from social relations.

Following Giddens, Shilling (1993) gives examples of increasing emphasis on the body in recent times, including the growing interest in self care in health. He also shows that investment in the body has its limitations. Indeed there are biological boundaries to the social construction and reconstruction of the body. Disease, pain, physical decline, although mediated by social and historical circumstances, pose challenges to the body-as-project. As Mellor notes, Bauman (1992) has seen recent self-care projects as specific attempts to overcome the body's limitations and in so doing deny the broader challenge which is posed by the biological irreducibility of the body.

What all this serves to emphasise is the important role which the body has in the reflexive ordering of identity. Bourdieu's contribution to this (Bourdieu, 1984), as Shilling points out, is the notion of 'physical capital', whereby the body is seen to create and possess value in certain social fields. Featherstone (1987) has noted the relevance of the ageing process to this and the related social-class dimensions. He suggests that, while working-class people, as they grow older, may come to accept the body as, in some sense, a machine in decline, members of the new middle classes may experience the deterioration of the 'body-as-project' as a source of acute anxiety. In the upper classes, by contrast, visible signs of ageing are worn unselfconsciously as a mark of status. Similarly, Hepworth (1987) has pointed out some of the key gender differences in the ageing process which are constructed and managed differently for men and women, not least as they relate to perceptions of sexuality and physical attractiveness.

Shilling highlights the importance of all this for a sociological understanding of death:

> I view death as having become a particular existential problem for people as a result of modern forms of embodiment, rather than being a universal problem for human beings which assumes the same form irrespective of time and place. (Shilling, 1993, p. 177)

We are sympathetic to this viewpoint. Both sexuality and death do pose existential dilemmas for individuals, but across time these will be mediated by other factors. Similarly, the ageing process will vary across generations. Our contention is that for those now entering later life (and many textbooks place this around age 50, in other words the generation of the 1960s) the generational experience of sexuality and the impact of changing discourses of sex has crucial implications for the ageing process. For these individuals, intimations of mortality are likely to proceed alongside of and enmeshed with changing sexual practices and awarenesses. Discourses of the ageing process recognise increasingly that for older people sex is not a thing of the past, a remnant from an earlier stage in the lifecourse. Indeed some of this forms a key theme within the prescriptive literature of old age and retirement which presents images of 'attractive' older people and promotes the social and sexual opportunities provided by the 'third age' (Featherstone and Hepworth, 1984). Nevertheless, older people are also likely to have increasing health care needs and their reflexive self-images and identities may thus be challenged in encounters with the 'abstract systems' of medical and nursing care. How such issues relate to the work of health professionals and how they are enacted in specific local contexts form the themes of the next section of this chapter.

HEALTH CARE ISSUES

In recent years the significance of sexuality has begun to be acknowledged in the health care literature. For example, in 1980 a well-known nursing textbook could observe:

even though doctors and nurses are beginning to acknowledge that illness and hospitalisation may cause sex-related problems, they are still reticent about discussing them openly with patients. Talking with patients about sexual problems is not easy; it requires tact, sensitivity, tolerance and knowledge. Perhaps most important it needs the helping person to be comfortable about his/her own sexuality. (Roper *et al.*, 1980, p. 250)

Various *models* of nursing have also emerged (Roper *et al.*, 1985). These seek to shift emphasis towards acknowledgement of the whole self, with mental, physical and spiritual needs being taken as necessary considerations to aid recovery or retain good health. Such models attempt to embrace sexuality as an important foundation for self-actualisation and positive self-esteem. As Jacobson puts it: 'if nursing is about caring for the whole patient, then body image and sexuality must be included in this care plan' (in Andrew and Andrew, 1991, p. 8).

In the terms we have been describing, facing death or life-limiting illnesses will clearly impact on the reflexive project of the self. An individual's ability to retain a positive self-image is threatened by illness and possible death and this in turn may be linked to questions of sexuality (Savage, 1987). The self may be further jeopardised if there is a need to be cared for by 'others' in the context of an *abstract system* of health care. In the discussion which follows, therefore, we consider the impact of illness, death and care-giving on both sexuality and the quality of life.

The effects of this need for care by others will depend on the extent to which the 'dependent's' body is sequestered to the trustee, the professional carer. For some this will involve committing the body for safe-keeping (residential care) with the consequent loss of (some) independence and control. For others, it may be a *fragment* of the self which is given over for care, for instance care in the home by a lover, spouse, child or by external agents such as community nurses and care assistants. Whatever the scale of the intervention into a person's private world, there is a potential impact on identity. Entering a system of dependence not previously encountered, will necessarily entail some reconstruction of identity. The individual's ability to maintain some process of *self-actualisation* (Berger and Luckmann, 1971) within this new world will vary. Those with the most genuine acceptance of the 'new' self are likely to have the greatest potential for positive well-being.

Such a position assumes, however, that those who deliver the care have a similar understanding of the impact of sequestration and the consequent reconstruction of identity which it can entail. When this is the case, care will be *offered* which is holistic, thoughtful, compassionate and in accordance with the observed and agreed needs of the individual, following sensitive consultation. Unfortunately, care is often likely to be *imposed* and the 'cared-for' person will encounter systems which isolate the body from the self. In other words, care will be administered without acknowledgement of the 'person' behind the symptoms or the infirmity, who is constructed solely as a passive object of the care process. The subsequent alienation of the 'body' from the individual's previous 'self-view' will have a variety of consequences, with direct implications for the maintenance of identity.

The willingness of individuals to give themselves over to an abstract system will, of course, vary, but the power of the health care system to encourage dependency has been widely acknowledged (Illich, 1975). The extent to which this sequestration is truly informed by personal decision-making will determine the extent of the potential alienation and fragmentation of self. This in turn will influence the quality of life and the potential for good health. It could be argued that it might even determine the longevity of the individual. On a domestic level, the loss of being able to fulfil certain roles may be devastating. Changes in gender roles are important here (e.g. a husband no longer able to fulfil his role as the 'sole' breadwinner may experience the erosion of a previous self-identity as father and spouse). Negative feelings may precipitate further personal doubt about wider abilities to function according to perceived cultural norms. Self definitions will be altered.

The ways in which these re-definitions manifest themselves will determine the reactions from significant others. Should these external reactions be perceived as endorsing the new fragile negative self, then internalisation of disapproval will be perpetuated. Sexuality encompasses human qualities – it affects the way we live, dress, think, act, our choice of partners, peers and lifestyle. (Hogan, 1980; Webb, 1985; Ingram-Fogel, 1990). Positive recognition of an individual's sexuality can bring both pleasure and pain (Weston, 1993). To ignore sexuality (or pay lip-service to it) in caring regimes will, therefore, affect directly an individual's ability to cope and to feel worthy of individual time, sensitivity and understanding.

As sexuality is a part of life and identity, so it must also be a part of dying. The literature, however, does not support acknowledgement of this aspect of our behaviour and life-path. Understanding of sexuality as it relates to older adults, sexuality and death, and nursing and sexuality is embryonic. There is a paucity of research to provide evidence of the relationship between sexuality and identity in later life. Typically, only those who have undergone considerable self-reflection or have had the opportunity for awareness-raising through education will feel able to raise the profile of sexuality as an important issue within this area of health care. Accordingly, the evidence available to us in preparing this chapter has been relatively patchy. In the following sections we examine some of the available literature before going on to discuss our own observations of professional practice, drawn principally from programmes of teaching and training for nurses.

Key Themes

The literature on the health and social care of elderly people is expanding considerably. There is also increased understanding of the needs of older people within the particular context of terminal care, palliative care and the hospice movement (Clark, 1993). Sexuality, however, receives only limited attention in this literature. Where it is discussed, the emphasis is on sexual behaviours and dysfunctions rather than a wider understanding of sexuality (Wilson-Barnett and Batehup, 1988; Wright, 1988; Weg, 1989). The sexual needs of people with a physical disability have suffered greater neglect but where these are addressed, sexual *behaviour* is again the central focus (Stuart, 1975). Research also suffers from sampling problems (for example Kinsey *et al.* in 1948 concluded that 75 per cent of men over 80 years were impotent – this was based on a sample of four) or the difficulties inherent in getting candid disclosures from older people about their sexuality (Kaye, 1993).

Such limitations in the literature are hardly surprising, given the negative views of ageing which exist in our society. Hostile stereotypes prevail with many unchallenged assumptions, in particular with reference to gender. Jokes about old men typically refer to sexual ability or interest – the 'dirty old man' syndrome (Huyck, 1974); whereas commentary on older women focuses on sexless widows and spinsters who are viewed as shrivelled, frustrated and lonely (Puner, 1979; Butler and Lewis, 1988). These jokes and images represent gross and misleading caricatures. They are, none the less, extremely powerful and often remain unchallenged, reflecting the structurally weak position of older people in society.

As we have noted already, sexual activity is not generally considered to be a positive part of the lives of older adults. They are burdened instead by their own internalised views and those of society at large – that sex is not for them. This view prevails despite evidence (albeit small) to the contrary which discounts some of the common myths about elderly people and sex. Starr and Weiner (1981) and Masters and Johnson (1970) found there is no age limit to sexual responsiveness and sexual behaviours. There are changes which stem from poor health, loss of partner, emotional and social problems and the effects of medication, but not enough to warrant the denial of sexuality among older people. Indeed, the acknowledgement of sex or expressions of sexuality for older adults are considered by many as foolish and inappropriate, and where sex and sexuality for older people do appear in the literature, discussion is restricted and fails to embrace the diversity of sexual identities and practices which would be considered for those in young or middle years. Morton Puner (1979), for example, acknowledges that sex and sexuality in the lives of older people warrant discussion, but then places his thoughts firmly within the context of sex and marriage.

The Starr–Weiner Report (1981) on sex and sexuality in the mature years, (significantly now out of print) addresses the myths and the realities and explores experiences and needs among older adults. Rather than focusing on physiological and behavioural aspects, this report offered insight into how older adults feel about sexual activities, whether they participate in them or not. Though these studies provide only limited knowledge, they are evidence of the need rigorously to re-order common understandings of older people and their sexuality. We live in a time where sexual self-determination is increasingly discussed and tolerated. Although still a contentious issue, discourse about sexuality has moved from being purely within the domain of married heterosexuals, to now include young people, unmarried people, gay, lesbian and bisexual people. But we cling to misconceptions and stereotypes about elderly people or those with a physical disability which enhance their exclusion and support misinformed assumptions about their lack of desire, physical unattractiveness and bodily fragility (Butler and Lewis, 1988). As Simone de Beauvoir observed, 'If old people show the same desires, the same feelings and the same requirements as the young, the world looks upon them with disgust' (de Beauvoir, 1972, p. 10).

Older people 'acting their age' may therefore be afraid to listen to their bodies. Shaped by their own upbringing, in the early part of this century, with parents who grew up in the Victorian age, sex may continue to be a topic of embarrassment, shame, even immorality (Greengross and Greengross, 1989). Not surprisingly, elderly people will be inclined to be reticent about disclosing publicly their experiences and desires. However, they live in a world where sexuality is seen (by degree) as less taboo, and they are cared for by people who enjoy greater freedom of expression and who are more likely to assert the right to sexual selfhood. At the same time, the attitudes and values of this younger generation collude with the sexual oppression of older people. Whilst it is considered 'normal' for older people to 'listen to their bodies' in the context of sickness and disease, the reverse is true on sexual matters. The sick or dying role suits, the sexual one does not.

Within nursing, sexuality began to receive greater attention in the late 1960s and came to be regarded by some as one of the basic tenets of nursing care. This was underpinned by the notion that an individual's health status cannot be fully understood without an awareness of sexual identity. Henderson (1969) argued that encouragement of healthy sexual expression was necessary to meet the total needs of the individual, particularly for those people who have to change or relearn their sexual behaviour following illness.

The World Health Organisation (WHO) in 1975 supported the recognition of sexuality as an individual issue and proposed that 'sexual health is the integration of the somatic, emotional, intellectual and social aspects of a sexual being, in ways that are positively enriching and that enhance personality, communication and love' (Weston, 1993, p. 26). However, WHO also reported that although sexuality and sexual needs were identified, there was little relevant teaching on sexuality being offered in schools of medicine or nursing. Jacobson's (1974) study, showed that nursing gave little attention to dealing with sexuality in patient and client care and found that few nurses or doctors gave patients information on how illness, drugs or procedures may affect their sexuality or more directly their ability to sustain previous sexual relationships. However in 1976 the profile of sexuality was heightened as a result of a research project which examined the clinical experience of student nurses (Roper, 1976). These findings proved to be influential in effecting changes in approaches to nursing care and culminated in the adoption of a new model of nursing in the 1980s. Thus, the Roper *et al.* (1985) model was accepted as a framework for the provision of all nursing care in the UK. The model sets out twelve 'activities of daily living' which require assessment and a subsequent care plan, which should be individually negotiated. 'Sexuality' and 'death and dying' represent two of these activities. The previous emphasis was broadened from a consideration of sexual behaviours alone, to embrace sexuality as a whole. However, though accepted as being generally successful, implementation of the model did not acknowledge the resources needed to equip 'carers' with the knowledge, skills and understanding to be able to honour the sentiments which underpin it. The evidence suggests that sexuality is still largely ignored, or at best has lip-service paid to it in health and social care settings. It is also given a very low priority or is entirely overlooked in care and training programmes (Weston, 1993). Some nurses continue to believe that sexuality is not a matter with which they should be concerned (Zalar, 1982) and as such continue to treat their clients as asexual beings or make the assumption that all clients are heterosexual (Weston, 1993). Yet research studies with nurses, patients and healthy adults support the assertion that patients' sexuality and sexual concerns *should* be a focus for nursing care (Gamel *et al.*, 1993). Furthermore, specific evidence from the UK, USA and Holland suggests that most patients want information about the effects of illness and treatment upon sexuality (Krueger *et al.*, 1979; Hanson and Brouse, 1983; Webb and Wilson-Barnett, 1983; Webb, 1986) and that patients want health-care professionals to initiate the relevant discussions (Krueger *et al.*, 1979; Baggs and Karch, 1987; Jenkins, 1988; Waterhouse and Metcalfe, 1991). At the same time it appears that patients' wishes are rarely heeded (Waterhouse, 1991).

Case Illustrations

We turn now to some illustrations of the status of sexuality in health-care settings. Within these the perspectives of both professional carers and those being cared-for are included. Our 'data' here are drawn from experience in teaching nurses at both pre- and post-registration levels and include ward observation, the marking of care plans for academic assessment and discussion with colleagues who are nurse tutors. Our insights into the feelings and experiences of the client have come principally from disclosures from professionals attending courses on 'sex and sexuality', where participation in experiential exercises has raised personal issues which have subsequently been shared with the course tutor (JH). To honour confidentiality, the case studies presented here are composites and typifications of a number of situations and accounts. It is notable that there are substantive parallels in the concerns raised by both the givers and receivers of care, where sexuality and concomitant effects on self-identity have been ignored. The solution to such dilemmas and problems is barred by almost imperceptible obstacles of ignorance, prejudice, denial and embarrassment. Concerned carers and anxious clients often can see what they want to do but nevertheless feel unable to act. The result, frequently, is frustration, sadness and disillusionment. We offer the following examples therefore to illustrate the overt denial of sexuality within health care. Though anecdotal in character, the material illustrates clearly some of the issues at stake and points the way to the need for more considered approaches through primary research.

At a recent Department of Health conference on the *Health of the Nation* (1992), concerned with targets for sexual health and the implications for the education of health and social work professionals, a senior nurse spoke of an incident in which an elderly male had undergone a penis amputation due to carcinoma. Within his care plan, under the sexuality section, the words 'not applicable' had been scribed. It transpired that this man had not received any guidance or counselling with respect to sexuality or sexual activity.

It seems that this example is not an exception to the rule. Over numerous training sessions and workshops, nurse teachers and practitioners readily offer up examples of similar experiences. With respect to care plans, they report that the sections on 'sexuality' and 'death and dying' (within the 'activities of daily living') are consistently ignored and left blank, apart from the occasional reference to sexual identity, where 'homosexual' may be recorded, irrespective of whether this is requested by the patient.

The acknowledgement of sexuality is further jeopardised where ageing can be taken as an excuse for excluding its consideration. Some of these points can be illustrated through the experience (JH) of teaching on a course specifically focused on the care of older people. Most participants on the course (generally those who are specialising in health care for elderly people) have had no previous education on sexuality during their training. During initial introductions they frequently register anxieties about the content and processes involved in sexuality education and some add that they are intrigued as to the significance of sex and sexuality to the people they care for. Furthermore, nurses in this specialism have rarely had the opportunity to attend specialist training on HIV/AIDS, since this has not been deemed relevant to caring for older adults.

It is significant that within all the various specialist areas of health care, (and with the exception of genito-urinary medicine) diabetes and leukaemia are the only conditions where items on sexuality are more routinely (but not always) included in the care plan for the patient. The reason for this is that prolonged diabetes can lead to premature impotence, and chemotherapy for the leukaemic patient may cause impotence and infertility. In these cases, sexuality and sexual abilities may be discussed at an early stage, albeit exclusively with young adult males. The implication of this in other specialisms/conditions or in other age groups is that the sexual ramifications of the condition do not need to be discussed since they are not relevant or not welcome. This is paradoxical since the majority of us will experience more ill health over age 40 and thus face increasing challenges to our self-identity as we grow older. There are obvious conditions which are more likely to occur in later years and which may threaten indirectly our sense of self (stoma-formation, mastectomy), and others which may more directly require modification of original behaviour – for instance incontinence, hysterectomy, prostate operations, stroke and cardiac problems. It is not the norm, however, for support and guidance on the direct effects on sexual ability to be offered here. Acknowledgement of the psychological and emotional impact of such conditions is also likely to be obfuscated. Nurse tutors and student nurses openly admit that this is indeed the case. Sexual behaviour and self-esteem do not get spoken of. They explain this in terms of their lack of confidence and knowledge and a perception that the patient would be embarrassed and would not welcome such an intimate intrusion. Research does not support the latter and teaching experience tells a different story. On several occasions, whilst teaching about sex and sexuality, often outside the context of 'older adults' (for instance, a course for those working with adolescents), at the slightest hint of sexuality being relevant to all age groups, including older people, individual participants have often requested 'a quiet word'. The following composite scenarios are taken from several disparate experiences, but share common themes of poignancy and isolation.

In two separate cases, a woman in her late 50s talked about her husband's prostate operation and another discussed her mastectomy. Such disclosures invariably begin with a sense of relief at older adults 'getting a mention', particularly from a younger person. Openings such as this articulate a sense of invisibility and marginalisation from wider discourse on sexuality.

The first woman describes her husband:

It's about my husband, don't get me wrong, we're very happily married, 38 years now. Then he had his operation. Now . . . there's nothing, he does nothing, stays in most of the time, has stopped running, he's putting on weight and our sex life has stopped dead. Nothing since his op. The doctors have given him the 'all clear'. Told him he's fine. So what's happened? I'm at my wits' end, I've got to talk to him about it, but don't know where to begin. He bought me a card on Mother's day, he's never done that before, it's as if he wants to remind me that he had some part in producing our children. The problem is getting out of hand, 'cos I'm finding that I don't want to take my clothes off in front of him, in case it feels like I'm teasing him, or maybe I'm beginning to feel I don't want him near me. Could you give me any advice or anything I could read?

The second woman had recently undergone a mastectomy and had also been given the 'all clear' from the doctors. However, she felt changed, 'completely different, a bit of me is missing'. A complete aversion to her husband touching her had gradually intensified since she left hospital. She described how she felt she would never be the same again – 'not just physically – but as a wife, mother and lover'. It is notable that she mentioned her gender roles as wife and mother before that of lover.

The onset of the dying process is often implicated in the denial of sexuality to the cared for patient and moreover provides an opportunity to dismiss the need for education on sexuality for carers of terminally ill people. Commonly explanations for reticent participation take the following line:

It's of no use to me or my patients. They're bed bound, near death, it's of no relevance.

Sex is no more on their mind than it is on mine. They've got enough on with their illness.

Whilst it is acknowledged that clients with severe infirmities may not be in a position to have sexual relationships, it is still relevant to consider their sexuality, no less because of an almost total dependency on the carer to attend to the very intimate aspects of personal care. Tenderness and sensitivity in daily routine tasks is of paramount importance. Sexuality, dignity and self-image will be affected by the way a patient is touched, spoken to, bathed and toileted. Some professionals appear

more threatened at confronting their role in acknowledging sexuality
through passive procedures (like touch) than through more direct actions (like discussions on sexual behaviour with a patient) and anger
may result, with other 'conditions' being introduced to qualify negative responses:

> I've told you . . . they're not only on death's door, they're also de-
> mented, brain-dead in fact. How I touch them has no bearing on
> what life they've got left.

Such comments reflect extremes of ignorance, fear and discomfort,
but leave another vital consideration. Does the sexuality of a senile
older adult warrant even less acknowledgement than that of the more
lucid?

The impact of growing old on sexuality and freedom of sexual expression is further threatened if there is dependency on external carers.
Public masturbation may indicate senility where the individual has lost
learned inhibitions, but still has a need for self-gratification. Negative
attention from carers may suppress the behaviour but is equally likely
to enhance it. The abstract system of health care colludes with the
taboos and denial of the human beings within it. The physical layout
of buildings, the policies, practices, priorities and pressurised working
conditions all militate against privacy, so that places for intimacy,
sensitive one-to-one discussions, and dignity for cleansing and bodily
functions, are frequently restricted. Individuality and privacy thus have
little place.

A further aspect of this is illustrated by examining the personal circumstances of professionals working within care for older people. One
particular teaching activity lends itself to providing evidence of the
constraints imposed by a gradual loss of independence and the need
for care from others. Participants are asked to consider their 'sexuality
lifeline' from birth to the present day. They record memorable people,
relationships, events, feelings, anxieties, messages and teachings which
they feel were significant in shaping who they are now. Usually they
decide unanimously that the most eventful (and often traumatic) times
are around their adolescence, new relationships, and changes in domestic relationships, for example the birth of children, or death of a
relative. Generally they express considerable surprise at the enormity
of the discoveries they make about themselves and the influences on
their self-esteem. Comments are made on how little regard they have
given to examination of the impact of external factors and how dy-

namic their sexuality and expression of it has been. However, the next stage of the activity brings about illuminating and quite often depressing insights – they are asked to look to the future and project their life-line to their death They need to consider ill-health, loss of a partner or parents, children growing up and leaving home, and dependency on 'others' for care. It is important to recognise that participants are usually from a mixture of community and institutional health care settings. The result is that they can, on the whole, envisage a life without their current domestic arrangements, but when they address being cared for by others, they are too well aware that the constraints are so massive as to create feelings of nothing but negativity at the prospect of old age. Being a part of care-giving (currently) leads them to believe that the system offers no guarantees for a continuation of choice, honesty, sexual affirmation or happiness. Not only do they think the system will halt their gradual self-actualisation (a factor which some perceive as a positive aspect of ageing) but that it will suppress it and deny them most of the things they currently take for granted. When they plot their 'sexuality curve' on the life-line (from birth to present day), in general it rises over time with occasional temporary descents. When they attempt to chart it within the context of needing external care, it always suffers a massive decline. The scale of this decline is directly proportional to the extent of their dependency on others. Being cared for in the home (with some degree of autonomy) is perceived as producing a gradual decline, being cared for in a residential home is significantly steeper, with a vertical slope for care within a long-stay hospital ward.

These nurses are aware that the system they view so negatively is created by people with a similarly poor understanding of sexuality and with attitudes and prejudices not unlike their own. Yet they resist change because the task feels daunting and enormous. They feel the main barrier to change is staff attitudes. This is substantiated by examples from their own practice where incidents related to sex and sexuality have been dealt with quickly and insensitively. Many of these relate to the syndrome of the 'dirty old man' where public masturbation is dealt with primitively ('shouted out', 'told to go to their room', or 'given drugs to calm them down'). The reasons behind the perpetrator's loss of inhibition are not addressed and staff continue to deal with these situations through crisis management, with no acknowledgement of the gender issues and with no safe forum for discussion. They feel too embarrassed or ignorant to question this method of treatment since it would require great confidence to initiate change in a situation where there would be very few allies. One feature of participating in the course, therefore, is a gradual acknowledgement that many of the problems arise from a lack of awareness of one's own sexuality; feelings of despondency often accompany this learning.

If this is the case for sexuality *per se* within health care and if it cannot acknowledge the sexuality of the heterosexual young or middle aged patient, how will it address the needs of the older gay man or lesbian, or the sexual desires of the gay, lesbian or bisexual older person who is dying? Concomitant with these dilemmas are those posed by HIV and AIDS. The anxieties evoked by caring for someone with HIV in a generic setting are the results of more deep-seated problems. HIV and AIDS merely serve to highlight the weaknesses in an already frail system. HIV and AIDS have forced an acknowledgement of gay bereavement, but it is doubtful whether this has really been addressed outside the gay community or specialist HIV services. There is scant evidence to suggest any favourable moves towards wider acknowledgement (Andrew and Andrew, 1991). If generic services are unable to embrace sexuality for the older, infirm heterosexual person, how will they offer sensitive care and compassion to the patient who is not only elderly but is gay and ill due to activities which are outside their experience or boundaries of permissibility. In other words, the expression of 'normal' sexuality is difficult for some to embrace. For example, a desire for guidance from an older patient to re-learn sexual satisfaction after an illness which results in a change in ability, lies beyond what some professionals consider as their responsibility. However, they do concede that such a patient has a right to self-gratification, but feel unable to assist in this endeavour. Whether or not it is the professional responsibility of a nurse to play a role here is hugely contentious, but warrants serious debate. Moreover, participants usually feel they would like to believe that a carer would do this for them, should they find themselves in the same position. This is the crucial point. Professionals *can* empathise with situations which bear some resemblance to their own life-world. The debate over 'guilty' and 'innocent' victims of HIV infection comes to the fore here. Caring for someone who is ill and has become infected with a pathogen through a sexually transmitted route raises feelings of 'right' and 'wrong' (perhaps subconsciously for some). This confirmation of undesirable sexual activity brings to the fore great fears and prejudices.

This scenario needs extending to include elderly people who are dependent on illegal drugs and people who work in the sex industry. Unquestioned labelling and discrimination jeopardise care. Studies on the attitudes of nurses to HIV have confirmed nurses' resistance to gaining knowledge, demonstrating negative attitudes and prejudices against patients with HIV (Bond *et al.*, 1988; Akinsanya and Rouse, 1991; McHaffie, 1993). Palliative care, the hospice movement and services for older people in general must also acknowledge HIV in order 'to prevent a social crisis developing as a growing number of people with HIV live longer and move into later life, and as increasing numbers of older people begin to experience HIV or AIDS at one remove' (Kaufmann, 1993, p. 2). There exists a widespread assumption that older people are not at risk from HIV, largely due to the conviction that they do not engage in high-risk behaviours. A survey of doctors and nurses working in Birmingham showed that 50 per cent did not believe that older people were at risk from HIV and AIDS (Jones, 1992). Statistics on prevalence and medical experience confirm otherwise, showing that in Britain 11 per cent of people with AIDS and over 1000 of those diagnosed with HIV infection are over aged 50 (Weiler, 1989; Mack *et al*, 1990; Kaufmann, 1993; PHLS, 1993). There are however some encouraging signs of HIV being taken seriously as an issue for older people, for example, with the Age Concern publication *A Crisis of Silence: HIV, AIDS and Older People* (Kaufmann, 1993). However, dissemination of this valuable resource appears limited, with a lack of awareness of its availability from nurses involved in the care of older people.

CONCLUSIONS

This paper has used some recent ideas on the body, identity and modernity as a call for the reappraisal and exploration of sexuality, ageing and illness within health care. Notions of identity as a reflexive project which incorporates the key dimensions of embodiment and gender help both to explain the use of more holistic models of health care and to problematise them. Within modernity, self-referential systems of meaning and understanding allow notions of the self to become closely entwined with the forms and surfaces of the body. Such reflexivity has proved possible even in health care, where biomedical models of the body and disease have been challenged by those incorporating psychological and social dimensions. In this way, 'the body as project' appears to have been carried right into the heart of the health care system. Herein lies a problem, however, for the bodily project is ultimately limited by certain irreducible biological determinants. All bodies must die.

How they die of course, is often socially determined. In a more generalisable sense therefore *ageing* becomes a key focus for under-standing how identity and embodiment are played out against a series of threats posed by illness and disease. We have been at particular pains to show how, in the modern context, sexuality is also implicated in this process. For in modernity, sexuality too is essential to identity and 'self-actualisation'. Changes in sexual mores across the generations, however, create difficulties for the recognition of sexual identities within the abstract system of health care. As our case illustrations show, tensions and problems appear at many levels, both for those giving and those receiving care, for individuals on either side are likely to be caught up in processes of self-surveillance and reflexivity.

The dual impact of ill health and ageing on sexuality and self-esteem, therefore, warrants careful scrutiny. Older adults and carers alike are marooned by a plethora of influences, including ignorance, misinformation, guilt, dependency, embarrassment and inhibition. Can such problems be overcome?

We learn from experience. We must look carefully to those in closest contact with our growing population of older people to learn from them and devise more proactive ways of creating safer places for older adults to feel confident in articulating their needs. Within the modern environment sexuality has become an integral part of an individual's identity. Webb says of sexuality: 'It involves the totality of being human' (Webb, 1985, p. 3). The acknowledgement and expression of sexuality from birth to death is a basic human right (Parke, 1991). It is a right which has no age-limit. Although health carers recognise the importance of treating the whole person, sexuality is rarely seen as integral to the treatment process. For older people and those who are dying, the importance of tenderness, touch and affection is paramount. For many, expressions of love and affection through sexual behaviours will not be possible. Is this not more reason to support a move towards a vigorous reappraisal of the focus of health care for this expanding group of service users?

NOTES

1. We are grateful to Sue Scott for detailed comments on an earlier version of this chapter.

REFERENCES

Akinsanya, J. and Rouse, P. (1991) *Who will Care? A Survey of the Knowledge and Attitudes of Hospital Nurses to People with HIV/AIDS* (Chelmsford: Anglia Polytechnic, Health and Social Work Centre).

Andrew, C. and Andrew, H. (1991) 'Sexuality and the Dying Patient', *Journal of District Nursing*, 10(5): pp. 8–10.

Baggs, J. G. and Karch, A. M. (1987) 'Sexual Counselling of Women with Heart Disease', *Heart and Lung*, 16(2): pp. 154–9.

Bauman, Z. (1992) *Mortality, Immortality and Other Life Strategies* (Cambridge: Polity Press).

de Beauvoir, S. (1972) *Old Age* (Harmondsworth: Penguin).

Berger, P. L. (1973) *The Social Reality of Religion* (Harmondsworth: Penguin).

Berger, P. L. and Luckmann, T. (1971) *The Social Construction of Reality* (Harmondsworth: Penguin).

Berger, P. L., Berger, B. and Kellner, H. (1973) *The Homeless Mind* (Harmondsworth: Penguin).

Bond, S., Rhodes, T. J., Phillips, P. R. *et al.* (1988) 'A National Study of HIV Infection, AIDS and Community Nursing Staff in England', Report 35, University of Newcastle upon Tyne, Newcastle Health Care Research Unit.

Bourdieu, P. (1984) *Distinction: A Social Critique of the Judgement of Taste* (London: Routledge).

Butler, R. N. and Lewis, M. I. (1988) *Love and Sex after Sixty* (New York: Harper & Row).

Clark, D. (ed.) (1993) *The Future for Palliative Care: Issues of Policy and Practice* (Buckingham: Open University Press).

Department of Health (1992) *The Health of the Nation* (London: HMSO).

Featherstone, M. (1987) 'Leisure, Symbiotic Power and the Life Course', in J. Horne, D. Jary and A. Tomlinson (eds) *Sport, Leisure and Social Relations* (London: Routledge, 1987).

Featherstone, M. and Hepworth, M. (1984) 'Changing Images of Retirement – An Analysis of Representations of Ageing in the Popular Magazine Choice', in D. Bromley (ed.), *Gerontology: Social and Behavioural Perspectives* (London: Croom Helm).

Foucault, M. (1984) *The History of Sexuality* (Harmondsworth: Penguin).

Frank, A. W. (1990) 'Bringing Bodies Back in: A Decade Review', *Theory, Culture and Society*, 7(1): pp. 131–62.

Gamel, C., Davies, B. D. and Hengeveld, M. (1993) 'Nurses' Provision of Teaching and Counselling on Sexuality: A Review of the Literature', *Journal of Advanced Nursing*, 18: pp. 1219–27.

George, R. (1992) 'HIV/AIDS Care in Hospices', paper presented to Help the Hospices Annual Conference (London: Royal College of Physicians).

Giddens, A. (1990) *The Consequences of Modernity* (Cambridge: Polity Press).

Giddens, A. (1991) *Modernity and Self-Identity: Self and Society in the Late Modern Age* (Cambridge: Polity Press).

Giddens, A. (1992) *The Transformation of Intimacy: Love, Sexuality and Eroticism in Modern Societies* (Cambridge: Polity Press).

Gorer, G. (1965) *Death, Grief and Mourning in Contemporary Britain* (London: Cresset Press).

Greengross, W. and Greengross, S. (1989) *Living, Loving and Ageing* (England: Age Concern).

Hanson, E. I. and Brouse, S. H. (1983) 'Assessing Sexual Implications of Functional Impairments Associated with Chronic Ulcers', *Journal of Sex Education Therapy*, **9**(1): pp. 39–45.

Henderson, V. (1969) *Basic Principles of Nursing Care* (Basle: Karger).

Hepworth, M. (1987) 'The Mid Life Phase', in G. Cohen (ed.), *Social Change and the Life Course* (London: Tavistock).

Hogan, R. M. (1980) *Human Sexuality: A Nursing Perspective* (New York: Appleton Century Crofts).

Huyck, M. H. (1974) *Growing Older – What you Need to Know about Ageing* (London: Prentice Hall).

Illich, I. (1975) *Medical Nemesis* (London: Calder and Boyars).

Ingram-Fogel, C. I. (1990) *Sexual Health Promotion* (Philadelphia, PA: W. B. Saunders).

Jacobson, L. (1974) 'Illness and Human Sexuality', *Nursing Outlook*, **22**(1): pp. 50–3.

Jenkins, B. J. (1988) 'Patients' Reports of Sexual Change after Treatment for Gynecological Cancer', *Oncology Nursing Forum*, **15**(3): pp. 349–54.

Jerrome, D. (1993) 'Intimate Relationships', in J. Bond, P. Coleman and S. Peace (eds), *Ageing in Society* (London: Sage).

Jones, H. M. (1992) 'The Human Immuno-deficiency Virus and Older People', unpublished MA dissertation, Keele University.

Jones, K. W. (1992) 'Dark Elegies' AIDS in Older People: The Kinship of Caring, Sharing and Loss', unpublished MSc thesis, Kings College, University of London.

Kaufmann, T. (1993) *A Crisis of Silence: HIV, AIDS and Older People* (London: Age Concern).

Kaye, R. A. (1993) 'Sexuality in the Later Years', *Ageing and Society*, **13**: pp. 415–26.

Kinsey, A. C., Pomeroy, W. B. and Martin, C. E. (1948) *Sexual Behaviour in the Human Male* (Philadelphia, PA: W. B. Saunders).

Krueger, J. C., Hassell, J., Goggins, D. B., Ishimatsu, T., Pablico, M. R., and Tuttle, E. J. (1979) 'Relationship between Nurse Counselling and Sexual Adjustment after Hysterectomy', *Nursing Research*, **28**(3): pp. 145–50.

Lash, C. (1980) *The Culture of Narcissism* (London: Abacus).

Mack, D. J., Green, T. S., Goldberg, J. D. and Fulton, J. D. (1990) 'AIDS: Elderly Patients are far from Immune', *Geriatric Medicine*, **20**(12): pp. 51–7.

Masters, W. and Johnson, V. (1970) *Human Sexual Inadequacy* (Boston, MA: Little Brown).

McHaffie, H. (1993) 'Improving Awareness', *Nursing Times*, 5 May, **89**(18): pp. 29–31.

Parke, F. (1991) 'Sexuality in Later Life', *Nursing Times*, 11 December, **87**: p. 50.

PHLS (1993) Statistics from the Public Health Laboratory Service, Communicable Disease Surveillance Centre, February.

Puner, M. (1979) *To the Good Long Life: What we Know about Growing Old* (London: Macmillan).

Roper, N. (1976) *Clinical Experience in Nurse Education* (Edinburgh: Churchill Livingstone).

Roper, N., Logan, W. and Tierney, A. (1980) *The Elements of Nursing* (Edinburgh: Churchill Livingstone).

Roper, N., Logan, W. and Tierney, A. (1985) *The Elements of Nursing*, 2nd edn (Edinburgh: Churchill Livingstone).

Savage, J. (1987) *Nurses, Gender and Sexuality* (London: Heinemann).

Scott, S. and Morgan, D. (eds) (1993) *Body Matters* (London: Falmer Press).

Sennett, R. (1977) *The Fall of Public Man* (Cambridge: Cambridge University Press).

Shilling, C. (1993) *The Body and Social Theory* (London: Sage).

Small, N. (1993) 'HIV/AIDS: Lessons for Policy and Practice', in D. Clark (ed.), *The Future for Palliative Care* (Buckingham: Open University Press).

Starr, B. D. and Weiner, M. B. (1981) *The Starr–Weiner Report on Sex and Sexuality in the Mature Years* (New York: McGraw Hill).

Stuart, W. F. R. (1975) *Sex and the Physically Handicapped*, National Fund for Research into Crippling Disease (Horsham: Sussex).

Turner, B. S. (1984) *The Body and Society* (Oxford: Blackwell).

Turner, B. S. (1992) *Regulating Bodies* (London: Routledge).

Waterhouse, J. and Metcalfe, V. (1991) 'Attitudes towards Nurses Discussing Sexual Concerns with Patients', *Journal of Advanced Nursing*, 16: pp. 1048–54.

Webb, C. (1985) *Sexuality Nursing and Health* (Chichester: John Wiley).

Webb, C. (1986) 'Professional and Lay Support for Hysterectomy Patients', *Journal of Advanced Nursing*, 11: pp. 167–77.

Webb, C. and Wilson-Barnett, J. (1983) 'Self-concept, social support and hysterectomy', *International Journal of Nursing Studies*, 25(3): pp. 235–44.

Weeks, J. (1981) *Sex, Politics and Society* (Harlow, Essex: Longman).

Weg, R. B. (1989) *Sexuality in Later Years: Roles and Behaviours* (New York: Academic Press).

Weiler, P. G. (1989) 'Why AIDS is Becoming a Geriatric Problem', *Geriatrics*, 44(7): pp. 81–2.

Weston, A. (1993) 'Challenging Assumptions', *Nursing Times*, May 5, 89(18): pp. 26–9.

Waterhouse, J. and Metcalfe, V. (1991), 'Attitudes towards Nurses discussing Sexual Concerns with Patients', *Journal of Advanced Nursing*, 16 1048–54.

WHO (1975) *Education and Treatment in Human Sexuality: The Training of Health Professionals*, Technical Report Series no. 572 (Geneva: World Health Organisation).

Wilson-Barnett, J. and Batehup, L. (eds) (1988) *Sexual Problems in Patient Problems: A Research, Base for Nursing Care* (London: Scutari).

Wright, S. (1988) *Nursing the Older Patient* (London: Harper Row).

Zalar, M. K. (1982) 'Role Preparation for Nurses in Human Sexual Functioning', *Nursing Clinics of North America*, 17: 3, pp. 351–63.

Index

AAAS *see* American Association
  for the Advancement of
  Science
Aberdeen, Lady, 123
abnormality *see* difference
abolitionist biologists, 69
  see also biological sciences
abortion:
  attitudes to, 208
  genetic engineering, 60, 63
  of homosexual foetuses, 60, 63
  selective, 60–1, 63
absconding fathers, 126, 128–30
  see also fathers
abstinence:
  from sexual relations, 88–91,
    104–5
  partial, 89–91
  see also celibacy
abstract systems concept, 264, 268,
  276
  see also health care
abused women:
  as prostitutes, 197
  see also violence
activists:
  on AIDS, 1
  gay, 61
  in scientific research, 59–60
ACT-UP, 149
The Adult (journal), 94
Advanced Industrial Society, BSA
  Conference, Kent (1975), 21,
  30
advertising *see* public advertising
AFDC *see* Aid to Families with
  Dependent Children
African Americans:
  AIDS/HIV groups, 172–3
  deprivation of, 116
  education for, 69–70
  see also racism
Age Concern:
  Crisis of Silence . . . , 279

age of consent:
  for homosexuals, 217
ageing process, 13, 274
  and AIDS/HIV, 278–9
  and the body, 265–6, 270–1,
    279–80
  and death, 263–4
  and dependence, 267–8, 276, 277
  and gender, 265–6, 268
  and health care, 266, 269–80
  personal experience of, 270,
    272–9
  and self identity, 267–9
  senility, 275, 276
  and sexuality, 263–4, 266, 268,
    269–80
  and social class, 265
  stereotyping of, 269, 270
Aid to Families with Dependent
  Children (AFDC) (US), 117,
  118–19
AIDS, 5–6, 8, 12–13
  in Britain, 11, 161–79, 201–19
  community responses to, 161–79
  cultural issues of, 158–9
  degaying of, 148, 166–71
  discourse on, 140–3, 147–8, 150,
    153
  and drug abuse, 165
  and ethnic groups, 165, 171–5
  as gay disease, 11, 129, 166–7,
    172
  gay response to, 162–3, 166–71
  government policy on, 162, 164,
    166, 167, 176–8
  and homophobia, 166
  language of, 143
  political attitudes to, 163, 164
  public attitudes to, 164, 202–3,
    206–7
  re-gaying of, 168
  and sexualities, 10, 26
  statistics on, 202–3, 216
  see also health care; health issues

AIDS activists, 11
  see also activists
AIDS clinics, 143–7, 150
AIDS organisations, 163, 164–6,
  171–5
  funding of, 165, 167, 172, 176–8
AIDS panics, 201–2, 205–7
  reactions to, 201, 205, 206–7, 217
AIDS, people with:
  Black, 165, 171–4
  buddying services, 164
  as communities, 162, 169–71
  death of, 57, 59, 166, 217, 278
  diagnosis, 147–53, 155–7
  dying, 278–9
  habits, 145–7
  health care, 147–53, 155–7, 163,
    261, 272–9
  hospice treatment, 263, 279
  knowledge of AIDS, 143–4, 145,
    147–53, 158–9
  older people, 278–9
  personal experience of, 140,
    143–7, 148–53
  reskilling of, 156–7
  self identity, 10, 140–1, 142–60
  self-help groups for, 163, 164,
    167, 213, 217–18
  voluntary organisations for, 163,
    164–6, 213–14, 217–18
  see also HIV-positive people
AIDS research:
  funding of, 11, 31
AIDS Service Organisations
  (ASOs), 166
AIDS transmission, 145–6, 162, 165
  risk of, 170, 171–5, 202–5
AIDS vaccines:
  testing of, 210
AIDS/HIV voluntary organisations,
  161–79
Aldred, Guy, 80
Allen, L., 59–60
Almahawi, Dr Yarab, 205, 206, 216
altruism, 210, 213–16, 217–18
  compulsory, 213
  gift-giving, 213
  social good, 215–16, 218
America *see* United States

American Association for the
  Advancement of Science
  (AAAS), 59
American Sociological Association,
  20
anal sex, 237
anarchism:
  and feminism, 77, 79, 80, 94
anglophone predominance:
  in sociological research, 23
animal nature:
  of sex, 80–1
anti-racism, 69–70
  see also racism
anti-social behaviour *see* delinquency
anxiety, 157
appropriate sex, 8, 9, 105, 106
  see also heterosexuality
arche-health concept, 218
  see also health issues
Arkley, Catherine, 210
articulating:
  in sexual storytelling, 41, 43
Askham, J., 131
ASOs *see* Aids Service
  Organisations
attitudes *see* public attitudes
authentic sex, 235–6
authority:
  balance of, 222–3
  and discourse, 140, 143, 147–8,
    150, 153
  disparities of, 12
  and gender inequalities, 222,
    239–57
  in heterosexual relationships, 12,
    221–4, 236, 240
  hierarchies of, 5, 6
  and identity, 10, 141–2, 154, 159
  individual, 252–3
  and knowledge, 141–2, 215
  in prostitution, 11, 182, 183–8,
    191–2
  social, 243–4, 251, 252
  strategies off, 141, 142, 151–3
  ubiquity of, 38
  of women, 12, 254–7, 258
auto-eroticism, 85, 95
  see also masturbation

autonomy *see* sexual autonomy
axial principle:
  of industrial societies, 203

Back to Basics campaign (UK),
  115, 133, 217
Bacon, Francis, 57
Bailey, J.M., 70
Barrett, Michèle, 64–5, 258
Barron, R., 30
Bartky, Sandra Lee, 257–8
bastardy *see* illegitimate children
Baudrillard, Jean, 37
Bauman, Zygmunt, 202, 211–12,
  265
BBC (UK), 132–3
de Beauvoir, Simone, 270
Beck, U.:
  Risk Society . . ., 202, 203, 205
Begg, Rev. Dr James, 123
Bell, C., 30
Bellah, R.N., 49
Bem Sandra, 255
benefits *see* welfare systems
Benton, T., 67
bereavement, 214, 278
  see also death
Berger, P.L., 264–5
Best, S., 142, 153
BHAN *see* Black HIV/AIDS
  Network
biological determinism, 66
  see also determinism
biological differences:
  gay brain theory, 8, 53–4, 58–60,
    62–71
  gay gene theory, 8, 53–4, 60–71
  third sex theory, 55–6, 69
biological politics, 66, 67–9
  sociobiology, 65
  see also politics
Biological Politics (Sayers), 65, 66
biological reductionism, 66
biological sciences, 55–7, 58, 64,
  69–70
  see also scientific research
biology as destiny, 65–6
  see also eugenics
Birkbeck College, London, 30

birth-control, 86, 89–91, 112, 126
  contraception, 89, 104–5
  Karezza technique, 90–1, 95
  Malthusian, 89
  natural, 89–91
  sterilisation, 89
  use of condoms, 145
birthrates:
  in Britain, 105–6, 107, 112
  decline in, 9, 105–6, 107, 112
bisexual men, 167–8, 278
  see also men
Black HIV/AIDS Network (BHAN)
  (UK), 165, 172, 174
Black men:
  inter-racial prostitution, 189–90
  see also men
Black people:
  with AIDS/HIV, 165, 171–4, 177
  African American, 69–70, 116,
    172–3
  in Britain, 165, 171, 172, 173–4
  in prostitution, 181
Blackliners (UK), 165, 171, 172,
  173–4, 177
Blackpool (UK), 100
blame:
  and risk behaviour, 204
  of the victim, 118–20, 129
Block, Iwan, 78, 85
blood transfusions, 213–14
BMA *see* British Medical Association
the body:
  ageing of, 265–6, 270–1, 279–80
  control of, 11–12, 47, 77, 240
  disciplined, 243
  essentialist theories of, 64–5, 66
  feminist attitudes to, 64–5
  and identity formation, 265–6
  missing body concept, 264
  as physical capital, 265
  self care of, 265
  sociological research on, 8, 64–9,
    264–6
Body Positive groups, 149, 170
the body as project, 266, 269–80
  see also health care
body rights, 208, 209, 210–11
  see also rights

Bolton (UK), 98
Bolton Health Authority (UK), 205,
  206–7
books *see* printing and books
Boord, C., 94
Bottomley, Virginia, 201
Bouchard, Thomas, 60
Bourdieu, P., 265
Boyle, Nina, 90
the brain *see* human brain
brain-imaging, 58
  see also human brain
breaking the silence, 45
  see also sexual storytelling
Bressanone group, 66
bridal pregnancy, 125
Britain:
  AIDS in, 11, 161–79, 201–19
  birthrate, 105–6, 107, 112
  Black people in, 165, 171, 172,
    173–4
  censorship in, 78, 94
  degaying movement, 166–71
  feminism in, 76, 84, 173–4
  illegitimacy in, 115, 117, 118–20,
    127–8
  immigration policies, 70, 191
  Poor Laws, 124, 126, 128
  poverty in, 9–10, 116, 117–18
  prostitution in, 11, 76, 77, 180–98
  responses to AIDS/HIV, 161–79
  sexual research, 9, 78, 94, 97–114
  sexology, 78
  welfare systems, 118, 127, 128–9,
    131
  see also Northern Ireland;
    Scotland
Britain and Her Birth-Rate
  (Mass-Observation), 105–6
British Medical Association (BMA),
  207, 208
British Psychological Society, 30
British Sociological Association
  (BSA), 2, 3, 5, 17
  conferences, 2, 17, 18–19, 21–8,
    29, 30
  Equality of Sexes committee, 20,
    21, 26
  history, 30

  organisational structure, 18–21,
    29
  Patriarchy Study Group, 21
  Position of Women . . . working
    party, 20
  Sexual Divisions conference
    (1974), 17, 18–19, 21–3, 24,
    28, 29
  Sexual Divisions Study Group,
    20, 30
  Sexualities in a Social Context
    conference (1994), 23–8
  Violence against Women Study
    Group, 21
  Violence, War and Social Change
    conference (1975), 21, 30
  women's caucus, 19–21, 24–5, 30
  Women's Caucus *Newsletter*, 21
Broadcasting Complaints
  Commission (UK), 132–3
Brodkey, Harold:
  Runaway Soul, 215
brothels, 85, 191
  see also prostitution
Brown, R.K., 30
Browne, Stella, 79–80, 81, 87–8,
  92, 95
BSA *see* British Sociological
  Association
buddying services, 164
  see also AIDS patients; HIV
    positive people
Butler, Judith, 22–3, 241, 254

Calman, Dr Kenneth, 206
Cambridge University, 63
Campbell, Beatrix, 115
Canadian Women's Temperance
  Union, 95
cancer:
  radiation-linked, 204
capitalism, 122–3
carers, 213, 267–9, 272
  see also health workers
Carpenter, Edward, 56, 79, 95
Carrie (film), 42
Carson, Johnny, 40
category policies, 172
  see also government policies

celibacy, 87, 232, 233
 see also self control
celebrity intellectuals, 40
censorship:
 in Britain, 78, 94
 of popular music, 40
 of sexual research, 2, 78, 94
 see also public reaction
Chalmers, Thomas, 121
change:
 in heterosexual relationships,
  248–53
 strategies for, 139–40
chaperonage, 121
chastity, 85, 86–9
chat shows *see* television
 programmes
Chesser, Eustace:
 *Sexual, Marital and Family
  Relationships . . .*, 107, 108,
  109, 110, 111–12
Chew, Ada Neild, 79, 94
Chicago University, 115–16
child abuse, 5, 36, 42
Child Helpline, 36
child prostitution, 180
 see also prostitution
Child Support Agency (CSA) (UK),
 115, 118, 130
children:
 delinquency among, 115, 118
 effect on married life, 22–8
 illegitimate, 9–10, 115–36
 parental responsibility, 209–10,
  217
 postnatal depression, 228–9
 of single mothers, 115, 117
 see also young people
Children's Liver Disease
 Foundation, 210
children's rights, 209–10, 217
choice:
 in health care, 173–4, 176
 for HIV workers, 11–12, 201–2,
  205–19
 limits of, 158
 moral, 11–12, 215–16
 rational, 132
 social, 47, 215–16

chromasomes:
 x-chromasomes, 61
the church *see* religious issues
'Churchtown', 98, 100
 see also 'Little Kinsey' survey
cinema *see* film; the media
citizenship, 46
 intimate, 7, 34, 45–52
 types of, 46–7
civil registration *see* registration of
 births
civil rights:
 for homosexuals, 54
 to know, 208–9
 liberty, 11
 for prostitutes, 192
 see also rights
class structure, 9–10, 77, 203
 and ageing, 265
 and illegitimacy, 120–9
 see also social structure
Clayton, Dr Peter, 205
clients:
 domination clients, 182, 185,
  186–7, 189
 married, 189
 motivations, 187, 188–9
 prostitute–client relationships,
  181, 182, 183–90, 194–5
 of street-walkers, 180, 197
clinical practitioners:
 attitudes to AIDS/HIV patients,
  143–7
 see also health care; health
  issues
clinics:
 for people with AIDS/HIV,
  143–7, 150
 for sexually transmitted diseases,
  145–6
 see also health issues
Clinton, President Bill, 117, 130
codes of conduct *see* guidelines
cohabitation, 119
 see also marriage
Cohen, David, 224
Cohen, Stan, 207
coitus interruptus, 89–90, 104–5
 see also birth control

coitus reservatus, 89–90
    see also birth control
collective identity, 6
    see also identity issues
collective risk, 204–5
    see also risk behaviour
collective welfare, 126, 127
    see also welfare systems
collusion:
    in heterosexual relationships, 241
coming out, 34, 35, 36, 45
    see also sexual politics; sexual
        storytelling
commitment, 139
communication, 49–50
    see also sexual storytelling
communications technology, 7, 35–6
    mass media, 38, 50
    the media, 36, 42, 43, 50, 62–3,
        69, 148, 206–7, 217
    newspapers and journals, 2–3,
        8–9, 39, 75–96, 98, 119,
        148, 149, 168
    printing and books, 35, 39, 85–6,
        148, 149
    and sexual storytelling, 34, 35–7,
        38–9
    television programmes, 34, 35–7,
        39–40
communitarianism, 49
communities:
    of people with AIDS/HIV, 162,
        169–71
    concept of, 161, 162, 177–8
    interpretive, 43–4
    response to people with AIDS/
        HIV, 161–79
    self-help groups, 163, 164, 167,
        213–14, 217–18
    sense of, 43
    and sexualities, 1, 6, 7, 101–11
    as support groups, 35, 36
    types of, 161–2, 167
    voluntary organisations as, 163,
        164–71
    women's organisations, 165, 171,
        174
community health care, 161, 162,
    163, 164

compulsory altruism, 213
    see also altruism
compulsory heterosexuality, 253, 256
condoms:
    use of, 145
    see also birth control
confidentiality issues, 12
    for health workers, 206, 207,
        216–17
    for patients, 206
consensual sex, 80
    see also sex
consent:
    and prostitution, 11, 180, 182
constraining:
    of sexual storytelling, 49
construction of self, 204
    see also self identity; risk
        behaviour
constructionism:
    social, 4, 61, 64–5, 66, 70
consumerism, 39–40, 44, 68
Contagious Diseases Act (UK), 76
continence:
    in marriage, 88–91
    see also self control
contraception, 89, 104–5
    see also birth control
contract work, 23–4
contrary sexual emotions, 53
    see also homosexuals
control issues:
    of the body, 11–2, 47, 77, 240
    and prostitution, 11, 183–98
    and sexual storytelling, 38, 42
    for women, 42, 77
Copeland, Peter:
    Science of Desire, 61, 63
coping strategies:
    of single mothers, 130–1
corpus callosum, 58
    see also human brain
counselling services, 206, 217
counsellors *see* clinical practitioners
the couple game, 221, 225
    see also heterosexual relationships
courtship, 121, 125–6
    see also marriage
Craig, Jane, 94, 95

Cramond, William, 123–4, 131, 132
creation:
  of identity, 139–40
  see also identity issues
crime *see* delinquency
criminalisation:
  of homosexuality, 57
A Crisis of Science: HIV, AIDS and Older People (Age Concern), 279
critical care, 208
  see also terminal care
cruelty *see* violence
CSA *see* Child Support Agency
cultural affirmation, 177
cultural conservatives, 48
cultural deprivation, 118–20, 121
  see also poverty
cultural intermediaries, 40
cultural issues, 47–8, 65, 77
  and AIDS/HIV, 158–9
  scientific culture, 65, 68–9
cultural progressives, 48
culture of public problems, 34, 35–7, 39–40
  creation of, 41, 44–5
culture war, 47–8
cultures of poverty, 129–33
  see also poverty

Daily Mirror, 3
Daily Star, 3
Daily Telegraph, 2–3, 207
data triangulation, 100–1, 113–14
  see also methodology
Davies, Laura, 209–10
Dawson, John, 208
death:
  and ageing, 263–4
  from AIDS/HIV, 57, 59, 166, 205, 217, 278
  attitudes to, 6, 261–2, 271, 280
  bereavement, 214, 278
  dying process, 13, 163, 261–3, 265, 268–9, 270, 275–6, 278–80
  euthanasia, 208
  and identity, 267
  and loneliness, 215

pornography of, 262
prospect of, 215
right to die, 208
sequestring of, 265, 268
and sex, 12–13, 214, 261–83
statistics of, 203
understanding of, 266
Victorian response to, 261–2
deception, 49–50
  self-deception, 49
decision making:
  for homosexuals, 160
  risk reduction, 160
deep act concept, 221
degaying:
  of AIDS, 148, 166–71
  in Britain, 166–71
delayed marriage, 125–6
  see also marriage
delinquency:
  amongst young people, 115, 118, 119–20
Delphy, C., 64–5
Dennis, N.:
  Families without Fatherhood, 118
Department of Health (UK), 201, 216–17, 257
  Health of the Nation conference (1992), 273
dependence, 267–8, 276, 277
  see also independence
deprivation *see* poverty
Derrida, Jacques, 218
desertion *see* absconding fathers
desire *see* sexual desire
determinism, 57–8
  biological, 66
Dews, Peter, 142
diabetes, 274
difference:
  concept of, 152
disciplinary societies, 151
  see also social structure
discipline, 141
Discipline and Punish (Foucault), 141, 151
discourse:
  on AIDS/HIV, 140–3, 147–8, 150, 153

and authority, 140, 141, 143, 158
  dominant, 140, 150, 153
  heterosexual, 223–4, 225–9
  on sexual reputations, 258
  sexual storytelling, 7–8, 34–58
diversity:
  of sexualities, 6–7
divorce, 119
  see also marriage
doctors *see* health workers
Domestic Workers Union, 87
dominant discourses:
  on AIDS/HIV, 140, 150, 153
domination clients:
  in prostitution, 182, 185, 186–7,
    189
  see also authority; prostitution
dormant stories, 35, 38
  see also sexual storytelling
double standards:
  in heterosexual relationships,
    109–10, 111, 240, 242–53,
    257, 258
Drapetomania, 69
drug abuse, 278
  and AIDS/HIV, 165
drug use:
  and prostitution, 186
Dubois, Ellen, 84
dying process, 13, 163
  and AIDS/HIV, 278–9
  attitudes to, 262–1, 272, 280
  hospice movement, 262–3, 269,
    270
  onset of, 275
  sequestring of, 265
  and sexuality, 268–9
  terminal care, 269, 275–6
  see also death
dysfunctional families, 115, 116–20
  see also family groups

economic independence, 76, 77
  see also independence
Economic and Social Research
    Council (ESRC), 23, 31, 70,
    163, 237, 257
education, 77
  for African Americans, 69–70

higher, 23–4
  ignorance, 77
  sexual, 103
  for women, 69, 103
The Egoist, 79
  see also Freewoman
electronic media *see*
    communications technology
elitism:
  in professional organisations, 30
Ellis, Havelock, 56, 75, 78, 85, 95
  Sexual Inversion, 94
Elton, Ben, 253
emancipation, 45
  see also sexual politics
Embattled Eros (Seidman), 50–1
embodied self concept, 265
  see also identity formation
emotion work, 220, 221
  see also sex work
emotional fulfilment, 220
  sexual, 220, 226–7, 229–30
empathising *see* imagining
employment rights, 217
empowerment, 152, 157
  through storytelling, 38
  of women, 253–7
England *see* Britain
England, Len, 100, 113
epistemology:
  of sexual research, 113–14
epidemics:
  illegitimacy seen as, 120–4
epidemiology, 5, 8, 66–9
equal opportunities, 122, 172
Equal Rights Amendment (USA), 70
Equality of the Sexes, BSA
    committee, 20, 21, 26
Erdos, G.:
  Families without Fatherhood, 118
ESRC *see* Economic and Social
    Research Council
essentialist theories, 4, 9
  of the body, 64–5, 66
  of homosexuality, 55–6
ethical responsibilities:
  of health workers, 206–7, 209
ethics:
  group, 209–12

individual, 209–12
medical, 210
postmodern, 202, 211–12
of sexual storytelling, 49–50
of sexualities, 61, 70
ethnic gay communities, 165, 171–4
ethnic groups:
and AIDS/HIV, 171–5
engaged in prostitution, 181
as prostitutes' clients, 189–90
voluntary, 165, 171–4
ethnicity:
and sexualities, 7
see also race
ethnomethodology, 27–8
Etzioni, Amitai, 49
eugenics, 8, 93
biology as destiny, 65–6
hereditarianism, 60, 69
inborn tendencies, 55–7, 60, 69
euthanasia, 208
Expert Advisory Group on Aids
(UK), 216–17
expert opinion, 207
expert systems, 157, 158
Exploring English Character
(Gorer), 110
extra-marital affairs, 233

faking orgasms, 233–4, 235–6
see also orgasms
Families without Fatherhood
(Dennis and Erdos), 118
family groups, 22, 76
dysfunctional, 115, 116–20
fathers, 118, 126, 128–30, 268
government policies on, 11, 115
grandparents, 117, 119, 126–8
husbands, 181, 274–5
parents, 117, 119, 126–8, 130,
209–10, 217
single mothers, 115, 116, 117,
118–36
single parent families, 115, 117
traditional, 118, 124–5, 126
wives, 181
see also children; mothers; social
structure
family myths, 221

family size preferences, 131
fantasising:
over sex, 78, 189–90
see also role playing; sexology
farm engrossment, 125
farming communities, 123, 125–6
see also rural areas
fateful moment concept, 10, 154–5,
157, 265
fathers, 118, 268
absconding, 126, 128–30
see also family groups; men
Faulkner, Wendy, 69
Fawcett, Millicent, 75
fear, 215
Featherstone, M., 265
feeling rules, 221
see also intimacy
female-in-the-head concept, 240,
241, 253–6
female hormones, 56, 70
see also hormones
female sexual autonomy, 6, 8–9
see also sexual autonomy
females see women
feminism, 5
and anarchism, 77, 79, 80, 94
attitudes to the body, 64–5
in Britain, 76, 84, 173–4
divisions in, 86–91
and heterosexual relationships,
8–9, 75–96, 221–2, 223, 241
and marriage, 221–2
materialist, 27
in nineteenth century, 76
postmodern, 27
and prostitution, 180–1
public attitudes to, 8–9
purposes of, 84
radical, 64–5, 66, 180–1, 187, 223
and sexualities, 17, 18–29, 76–8
in United States, 84
women's studies, 25–6, 27, 31
see also sexual politics; women
feminist biologists, 69, 70
see also biological sciences
feminist critiques, 27
of gender studies, 5
of scientific research, 5, 8, 53–71

feminist morality, 86–91
  see also morality
feminist politics, 5, 8–9, 17, 18–29,
  64–5, 258
  see also sexual politics
feminist writing, 81–4
  see also Freewoman
femininity, 240, 241, 242, 247,
  248–53, 257–8
  see also women
fertility levels, 131
  see also pregnancy
fetishes, 78
  see also sexology
Field, Nicola, 174–5
film, 42, 69
Fisher, Dr Fleur, 207
fit motherhood, 93
  see also mothers
Flax, Jane, 50
Fletcher, R.C., 94
the foetus:
  rights of, 209
  status of, 209
  see also pregnancy
forced prostitution, 180
  see also prostitution
Forel, August, 78, 85
foreplay, 93, 227
Foucault, Michel, 7, 10, 37–8, 57,
  147, 153, 262
  Discipline and Punish, 141, 151
  History of Sexuality, 5, 53, 55,
    142, 214–15, 222
  on identity, 140, 141–2, 143,
    150–1, 158, 159, 257–8
  on the soul, 160
Fox, N., 218
Frances, Hilary, 94, 95
Frankenberg, R., 30
Frankie Goes to Hollywood, 40
free choice prostitution, 180, 181
  see also prostitution
Free Church of Scotland, 123
free love movement, 77, 83–4
Freewoman (journal):
  articles in, 80
  ban on sale of, 79
  contributors to, 75, 76, 79–80

impact of, 8–9, 75–6, 79–96
opposition to, 75–6
publication run of, 79
Freud, Sigmund, 56
Friedan, Betty, 42
frigidity:
  in women, 78–9
Frontliners (UK), 165
Frost, Robert, 214
frustration *see* sexual frustration
fundamentalism:
  attitudes to homosexuals, 61
  in sexual storytelling, 48–50
  tribalism, 48–50
funding:
  of AIDS research, 11, 31
  of AIDS/HIV organisations, 164,
    167, 168–9, 172, 176–8
  of HIV prevention initiatives,
    168–9
  of National Health Service,
    176–8, 206
  public, 11, 164, 167, 168–9, 172,
    176–8
  of sociological research, 21, 23–4,
    30, 31
  voluntary, 164
funding crises, 176–8
Fuss, Diana, 254

Gagnon, John T., 7
  Sexual Conduct . . ., 4–5
Gawthorpe, Mary, 75–6
gay activists, 61
  see also activists; gay liberation
    movement
gay bereavement, 278
gay brain theory, 8, 53–4, 58–60,
  62–71
  see also homosexuals
gay clubs, 148, 149
gay communities, 148–9, 162
  ethnic, 165, 171–4
  response to HIV/AIDS, 162–3,
    166–71
gay disease, 11, 129, 166–7, 172
  see also AIDS
gay gene theory, 8, 53–4, 60–71
  see also genetics; homosexuals

gay liberation movement, 5, 8,
     262–3
   homosexual underworld, 36
   see also homosexuals; lesbians;
     sexual politics
Gay Men Fighting AIDS (GMFA)
     (UK), 163, 168–70, 174–5
Gay Men's Health Crisis (US), 166
gay politics, 5, 8, 164, 262–3
   see also sexual politics
gay press, 148, 149, 168
   see also newspapers and journals
gay studies:
   funding of, 31
gay writers, 166
gender balance, 20
gender differentiation, 7, 22–8, 31,
     222
   sexual divisions, 4, 17, 23
   and sexualities, 26
gender inequalities, 22, 180, 222
   and authority, 222, 239–57
   institutionalised, 222
gender studies, 2, 5, 22–8, 31
   and aging process, 265–6, 268
   feminist critiques of, 5
gendered power relationships,
     239–57
   see also authority
gendering:
   of sexual reputations, 241–57
generic process:
   of sexual storytelling
genetic engineering, 60–1, 63
genetic markers, 60, 61, 62
genetics, 5, 8, 70
   gay gene theory, 8, 53–4, 60–71
   gene determination, 54
   molecular, 60–2
   political economy of, 68
   see also scientific research
genital contact, 110–11
genito-urinary medicine (GUM),
     162, 164
   see also health care
Germany:
   Nazism, 69
   sexual research, 55–6
Geschwind, 58

Giddens, Anthony, 10, 140, 153–9,
     214–15, 223, 264–5
   Modernity and Self Identity,
     153–5, 203, 264–6
   Transformation of Intimacy, 202,
     220
gift-giving, 213
   see also altruism
Gilder, G., *Visible Man . . .*, 118
Gilligan, Carol, 255
Glasgow Experiment, 121
GMFA *see* Gay men Fighting Aids
Goldsmith's College Research Fund
     (UK), 257
Gordon, Linda, 84, 90
Gorer, Geoffrey, 262
   Exploring English Character, 110
   *Sex and Marriage in England
     Today*, 107, 108, 109, 110, 112
government policies:
   on AIDS/HIV, 162, 164, 166,
     167, 176–8
   category policies, 172
   on the family, 11, 115
   on immigration, 70, 191
   see also politics
Graham, Hilary, 131
grandparents, 117, 119, 126–8
   see also family groups
Greater Glasgow Health Board
     (UK), 217
Greenway, Judy, 94
Greig, Teresa Billington, 79
group ethics, 209–12
   see also ethics
Guardian, The, 2, 217
guidelines:
   for health workers, 201, 206,
     216–17, 271–2
GUM *see* genito-urinary medicine

Habermas, Jürgen, 49
habits, 102
   of people with AIDS/HIV, 145–7
Hall, Stuart, 207, 217
Halson, J., 258
Hamblin, A., 223
Hamer, Dean, 53, 60–2, 63, 68
   Science of Desire, 61, 63

Hamilton, Cecily, 88
Hanmer, Jalna, 29
harassment *see* sexual harassment
Harvard University, 63, 70
Hay, Anne, 128
health care, 13
  abstract system of, 267, 268, 276
  and ageing, 226, 269–80
  AIDS/HIV clinics, 143–7, 150
  AIDS/HIV, people with, 147–53,
    155–7, 163, 261, 272–9
  approach to sexuality, 266–88
  changed attitudes in, 276–8
  choice in, 173–4, 176
  in the community, 161, 162, 163,
    164
  dependence on, 267–8
  genito-urinary medicine, 162, 164
  hospice movement, 149, 262–3,
    269, 279
  imposed, 268
  models of, 267, 271–2
  public, 164
  quality of, 176
  self care, 265
  statutory, 164, 176
  STD clinics, 121, 145–6
  terminal care, 269, 275–6
health education, 11–12, 164, 169,
    172, 202–3
health issues, 5–6, 85
  arche-health concept, 218
  clinics, 143–7, 150
  public health, 120, 164
  sexually transmitted diseases,
    121, 145–6
  women's health, 66–7
  see also AIDS; HIV
Health of the Nation conference,
    1992 (UK), 273
health promotion *see* health
  education
health risks *see* risk behaviour
health workers:
  carers, 213, 267–9, 272
  confidentiality issues for, 206,
    207, 216–17
  dangers to, 216
  ethical responsibilities, 206–7, 209

guidance for, 201, 206, 216–17,
    271–2
HIV positive people as, 11–12,
    201–2, 205–19
professional standards, 206–7
responsibilities, 201, 206–7
screening of, 206
sexuality of, 276–7
and sexuality of patients, 263–4,
    266, 268, 270–8
training, 266–7, 271–3, 276–7
treating AIDS/HIV patients,
    147–53, 155–7, 163, 261,
    272–9
help lines, 36, 163, 206, 217
Henderson, S., 144
Hendrix, Jimi, 40
Hepworth, M., 265–6
hereditarianism, 60, 69
  see also inborn tendencies
heterosex discourse, 223–4, 225–9
heterosexism *see* homophobia
heterosexual prostitution, 182–96
  see also prostitution
heterosexual relationships:
  authentic sex, 235–6
  and authority, 12, 221–4, 236,
    240
  balance of, 22–3
  celibate periods, 232, 233
  changes in, 248–53
  collusion in, 241
  communication in, 234
  the couple game, 221, 225
  criticism in, 221
  declining passion, 225–7
  declining sexual activity, 225–6,
    237
  discourse on, 223–4, 225–9
  disruptions in, 227–9
  double standards in, 109–10, 111,
    240, 242–53, 257, 258
  empathy in, 223–4
  extra-marital affairs, 233
  feminist attitudes to, 8–9, 75–96,
    221–2, 223, 241
  habituation effects, 234
  initiative in, 225, 234
  instability of, 220

long-term, 220, 225–36
male domination, 12, 140, 221–4,
    236, 240, 241
marital, 88–91
personal experience of, 242–57
phases of, 221
pure relationships, 220, 223
resentment build up, 231–2, 234,
    235
as sex work, 11, 220, 221–4,
    233–6
sexual empathy in, 223–4
sexual experimentation, 229–31
studies of, 225–33
unfulfilling, 26
use of masturbation, 229, 230
use of pornography, 229–31, 237
heterosexual sex, 12, 26, 63
anal sex, 237
exchange value of, 234–5
oral sex, 230, 237
see also men; sexual act; women
heterosexuality, 8, 82
appropriate sex, 8, 9, 105, 106
assumption of, 53–4, 80, 104,
    105–7, 109–11
compulsory, 253, 256
feminist views of, 8–9, 75–96,
    241
institutionalised, 5
resistance to, 241
see also homophobia
hierarchies of authority, 5, 6
see also authority
Terrence Higgins Trust, 163, 164
higher education, 23–4
see also education
Hill, Anita, 35
Hill, Dave, 217–18
Hirschfeld, Magnus, 55, 56, 69
historical analyses:
essentialist, 9
of homosexuality, 53–7
of sexual knowledge, 8–10
of sexual research, 4–6, 8–10,
    55–7
of sexualities, 10–11, 17–33, 54
The History of Sexuality (Foucault),
    5, 53, 55, 142, 214–15, 222

Hite, Shere, 114
HIV, 5–6, 8
community responses to, 161–79
cultural issues, 158–9
discourse on, 140, 143, 147–8,
    150, 153
and drug abuse, 165
and ethnic groups, 165, 171–5
gay response to, 162–3, 166–71
government policy on, 162, 164,
    166, 167, 176–8
language of, 143
political attitudes to, 163, 164
public attitudes to, 164, 202–3,
    206–7
scientific knowledge of, 143–4
and sexualities, 10, 26
statistics on, 216
see also health care; health issues
HIV clinics, 143–7, 150
HIV organisations, 163, 164–6,
    171–5
HIV positive people:
Black, 165, 171–4
buddying services, 164
as communities, 169–71
as a danger to others, 216
deliberate infection of others, 213
death of, 205, 278
diagnosis, 147–53, 155–7
habits, 145–7
health care, 147–53, 155–7, 163,
    261, 272–9
as health workers, 11–12, 201–2,
    205–19
hospice treatment, 263, 279
knowledge of HIV, 143–4, 145,
    147–53, 158–9
moral choice for, 11–12
older people, 278–9
personal experience of, 140,
    143–7, 148–53
reskilling of, 156–7
self identity, 10, 140–1, 142–60
self-help groups for, 163, 164,
    167, 213, 217–18
statistics of, 216
voluntary organisations for, 163,
    164–6, 213–14, 217–18

women as, 144
see also AIDS, people with
HIV prevention, 159–60, 167–8, 175
public funding of, 168–9
see also safer sex
HIV transmission, 145–6, 162, 165,
206, 216
risk of, 11–12, 171–5, 202–5,
206
Hobbes, Thomas, 204
Hochschild, Arlie R., 221, 236
Hodgkinson, K., 224
Hogben, Lancelot, 64
holistic care see hospice movement
home ownership, 123
see also housing conditions
homophobia, 5, 56–7, 63
and AIDS, 166
institutionalised, 169
homosexual literature, 166
homosexual prostitution, 182
see also prostitution
homosexual underworld, 36
homosexuals, 82
age of consent for, 217
attitudes to, 97
civil rights, 54
as criminals, 57
decision-making by, 160
as diseased, 55–7
essentialist theory of, 55–6
ethnic, 165, 171–4
explanations of, 55–62
fundamentalist attitudes to, 61
gay brain theory, 8, 53–4, 58–60,
62–71
gay communities, 148–9, 162
gay gene theory, 8, 53–4, 60–71
health care for, 278–9
HIV prevention, 159–60, 167–8,
175
identification of, 78
morality of, 61, 169
organism as origin of, 57–62
scientific research on, 53–71
and sexual reputations, 257
as a species, 53–4
statistical surveys of, 56, 69, 110,
116

theories about, 55–71
third sex theory, 55–6, 59
young people as, 110
see also gay liberation
movement; lesbians
hooks, bell, 189
hormones:
female, 56, 70
male, 56
hospice movement, 149, 262–3,
269, 279
see also dying; health care
housing conditions:
in farming communities, 123
lack of housing, 126
and poverty, 119, 122, 123–4
rented housing, 125
of social underclass, 119, 125,
131–2
human brain:
brain-imaging, 58
corpus callosum, 58
gay brain theory, 8, 53–4, 58–60,
62–71
hypothalamus, 59–60
men's, 58–9
sexual dimorphism in, 54, 56, 58
women's, 58, 69, 69
Human Fertilisation and
Embryological Authority (UK),
63
Human Genome Project, 58
human rights, 180, 280
see also rights
Human Sexual Behaviour see
Kinsey Reports
human-interest stories, 44
see also sexual storytelling
Hurdy, S., 65
husband, 181, 274–5
see also family groups;
heterosexual relationships;
men
hypothalamus, 59–60
INAH 3 region, 59–60
see also human brain

ideal marriage, 225
identity formation, 10, 140–3

and authority, 141
and the body, 265–6
embodied self, 265
female construction of, 240
Giddens on, 153–9, 203, 264–6
and modernity, 154–7, 264–7,
    279–80
and reflexivity, 10, 153–9
self-actualisation, 267
identity invention:
in sexual storytelling, 41, 43
identity issues, 6, 27, 139–40
and AIDS/HIV, 10, 140–1, 142–60
and authority, 10, 141–2, 154,
    159
collective, 6
complex, 158–9
and death, 267
fateful moments, 10, 154–5, 157,
    265
Foucault on, 140, 141–2, 143,
    150–1, 158, 159, 257–8
lifestyle choices, 154–5
politics of, 43
and reflexivity, 10, 153–9
and strategies for change, 139–40
subjectivity, 139–40, 158
understanding of, 139–40
see also self identity; sexual
    identities
identity reconstruction, 222, 237,
    268
ignorance:
sexual, 77
. see also education
illegal sexual acts, 145–6
see also sexual act
illegitimate children, 9–10, 115–36
attitudes to, 115, 118–33
in Britain, 115, 117, 118–20,
    127–8
causation, 120–9, 131–3
delinquency among, 115, 118,
    119–20
as an epidemic, 120–4
as a moral issue, 121–9, 132
moral panic over, 115, 118–33
patterns of, 125–9
and race, 116–17

in Scotland, 9–10, 117–18,
    120–36
and social class, 120–9
as social underclass, 115–36
statistics on, 115, 117, 118–19,
    120–2, 126–7
in United States, 115, 116–17,
    118–19, 128–9
see also children
imagining:
blocks to, 42
in sexual storytelling, 41–2
immigration policies:
in Britain, 70, 191
immorality:
concept of, 9–10, 121–9
see also moral issues
imposed health care, 268
see also health care
impotence, 269, 274
imprisonment:
of women, 83
inborn tendencies, 55–7, 60, 69
see also eugenics
incontinence, 88–91, 124–5
see also illegitimate children
independence:
economic, 76, 77
and health care, 267–8
loss of, 267–8, 276, 277
social, 76
for women, 76, 77
Independent, The, 2
indissoluble monogamy, 86
see also monogamy
the individual see identity issues
individual authority, 252–3
see also authority
individual ethics, 209–12
see also ethics
individual insecurity, 155
individual morality, 209–12
industrial societies, 203
initiation:
in heterosexual relationships, 225
inner lives, 41–2
insecurity, 155
Institute of Historical Research
    (UK), 30

Institute of Sexual Science (Berlin), 69
institutionalised gender inequalities, 222
institutionalised heterosexuality, 5
  see also heterosexuality
institutionalised homophobia, 169
  see also homophobia
interactionist approach:
  to sociology, 7
  symbolic, 27–8, 34
International Sociological Association:
  Research Committee on Women, 30–1
interpretive communities, 43–4
  see also communities
inter-racial prostitution, 189–90
  see also prostitution
intersex, 56
  see also homosexuals; lesbians
intimate citizenship, 7, 34, 45–52
  see also sexual storytelling
intimate gifts *see* gift-giving
intimacy:
  concept of, 11–12, 225–6
  democratisation of, 38
  expression of, 221, 229
  feeling rules, 221
  loss of, 234–5
  and sexualities, 1, 221, 229
  transformation of, 220–1
IQ theories, 69–70
irresponsibility:
  as a male trait, 245–6

Jackson, Margaret, 258
Jacobson, L., 269, 271
Jakobovits, Chief Rabbi Lord, 63
James, William, 51
Japan, 85
Jarman, Derek, 217
Jeffreys, Sheila:
  The Spinster and her Enemies, 84
Jenkins, Rosemary, 206–7
job creation, 117
  see also labour market
jobs *see* labour market
Johnson, Martin, 63

Joseph, Sir Keith, 116
journals *see* newspapers and journals

Karezza technique, 90–1, 95
  see also birth control
Kaufmann, T., 279
Keller, E.F., 68–9
Kellner, D., 142, 153
Kennedy, President John F., 116
Kertbeny, Karl, 94
Kiernan, Nora, 81, 82
King, Edward, 148, 159–60, 166, 174
Kinsey Reports, 39, 62, 98, 102, 121, 269
  'Little Kinsey' survey, 9, 97–114
knowledge, 142
  patients of AIDS/HIV, 143–4
  and authority, 141–2, 215
  medical, 143–4
  self, 142, 153
  sexual, 12, 104–5
  types of, 144
von Krafft-Ebbing, Richard, 56

labour:
  division of, 22, 30, 31
  Marxian concept of, 30, 191, 193
  waged, 192–4
labour market, 22, 76, 123
  job creation, 117
  unemployment, 117, 118
  workfare programmes, 117
Land, Hilary, 213
Landmark Trust, 263
Landström, Catherina, 69
lang, k.d., 36
language:
  of AIDS/HIV, 143
  and meaning, 81, 143
  of sex, 81–4, 105
Lash, Scott, 157–8, 203
Laws of Love (film), 69
leasehold property *see* rented housing
Leatham, Isabel, 80, 89, 95
legal issues:
  in prostitution, 182, 192, 196

legalisation:
  of prostitution, 181, 195
legitimate sex, 85
  see also sex
Leonard, Diana, 31
lesbian movement, 5, 8, 36
  see also sexual politics
lesbian politics, 5, 8, 36, 164
  see also sexual politics
lesbian sex, 93
  and sexual reputations, 257
lesbians, 53–4, 61, 79, 80, 254
  Black, 174
  health care for, 278–9
  identification of, 78
  naming women as, 79
  romantic friendships, 79
  theories of, 55–7
  see also gay liberation
    movement; homosexuality
leukaemia, 274
LeVay, Simon, 53, 59–60, 61, 62, 68
  The Sexual Brain, 59
Leverhulme Trust (UK), 257
Lewis, Oscar, 131
liberals, 48
liberty:
  right to, 11
  see also civil rights
life *see* death; quality of life
lifestyle choices, 154–5
  see also identity
Lilley, Peter, 130
limited monogamy, 86
  see also monogamy
limiting *see* constraining
listeners, 7, 35–7
  importance of, 43–4
  social worlds, 36
  as support groups, 35, 36
  see also sexual storytelling
'Little Kinsey' survey, 9, 97–114
  contents, 98–9, 102–13
  contribution of, 112–13
  methodology, 98, 99–101
  publication of, 98
  text of, 100
  use of data, 100–1
  see also Kinsey Reports

Littlewood, Margaret, 31
London Lighthouse, 163, 263
London School of Economics, 64
loneliness, 212, 215
loving:
  falling in love, 234
  free love, 77, 83–4
  and passion, 94–5
  and sex, 77
  womens need for, 243–53
low income families *see* poverty
loyalty, 139
lust, 83, 84, 94–5

McIntosh, Mary, 53, 64–5
MacIntyre, Alasdair, 49
McKellan, Ian, 61
McKenna, Dr James, 205
MacNicol, J., 132
McRobbie, R., 127, 130, 131
Madonna, 39, 40
magazines *see* newspapers and
    journals
Mainliners (UK), 165, 174–5
maintenance payments, 118, 130
  see also single mothers
male domination:
  of heterosexual relationships, 12,
    180, 221–4, 236, 240, 241
male-in-the-head concept, 240, 241,
    243, 253, 255, 257–8
male hormones, 56
  see also hormones
male impotence, 269, 274
male oppression:
  in heterosexual relationships,
    223–4
  prostitution seen as, 180, 187
male right of access:
  to women's bodies, 180, 181,
    187
male sexual problems, 190, 269,
    274
male/female dualism, 240, 241
Malthusian appliances, 89
  see also birth control
manipulation *see* political
    manipulation
Mansfield, P., 225, 233–4

marital behaviour:
  of women, 9
marital law:
  reform of, 77
marital relations, 88–91, 270
  see also heterosexual
    relationships
marital satisfaction, 237
market forces, 193–4, 212
marriage, 76, 93, 119
  courtship, 121, 125–6
  delayed, 125–6
  effect of children on, 228–9
  effect of work on, 227–8
  extra-marital affairs, 233
  ideal of, 225
  improvident, 121
  mercenary, 77
  monogamy, 77, 86, 237
  rape in, 42
  sex before, 125–6
  sex outside, 104
  see also cohabitation; divorce
Marsden, Dora:
  as *Freewoman* editor, 75–6, 79
  life, 79
  opinions, 76, 80, 81, 82–3, 84,
    86, 89, 91–2
  Rebecca West on, 94
Marshall, T.H., 46, 208
Marx, Karl, 191, 193
Marxism:
  concept of labour, 30, 191, 193
  and sociological research, 18, 30,
    64–5, 66
masculinity, 248–53, 258
  see also men
mass media, 38, 50
  see also the media
massage parlours, 182, 183, 197
  see also prostitution
Mass-Observations, 98
  'Little Kinsey' survey, 9, 97–114
mastectomies, 274, 275
Masters, William, 270
masturbation, 85, 95, 104, 229,
    230, 234, 235, 237, 252–3, 276
materialist feminism, 27
  see also feminism

Maynard, Mary, 26
means-testing, 129
  see also welfare systems
media, the, 36, 43
  film, 42, 69
  mass media, 38, 50
  misrepresentation by, 62–3,
    132–3, 217
  reaction to AIDS panics, 206–7,
    217
  as source of knowledge, 148
  see also communications
    technology
medical analogies:
  for social underclass, 120–4, 129
medical ethics, 210
  see also ethics
medical knowledge, 143–4
Medical Research Council (MRC)
  (UK), 70
medical technology, 209
medicalisation:
  and identity formation, 142–3
  of sexualities, 55–7, 70
medicine *see* health care
Medway Health Authority (UK),
    205, 206–7
men:
  attitudes to sex, 103
  and authority, 12
  bisexual, 167–8
  Black, 189–90
  brains of, 58–9
  as fathers, 118, 126, 128–30, 268
  heterosexual relationships,
    220–38
  heterosexual sex, 12, 26, 63, 230,
    234–5, 237
  as husbands, 181, 274–5
  irresponsibility of, 245–6
  masculinity, 243–53, 258
  New Men, 34, 251–3
  self-control by, 77–8, 88–91
  sexual difficulties, 190, 269, 274
  sexual pleasure, 77–8, 84, 240
  sexual reputations, 239–57
  social control of women, 180
  as social group, 26
  in sociological research, 18–29

use of prostitutes, 180–96
as victims, 224
and violence, 65
young men, 118, 239–57
see also family groups
Men, Risk and AIDS Project (UK),
  239, 257
menopausal women, 66–7
see also women
men's needs, 243–53
men's studies:
  funding of, 31
menstruation, 42, 103
see also women
mental ability, 58
mental dysfunctions, 58
mercenary marriages, 77
see also marriage
Mercer, Kobena, 139
methodological failure, 115–16
methodology:
  data triangulation, 100–1, 113–14
  prostitution studies, 196
  sampling techniques, 116
  of sexual research, 98, 99–101,
    108–9, 116, 239, 257, 258
  see also scientific research
Middlesborough (UK), 98
Miller, G.N., 95
minority communities *see* ethnic
  groups
misrepresentation:
  by the media, 62–3, 132–3, 217
  of scientific research, 62–3
  see also political manipulation
missing body concept, 264
  see also the body
Mitchel, Elizabeth, 128
Mitchel, Jane, 128
Mitchel, William, 128
modernity:
  and identity formation, 154–7,
    264–6, 279–80
  repressive nature of, 153
Modernity and Self Identity
  (Giddens), 153–5, 203, 264–6
molecular genetics, 60–2
  see also genetics
monogamy, 77, 237

indissoluble, 86
limited, 86
see also marriage
moral choice, 11–12, 215–16
  see also choice
moral issues:
  concept of sin, 56
  illegitimacy seen as, 121–9, 132
  immorality, 9–10, 121–9
  political manipulation of, 116,
    121, 124–5, 129, 132, 153
moral panic:
  over AIDS/HIV, 207, 217
  over illegitimacy, 115, 118–33
morality:
  feminist, 86–91
  group, 209–12
  of homosexuals, 61, 169
  individual, 209–12
  new, 86
  old, 86
  of sexual storytelling, 40–1, 45,
    47–8
Morgan, E. Noel, 95
mortality statistics, 203
  see also death
mothers:
  fit motherhood, 93
  teenage, 9
  voluntary motherhood, 77
  see also pregnancy; single
    mothers; women
motivations, 116
Moynihan, Senator Daniel P.:
  The Negro Family . . ., 116, 118,
    120
MRC *see* Medical Research Council
MTV, 36, 40
  see also television programmes
mugging, 207, 217
  see also violence
Murphy, R., 67
Murray, Charles, 116–17, 118, 119,
  130, 131, 132
mutual orgasms, 225
  see also heterosexual
    relationships; orgasms

narratives *see* sexual storytelling

National Council for One Parent Families (NCOPF) (UK), 132–3
National Health Service (UK): funding of, 176–8, 206
see also health care; health workers
National Health Service and Community Care Act, 1990 (UK), 176
National Institutes of Health (USA), 54
National Organisation of Gay and Lesbian Scientists and Technical Professionals (NOGLTSP) (USA), 59–60
National Survey of Sexual Attitudes and Lifestyles (Wellcome Trust), 107, 108–12, 113, 115–16
National Union of Women's Suffrage Societies, 75
natural birth control, 89–91
see also birth control
natural sciences, 54–5, 59–60
see also scientific research
natural sex *see* appropriate sex
nature/nurture arguments, 60, 61
NAZ project, 171
Nazism, 69
see also Germany
NCOPF *see* National Council for One Parent Families
negative sexual reputations, 250, 258
see also sexual reputations
The Negro Family: The Case for National Action (Moynihan), 116, 118, 120
Nelkin, D:
Selling Science, 59, 60–1
Netherlands:
prostitution in, 181
New Age culture, 40, 65
New Freewoman (journal), 79
see also Freewoman
New Men, 34, 251–3
see also men
new morality, 86
see also morality

New Right politics, 64, 132, 164, 165
see also politics
Newby, H., 30
newspapers and journals, 2–3, 39, 98, 119
Freewoman, 8–9, 75–96
gay press, 148, 149, 168
see also communications technology
NOGLTSP *see* National Organisation of Gay and Lesbian Scientists and Technical Professionals
non-penetrative sex, 93, 145, 159–60
see also penetration
normalisation strategies, 141
normality:
perception of, 146–7, 278
Norris, G., 30
Northern Ireland, 205, 206–7
see also Britain
Noyes, John Humphrey, 90
nuclear families *see* traditional families
nursing *see* health care
Nuss, Shirley, 31
nymphomania, 78

Oakley, Ann, 29
Sex, Gender and Society, 30
Oakley, Robin, 29
Observer, The, 217
old morality, 86
see also morality
older women, 92–3, 197
see also ageing process; women
Oliver, Kathlyn, 87–8, 89
onanism *see* auto-eroticism; masturbation
Oncomouse, the, 63
Oneida Colony (US), 90
Onward and Upward Association, 123, 132
open relationships, 231
opinion leaders, 99, 102
oppression:
of women, 27, 30, 31

oral cultures, 35
  see also sexual storytelling
oral sex, 230, 237
  see also heterosexual sex
organ transplants, 209–10
organisations *see* voluntary
  organisations
the organism:
  as origin of homosexuality,
    57–62
orgasms, 111, 223, 224
  faking of, 233–4, 235–6
  fantasising during, 235
  mutual, 225
  self-stimulation, 223
  see also women
Other than the Others (film), 69

Pagan, Leighton, 94
paid prostitutes, 180
  see also prostitution
palliative care *see* health care
panic:
  AIDS panics, 201–2, 205–7
  moral, 115, 118–33, 207
  postmodern, 207
  public anxiety, 207
Pankhurst, Christabel, 88
Pankhurst family, 75, 94
parents:
  responsibilities of, 209–10, 217
  of single mothers, 117, 119,
    126–8, 130
  see also children; family groups
partial abstinence, 89–91
  see also abstinence; celibacy
passion, 89, 92
  definition of, 82–4, 94–5
passive women, 78, 84–5
Pasteur, Merieux, 210
Pateman, C., 187
patents, 63
patients *see* AIDS patients; health
  care; HIV patients
Patriarchy Study Group (BSA), 21
Patterns of Marriage (Slater and
  Woodside), 107–8, 109, 110
Patterson, O., 191
Patton, Cindy, 145, 166, 172–3

Pearson, Karl, 94
penetration, 223–4
  non-penetrative sex, 93, 145,
    159–60
  in prostitution, 182, 183–4
  synonimity with sexual act, 9,
    82, 93, 104, 106, 110–11
  see also sexual act
people as property, 180, 181, 187,
  195–6
  see also prostitution
personal experience:
  of ageing process, 270, 272–9
  of AIDS/HIV, 140, 143–7,
    148–53
  hidden, 41, 42
  of prostitution, 181–96
  and sexual storytelling, 41–3
  of sex, 222, 239–57
personal identity *see* self identity
personal inadequacy, 132
personal risk, 202–3
  see also risk behaviour
perversions, 78
petting, 104
phallocentric sex, 223
  see also heterosexual
  relationships
philanthropic organisations, 123,
  129
  see also voluntary organisations
Phoenix, A., 132
physical appearance, 266, 270
  importance of, 243–4, 254
physical capital concept, 265
  see also the body
physical disabilities, 269, 270
physical sensation:
  sex as, 77–8, 86, 91–3
Pillard, R.C., 70
pimps, 190, 191
  see also prostitution
Pinching, Professor A.J., 217
plastic sexuality concept, 214–15
  see also sexualities
pleasure:
  limits of, 240
  sexual, 77, 778–9, 94, 240
Plotkin, Stanley, 210

Plummer, Trisha, 177
pluralism *see* diversity
political manipulation:
  of moral issues, 116, 121, 124–5,
    129, 132, 153
  see also misrepresentation
Political Science Association (UK),
  30
political subordination:
  of women, 180, 194–5
politicians, 207
politics:
  of AIDS/HIV, 163, 164
  biological politics, 66, 67–9
  new politics, 45–6
  New Right, 64, 132, 164, 165
  of prostitution, 180
  Right wing, 116, 117
  of sexual storytelling, 7, 34,
    45–52
  see also government policies;
    sexual politics
politics of identity, 43
  see also identity issues
politics of research, 57
  see also scientific research
Poor Law Report, 1834 (England),
  117
Poor Laws (UK), 124, 126, 128,
  131
poorhouse, the, 129
  see also poverty
popular music, 40
pornography, 234, 237
  use of during sex, 229–31
  women's attitudes to, 35
pornography of death, 262
Portillo, Michael, 217
Position of Women in the
  Profession [of sociology], BSA
  working party, 20
Positively Irish Action on AIDS,
  171
Positively Women (UK), 165, 171,
  174
postmodern ethics, 202, 211–12
  see also ethics; moral choice
postmodern feminism, 27
  see also feminism

postmodern panic, 207
  see also panic
postmodernism, 7, 50–1, 55
post-mortem research, 59–60
  see also scientific research
post-natal depression, 228–9
  see also children; pregnancy
post-structuralism, 5, 65
Pound, Ezra, 79
poverty:
  acute, 119
  in Britain, 9–10, 116, 117–18
  cultural deprivation, 118–20, 121
  cultures of, 129–33
  geographical analysis of, 119
  housing conditions, 119, 122,
    123–4
  and illegitimacy, 120–36
  in Scotland, 120–36
  and single mothers, 120–36
  social analysis of, 119
  in United States, 116–17, 122
power *see* authority
pregnancy:
  bridal, 125
  fertility levels, 131
  the foetus, 209
  teenage, 9, 115
  unwanted, 103
  see also women
President's National Advisory
  Committee on Equal
  Opportunity (US), 122
Presley, Elvis, 40
press coverage:
  of AIDS/HIV, 148, 201, 205,
    206–7, 217
  of sexual research, 2–3, 116
  see also the media; newspapers
    and journals
Preston, Jane, 257
prevention strategies:
  for HIV, 159–60, 167–9
preventive checks, 89
  see also birth control
printing and books, 35
  gay press, 148, 149
  paperbacks, 39
  sexology publications, 85–6

see also communications technology
Prison Board (UK), 122
privacy:
  right to, 208–9
  and sexual storytelling, 36, 41, 42
problem families *see* dysfunctional families
procreation *see* reproductive sex
professional standards:
  of health workers, 206–7
promiscuity, 82–3
property:
  home ownership, 123
  people as, 180, 181, 187, 195–6
prostitute organisations, 180, 195
prostitute–client relationship, 181, 182, 183–90, 194–5
prostitutes' rights, 180
prostitution:
  abused women in, 197
  attitudes to, 77, 89, 93, 180–1, 187, 221–2
  authority issues, 11, 182, 183–8, 191–2
  Black people in, 181
  in Britain, 11, 76, 77, 180–98
  brothels, 85, 191
  as a business, 182–3
  charges for, 182, 183
  child prostitution, 180
  client motivation, 187, 188–90
  client requirements, 182, 185–6, 188–90
  consent in, 11, 180, 182
  control issues, 11, 183–98
  domination clients, 182, 185, 186–7, 189
  and drug use, 186
  ethnic groups engaged in, 181
  female, 1, 76, 180–98
  feminist attitudes to, 180–1, 187
  forced, 180
  free choice, 180, 181
  heterosexual, 182–96
  homosexual, 182
  inter-racial, 189–90
  legal issues, 182, 192
  legislation on, 181, 195
  as male oppression, 180, 187
  male use of, 180–96
  married clients, 189
  massage parlours, 182, 183
  masturbation as alternative to, 85
  for money, 180, 191–2, 194–6
  in Netherlands, 181
  penetrative sex, 182, 183–4
  personal experience of, 181–96
  pimps, 190, 191
  politics of, 180
  profits from, 182–3
  reduction of, 77
  role playing in, 182, 183, 186–7, 189–90
  saunas, 190, 197
  sex tourism, 196, 197
  as slavery, 180, 191–2
  socio-economic background, 181
  soliciting, 182
  street-walkers, 180, 197
  in United States, 181
  and violence, 197
  as wage labour, 192–4
prurience:
  as reaction to sexual research, 2, 3
psychology:
  and risk analysis, 204–5
public advertising, 11, 39
public anxiety, 207
  see also panic
public attitudes:
  to AIDS/HIV, 164, 202–3, 206–7
  to feminism, 8–9
  to *Freewoman*, 8–9, 75–6, 79–96
  to prostitution, 77, 89, 93, 180–1, 187, 221–2
  to scientific research, 2–3, 102–3, 116
  to women's suffrage, 75
  see also censorship
public discussion:
  of sex, 76–7, 79–96
public funding, 164
  of AIDS organisations, 165, 167, 172, 176–8
  of AIDS research, 11

cuts in, 176–8
of HIV prevention, 168–9
targeting of, 175–8
see also funding
public health, 120
see also health issues
public health care, 164
see also health care
public problems:
creation of, 44–5
culture of, 34, 35–7, 39–40, 41,
44–5
human-interest stories, 44
public reaction *see* public attitude
Puner, Morton, 270
punters *see* clients
pure relationships, 8, 220, 223
see also heterosexual relationships

quality of life, 267
queer theory, 31
see also homosexuals

race:
and illegitimacy, 116–17
and sexualities, 7
see also ethnicity
racism:
anti-racism, 69–70
scientific, 65, 69
in United States, 116, 118, 120,
173
Radcliffe, Polly, 257
radiation-linked cancer, 204
radical change *see* change
radical feminism, 64–5, 66, 223
and prostitution, 180–1, 187
see also feminism
radical science, 64–7, 70
see also scientific research
rampant women, 242–3, 247, 252–3
see also women
Ransom, Janet, 257
Ranzen, Esther, 36
rape, 5
in marriage, 42
see also sexual abuse
rape survivors, 45
see also survival stories

rational choice, 132
see also choice
reductionism:
biological, 66
Redwood, John, 133
reflexive risk, 202, 203
see also risk analysis
reflexivity:
and identity formation, 10, 153–9
limits of, 157–9
re-gaying:
of AIDS, 168
registration of births, 120–1, 126
relationships:
heterosexual, 8–9, 75–96, 220–38
religious issues, 47–8, 103, 120,
123–4, 125
hospice movement, 149, 262–3,
269, 279
the soul, 140–1, 158, 160
rented housing, 125
see also housing conditions
reproductive sex, 8, 80–1, 82, 93,
94
see also sex
research *see* scientific research
Research Committee on Women
(International Sociological
Association), 30–1
resentment:
in heterosexual relationships,
231–2, 234, 235
resistance:
strategies of, 140, 142, 241
reskilling:
for people with AIDS/HIV,
156–7
resource allocation *see* funding
responsibilities:
of health workers, 201, 206–7
Rhodes, Tim, 257
right to die, 208
euthanasia, 208
see also death; rights
right-wing politics, 117
New Right, 132
see also politics
rights:
body rights, 208, 209, 210–11

of children, 209–10, 217
civil, 11, 54, 192, 208
of the foetus, 209
human, 180, 280
to know, 208–9
to liberty, 11
to privacy, 208–9
to sex, 76, 85, 91–3
women's, 209–10
risk:
    of AIDS, 170, 171–5, 202–5
    of HIV transmission, 11–12,
        171–5, 202–5
risk analysis, 202, 203
    existence of risk, 204–5
    personal risk, 202–3
    psychology of, 204–5
    reflexive, 202, 203
    scientific, 202, 203, 204
    sociology of, 203–4
risk behaviour, 202
    and blame, 204
    collective, 204–5
    concept of, 203
    construction of self, 204
    health risks, 203, 204
    personal risk, 202–3
risk choices, 203–4
risk monitoring *see* risk analysis
risk reduction, 160
risk society, 202–5
Risk Society . . . (Beck), 202, 203
role playing:
    in prostitution, 182, 183, 186–7,
        189–90
romantic friendships, 79
    see also lesbians
Roper, N., 266–7, 271
Rorty, Richard, 50
Rose, Steven, 66, 69
Rousseau, Jean-Jacques, 42
Royal College of Midwives (UK),
    206–7
Royden, Maude, 75
Rubin, L.B., 220, 225–6, 233–4,
    237
The Runaway Soul (Brodkey), 215
rural areas, 9, 121, 123–4, 125–6
Ryan, W., 120, 129

sacred nature:
    of sex, 80, 82, 94
    see also sex
sado-masochism, 78
    domination, 182, 185, 186–7, 189
safe periods, 89
    see also birth control
safe sex, 11, 145–6, 159–60, 169
    see also sexual act
safer sex, 145–6, 159–60, 163, 164,
    167, 169
    HIV prevention, 159–60, 167–8,
        175
Saggers, Kathy, 119
Salk Institute (US), 54, 59
sampling techniques, 116
    see also methodology
saunas, 190, 197
    see also prostitution
Sayers, Janet, 66
    Biological Politics, 65, 66
Scase, Richard, 30
Schofield, Michael:
    Sexual Behaviour of Young People,
        107, 108, 109, 111–12
Schreiner, Olive, 75, 76
Science (journal), 59, 60, 61
The Science of Desire (Hamer and
    Copeland), 61, 63
scientific culture, 65, 68–9
    see also cultural issues
scientific racism, 65, 69
    see also racism
scientific research:
    activists in, 59–60
    biological sciences, 55–7, 58, 64,
        69–70
    feminists critiques of, 5, 8, 53–71
    funding of, 11
    genetics, 5, 8, 53–4, 60–2
    on homosexuality, 53–71
    misrepresentation of, 62–3
    natural sciences, 63–4, 59–60
    politics of, 57
    post-mortem, 59–60
    radical science, 64–7, 70
    on sexualities, 5, 8
    on twins, 60
    vaccine testing, 210

see also methodology; sexual research
scientific risk, 202, 203, 204
see also risk analysis
Scotland:
Glasgow, 217
Glasgow Experiment, 121
illegitimacy in, 9–10, 117–18, 120–36
poverty in, 120–36
see also Britain
Scott, Peter, 166
Scott, Sue, 257, 280
screening:
of health workers, 206
'Seatown', 100
see also 'Little Kinsey' survey
security:
sense of, 158
Segal, Lynne, 222, 235
Seidman, Steven:
Embattled Eros, 50–1
selective abortion, 60–1, 63
self care, 265
see also health care
self control:
celibacy, 87, 232, 233
continence, 88–91
in marriage, 88–91
by men, 77–8, 88–91
sexual, 86–91
self identity, 7, 43, 264–6
and ageing, 267–9
of people with AIDS/HIV, 10, 140–1, 142–60
construction of self, 204
Giddens on, 153–9
for women, 76
see also identity issues
self knowledge, 142, 153
see also knowledge
self narratives, 40
see also sexual storytelling
self-actualisation, 267
see also identity formation
self-deception, 49
self-help groups:
for people with AIDS/HIV, 163, 164, 167, 213–14, 217–18

see also voluntary organisations
self-stimulation:
for women, 223
see also orgasms
Selling Science (Nelkin), 59, 60–1
senility, 275, 276
see also ageing process
sensuality, 94–5
separatism see tribalism
servants:
sexual behaviour of, 121–4, 125–6
sex:
animal nature of, 80–1
attitudes to, 103–13, 261–2, 271
authentic, 235–6
before marriage, 125–6
consensual, 80, 94
and death, 12–13, 214, 261–83
definition of, 81–2
importance of, 104
language of, 81–4, 105
legitimate, 85
as loving experience, 77
marital, 88–91, 220
non-penetrative, 93, 145, 159–60
personal experience of, 222, 239–57
phallocentric, 223
as purely physical, 77–8, 86, 91–3
public discussion of, 76–7, 79–96
reproductive, 8, 80–1, 82, 93, 94
right to, 76, 85, 91–3
as sacred, 80, 82, 94
sequestring of, 265
as spiritual experience, 77
Victorian attitude to, 261–2, 271
women's attitudes to, 76, 85, 91–3, 103–13
see also sexology; sexual act
sex drive, 103, 224, 226–7
sex for money see prostitution
Sex, Gender and Society (Oakley), 30
Sex and Marriage in England Today (Gorer), 107, 108, 109, 110
sex outside marriage, 104

Sex Pistols, 40
sex psychology, 78, 94
  see also sexology
sex roles, 22, 30–1
Sex Roles and Society *see* Research
  Committee on Women
sex theorists *see* sexology
sex tourism, 196, 197
  see also prostitution
sex work, 11, 180, 181, 192–4, 278
  heterosexual relationships seen
    as, 11, 220, 221–4, 233–6
  see also prostitution
sexist fantasies, 78, 189–90
sexology, 55–7, 76–7
  in Britain, 78
  difficulty of obtaining works on,
    85–6
  history of, 76–7, 78–9, 93, 94
  in United States, 84
  uses of, 84–6
  see also sexual research
sexual abuse, 77
  rape, 5, 42, 45
sexual act:
  abstinence from, 88–91, 104–5
  advice on, 145
  definition of, 81–2
  illegal, 145–6
  importance of, 26, 232, 237
  initiation of, 224
  non-penetrative, 93, 145, 159–60
  penetration, 182, 183–4, 223–4
  safer, 11, 145–6, 159–60, 163,
    164, 167, 169
  synonimity with penetration, 9,
    82, 93, 104, 106, 110–11
  types of, 145–6
  see also heterosexual
    relationships; sex
sexual assertiveness, 225
sexual autonomy, 11–12
  female, 6, 8–9
sexual behaviour, 7, 12, 77, 98–9,
    102–13
  changes over time, 111–12, 114
  double standards in, 109–10, 111,
    240, 242–53, 257, 258
  of servants, 121–4, 125–6

of young people, 107, 108, 109,
    239–57
Sexual Behaviour of Young People
  (Schofield), 107, 108, 109,
    111–12
The Sexual Brain (LeVay), 59
Sexual Conduct . . . (Gagnon and
  Simon), 4–5
sexual conservatism, 103–4
sexual cultures *see* sexualities
sexual danger, 38, 85
sexual desire *see* sexual
  expectations
sexual difficulties, 190, 227–9, 231–2
  male, 190, 269, 274
sexual dimorphism:
  in human brain, 54, 56, 58
sexual diversity *see* sexual divisions
sexual divisions, 4, 6–7, 17, 23, 85
  see also gender differentiation;
    sexualities
Sexual Divisions in Society, BSA
  Conference, Aberdeen (1974),
    17, 18–19, 21–3, 24, 28, 29
Sexual Divisions Study Group
  (BSA), 20, 30
sexual domination:
  of women, 180
sexual education, 12, 103, 104–5
  see also education
sexual empathy, 223–4
  see also heterosexual
    relationships
sexual equality, 3, 8
sexual expectations, 12, 26, 82–3,
    221, 232, 237, 240
  of women, 8, 9, 105, 107, 112,
    232, 243–53
sexual experimentation, 229–31
sexual frustration, 87
  see also self control
sexual fulfilment, 220, 226–7,
    229–30
sexual habits *see* sexual act
sexual harassment, 5, 258
  see also violence
sexual identities, 76–7, 222, 255–7
  see also identity issues; sexual
    reputations

sexual ignorance, 77, 104–5
sexual intercourse *see* sexual act
Sexual Inversion (Ellis), 94
sexual knowledge *see* sexual
  education
*Sexual, Marital and Family
  Relationships . . .* (Chesser),
  107, 108, 109, 110, 111–12
sexual needs *see* sexual expectations
sexual nonconformity, 9, 115–16
sexual partners, 144–5
  see also heterosexual
  relationships; homosexuals;
  lesbians
sexual passivity *see* passive women
sexual pleasure:
  for men, 77–8, 84, 240
  for women, 77, 78–9, 84, 94, 240
sexual politics, 5–6, 116
  coming out, 34, 35, 36, 45
  emancipation, 45
  feminist, 5, 8–9, 17, 18–29,
    64–5, 258
  gay, 5, 8, 164, 263
  lesbian, 5, 8, 36, 164
  and sociological research, 5–6,
    17–33
  see also politics
sexual preference *see* heterosexual
  relationships; homosexuals;
  lesbians
sexual pressures, 243–4
sexual problems *see* sexual
  difficulties
sexual progressivism, 103–4
sexual protection, 76, 145
sexual reform, 6, 56, 69, 76–7, 84,
  121
  see also sexology
sexual regrets, 225–6
sexual reputations, 12, 239–60
  discourse on, 258
  double standards in, 109–10, 111,
    240, 242–53, 257, 258
  gendering of, 241–57
  homosexual, 257
  lesbian, 257
  male, 239–57
  negative, 250, 258

personal experience of, 240,
    243–53
  and virginity, 244, 258
  women's, 239–57
  of young people, 239–53
  see also sexual identities
sexual research:
  in Britain, 9, 78, 94, 97–114
  censorship of, 2, 78, 94
  epistemology of, 5, 8, 113–14
  in Germany, 55–6
  on heterosexual relationships,
    225–33
  historical survey of, 4–5, 8–10,
    55–7
  on homosexuals, 53–7
  press coverage, 2–3, 116
  prurience about, 2, 3, 116
  public attitude to, 2–3, 102–3,
    116
  sexology, 55–7, 76–7
  in United States, 53–71
  see also methodology
sexual responsibility, 239
sexual scripts *see* sexual
  storytelling
sexual self control *see* self control
sexual self-determination, 270–1
sexual stereotypes, 116
sexual storytelling, 7–8, 34–52, 222
  articulation of, 41, 43
  blocks to, 42
  in books, 39
  breaking the silence, 45
  coming out, 34, 35, 36, 45
  and communications technology,
    34, 35–7, 38–9
  constraining of, 49
  and consumerism, 39–40, 44
  control issues, 38, 42
  cultural context, 222
  cultural intermediaries, 40
  culture of, 35–44
  culture of public problems, 34,
    35–7, 39–40, 41, 44–5
  dormant, 35, 38
  and empowerment, 38
  ethics of, 49–50
  generic process of, 41–5

history of, 37–9
identity inventions, 41, 43
imagining of, 41–2
intimate citizenship, 7, 34, 45–52
listeners, 7, 35–7, 43–4
morality of, 40–1, 45, 47–8
and personal experience, 41–3
politics of, 7, 34, 45–52
private, 36, 41, 42
reality of, 37–8
relevance of, 41
self narratives, 40
social context, 222
survival stories, 34, 35
as television programmes, 34,
    35–7, 39–40
as therapy, 40
traditional, 47–50
types of, 47–52
sexual subjects:
women as, 223–4
sexual surveys *see* sexual research
sexual techniques, 229, 237
sexual values, 1, 6, 11–12
sexual variation *see* sexual divisions
sexual violence *see* sexual
    harassment
sexual vocabulary, 81–4
sexualities:
and ageing, 263–4, 266, 268,
    269–80
and AIDS/HIV, 10, 26
and communities, 1, 6, 7, 10–11
definition of, 1, 6
discourse on, 7
of the dying, 268–9
ethics of, 61, 70
and ethnicity, 7
and feminism 17, 18–29, 76–8
and gender differences, 26
and health care, 263–4, 266–88
historical survey, 10–11, 17–33,
    54
and intimacy, 1, 221, 229
medicalisation of, 55–7, 70
of patients, 263–4, 266, 268,
    270–8
plastic, 214–15
purpose of, 80–1

and race, 7
scientific research on, 5, 8
and social relations, 3–6
sociological analyses of, 1–2, 3,
    5–13
theory of, 6–8
types of, 78
and values, 1, 6
see also sexual divisions; sexual
    research
Sexualities in a Social Context,
    BSA Conference (1994), 23–8
sexually transmitted diseases (STD),
    121, 145–6
see also AIDS; health issues;
    HIV
'Sexualogy', 94
see also sexology
Shafts (journal), 94, 95
shallow act concept, 221
Shaver, S., 208
Sherwen, Mrs, 89, 94
Shilling, C., 157, 265–6
Shuttleworth, Terence, 205, 206
Sibthorp, Margaret Shurmer, 94–5
Simon, William:
    Sexual Conduct . . . , 4–5
Simpson, J.A., 94
sin:
concept of, 56
see also moral issues
Sinclair, Upton, 87
single mothers, 115, 116, 117,
    118–36
attitudes to, 115, 118–33
children of, 9–10, 115–36
coping strategies, 131–1
maintenance payments, 118, 130
motivation of, 125–9
and their parents, 117, 119,
    126–8, 130
poverty of, 120–36
and welfare systems, 117, 118–19,
    127, 129–30, 131
see also children; mothers
single-parent families, 115, 117
see also family groups
single women, 85
chastity for, 86–9

sexual status of, 86–8
see also women
Skelhorn, S., 94
Slater, Eliot:
Patterns of Marriage, 107–8,
109, 110
slavery:
prostitution seen as, 180, 191–2
Smart, C., 243
W.H. Smith, 79
Smith-Rosenberg, Caroll, 78, 93
snacking:
at sex, 83, 84
Snell, Dr Paul, 205
social change, 111–12, 114
social choice, 47, 215–16
see also choice
social constructionism, 4, 61, 64–5,
66, 70
social control:
of women by men, 180
see also control issues
social good, 215–16, 218
see also altruism
social independence, 76
see also independence
social policy *see* government
policies
social pressures, 243–4, 251, 252,
258
social problems, 44
see also poverty; sexual
storytelling; social underclass
social relations:
and sexualities, 3–6
Social Science Research Council
(SSRC), 21, 30
social structure:
anthropological view, 31
class structure, 9–10, 77, 120–9,
203, 265
disciplinary societies, 151
rural areas, 9, 121, 123–4, 125–6
urban areas, 9, 121, 127
see also family groups
social underclass, 9–10
housing conditions, 119, 125,
131–2
illegitimacy amongst, 115–36

medical analogies for, 120–4, 129
and poverty, 116–18
social worlds:
in sexual storytelling, 36, 41, 43–4
see also listeners; support groups
sociobiology, 65
see also biological politics
Sociobiology (Wilson), 70
sociological research:
anglophone predominance in, 203
on the body, 8, 64–9, 264–6
as critical discipline, 18
criticism of, 27
difficulties of, 3, 18, 22–3, 31
funding of, 21, 23–4, 30, 31
interactionist, 7
male predominance in, 18–29
Marxist, 18, 30, 64–5, 66
and sexual politics, 5–6, 17–33
of sexualities, 1–2, 3, 5–13
theoretical, 21–3, 26–8
women in, 18–29
women's studies, 25–6, 27, 31
see also identity issues
sociological researchers, 18–29
sociology:
and risk analysis, 203–4
sodomites *see* homosexuals
soliciting, 182
see also prostitution
Sontag, Susan, 121
the soul, 140–1, 158, 160
see also religious issues
The Spinster and her Enemies
(Jeffreys), 84
spinsters *see* single women
spiritual experience:
sex as, 77
SSRC *see* Social Science Research
Council
Stanley, L., 98, 99, 113, 114
Starr–Weiner Report . . . (US), 270
statistical analyses, 56, 61, 69
statutory health care, 164, 176
see also health care
STD *see* sexually transmitted
diseases
'Steeltown', 98, 100
see also 'Little Kinsey' survey

sterilisation, 89
  see also birth control
stereotypes *see* sexual stereotypes
Stockham, Alice B., 90, 95
storytelling *see* sexual storytelling
Strachan, Dr J.M., 121
strategies:
  of authority, 141, 142, 151–3,
    159
  of HIV prevention, 159–60,
    167–9
  of knowledge, 142
  normalisation, 141
  of resistance, 140, 142
  street-walking prostitutes, 180,
    197
  see also prostitution
Strong, P., 204
subjectivity, 139–40, 158
  see also identity issues
suffrage *see* women's suffrage
Sun, The, 3
Sunday Pictorial, 98
Sunday Times, 2, 119
support groups:
  communities as, 35, 36
  listeners as, 35, 36
  social worlds, 36, 41, 43
  see also voluntary organisations
survival stories, 34, 35
  see also sexual storytelling
Swaab, D., 59
Sweden, 119
symbolic interactionism, 27–8, 34
  see also interactionist approach

Taitz, Dr Leonard, 205, 216
Taylor-Gooby, P., 208
technological advances:
  in medicine, 209
teenage mothers, 9
  see also mothers
teenage pregnancy, 9, 115
  see also pregnancy
telephones:
  help lines, 36, 163, 164, 206,
    217
television programmes, 34, 35–7,
  39–40

  see also communications
    technology; culture of public
    problems
terminal care, 269, 275–6
  critical care, 208
  see also dying process
therapy:
  sexual storytelling as, 40
Thatcher, Margaret, 217
third sex theory, 55–6, 59
  see also homosexuals
Thomas, Clarence, 35
tippling *see* snacking
Titmuss, Richard, 213
tourism *see* travel and tourism
traditional families, 118, 124–5, 126
  see also family groups
traditional stories, 47–50
  see also sexual storytelling
traditionalists, 48
training:
  of health workers, 266–7, 271–3,
    276–7
transformation of intimacy, 220–1
  see also intimacy
Transformation of Intimacy
  (Giddens), 202, 220
transmission:
  of AIDS/HIV, 145–6, 162, 165,
    170, 171–5, 202–5, 206, 216
travel and tourism, 36
  sex tourism, 196, 197
tribalism, 48–50
Triechler, P., 143
Turner, B.S., 64, 264–5
twins:
  studies of, 60

Ulrichs, Karl Heinrich, 55–6
uncertainty, 211–12
underclass *see* social underclass
undesired sex *see* sexual protection
unemployment, 117, 118
  see also labour market
UNESCO, 66
United Kingdom *see* Britain
United States:
  African Americans, 69–70, 116,
    172–3

birth control in, 90–1, 95
degaying in, 166
education in, 69–70
feminism in, 84
illegitimacy in, 115, 116–17,
  118–19, 128–9
Kinsey Reports, 39, 62, 98, 102,
  121, 269
Oneida Colony, 90
patent protection in, 63
poverty in, 116–17, 122
prostitution in, 181
racism, 116, 118, 120, 173
sexology in, 84
sexual research in, 39, 53–71, 98
War on Poverty, 116–17
welfare system, 117, 118, 128
unmarried mothers *see* single mothers
unwanted pregnancy, 103
  see also pregnancy
urban areas, 9, 121, 127
  see also social structure
Urnings, 56
  see also homosexuals; lesbians
uterus, the, 69
  see also women

vaccine testing, 210
  see also scientific research
value systems, 118, 261
  sexual, 1, 6, 11–12
Veritas Splendor (Papal Encyclical),
  215
victim-blaming, 118–20, 129
victimisation *see* oppression
Victorian Values Campaign (UK),
  133
Vietnam Solidarity Campaign (UK),
  25
violence:
  against women, 197, 243
  as a male trait, 65
  mugging, 207, 217
  sexual harassment, 5, 258
Violence against Women Study
  Group (BSA), 21
Violence, War and Social Change,
  BSA Conference, Hull (1975),
  21, 30

virginity, 244, 258
Visible Man . . . (Gilder), 118
visualising *see* imagining
vocalising *see* articulating
voluntary funding, 164
  see also funding
voluntary motherhood, 77
  see also mothers
voluntary organisations:
  for people with AIDS/HIV,
    161–79, 213–14, 217–18
  degaying of, 166–71
  diversification of, 175
  ethnic, 165, 171–4
  expertise of, 165
  funding, 165, 167, 172, 176–8
  need for, 172–4
  non-gay, 165–6
  self-help groups, 163, 164, 167,
    213–14, 217–18
  structure of, 165, 176
  for women, 165, 171, 174
voluntary prostitution *see* free
  choice prostitution
Voluntary Sector Responses to
  HIV and AIDS: Policies,
  Principles, Practice (research
  project), 163
votes for women *see* women's
  suffrage

War on Poverty (US), 116–17
Ward, David, 2
Watney, Simon, 166
Watson, E.M., 85, 87, 88–9, 90
  identity of, 90–1
Watson, Edith M., 90–1, 94, 95
Watson, Ernest, 90–1
Watson, Sheriff W., 122
Wavell, Stuart, 2
Webb, C., 280
Weeks, Jeffrey, 51, 262
Weiner, E.S.C., 94
welfare states, 208, 212
welfare systems:
  in Britain, 118, 127, 128–9, 131
  collective, 126, 127
  means-testing, 129
  the poorhouse, 129

for single mothers, 117, 118–19, 129–30, 131
in United States, 117, 118, 128
Wellcome Trust:
'National Survey of Sexual Attitudes . . . ', 107, 108–12, 113, 115–16
Wells, H.G., 79
West, Rebecca, 79, 90, 94
Westphal, Karl, 53
WHO *see* World Health Organisation
Wilde, Oscar, 42
Wilson, E.O.:
Sociobiology, 70
Witcop, Rose, 80
wives, 181
see also family groups; women
WLM *see* Women's Liberation Movement
women:
abused, 197
with AIDS/HIV, 144
attitudes to sex, 103–13
authority of, 12, 254–7, 258
brains of, 58, 59, 69
as carers, 213
control over their own bodies, 11–12, 47, 77, 240
education of, 69, 103
empowerment of, 253–7
femininity, 240, 241, 242, 247, 248–53, 257–8
frigid, 78–9
heterosexual relationships, 220–38
identity formation, 240
independence for, 76, 77
as initiators, 78
male right of access to, 180, 181, 187
male/female dualism, 240, 241
marital behaviours, 9
mastectomies, 274, 275
masturbation by, 85
menopausal, 66–7
menstruation, 42, 103
nymphomania, 78
older, 92–3, 197
oppression of, 27, 30, 31, 180, 187, 223–4

orgasms, 111, 223, 224, 225, 233–6
passive, 78, 84–5
political subordination of, 180, 194–5
and pornography, 35
as post-graduates, 21, 30
pregnancy, 9, 103, 11, 125, 131, 209
right to sex, 76, 85, 91–3
self identity for, 76
self-stimulation, 223
sexual divisions among, 85
sexual domination of, 180
sexual expectations, 8, 9, 105, 107, 112, 223, 243–53
sexual harassment, 5, 258
sexual pleasure, 77, 78–9, 84, 94, 240
sexual reputations, 239–57
as sexual subjects, 223–4
single, 85, 86–9
social control by men, 180
as social group, 26
as sociological researchers, 18–29
the uterus, 69
violence against, 197, 243
as wives, 181
young, 92, 239–57
see also feminism; lesbians; men; mothers; prostitutes
women prisoners, 83
Women, Risk and Aids Project (UK), 239, 257
women's caucus (BSA), 19–21, 24–5, 30
Women's Caucus Newsletter (BSA), 21
women's health movement, 66–7
see also health issues
Women's Liberation Movement (WLM), 18, 19, 20, 26, 28
women's movement *see* feminism
women's needs *see* sexual expectations
women's organisations, 165, 171, 174
women's rights, 209–10

Women's Social and Political
    Union (WPSU) (UK), 75–6,
    79, 83
women's studies, 25–6, 27, 31
    see also sociological research
women's suffrage, 75, 77, 94
Woodside, Moira:
    Patterns of Marriage, 107–8,
    109, 110
workfare programmes, 117
    see also labour market
working life:
    effect on marriage, 227–8
'Worktown', 98
    see also 'Little Kinsey' survey
World Health Organisation (WHO),
    271
Worsley, Peter, 27–8
WPSU *see* Women's Social and
    Political Union
Wrench, Dr, 85

writing:
    by feminists, 81–4
    by homosexuals, 166

X chromosones, 61

Yingling, Thomas, 140
young men:
    sexual reputations, 239–57
    see also men
young people:
    delinquency among, 115, 118,
    119–20
    as homosexuals, 110
    sexual behaviour, 107, 108, 109,
    111–12, 239–57
    see also children
young women, 92
    sexual reputations, 239–57
    see also women
youth culture, 39–40